Corporate Reporting and Company Law

The importance of disclosure as a regulatory device in company law is widely recognised. This book explores the disclosure requirements of companies in their reporting activities, and seeks to bring together the main features of the reporting system. The book considers the theoretical basis of the corporate reporting system and describes the regulatory framework for that system. It explores financial reporting and 'narrative' reporting, highlighting the fact that financial reporting requirements are more substantially developed than narrative reporting requirements – a consequence of the shareholder-centred vision that persists in company law. The roles of those responsible for providing corporate reports and those entitled to receive such information are examined. The book concludes with some broad suggestions for future development, with particular focus on the need to recognise the relevance of the communicative role of corporate reporting. The use of new technology also presents both challenges and opportunities for improving the regime.

CHARLOTTE VILLIERS is Professor of Company Law in the Law School at the University of Bristol, specialising in company law and employment law. She has also taught at the universities of Sheffield and Glasgow and has been a visiting lecturer at the University of Oviedo, Spain.

Cambridge Studies in Corporate Law

Series Editor

Professor Barry Rider,
University of London

Corporate or Company Law encompasses the law relating to the creation, operation and management of corporations and their relationships with other legal persons. **Cambridge Studies in Corporate Law** offers an academic platform for discussion of these issues. The series is international in its choice of both authors and subjects, and aims to publish the best original scholarship on topics ranging from labour law to capital regulation.

Books in the series
Janet Dine, *The Governance of Corporate Groups*
A. J. Boyle, *Minority Shareholders' Remedies*
Gerard McCormack, *Secured Credit under English and American Law*
Janet Dine, *Companies, International Trade and Human Rights*
Charlotte Villiers, *Corporate Reporting and Company Law*

Corporate Reporting and Company Law

Charlotte Villiers

CAMBRIDGE
UNIVERSITY PRESS

CAMBRIDGE UNIVERSITY PRESS
Cambridge, New York, Melbourne, Madrid, Cape Town, Singapore, São Paulo

CAMBRIDGE UNIVERSITY PRESS
The Edinburgh Building, Cambridge CB2 2RU, UK
Published in the United States of America by Cambridge University Press,
New York

www.cambridge.org
Information on this title: www.cambridge.org/9780521837934

First published 2006

Printed in the United Kingdom at the University Press, Cambridge

A catalogue record for this book is available from the British Library

ISBN-13 978-0-521-83793-4 hardback
ISBN-10 0-521-83793-6 hardback

To the memory of my father
John Villiers
(4 February 1940 to 3 June 2005)

Contents

PART II: FINANCIAL REPORTING

PART III: NARRATIVE REPORTING

Contents ix

Preface

This book seeks to provide an overview of the system of corporate reporting in company law. Disclosure is fundamental to company law and requirements for disclosure exist at many levels. As an evolving process the disclosure regime changes to reflect new developments in business activity. However, many problems exist in the disclosure regime, partly because it fails to keep pace with the speed of changes in business and partly because its character is shaped by the traditional, shareholder-centred legal model of the company. The introduction of the operating and financial review attempted to resolve some of the problems identified in the disclosure system, but in this book I seek to argue that the OFR would not have been a sufficiently radical development. The recent repeal of the OFR by the Chancellor of the Exchequer, Gordon Brown, perhaps demonstrates the inadequacy of the Regulation before it came into effect.

Most company law textbooks consider disclosure rules as part of their general discussion of the company law regime. Disclosure usually also takes a central position in discussions of corporate governance. Increasingly there is recognition in the company law debates of the importance of disclosure. In this book I therefore attempt to bring together the various aspects of disclosure and corporate reporting and to provide an overall assessment of the regime. Of course it must be understood within its company law context and as part of the commercial environment in which it occurs. I hope to show, however, that the disclosure system itself is relevant to future directions for company law and that provides a reflection of the limits inherent in the company law system as a whole. Within the confines of this monograph it is not possible to provide great detail about the practical intricacies of specific rules. Such work is arguably better left to academics in the field of accounting and auditing. However, for company lawyers, the form of regulation adopted within the disclosure system is relevant to the objectives of that system. If the regulatory mechanisms are not appropriate the system will not achieve what it sets out to do.

My basic argument in this book is that the corporate reporting and disclosure system is closely tied to the profit maximisation goal of shareholders and therefore focuses primarily on financial accounting and reporting. This narrow focus influences developments relating to social and environmental reporting so that stakeholder advocates are likely to be disappointed if they rely on the disclosure system in its present form to take their objectives forward. More research will need to be done but I hope that this book at least begins a serious debate about the role of disclosure in modern company law, faced with the challenges of globalisation and information technology. Those challenges also present opportunities for improving the disclosure system and I hope that this book will help to set that process in motion.

I have a long list of people to thank. Andrew McGee gave me the idea for this project half a decade ago, and Barry Rider helped me to get it started by supporting me with the book contract with Cambridge University Press and through a research fellowship at the Institute of Advanced Legal Studies, for which I gained financial assistance from the Nuffield Foundation. I began the research during my time at Glasgow University where I was inspired by many colleagues, not least Laura MacGregor and Fraser Davidson. I was lucky to have a couple of weeks' research assistance from Lloyd Embleton there too. At the University of Bristol my present colleagues are a constant source of support and inspiration: especially Marc T. Moore, Harry McVea, Tonia Novitz and Rachel Murray. I have presented papers related to the research for this book at a number of institutions: the University of Warwick, the University of Dundee and the University of Leicester as well as at conferences including the Society of Legal Scholars Conference at the University of Sheffield 2004, and the British Association of Chartered Accountants' Annual Conference in Cardiff in 2001. Kim Hughes at Cambridge University Press has given to me heaps of encouragement and enduring patience and Jan Green and Matthias Punt have helped me with printing various drafts. Finally, a huge thanks to Tony, who has held the fort on too many weekends, and for being so supportive at my low points.

I cannot let this book go without mention of its coincidence with a number of important personal events that have interrupted its completion. My two beautiful children, Amelia and Laurence, were born during the research and held it up and distracted it along the way. My mother, thankfully, came through a serious illness. Sadly, my father died just as I was in the finishing stages of the book. He was always eager to talk about my research and I will miss his infinite common sense and level-headedness. It is to his memory that I dedicate the book. My uncle also died even more recently. The book therefore will retain a personal significance for me and I hope it will have some academic significance for my company law colleagues.

Stop press

As this book reaches proof stage two significant developments occurred: the publication of the Company Law Reform Bill and the decision of the Chancellor of the Exchequer, Gordon Brown, to scrap the OFR Regulations. Both events are relevant to the subject of this book but occur at a time when it is difficult to incorporate them fully or comment on them in depth without delaying the book's publication intolerably. I have therefore decided to add limited reference to the developments where possible, in particular in Chapter 9. In any event, such developments arguably confirm the observations made in my overall thesis.

Bristol, July 2005   CHARLOTTE VILLIERS

Table of legislation

Table of cases

Introduction

> Good company reporting is essential. It provides information to shareholders, as well as creditors, employees and others who may have an interest in companies and their activities. Equally, the need for information has to be balanced against the cost to the company of collecting and publishing that information, as well as the cost to the readers in finding the information they are seeking. More information is not necessarily better information; and the Government is firmly committed to improving the quality rather than the mere quantity of company reporting.[1]

Disclosure and information sharing represent a substantial portion of company law. The briefest of glances at the legislation and legal texts will highlight to the reader the importance of the so-called 'disclosure philosophy'. Disclosure requirements appear in statutes, in codes of practice and in rule books of various institutions with which many companies are connected, such as the Financial Services Authority. Information is delivered and shared in a variety of different forms and by using a broad range of media including written reports, newspaper reports, internet and advertising. There are many participants involved in the company's disclosure activities, especially for larger public listed companies.

Despite this emphasis on disclosure a considerable degree of scepticism also exists about the effectiveness of the disclosure system in the UK. The main criticisms focus on the complexity and cost burdens that pervade the disclosure system and the lack of clear measures used for assessing a company's performance, as well as the poor quality of the verification process, the failure of such disclosure to provide users with what they need and, finally, reactions to information that is produced. The fact that such criticisms exist leads naturally to the question of the role of disclosure and the appropriateness of the system currently in place. Before answering this question one needs to settle on the aims of company law and more particularly, the aims of disclosure.

[1] White Paper, *Modernising Company Law* (July 2002), Cm. 5553–I, para. 4.1, at p. 33.

Is disclosure itself an appropriate system for achieving the objectives of company law generally? The answer to this question depends upon a clear understanding of the goals of companies and company law and the purpose of disclosure, a knowledge of the features of the disclosure regime and what disclosure requirements exist, as well as the practice of disclosure by companies and empirical evidence on communication processes.

The UK's disclosure regime is part of a legal framework that assumes a shareholder-centred model of the company. Mary Stokes, for example, describes the various phases of the legal model, highlighting first the traditional model, which 'originally treated the directors of the company as agents of the company', whose authority could 'at any moment be revoked by the shareholders' and the 'shareholders as the principal were entitled to issue specific instructions to the directors which as agents they were obliged to implement.' Then when the traditional model was abandoned and the board of directors 'came to be viewed as an organ of the company' with the shareholders no longer exercising the direct control of principals over the directors as their agents, nevertheless the model gave 'power to the shareholders to appoint and dismiss the directors and power to supervise them' and the fiduciary duties imposed upon directors meant that directors would be under a duty to act in the best interests of the shareholders. They cannot place their own interests above those of the shareholders.[2] Under this model, the primary interest attributed to shareholders is profit. Again, Mary Stokes asserts that the legal model adopts two mechanisms for ensuring that the directors of the company are subject to the control of the shareholders: by the structure of the internal division of power within the company so that shareholders can appoint and dismiss the directors and supervise them whilst in office and by the fiduciary duties that require them to act in the best interests of the shareholders. Stokes adds: 'the common aim of both legal mechanisms is to force managers to maximise profits for their company and prevent them from maximising their own utility'. Stokes says further, 'Corporate managers' discretion will be legitimated since their power will be severely limited by the requirement that all their decisions must aim simply at profit-maximization.'[3]

---

[2] See Mary Stokes, 'Company Law and Legal Theory' in W. Twining (ed.), *Legal Theory and Common Law* (Blackwell, Oxford, 1986) 155, esp. at pp. 160–1. See for a similar analysis of US corporate law developments, David Millon, 'Theories of the Corporation' (1990) 193 *Duke Law Journal* 201.

[3] Stokes, *ibid.*, at pp. 165–6.

The potential benefits of disclosure make this generally an attractive form of regulation. In the context of the American health care system, Sage remarks that 'because disclosure laws influence private transactions without substituting direct government regulation, they illuminate all parts of the political spectrum, appealing equally to conservatives, who applaud "market facilitation" and "bootstrapping" and to liberals who favour "empowerment" and the "right to know"'.[4] This same observation could also be made of corporate disclosure laws. The Cadbury Committee, for example, advocated disclosure as a mechanism for accountability, emphasising the need to raise reporting standards in order to ward off the threat of regulation.[5] The Hampel Committee also regarded disclosure as 'the most important element' of accountability[6] and in introducing a new code and set of principles stated that their objective was 'not to prescribe corporate behaviour in detail but to secure sufficient disclosure so that investors and others can assess companies' performance and governance practice and respond in an informed way'.[7]

There also exist more positive reasons for a disclosure system than merely the avoidance of regulatory intervention. For example, disclosure could enable investors to make more accurate investment decisions and that disclosure could protect them and others from fraud by managers or directors. Additionally, some advocates suggest that a disclosure system could contribute to corporate democracy by enabling participants to make and influence decisions more effectively. Eccles and Mavrinac emphasise the interactive role of disclosure that brings about positive results for the firm since the intent of disclosure 'is to create shared perspectives and perceptions, build a context for constructive debate, and develop a supporting context to ensure effective capital allocation both inside and outside the firm'.[8] Disclosure of information

---

[4] William Sage, 'Regulating Through Information: Disclosure Laws and American Health Care' (1999) 99 *Columbia Law Review* 1701, at pp. 1825–6.

[5] Cadbury Committee, *Report on the Financial Aspects of Corporate Governance* (Gee, London, 1992), at para. 3.6. See also para. 1.10 at which the Committee stresses the advantages of a voluntary code and best practice over statutory regulation.

[6] Hampel Committee, *Final Report on Corporate Governance* (Gee, London, 1998), at para. 1.2.

[7] Hampel Committee Report, at para. 1.25. See also para. 1.9 at which the Hampel Committee observes that the primary aim of the Greenbury Committee, which reported on directors' remuneration, was full disclosure rather than control of board remuneration. See further, Greenbury Committee, *Report on Directors' Remuneration* (Gee, London, 1995).

[8] Robert G. Eccles and Sarah C. Mavrinac, 'Improving the Corporate Disclosure Process' (1995) *Sloan Management Review*, Summer Issue, 11, at p. 23.

also provides participants with choice and the opportunity to make judgements.[9] Information connects choice and accountability and participation.[10] Choice provides participants with opportunities for exit from the organisation. In this way existing shareholders require information in order for them to give their consent to or to influence the way in which the managers perform their functions. Ultimately, as Sage remarks, 'lasting benefit from disclosure generally requires the availability of choice through entry and exit, ongoing control, political voice, or other forms of self-help through legal or extralegal mechanisms.'[11] It can be concluded then that disclosure has the potential to improve corporate behaviour and relationships and in doing so might also ward off more demanding forms of external regulation.

However, despite its appeal disclosure risks being an ineffective form of regulation if it is not designed appropriately to meet its objectives. For example, investors cannot make good investment decisions without relevant information. This might require predictions and details of future projections by directors and managers rather than just historical information. In addition, if attention is not paid to providing meaningful disclosure over time then this will result in 'boiler plates' that are of no real benefit to any of the participants.[12] Similarly, if information is provided in obscure or over-technical language or is not made widely available or not presented in good time then it could be ignored or missed despite its relevance to a decision. A poorly designed disclosure system could also lead to information overload by which the participants are unable to process the information effectively.[13] Ernst and Young made such an observation when the requirements introduced by the Greenbury Committee on disclosure of directors' remuneration had the effect of increasing the length of annual reports substantially, causing shareholders to discard or ignore the information because of the burden

---

[9] Patrick Birkinshaw, *Freedom of Information: The Law, the Practice and the Ideal* (2nd edn, Butterworths, London, 1996), at p. 14. According to Birkinshaw, 'information in the form of facts constitutes the basis of order in our lives, of community, regularity and knowledge'. *Ibid.*

[10] Lewis states that, 'as part of the argument surrounding accountability it is important to develop the innate relationship between choice and debate or discourse and freely available information'. See Norman D. Lewis, *Choice and the Legal Order:Rising Above Politics* (Butterworths, London, 1996) at p. 17.

[11] Sage, *op. cit.*, at pp. 1827–8.

[12] Boiler plates are rhetorical statements of policy or practice with stock phrases that fail to contain any meaning. Ernst & Young give the example of the phrase 'attract, retain and motivate' that is used in so many accounts that it has lost its meaning: *ibid.*, at p. 22. See also KPMG, *The Combined Code: A Practical Guide* (Gee, London, 1999), at p. 58.

[13] See, for example, R. Groves, 'Financial Disclosure: When More is Not Better' (May–June 1994) *Financial Executive* 11–4.

it imposed on them.[14] In this way, Ernst & Young saw the 'sheer volume of information' as 'a barrier to effective communication'[15] and suspected that 'all but the most determined readers, when faced with a page or more of dense figurework simply skip to the next paragraph of narrative'.[16] These shortcomings in the disclosure system could result in poor decisions, causing loss to the participants or, perhaps in extreme cases, even failure of the company. In any event, if the disclosure system is not designed appropriately it is likely at best that the costs will exceed the benefits that might be gained.

The above paragraph makes it clear that simply to demand disclosure is not sufficient. Rather, some thought has to be given to the content and form of the required information. Such disclosure rules, if they are to be meaningful, should be cohesive and should address the specific objectives that they claim.[17] An example is provided by Lewis, who makes direct reference to information and its importance for consumer choice in the market place. He points out that to make free and effective choices price is not the only information needed. Rather, the seller as manufacturer or retailer must provide the purchaser with all the available information in his possession. Otherwise, according to Lewis, 'choices are partial, forced or even fake'.[18] Consequently, as Lewis asserts, this necessitates information of a constructive nature on safety, quality, durability, servicing, repair and replacement costs and the like.[19] Of course, the more purposes that are attributed to the system the more difficult it will be to design an appropriate system. This may be further complicated by the existence of a potentially wide range of interest groups seeking to participate in the disclosure and information-sharing process within the company. Thus the existence of different objectives as well as different interests gives rise to the need for a sophisticated disclosure system based on more than merely a principle of openness.

This book will show that the disclosure regime reflects a shareholder-centred structure, giving priority to shareholders over other constituents with regard to information entitlements and with an emphasis on their financial interests. A sophisticated and complex financial regulatory disclosure system has been developed over time, in which legislative

---

[14] Ernst & Greenbury Implementation (Ernst & Young, London, 1996) at para. 2.2, p. 6.
[15] Ibid., para. 2.2., at p. 6.
[16] Ibid., para. 2.2., at pp. 6–7.
[17] Sage, op. cit., at p. 1827.
[18] Lewis, Choice and the Legal Order, at p. 18.
[19] Lewis, at p. 18.

requirements are backed up by professional mandatory standards and are bolstered also by a developed verification process. The securities field is also heavily regulated with strong disclosure requirements designed to protect investors and to maintain creditable capital and financial markets.

The emphasis on equity capital and consequent focus on the interests of shareholders has resulted in a specific kind of accounting and disclosure system. The equity capital base of companies in the UK leads to a focus on shareholders. Coinciding with the existence of a common law jurisdiction, this lead to an accounting system that relies on private regulation to supplement basic statutory regulatory rules. By contrast, some other systems, in which companies rely more on loan capital, are characterised by the existence of more government-based rules and less developed private regulatory functions.

The complex and sophisticated financial reporting regulation may be contrasted with the disclosure requirements that would support a corporate social responsibility or social contract vision of the company. Social and environmental reporting requirements are indeed relatively underdeveloped, comprising mainly an array of voluntary guides and codes, which are left to the discretion of corporate managers to follow. Companies are encouraged to follow such codes as a way of improving the company's competitive position and helping it to improve its long-term profit opportunities. Thus even this aspect of disclosure has ultimately a shareholder interest objective.

The disclosure regime entails an expensive process of information gathering, reporting and analysis. Yet the evidence suggests that shareholders do not use such information to full advantage. They are inclined to use 'exit' strategies rather than seek to improve the company's long-term prospects. At the same time there are problems with the different types of information disclosed. Financial reports, for example, are typically complex and difficult to read. Social information, on the other hand, tends to lack comparability, which reduces its usefulness. As a corporate governance device disclosure is a questionable form of corporate control. Indeed, it could be accused of making matters worse. For example, disclosure rules relating to executive directors appear to have encouraged further increases in their pay levels rather than result in a ceiling over what they receive. Thus, in *The Guardian*'s recent executive pay survey, the Notebook article states,

The remuneration consultants blame executive salary demands on the trend for greater disclosure. With full details of every pay deal now revealed in annual reports and newspapers, they say, directors are bound to compare their own pay with their peers and rivals. They then demand parity – or more – and average pay is remorselessly cranked up.[20]

Recent corporate disasters across Europe and the United States underline the problems with the disclosure regime. The Enron debacle, for example, highlighted the dangers of creative accounting and poor gatekeeping. Special purpose vehicles were used to hide financial discrepancies. The auditors were too close to the managers and were accused of shredding documents. One commentator described Enron's financial statements as 'impenetrable'.[21] Similar descriptions were made of MG Rover's accounts following the company's demise.[22] There are failures at different stages of the disclosure process: failures about what is disclosed; failures in the gatekeeping functions; failures with regard to the reaction to such information; failures in dialogue between the corporate constituents; and failures of enforcement of requirements.

The lack of a clear conceptual framework might be a root cause of its problems. This may be because accounting is an evolving process with objectives that 'will change over time as a result of changes in the economic, legal, political and social environment'.[23] Stamp was led by this fact to argue that the focus should not be so much on definitions and objectives but instead on the needs and priorities of the users, also noting that these may be varied and sometimes conflicting as the potential body of users and interests grows. The ASB also notes in its *Statement of Principles of Financial Reporting* that 'accounting thought is continually evolving and it is only to be expected that the statement will need to be revised from time to time to reflect such developments'.[24]

According to Litan et al, three challenges face the disclosure environment today: globalisation, technology and the internet, and the growing importance of intangible assets to the creation of shareholder wealth.[25]

---

[20] *The Guardian*, 27 August 2004, Notebook, 'Curbs have done little to shrink bosses' pay', p. 27.

[21] See e.g., Anthony H. Catanach and Shelley Rhoades-Catanach, 'ENRON: A Financial Reporting Failure?'(2003) 48 *Villanava Law Review* 1057; Macey, 'Efficient Capital Markets, Corporate Disclosure, and Enron' (2004) 89 *Cornell L Rev* 394.

[22] Ian Griffiths, 'Breaking Down the Mechanics of the Money', *The Guardian*, 15 April 2005; Ian Griffiths, 'Rover's £400m accounting puzzle', *The Guardian*, 15 April 2005.

[23] Financial Accounting Standards Board, Statement of Financial Accounting Concepts No 1, Stamford FASB. Discussed in M.R. Mathews and M.H.B. Perera, *Accounting Theory and Development* (3rd edn, Nelson, Melbourne, 1996), ch. 6. See also Edward Stamp, 'First steps towards a British conceptual framework' (1982) *Accountancy* 123.

[24] See *Statement of Principles of Financial Reporting*, (December 2000).

[25] Robert Litan and others, *Following the Money: The Enron Failure and the State of Corporate Disclosure* (Brookings, US, Mass., 2002).

In their view, the best approach for dealing with globalisation is to inject competition at a low level and to ensure that capital flows can be maintained. They note that the internet provides many possibilities: interactive communication with investors, use of tags through XBRL (eXtensible Business Reporting Language) so that investors can look at information given from many different angles. In this way it becomes more difficult for the company to use presentational methods to hoodwink the investors and others. The increasing relevance of intangible assets means that financial reporting will not be sufficient on its own as it does not highlight sufficiently the contribution of intangibles to the performance of the business.

What has resulted is a disclosure system that is asymmetrical, being overly complex and multi-layered for financial reporting and underdeveloped for narrative, social reporting. In both broad areas international influences are important, more formally through international accounting standards and European Directives with regard to financial reporting requirements and more informally through the publication of voluntary codes of conduct and award schemes for social and environmental reporting and management.

A number of solutions are required. First it is important to address the different challenges, for example by including information relevant to the contribution of intangible assets or by making use of technological developments to improve the delivery and accessibility of information. More fundamentally, it is necessary to consider the different user needs and address them all by managing competing requirements appropriately. A system of communication needs to be more clearly developed that recognises the different users and leads to better rules and instruments and better presentation of information and that facilitates dialogue between the company and all parties affected by its activities. A new morality is required that reduces the profit motivation, that sorts out the problems involved with large institutions, that stops using nonshareholders instrumentally for profit and sees them in their own right.

This book explores the disclosure regime and suggests a number of possible solutions to the problems and limitations of the existing framework. Part one deals with the general aspects, including theoretical bases for the disclosure regime as it currently exists, an overview of the regulatory structure, and a discussion of the key players including those responsible for providing information and those who use the information produced. The official information requirements and the role of the companies registrar are also considered. Part two explores the financial reporting aspects of disclosure and covers the development of the UK's financial reporting rules and the contribution of international and European financial reporting requirements as well as the protections available within the securities markets. Part three is concerned with narrative reporting. In particular the Operating and Financial Review, social and environmental reporting and human capital management reporting are explored. Part four concludes with an overview of the current regime and concludes by offering specific solutions to some of the problems identified and suggestions on how the regime might be developed in the future.

Part I

General issues

1   Disclosure theory and the limitations of corporate reports

Introduction

In the twenty-first century the disclosure concept might be taken very much for granted in company law. The standard justification for a disclosure system in the literature in the UK is that disclosure is the price to be paid for the privileges of incorporation and limited liability. The appearance is that of tremendous faith in the disclosure philosophy with increasing demands for more information to be shared. The corporate governance debate that has dominated company law since the 1990s has generated more disclosure requirements and demands for information on issues much broader than a company's financial condition. Disclosure has many theoretical objectives. In practice, however, the disclosure system is burdened with numerous problems and the costs inherent in the system lead to questions about its validity as a regulatory technique.

This chapter will explore the theoretical bases for disclosure and the problems identified with the system. The chapter will therefore begin with a brief description of the corporate reporting and disclosure system currently in place in the UK. The second section of the chapter will explore the traditional company law arguments supporting the existence of a mandatory disclosure system. That section will be followed by a description of the problems that pervade the current system. This will lay the foundation for the remainder of this book which will explore in more depth the features of corporate disclosure regulation and the challenges the system faces.

Summary of the disclosure system in English Company Law

The disclosure system in the UK operates on a number of levels. There is an extensive body of statutory requirements. Besides these requirements there have developed several common law principles that depend on disclosure. For example, company promoters and company directors are subject to disclosure duties as a consequence of their positions as agents and fiduciaries of the company. In addition to these formal legal requirements disclosure obligations have been imposed by a number of institutions and organisations with which companies or their officers might be associated. Such obligations are laid down in codes of practice, institutional rules and organisational and professional standards and guidance. Finally, companies may choose to produce information voluntarily. Often this information is less formal and because it is voluntary is perhaps less easy to subject to evaluative comparisons or judgements. The accuracy of such information may be more insecure.

A wide variety of methods of disclosure and forms of presentation are employed. These range from information provided in the commercial register, to information maintained on company registers, and to written reports delivered at the general meeting or personally to each shareholder. Disclosure may also be forced by investigations in certain situations. Information may also be obtained through a variety of sources beside the formal legal or regulatory sources. For example, newspaper reports and internet information may provide valuable information. So also might advertising materials and information contained on product packaging. Additionally, customers or investors may obtain comparative information from external bodies such as investment analysts or consumer associations such as *Which?* Television programmes and investigative reporting may also provide the public with information not willingly disclosed by the company. As with voluntary corporate disclosure, some of these 'extra-legal' sources of information are less likely to offer guaranteed accuracy and the quality of such information will depend upon the level of professionalism and expertise of those presenting it.

The wide range of methods and forms of presenting information reflects the diversity of subjects upon which information is given. Many mandatory disclosure provisions concern financial information and information that is relevant to monitoring the management's stewardship. Within these two broad categories there is also a variety of material. For example, financial information may cover historical as well as forward-looking information. Sometimes financial information is broken down into categories of hard information, comprising statements concerning objectively verifiable facts, and soft information which comprises opinions, predictions, analyses and other subjective evaluations.[1] Management monitoring information ranges from personal details about

---

[1] See Janet E. Kerr, 'A walk through the circuits: the duty to disclose soft information' (1987) 46 *Maryland LR* 1071, footnote 2 at 1071.

directors, to levels and breakdown of their compensation packages to past experience. Some social aspects must also be disclosed such as health and safety matters in large companies. Voluntary disclosures may be more diverse covering issues such as environmental impact, community relations with the company, employee promotions.

A broad range of participants are involved in the disclosure process. The process involves both top-down and bottom-up information transfer so that directors and managers deliver and receive information. The most obvious participants are those identified in the statutory provisions: directors, members, creditors, auditors, the companies registrar, investigators, administrators, the company secretary. Yet the field of participants is much wider than traditional company law would at first suggest. Analysts, lawyers, accountants, employees, consumers, brokers, HMRC, journalists, and the wider community all have a role in the disclosure process. Indeed, it would be fair to suggest that corporate disclosure is more generally a matter of public interest.

In summary, the extent of information sharing and the breadth of interest in the delivery and receipt of information demonstrate the importance that disclosure has for company law. In the words of Professor Sealy,

If there is one key word which more than any other sums up the underlying principles of company law in this country it is disclosure. . . . . Investors are plainly entitled to be adequately informed, and creditors to be safeguarded, and society can reasonably demand nowadays that large corporations conduct their business on terms of public accountability. . . . . lawyers and company secretaries are required to go on compiling information, and the Registrar of Companies and his staff to receive it; and the cry of the would-be reformers is only for more and yet more.[2]

These words of Professor Sealy illustrate the impact of the disclosure phenomenon on company law and its significance for those participating in corporate activities. However, Professor Sealy was writing in 1981 in an article in which he expressed doubts about the efficacy of the disclosure system as it had developed by then. The doubts expressed by Professor Sealy arose mainly from the volume and consequential costs of the disclosure system leading him to ask whether the system warranted such costs. Since that date there have been introduced many more disclosure obligations.

---

[2] Leonard Sealy, 'The Disclosure Philosophy and Company Law Reform' (1981) 2 *Company Lawyer* 51, at p. 51.

Is a mandatory corporate disclosure system necessary?

An extensive legal literature has evolved, much of it in the US, on the value of a mandatory disclosure system. That debate has been largely influenced by economic considerations and has focused on the efficiency levels achieved by disclosure. The key arguments in favour of disclosure include, prevention of fraud, investor protection, corporate governance and accountability of managers to the shareholders, corporate democracy, efficiency through reduction of monitoring and information search costs, reduction of competitive injury, standardisation of information making comparison easier, alternative to regulatory intervention and political and social benefits arising from disclosure. These arguments need to be weighed against the perceived and observed problems of mandatory disclosure. In short these consist of complexity, overload, cost of providing and of interpreting information, potential threat to confidentiality, lack of relevance, lack of interest on the part of the shareholders, misleading and incomplete information. In this section I will explore these different rationales for disclosure in more detail.

Incorporation and limited liability

Traditionally, the main reasons for disclosure in English company law have been incorporation and limited liability. Indeed, Sealy notes that disclosure has been an underlying principle of company law in the UK 'ever since companies were accorded the twin privileges of incorporation and limited liability by the legislation of 1844 and 1855'.[3] The leading text books adopt this reasoning.[4] Clearly this claim does bear weight but there is evidence that disclosure was relevant even before the advent of limited liability at least, and also that from a very early date there existed other reasons for mandatory disclosure. Thus, as Mahoney has shown, periodic public disclosure by corporations for the benefit of creditors was a settled feature of English company law from its beginning.[5] In fact, even before limited liability was provided companies would be required to make a biannual public statement noting transfer of their shares so that creditors would know the names and addresses of current investors

---

[3] Sealy, *ibid.*, at p. 51.
[4] See e.g., Paul L. Davies (ed.), *Gower's Principles of Modern Company Law* (6th edn, Sweet and Maxwell, London, 1997) at p. 512.
[5] Paul G. Mahoney, 'Mandatory Disclosure as a Solution to Agency Problems' (1995) 62 *University of Chicago Law Review* 1047, at pp. 1056–7.

in the event of non-payment.[6] Even after limited liability had been introduced when partly paid shares were usual there were to be filed annually shareholders' names and addresses and the amount of their unpaid subscriptions.[7]

Another indication that limited liability and incorporation might not be the sole reasons for a mandatory disclosure system is the fact that disclosure is not just relevant to third parties, outsiders dealing with the company. Yet a logical consequence of disclosure based on these reasons would be disclosure of information concentrating on third party needs. Of course the information published and retained on the companies register is available for public inspection; indeed, the existence of a public register and the *Gazette* might suggest that third party needs are primary. Yet there is much information that is not available to third parties and they are not the group always given priority in the legislation. Rather, most information is provided to investors and potential investors. This fact gives rise to the suggestion that there are reasons beyond the incorporation and limited liability of companies for having a mandatory disclosure system, with the implication that a disclosure system may be more complex and consist of several more different levels and participants than would be necessary for responding to incorporation and limited liability. Indeed, the debate that surrounds securities disclosure concentrates mainly on the prevention of fraud and investor protection, which would possibly require different disclosure mechanisms than might be needed for third parties only.

Prevention of fraud

The early history of English company law shows that fraud was considered relevant to disclosure. One reason for the enactment of the Companies Clauses Consolidation Act 1845 was a response to the history leading from the South Sea Bubble scandal. One of the two key objectives of the Act was to 'obviate the evils of fraudulent and fictitious companies'. Gladstone stated then that 'publicity is all that is necessary. Show up the roguery and it is harmless'.[8] The Companies Act 1900 has been described as the 'first statute in Anglo-American law to impose

---

[6] Joint Stock Companies Act 1844, at para. XI. See Mahoney, *ibid.*
[7] See Companies Act 1862, para. 26. Mahoney, *ibid.*
[8] Robert L. Knauss, 'A Reappraisal of the Role of Disclosure' (1964) 62 *Michigan Law Review* 607, at pp. 610–1. See also Louis Loss, 'Disclosure as Preventive Enforcement' in K. Hopt and G. Teubner, *Corporate Governance and Directors' Liabilities* (de Gruyter, New York, Berlin, 1985) 327, at p. 327, quoting *The Times*, 4 July 1844.

comprehensive disclosure requirements on companies selling securities to the public'.[9] It has been suggested again that the 1900 Act aimed to deal with the problem of frauds on shareholders by promoters.[10] Thus the early history of English company law would suggest that prevention of fraud does contribute as an explanation for a mandatory disclosure system.

In theory, the problem for a person buying securities is that he or she is 'unable to make an immediate value judgement, as they would with tangible items'.[11] As is explained by Knauss, the investor

must look behind the piece of paper and examine the merits of the company which has issued the security. The buyer must of necessity rely on this information given to him and on material generally available from the company. The less information available the less the market price will be representative of the security's true value and the greater will be the opportunity for fraud.[12]

This leads to the suggestion that government regulation is necessary and one form of such regulation would be to impose a disclosure requirement on those offering the securities for sale. Mandatory disclosure would arguably deter the concealment or the misrepresentation of information material to investment decisions.[13]

Fraud prevention appears as a reason in much of the literature concerned with securities disclosure. Small and uninformed investors are considered to be particularly vulnerable to the possibility of fraud. However, although there is evidence to suggest that the adoption of disclosure rules helped to reduce fraudulent behaviour or misrepresentations,[14] the ability of a mandatory disclosure regime to prevent fraud is not complete; fraud continues to occur even after disclosure schemes have been established.[15] However, some steps towards prevention are better than none and it could be argued that disclosure has brought at least some

---

[9] Mahoney, at p. 1063.

[10] Cottrell, *Industrial Finance: 1830–1914*, (Methuen,1979) at p. 74, cited by Mahoney, *supra*, at p. 1065.

[11] Knauss, at p. 610.

[12] *Ibid.*, at p. 610.

[13] Joel Seligman, 'The Historical Need for a Mandatory Corporate Disclosure System' (1983) 9 *Journal of Corporation Law* 1, at pp. 10–45.

[14] Seligman, who reveals evidence that fraud was more prevalent among firms who were not subject to the disclosure rules introduced in the United States in 1933 and 1934, *ibid.*

[15] Widely publicised examples in the UK include the fall of the Maxwell empire, Polly Peck and the Bank of Credit and Commerce International. More recent scandals highlighting fraud include ENRON, Parmalat, Worldcom and Tyco. See also Christian J. Meier-Schatz, 'Objectives of Financial Disclosure Regulation' (1986) 8 *Journal of Comparative Business and Capital Market Law* 219, at p. 221.

protection since it appears that some schemes will not even be begun because disclosure is in place.[16] Thus disclosure can claim at least to reduce if not eliminate fraud.

The reduction of fraud should have the positive consequence of increasing confidence in the capital market. Indeed, if formally presented data is able to confirm data received by less formal channels[17] that ought eventually to build trust and encourage larger investments to be made. This leads to the suggestion that fraud may be a first instance motive but may be accompanied by a longer term, and perhaps stronger, objective of creating a free and open securities market.[18] Of course that result depends on confidence and confidence is not only connected with fraud prevention but also with making accurate investment decisions. This provides a link between the two claims that disclosure helps to prevent fraud and protects investors.

Investor protection

The close connection between fraud prevention and investor protection is self-evident. Investors, as well as potential creditors, are most likely to be the victims of securities fraud.[19] Investor protection thus entails protection from fraud or mismanagement[20] as well as helping investors to make more accurate investment decisions. This was certainly regarded as a relevant consideration in the earlier English company law when the public were encouraged to finance investments, many of which turned out to be unsound. As Mahoney has argued, the inspiration for the English disclosure system was the activities of promoters who had a reputation for unsound behaviour. An agency position arose for them which required disclosure.[21] In the case of *New Brunswick and Canada Railway Holding* v. *Muggeridge*[22] it was stated that:

those who issue a prospectus holding out to the public the great advantages which will accrue to persons who will take shares in a proposed undertaking, and inviting them to take shares on the faith of the representations therein contained, are bound to state

---

[16] Meier-Schatz, *ibid.*, at p. 221.
[17] Meier-Schatz, *ibid.*, at p. 221.
[18] Knauss, at pp. 613–4.
[19] Professor Gower actually regards investors as creditors in the context of fundraising (see 4th edn of his *Principles of Modern Company Law* (Sweet & Maxwell, London, 1979), at p. 356), though this view has been doubted by John Azzi, 'Disclosure in Prospectuses' (1992) 9 *Company and Securities Law Journal* 205, at pp. 211–2. Employees often suffer in the fall-out too: see e.g., Enron.
[20] Knauss refers to unsound calculations and inadequate management, at p. 610.
[21] Mahoney.
[22] 1 Dr and S, 381.

everything with strict and scrupulous accuracy, and not only to abstain from stating as fact that which is not so, but to omit no one fact within their knowledge the existence of which might in any degree affect the nature, or extent, or quality of the privileges and advantages which the prospectus holds out as inducements to take shares.

However, Mahoney does not deny that accuracy enhancement has relevance and this is certainly a claim made by other commentators. In theory more information will lead to greater accuracy and not only does this allow for a greater diversity of approaches but, further, if investors could make informed decisions their confidence in the markets would increase.[23] This would appear to lie behind governmental and legislative claims for 'timely' and 'material' disclosure that would be necessary for making investment decisions.[24]

Despite the theoretical logic of this claim the reality appears to lead to more circumspection. Meier-Schatz for example argues that the investor protection argument is not so strong because often the investors are affluent and experienced and are capable of protecting themselves, though he does concede that smaller investors who have private savings in shares might require protection. In that case there might be an argument for tailoring prospectuses to the needs and levels of understanding of those smaller investors. Yet, as Meier-Schatz observes, often they do not read prospectuses, and often the information is available on the market anyway so those smaller investors can free ride on information sought by active investors, usually larger or institutional investors.[25] In addition, Azzi asks who are the users of prospectuses and should the information be understandable by ordinary people? On the one hand an investor could be anybody.[26] But on the other hand, in reality an investor might need to be a professional trained in accounting to be able to understand the information supplied.[27] One problem is that disclosure appears unable to protect less experienced investors from high pressure selling techniques.[28] These factors could lead to some scepticism as to the extent that disclosure actually brings returns for

---

[23] Seligman, 'Disclosure System'.

[24] Corporate Law Reform Bill (No. 2) 1992 second reading speech, Senator N. Balkus, 26 November 1992: 'essential that there be timely disclosure . . . Disclosure of relevant information about an investment and access to such information, either directly or through advisers, is necessary to ensure an equitable and efficient investment system.' Quoted by Mark Blair and Ian M. Ramsay, 'Mandatory Corporate Disclosure Rules and Securities Regulation' in G. Walker and B. Fisse (eds.), *Securities Regulation in Australia and New Zealand* (Oxford University Press, Melbourne, 1994) ch. 12, 264, at p. 264.

[25] Meier-Schatz, at p. 222.

[26] Azzi, 'Disclosures in Prospectuses. . .' at p. 207.

[27] Azzi, *ibid.*, at pp. 207–8, citing Homer Kripke, *The SEC and Securities Disclosure* (1979).

[28] Knauss, at pp. 617–8.

investors. However, investors may be protected by the use of disclosure as a mechanism for accountability.

Accountability

The claim by Mahoney that disclosure has an important monitoring function, made necessary from the agency relationship that exists between the corporate managers and the shareholders, carries some weight. In the context of public companies this agency relationship entails a particular structure. While it is not entirely representative of public companies today, Berle and Means' analysis, based on the theory of separation of ownership and control, still has authority.[29] This analysis suggests an evolution by which the two functions of ownership and control of the enterprise have been separated. When the owner was also in control of his enterprise he could operate it in his own interest and the philosophy surrounding the institution of private property had assumed that he would do so. This assumption, according to Berle and Means, was carried over to present conditions and it is still expected that the enterprise will be operated in the interests of the owners. However, the practical effect of the separation of ownership and control is that, 'the position of the owner has been reduced to that of having a set of legal and factual interests in the enterprise while the group which we have called control, are in the position of having legal and factual powers over it'.[30] The danger within this evolved structure is that if the interests of those in control grow primarily out of the desire for personal monetary gain, there is created a potential divergence of interests between those in control of the firm and those who own the firm.

This divergence of interests could encourage the managers or controllers to direct the firm in their own interests rather than in the interests of the owners, or the stockholders. This may be made possible by the information asymmetry which arises from the divorce between ownership and control.[31] From this analysis, in which the shareholder is said to have surrendered a set of definite rights for a set of indefinite expectations, it might be presumed that the law should seek to protect the shareholder by imposing disclosure obligations on the controller. First,

---

[29] Adolf A. Berle and Gardiner C. Means, *The Modern Corporation and Private Property* (1991) (originally published in 1932 by Harcourt, Brace and World Inc.).
[30] Berle and Means, *ibid.*, at p. 113. Note that the owner of the company is the stockholder or the shareholder.
[31] P. Ormrod and K. C. Cleaver, 'Financial Reporting and Corporate Accountability' (1993) 23 *Accounting and Business Research* 431, at p. 431.

disclosure regulations might help to redress the informational imbalance between managers and investors, and indeed between promoters and investors[32], against whom it appears that disclosure obligations first arose. Secondly, such disclosure obligations might prevent actions by the controller which contravene the interests of the owner. Both possibilities could have the effect of empowering shareholders to take a more active role in monitoring the managers and in participating in corporate decision-making.

If shareholders are given a more equal access to information with the managers it is likely that they will have a better understanding of management decisions and be able to participate in decision-making. One key aspect of participation is monitoring of management and managerial activity. Disclosure is necessary for the managers to be able to explain their actions. The existence of such disclosure requirements might of itself encourage higher standards of behaviour by the company directors. A frequently quoted statement is that of US Supreme Court Justice Brandeis: 'publicity is justly commended as a remedy for social and industrial diseases. Sunlight is said to be the best of disinfectants; electric light the most efficient policeman.'[33] Brandeis's words have been used in support of the suggestion that disclosure and publicity create incentives to forego, rescind or restructure transactions or relationships that cannot stand the light of day. The opportunistic reporting hypothesis claims that without such regulations management would be encouraged to conceal information that would damage their own interests.[34] Thus disclosure regulation arguably encourages 'housecleaning' so that companies can eliminate unproductive, inequitable or simply embarrassing self-dealing transactions between insiders and the company.[35] For example, in tender offer situations mandatory disclosure rules may inhibit the manipulation of information by managers to protect their own interests.[36] In fact, disclosure may even be used more positively as a way of influencing corporate behaviour. In this way, the knowledge that transactions would have to be disclosed might influence corporate managers to use their power prudently and properly.[37] For example, disclosure may encourage revision of compensation policies and stock

---

[32] Mark A. Sargent, 'State Disclosure Regulation and the Allocation of Regulatory Responsibilities' (1987) 46 *Maryland LR* 1027, at p. 1045.

[33] L. Brandeis, *Other People's Money* (1933), at p. 62.

[34] Blair and Ramsay, at p. 267.

[35] Sargent, at p. 1045.

[36] Meier-Schatz, at p. 228.

[37] Elliot Weiss, 'Disclosure and Corporate Accountability' (1979) 34 *The Business Lawyer* 575, at p. 580.

option programmes in order to make them more equitable.[38] By creating such incentives disclosure can have a positive effect as well as a defensive purpose that seeks to avoid bad behaviour – it can be used to improve behaviour. In this way disclosure is seen potentially to have normative goals and effects and has a functional quality.[39] By deterring self-dealing and other questionable practices disclosure can encourage and promote greater loyalty.[40]

One way in which these positive effects can be achieved is by empowering shareholders through ensuring that they receive the information they need to make decisions and assert their influence on the directors. In this way disclosure helps to restore the power balance that has been lost in the agency relationship and the separation of ownership and control. Disclosure thus encourages shareholders to exercise 'voice' rather than run for 'exit' in Hirschman's terminology.[41] Where disclosure regulation is weak this serves only to strengthen the position of power enjoyed by the corporate executives.[42]

Corporate democracy

Encouraging shareholders to participate enfranchises them and, in theory, enables them to use their voting powers more effectively. This improves the quality of corporate democracy. Indeed, promotion of 'fair corporate suffrage' was an explicit legislative objective of the corporate disclosure provisions of the Securities Act of 1934 in the US.[43] Many commentators have also drawn parallels between the company and government.[44]

Yet despite these claims to better corporate democracy there are limits to the potential of disclosure in this regard. Indeed, even though Berle

---

[38] Sargent, at p. 1045.

[39] *Ibid.*, at p. 1045.

[40] Meier-Schatz, at p. 228.

[41] Elliott J. Weiss and Donald E. Schwartz, 'Using Disclosure to Activate the Board of Directors' 63, at pp. 80–2. See also Albert O. Hirschman, *Exit Voice and Loyalty: Responses to Decline in firms, Organizations and States* (Harvard University Press, Cambridge, Mass., 1970).

[42] Bayless Manning, 'Thinking Straight About Corporate Law Reform' (1977) 41 *Law and Contemporary Problems* 3, at p. 27.

[43] HR Rep. No. 1383, 73d Cong., Sess. 13–4 (1934): see Elliot Weiss, 'Disclosure and Corporate Accountability' (1979) 34 *The Business Lawyer* 575, at p. 580.

[44] See for example, Russell B. Stevenson, 'The Corporation as a Political Institution' [1979] 8 *Hofstra LR* 39; Julian Blanchard, 'Corporate Accountability and Information – Lessons from Democracy' (1997) 7 *Australian Journal of Corporate Law* 326; Mary Stokes, 'Company Law and Legal Theory' in W. Twining, (ed.), *Common Law and Legal Theory* (Blackwell, London, 1986) 155.

and Means advocated disclosure as an appropriate form of regulation
their attention focused on a more general disclosure of information to
the market rather than disclosure to the shareholders within the company. Even then, the disclosure requirements of the company would not
be significantly onerous.[45] Moreover, the weakness in the notion of
shareholder democracy is identified by the separation of ownership and
control theory because it attributes to the shareholders a very limited
electoral role.[46] The reality of the apathy of shareholders is well known
and signifies the disincentives in place for shareholders to participate and
seek to influence corporate activity. This 'rational apathy' is often due to
the unattractive economics of shareholder activism, and the costs of
carrying out a proxy campaign are very high – that problem made worse
by the fact that the dissenting shareholder cannot recover his or her
expenses if the action fails.[47]

In reality the parallels with political government and democracy are
limited.[48] For example, governments usually have to answer to an opposition party whereas boards of directors present themselves for re-election
on a rotation basis; governments are usually subjected to independent
scrutiny whereas independent monitoring of management boards has
proven difficult to achieve in the corporate environment; unlike governments management has often been able to control votes made at
company meetings; and, finally, media attention on government activities is generally more comprehensive than is the case for individual
companies which tend only to come under media spotlight in limited
circumstances such as in the context of a takeover bid, major fraud or
a boardroom crisis. Ultimately, to claim that disclosure improves
corporate democracy is perhaps to make too strong a claim for the
effectiveness of disclosure in its current form. An alternative case in
favour of disclosure regulation has been that of efficiency. Indeed,
Meier-Schatz suggests that the emphasis has shifted from protection
and fairness towards information and efficiency.[49] Thus, mandatory
disclosure may provide necessary information more efficiently than can
the marketplace.

---

[45] In this respect Berle and Means expressed the following view: 'It will be noticed that in
dealing with corporate information the underlying assumption is that such information
must be considered as a private matter, of interest only to its shareholders; and even
in that regard limits in the extreme the information which the corporate management
must make available, even to its own shareholders' at p. 279.
[46] Stevenson, at pp. 39–40.
[47] Weiss, at p. 581.
[48] Blanchard.
[49] Meier-Schatz, at p. 221.

Efficiency

Meier-Schatz observed in the 1980s a shift towards a greater focus on information and efficiency.[50] Indeed, efficiency has evolved into a key issue in the debates upon disclosure obligations in company law.[51] The Department of Trade and Industry's company law review also high-lighted the influence of economics and efficiency considerations upon law reform policy:[52] 'transparency should lead to the efficient operation of market forces and the exercise of beneficial economic choices without the need for legal or regulatory intervention with its distorting and costly effects'.[53] Disclosure might, from this perspective, be regarded as an efficient alternative to substantive regulation.

The phases of the economic debate There have been a number of shifts in the economic arguments concerned with disclosure. In the US, where the literature is plentiful, Coffee observes three distinct phases in the progress of the economic debate upon disclosure: the 'motherhood' phase in which mandatory disclosure was said to protect investors; the revisionist phase in which empirical evidence was produced doubting the alleged benefits of a mandatory disclosure system; and the efficiency capital markets hypothesis phase which has since dominated the arguments surrounding disclosure and which has undergone changes of its own.[54]

The efficient capital market hypothesis A simple description of the efficient capital market has been provided by Sharpe: 'in a well-functioning market, the prices of securities will reflect predictions based on all relevant and available information'.[55] The important feature is that even when information is not immediately and costlessly available to all participants, the market will behave as if it were. Fama identified three different possible strengths of the efficient market at which securities prices would reflect information.[56] In its strong form the share prices

---

[50] *Ibid.*, at p. 221.
[51] Boyle sees a clear link between economic considerations and disclosure regimes: A. J. Boyle, 'Economic considerations in Part 3 of the Law Commission's paper on company directors' (1999) 20 *Co Lawyer* 210, at p. 211.
[52] See for example, Department of Trade and Industry, *Modern Company Law for a Competitive Economy: Developing the Framework* (HMSO, London, March 2000) ch.5.
[53] DTI (2000), para. 5.3, at p. 152.
[54] John C. Coffee, 'Market Failure and the Economic Case for a Mandatory Disclosure System' (1984) 70 *Va L Rev* 717.
[55] Sharpe, Note, (1970) 25 *J Fin* 418, at p. 418, quoted in Ronald J. Gilson and Reinier H. Kraakman, 'The Mechanisms of Market Efficiency' (1984) 70 *Va LR* 549, at p. 552.
[56] Eugene Fama, 'Efficient Capital Markets: A Review of Theory and Empirical Work' (1970) 25 *J Fin* 383.

would reflect all information publicly available or otherwise. In its semi-strong form the prices would reflect all publicly available information. In its weak form current prices would reflect the information supplied by the historical sequence of prices. This information will be the most widely available. The occurrence of insider dealing suggests that the strong form of the efficient capital market does not operate in practice.[57] Instead, commentators generally conclude that the empirical evidence supports the semi-strong version of market efficiency, since tests have indicated that share prices adjust quickly to reflect new relevant information.

The general claim advanced for the semi-strong form of the efficient market is that all available public information is impounded unbiasedly in share prices as soon as it becomes available[58] and also to the point of anticipating new information prior to its public announcement and dissemination.[59] The securities prices behave as if everyone observes the signals from the information system.[60]

This form of market efficiency is by definition limited. The most obvious limitation is that private information will not be reflected in the securities prices. There may also be differences in levels of information efficiency between large and small companies.[61] Some shares are also more actively traded than are others.[62] Additionally, the majority of companies are not listed on stock exchanges or investment markets and information relating to such companies will not be released to the public so easily.[63] A further problem is that the semi-strong version of market efficiency does not provide any guarantees against the market mispricing securities. A number of factors can cause securities to be mispriced, ranging from 'noise' to overreaction of investors and cognitive biases.[64] A further limitation identified by Beaver is that the semi-strong efficient

---

[57] Brian R. Cheffins, *Company Law: Theory, Structure and Operation* (Clarendon Press, Oxford,1997), at p. 56. See also Eilís Ferran, *Company Law and Corporate Finance* (OUP, Oxford, 1999), at pp. 64–5.

[58] R. D. Hines, 'The Usefulness of Annual Reports: the Anomaly between the Efficient Markets Hypothesis and Shareholder Surveys' (1982) *Accounting and Business Research* 296, at p. 296.

[59] Meier-Schatz, at p. 224.

[60] William H. Beaver, *Financial Reporting: An Accounting Revolution* (3rd edn, Prentice Hall, New Jersey, 1998) at p. 127.

[61] Mark Blair and Ian M. Ramsay, 'Mandatory Corporate Disclosure Rules and Securities Regulation' in G. Walker and B. Fisse (eds.), *Securities Regulation in Australia and New Zealand* (Oxford University Press, Melbourne,1994) ch. 12, 264, at p. 276.

[62] *Ibid.*

[63] Meier-Schatz, at p. 224.

[64] Blair and Ramsay, at pp. 276–7.

market is concerned only with financial information and focuses more on short-term issues. It is not particularly concerned with social goals or long-term decision-making.[65]

As has been noted, this form of efficiency is related to publicly available information and so it is possible that investors could still gain abnormal returns or unfair information advantages with regard to private information.[66] The key question then becomes whether or not it is necessary to regulate the provision of private information. The answer to this question has varied during the course of the debate on efficient capital markets. Clearly, under the semi-strong version, companies may be able to adopt policies of less than full disclosure which can give to some investors opportunities to trade on private information while other investors cannot.[67] Thus, whilst some commentators have criticised the need for and the character of mandatory disclosure provisions,[68] there exist also some justifications for regulation of disclosure by companies in a semi-strong efficient information environment. As regards private information, for example, a mandatory disclosure system may improve fairness of access to that information. It could also improve cost effectiveness by reducing the need to search for information, since it will provide a central repository for information and will also enhance comparability of information provided by different companies and by each company over time. A mandatory disclosure system could also steer management away from any temptation to suppress unfavourable information.[69] Ultimately, in view of the mixed claims, Blair and Ramsay suggest that it is not possible, using the semi-strong version of market efficiency, to reach definitive conclusions regarding the extent to which governments should mandate the nature and amount of corporate financial disclosures. Nor, in their opinion, do the justifications for disclosure provide clear guidance concerning the desirable form and content of corporate reports.[70] Beaver, also suggests that the substance rather than the form of disclosure may under this model be the more important policy issue. However, he does suggest that there might be a possible

---

[65] Beaver, at pp. 148–9.

[66] *Ibid.*, at p. 127.

[67] *Ibid.*, at p. 147.

[68] Classic opponents of the mandatory disclosure provisions on the grounds that the benefits outweigh the costs are: Stigler, 'Public Regulation of the Securities Markets' (164) 37 *J Bus* 117; G. Benston, 'Required Disclosure and The Stock Market: An Evaluation of the Securities Exchange Act of 1934' (1973) 63 *American Economic Review* 132.

[69] For further elaboration of these arguments see Meier-Schatz, at pp. 225–6; and Beaver, ch. 7.

[70] Blair and Ramsay, at p. 280.

significance in the location of data in the information provided since where it appears may indicate its level of importance not only to investors but also to managers and auditors.[71]

Despite these claims that express a preference for a market-based disclosure mechanism there are problems with this analysis. First, markets are universally imperfect. In reality, the market continues to function subject to major structural imperfections and corporate managers continue to exercise great discretionary power.[72] Thus the incentives supposedly existent in the marketplace are unlikely to guarantee openness. Competition is likely in fact to be a positive disincentive to disclosure for fear of other companies gaining a competitive advantage since they do not spend the costs of that disclosure. On the other hand it could be argued that disclosure itself would improve the operation of competition since it would remove the competitive advantage that firms gain by not disclosing material information. Additionally, competition itself might encourage disclosure since the more information investors have, the more confidence they feel in the company and therefore the more likely they will be to invest. Thus arguably the company performs better. Additionally, the impact of market forces is often diluted or delayed, thereby reducing management's sensitivity to stockholder's exit.[73] Furthermore, not everyone follows market movements and also analysts concentrate on a small percentage of companies listed. The market does little to protect shareholders in non-listed companies.[74]

One of the main arguments in opposition to a mandatory disclosure regime is that disclosure would create unjustifiable cost burdens for companies. Such costs would be both direct and indirect. Direct costs would include compiling and recording, processing, printing, auditing, disseminating and mailing the information to the recipients.[75] Indirect costs would include having information reported that complies with regulatory requirements but which is inappropriate for the purpose of the report's user, or information that would be useful but which the company is not permitted to report, as well as the requirements having the effect of preventing firms from continuing with projects that might have been profitable.[76] For a number of commentators these costs would outweigh the alleged benefits of disclosure and empirical reports have

---

[71] Beaver, at pp. 145–6.
[72] Weiss, at p. 580.
[73] *Ibid.*, at pp. 584–6.
[74] Meier-Schatz, at pp. 222–3.
[75] Azzi, at pp. 212–3; Blair and Ramsay, at p. 265.
[76] Azzi, at pp. 212–3; Blair and Ramsay, at p. 265.

revealed the cost problems.[77] However, these findings have been doubted by others.[78] For example, cost savings may be made for those requiring the information since a central resource makes investigation easier and also prevents wasteful overlapping requests for information.[79] One such cost saving may also arise from standardisation.

Standardisation of information

A mandatory disclosure system in which companies are required to provide specified information is likely to produce a greater quantity of standardised data from firm to firm. For example the use of prescribed forms and the request for particular data and details all help to create a more standardised system. This may have a number of benefits which would ultimately have a positive cost impact. For example, with increased standardisation would arise greater comparability. Shareholders and other readers might eventually become more familiar with the form and language that such a system would produce that they would eventually require less time and cost in seeking to interpret the data they collect.[80] The language might ultimately evolve into a uniform language, again making understandability more feasible.[81] Comparison of situations from firm to firm would also be more possible as would verification of data produced.

Alternative to regulatory intervention

One possible advantage of a disclosure regime is that it could provide companies with an alternative to other forms of regulation. In some circumstances, disclosure itself could resolve problems. This suggestion is connected with the above claim that disclosure could help to influence corporate behaviour. For example, rather than punish certain transactions such as loans to directors, disclosure could lead to ratification. As long as a director's conflict of interest is brought into the open the shareholders have an opportunity to decide whether or not that will damage the company's position. If not then there should be no problem

---

[77] Notably, Stigler and Bentson.
[78] Meier-Schatz, at p. 225.
[79] See e.g., Weiss, who claims that information would reduce shareholders' monitoring costs, at p. 592.
[80] Meier-Schatz, at p. 225.
[81] Azzi, at pp. 214–5.

in granting consent. That would not be possible without a mandatory disclosure system.

Disclosure might be attractive because it is less intrusive compared with other forms of regulation. As is claimed by Hopt,

> this type of regulation is most compatible with a market economy because it interferes least with freedom and competition of enterprises in the market. This is particularly relevant when ... there is considerable uncertainty and difference of opinion on what the right rules ... are. Under such circumstances, disclosure allows for greater flexibility, and in a way, can function as an experimental tool before the imposition of substantive legal provisions. Disclosure also avoids the well-known petrifying effect of [European] substantive law.[82]

Some forms of regulation might not be practical. For example, the litigation system does not generally offer incentives to shareholders to enforce directors' legal duties of care and loyalty,[83] but disclosure could avoid such conflicts arising in the first place. Disclosure can by itself act as a deterrent to undesirable conduct. In addition public opinion may itself lead to regulatory changes not welcomed by companies. A good example in the UK might be that of board structure and length of service contracts. Public outcry at the level of compensation directors were receiving when leaving companies led to the reduction of appointment periods for directors. Additionally, the industry itself has settled on a stricter disclosure regime for remuneration packages as an alternative to measures such as imposing ceilings on levels of pay. Disclosure in recognition of public opinion can be a preferred alternative to stricter regulation.[84] Recognition of the public interest presents a further dimension in the debate on disclosure regulation.

Disclosure and the public interest

An important aspect of disclosure is its social impact. This is one of the aspects of disclosure that is gaining in significance. A company may be performing well in terms of economics and market efficiency but this performance must be distinguished from a company's social performance. Many corporate activities have external effects that could be either positive or negative.[85] If they are negative it may be necessary to weigh

---

[82] Klaus J. Hopt, 'Modern Company and Capital Market Problems: Improving European Corporate Governance after Enron' (2003) 3 *JCLS* 221, at p. 241.

[83] Weiss, at pp. 586–8.

[84] Stevenson, at pp. 50–1.

[85] Weiss, at p. 575.

these against the efficiency returns to judge how well the company is performing. For this reason social disclosure has a potentially important role.

Another reason for the need for social as well as economic and financial information is that there are a number of interested parties who contribute to the company's continued existence but who do not have a direct financial or economic interest in that company. Such parties should be included in the list of recipients of information from the company and such parties might request information beyond monetary figures. For example, customers will not necessarily be interested in the share price of a company but they will have an interest in the safety and quality of the products they buy or the services they use. Such information will, of course, impose an extra cost for the company to produce. Additionally, employees and/or their representatives might wish to see both financial and social information about the company as part of a collective bargaining strategy. Indeed, it is likely that the obligation on companies to disclose information about directors' remuneration will influence the pay negotiations for other employees of the company.[86] Additionally, the inclusion of parties such as the employees as recipients of company information may help to build trust in the relationships within the firm thereby leading to greater cooperation between different groups, such as labour and management.[87]

It can also be to a company's advantage to disclose information if that has the effect of dispelling erroneous beliefs the public may have about a company or its activities. That might also help the company to avoid more intrusive forms of regulation since public opinion tends to influence considerably legislative policy. Indeed, an important advantage of disclosure is its role in enabling the public to impose pressure for change either on companies themselves or on the government to make legislative change. Thus the political role of disclosure is potentially very important.[88]

---

[86] Knauss, at p. 647. See also Cary, who discusses the role of disclosure in enforcing higher standards on matters such as executive pay: 'The existence of bonuses, of executive commissions and salaries, of preferential lists and the like, may be all open secrets among the knowing, but the knowing are few. There is a shrinking quality to such transactions; to force the knowledge of them into the open is largely to restrain their happening. Many practices safely pursued in private lose their justification in public. Thus social standards newly defined gradually established themselves as new business habits.' See W. Cary, 'The Case for Higher Corporate Standards' (1962) *Harv Bus Rev*, Sept.–Oct., p. 53.

[87] See Meier-Schatz, at pp. 233–4.

[88] Knauss, at p. 647 and Weiss, at p. 600.

These are all clearly positive arguments in favour of extending disclosure to other groups, allowing a wider audience for financial and economic details about the company alongside the shareholders, as well as disclosing a broader range of information. However, such an approach is not without problems of its own. One such problem is that of measuring or evaluating social information. Coupled with that problem is the issue of deciding what is appropriate for social disclosure. Weiss recounts that when the SEC asked what information would be relevant for social disclosure in 1974, groups suggested that it mandate disclosure about corporate activities in more than 100 areas of social concern, ranging from environmental protection and equal employment opportunity to charitable contributions, receipt of federal subsidies and discrimination against persons less than six feet tall.[89] Connected with this problem is the so-called public choice theory by which those lobbyists with the loudest voice or best resources would dominate the debate and impose their wishes on the eventual structure. This has been claimed by some writers against the mandatory disclosure system already in existence. Some commentators suggest that the system exists because analysts have influenced the debate and it saves analysts lots in time and expense of gathering information.[90] Even when areas have been identified as appropriate the question remains what data would be needed to provide an accurate picture of the company's performance? Another problem is that even if outsiders have possession of information that incriminates a company their opportunities for litigation will be extremely rare since as outsiders they will seldom have *locus standi* against corporate executive wrongdoing.[91]

An alternative to mandatory social disclosure is reliance on voluntary disclosure from companies. A number of companies have made public gestures towards greater social and environmental disclosure beyond their legal and regulatory disclosure obligations. The Body Shop, Traidcraft and Shell are prominent examples. Such steps may have a positive impact on a company's image, enabling that company to recover some of the costs incurred in such disclosure. However, one problem is that reliance on voluntary disclosure would allow companies to avoid disclosing negative information connected with their activities. Any disclosures made would also be difficult to verify or even compare with other companies. Effectively such an approach would potentially give to companies an opportunity for advocacy advertising and possibly also to mislead.[92]

---

[89] SEC Release No. 33–5704, 6 May 1976: see Weiss, *supra*, at p. 600.
[90] See e.g., Blair and Ramsay.
[91] Weiss, at p. 600.
[92] *Ibid.*, at pp. 602–3.

Criticisms of corporate information and disclosure

Annual reports have frequently been criticised for their failure to address users' needs: notably such a criticism was made in a widely cited discussion paper produced by the Accounting Standards Steering Committee in 1975 entitled *The Corporate Report*.[93] The Institute of Chartered Accountants of Scotland in 1988 stated that the accounts have 'almost invariably lagged behind the current needs of their users'.[94] One reason for this failure to meet users' needs is that terminology used in the accounts has, according to the Institute, 'outgrown common sense'. For example, the balance sheet 'is a hotch potch of costs, valuations and adjusted figures which indicate neither the worth of an entity as a whole nor the separate worths of its individual components'.[95] Concepts upon which financial statements are based are not consistent or logical and do not lead to a portrayal of economic reality.[96] In addition, the directors' report has been described as reflecting a 'hotchpotch of requirements' and lacking in structure.[97]

The emphasis on numbers is also problematic. First, the profit figure is the 'key note' of financial reports, encouraging short-termism, and the audited profit figure is itself subject to uncertainties.[98] Secondly, Lowenstein, notes 'enormous emphasis' upon earnings per share represented by a single number which urges managers to manage for the measured outcome rather than the economically better outcome. He also argues that reliance on numbers enables financial reports to be manipulated.[99] Charkham and Simpson suggest that numbers have prevailed over words in information published to shareholders but that numbers tend to look backwards whilst investors are looking instead for information about the present state of the company and its future.[100]

Accounting procedures are regarded as too flexible, permitting companies to hide problems for too long. Accounting rules are determined by

---

[93] Accounting Standards Steering Committee, *The Corporate Report*, (ASSC, London,1975), at p. 47 (hereinafter 'ASSC').

[94] Research Committee of the Institute of Chartered Accountants of Scotland, *Making Corporate Reports Valuable* (ICAS, Kogan Page, London, 1988), at p.34 (hereinafter 'ICAS').

[95] *Ibid.*, at p. 34.

[96] *Ibid.*, p. 20 and also ch. 4.

[97] DTI, 2000, para. 5.19, at p. 158.

[98] ASSC, at p. 47.

[99] Louis Lowenstein, 'Financial Transparency and Corporate Governance: The United States as a Model?' in Ross Grantham and Charles Rickett, *Corporate Personality in the 20th Century* (Hart, Oxford, 1998) 279, at p. 289 (hereinafter 'Lowenstein').

[100] Jonathan Charkham and Anne Simpson, *Fair Shares: The Future of Shareholder Power and Responsibility* (Oxford University Press, Oxford, 1999), at pp. 198–9.

private sector organisations. The major accounting firms which handle the bulk of the audit work are also criticised for being too cosy with their clients.[101] The accounting methods used tend to reveal a preference by auditors for conservative accounting practices such as reporting actual expenditures, but again this provides a poor guide to decisions about future investments.[102] In part, this approach is encouraged by the legal framework since the legal requirements themselves, having been described as a 'legislative straightjacket',[103] lean towards historical information rather than forward looking information.[104] Additionally, the evidence suggests that managers, 'understandably, for fear of giving hostages to fortune, stick to what the existing regulations require'.[105] This may not be adequate for users' needs. It is hardly surprising, in the light of these criticisms, that one commentator recently described annual accounts and reports as 'unintelligible'.[106]

Empirical evidence in the UK and in the US has consistently revealed that annual reports are neither useful nor of interest to many shareholders. Lee and Tweedie during the 1970s[107] and Bartlett and Chandler at the end of the 1990s[108] lament the inappropriate nature of the annual report for private shareholders. Brown and De Tore for example indicate that less than five minutes is spent by 40 per cent of stakeholders on reading the annual reports and that 37 per cent of shareholders do not read or even look at it.[109] Another problem is that of information overload, much of the information serving to muddy the water rather than providing a clear picture.

Interested parties are not always given access to the information they consider to be essential to their judgements and decisions. This is

---

[101] Margaret M. Blair, *Ownership and Control: Rethinking Corporate Governance for the Twenty-First Century* (Brookings Institution, Washington DC, 1995), at pp. 84–8.

[102] *Ibid.*, at pp. 86–7.

[103] DTI, 2000, para. 5.20, at p. 160.

[104] DTI, 2000, para. 5.19, at p. 158.

[105] ICAS, at p. 19.

[106] R. Turner, 'Clear and Simple', *Accountancy*, October 2000, vol. 126, No. 1286, 156, at p. 156 (hereinafter 'Turner').

[107] T. A. Lee and D. P. Tweedie, 'Accounting Information: An Investigation of Private Shareholder Understanding' (1975) *Accounting and Business Research* 3; 'Accounting Information: An Investigation of Private Shareholder Usage' (1975) *Accounting and Business Research* 280; 'The Private Shareholder: his Sources of Financial Information and his Understanding of Reporting Practices' (1976) *Accounting and Business Research* 304.

[108] Susan A. Bartlett and Roy A. Chandler, 'The Corporate Report and the Private Shareholder: Lee and Tweedie Twenty Years On' (1997) 29 *British Accounting Review* 245.

[109] J. Robert Brown, Jr and Stephen M. De Tore, 'Rationalizing the Disclosure Process: The Summary Annual Report' (1988–89) 39 *Case Western Reserve Law Review* 39, at p. 56 and footnote 77.

particularly true of those seeking environmental and social reports which are frequently criticised as 'greenwash' and vehicles for public relations.[110] Additionally, often there is poor access to the information required and when provided it is not always timely. In short, according to Charkham and Simpson, 'standards are patchy and access is poor'.[111]

Why do these problems exist with company reports?

A number of limitations are present in the disclosure system despite the clear justifications for its existence and despite the appearance of a complex and sophisticated structure. First there is a lack of a conceptual framework for the principles and standards intended to meet the objectives of the disclosure system. Accounting and reporting are evolutionary practices, which are influenced and affected by a continuously changing commercial environment. Second there are different types of entity and different participants and interests to be accommodated by the disclosure regime. Clearly, the different needs of small, medium and large companies are appreciated in the UK but how their different needs have been addressed is not necessarily adequate. This fact is recognised by the 'think small campaign' that has featured strongly in the latest proposals for company law reform. The disclosure regime has to make possible the provision of information to many possible users and user groups. One might argue that the emphasis upon shareholder needs is both too narrow and too simplistic: too narrow because third parties beyond the shareholders may have a legitimate claim to corporate information different from the information in which shareholders are interested; too simplistic because even the shareholders may not necessarily form a homogenous group that shares entirely the same information needs. In addition the information presented to shareholders may not be what they really seek. The emphasis on financial and economic information misses the point that there is a growing body of socially responsible investors and others who seek more social information.

Another problem is the failure to coordinate the roles of the different participants in the disclosure process. To what extent are those responsible for providing information encouraged in the disclosure process to establish the needs of the information recipients? How much opportunity is there for dialogue between the different parties?

---

[110] See Michele Sutton, 'Between a rock and a judicial hard place: corporate social responsibility reporting and potential legal liability under *Kasky v Nike*' (2004) 72 *UKMC L Rev* 1159, at pp. 1165–6.

[111] Charkham and Simpson, at p. 200.

Conclusion

Clearly, there are strong reasons to support a mandatory disclosure system in company law. Transparency is an important aspect of any society. In politics and in business information generates power and in order to avoid abuse of power it is important to share information. Sharing information empowers those who are led whether by governments or by executive boards of companies. Thus voters of governments or in companies will be able to make more effective decisions if they have the benefit of information. Transparency may also deter abuse of power since actions will be examined and judged. Disclosure therefore has a housecleaning function and can be justified also on other grounds including prevention of fraud, protection of investors, informed decision-making, accountability and legitimacy of corporate action. Despite these justifications the process lacks overall a conceptual framework to guide the development and implementation of accounting and reporting standards and principles. Consequently the disclosure requirements concentrate on matters that are not always relevant or appropriate to the needs they are trying to cater for. For example, financial reports are dominated by numbers and are historically oriented, even though they are presented to investors and shareholders seeking to predict the future of their investments.

Increasingly, information relevant to corporate social responsibility is requested but currently this remains underdeveloped as an aspect of the disclosure system. The largely voluntary guidance gives to companies the opportunity to greenwash their activities and use such reporting facilities as public relations exercises. The position of users, other than shareholders, remains precarious and in the shadow of the shareholders' interests, despite the fact that the limited liability principle might justify putting third parties into the central position as recipients of corporate information. Yet this situation reflects generally the traditional company law view of the corporate structure – that shareholders own the company and managers, as agents, must account to the shareholders. This point is illustrated in the regulatory structure of disclosure which will be explored in the next chapter.

2   The regulatory framework

Introduction

The structure of the regulatory framework for corporate reporting and dialogue strongly influences the character and development of the disclosure regime. Effective disclosure depends in the first place on knowledge and understanding of the reporting obligations both by those required to provide and prepare the information and by those entitled to receive such information. The existence of a clear and transparent regulatory framework contributes to that knowledge. A balance between standardisation and accommodation of specific company needs is also required. Standardisation aids discipline in reporting and allows for comparability and credibility. At the same time, different companies have their own needs and one aspect of the reporting regime is to recognise and accommodate the individual needs of companies and information users. The major objectives of disclosure, as was observed in chapter 1, are to enable companies to take stock of their position financially and in the market place, as well as to encourage more informed and better quality decision-making and finally to improve corporate behaviour and behaviour of those acting within the company or to maintain best practice. Information, followed by effective dialogue and decision-making, is a stepping-stone to those objectives. To what extent does the regulatory disclosure regime enable the objectives to be achieved in the UK?

The UK's disclosure regime is multi-layered and has input from a variety of institutions internationally as well as nationally. The legal framework is therefore complex. According to McBarnet and Whelan, 'following the Dearing Report, a new structure for the making and enforcement of accounting regulation was created in the Companies Act 1989 and related legislation. The role of law in accounting was enhanced. . . . A multi-tiered regulatory structure was set up.'[1] This system

---

[1] Doreen McBarnet and Christopher Whelan, *Creative Accounting and the Cross-Eyed Javelin Thrower* (Wiley, Chichester, 1999), at p. 17.

consists of legislative provisions in the Companies Act 1985, as amended by the Companies Act 1989 (many of the legislative provisions implementing the requirements set out in the Fourth and Seventh European Company Law Directives on provision of accounts and on consolidation of accounts), and a variety of related statutory instruments; accounting and reporting standards set by institutions such as the Financial Reporting Council and its subsidiaries, including the Accounting Standards Board, which in turn set up the Urgent Issues Task Force to assist the Accounting Standards Board and to provide 'authoritative guidance'; and the Financial Reporting Review Panel, which monitors compliance with accounting standards and legislative accounting requirements of published accounts;[2] expert, professional regulatory bodies such as the Institutes of Chartered Accountants of England and Wales, Scotland and Ireland, the Chartered Association of Certified Accountants, and the Auditing Practices Board which issues Statements of Auditing Standards, Practice Notes and Bulletins.

Essentially, the regulatory framework consists of three layers of legislative mandatory rules, self-regulatory mandatory requirements and voluntary codes and conventions. A significant number of the statutory and self-regulatory provisions originate from a series of European Directives in which various reporting requirements are laid out. Most of the Directives have recently been or are currently being modernised partly to take account of the international standards issued by the International Accounting Standards Board. The UK's accounting profession – notably the Accounting Standards Board – has been influential in the creation of international accounting standards and the UK's own domestic rules are influenced in turn by those standards created.

This chapter will provide a brief overview of the different layers of regulation and will consider how they relate to each other. In short, the legislative mandatory rules implement the European requirements and they set out broad principles and reporting obligations for different types of company. The legislative provisions are supplemented and supported by requirements and standards drawn up by the professional regulatory bodies. In particular, the Accounting Standards Board issues authoritative standards founded on stated principles. The legislative and self-regulatory requirements predominantly focus on financial reporting aspects of corporate disclosure. Alongside those provisions there has emerged a range of voluntary and best practice guidance on corporate reporting. Such best practice guidance is supported by codes of conduct

---

[2] See, for example, Companies (Defective Accounts) (Authorised Person) Order 1991, SI 1991/13.

published by individual companies, as well as by specific sectors or more generally by broader institutions. Often these pertain to the narrative reporting aspects of corporate disclosure and are usually reports or statements on corporate governance matters or social and environmental reports. These areas are currently mostly left to market-led innovations, though increasingly they are becoming the subject of mandatory requirements.

The regulatory structure exhibits an emphasis on the shareholder interest in company law in the UK and complies with the legal model of the company, which, as was noted in the introduction, highlights the relationship between the managers and shareholders. Under that model the primary interest attributed to shareholders is profit.[3] Financial reporting is directed towards establishing profits and profit forecasts through the profit and loss account and balance sheet of the company. It is this aspect of disclosure and reporting requirements that has developed most. Stewardship of a company also tends to be gauged by financial indicators. The social responsibility aspects of reporting, which tend to be of greater interest to other stakeholders, as well as the shareholders, have not been developed to the same extent. Social and environmental disclosures are regulated by softer legal devices with a less formal character. The stronger, more developed, reporting requirements and procedures for financial reporting allow financial reporting to dominate the disclosure regime, leaving the impression that reporting for corporate social responsibility is less important.

Legislative requirements

The most significant legislation in the UK's disclosure regime comprises the Companies Act 1985 and the Financial Services and Markets Act 2000. The Companies Act 1985 contains a broad range of general disclosure requirements, whilst the Financial Services and Markets Act 2000 makes provision for disclosure relating to public offers of securities.

The Companies Act 1985 requires companies to make disclosures to the registrar of companies,[4] who, via the registry, acts as a main source of public information on registered companies. The Act also requires

---

[3] Mary Stokes, 'Company Law and Legal Theory' in W. Twining (ed.), *Legal Theory and Common Law* (Blackwell, Oxford, 1986) 155, at pp. 165–6.

[4] See for example Companies Act 1985, s. 10 which specifies which documents must be sent to the registrar for the purposes of registration. See also Part XXIV of the Companies Act 1985 which sets out the functions of the registrar. See further ch. 5 below for more details on information to be delivered to the registrar as well as the role and functions of the companies registry.

companies to keep accounting records 'which are sufficient to show and explain the company's transactions and are such as to (a) disclose with reasonable accuracy, at any time, the financial position of the company at that time, and (b) enable directors to ensure that any balance sheet and profit and loss account prepared . . . complies with the requirements of [the] Act'.[5] Section 221 also sets out generally what information the accounting records must contain. Part VII of the Act contains detailed requirements relating to the provision of financial information about the company. The Act requires the company's directors to prepare for their shareholders each financial year company accounts,[6] a directors' report,[7] and a directors' remuneration report if the company is a quoted company.[8] Auditors must prepare (where the company is not audit exempt) an auditors' report.[9] As well as sending these documents to members, debenture holders and persons entitled to receive notice of general meetings,[10] the documents must be laid before the meeting[11] and must also be delivered to the companies registrar.[12] Whilst the main body of the Act sets out the general principles relating to preparation and disclosure of the company's accounts and reports as well as the requirement that the accounts must give a true and fair view of the state of the affairs of the company and its profit or loss for the financial year,[13] the form and contents of the accounts to be followed are set out in Schedules 4 and 4A of the Act. The requirements in Schedule 4 implement the Fourth Company Law Directive[14] and Schedule 4A's requirements implement the Seventh Company Law Directive.[15] Those Directives lay out as part of the European company law harmonisation programme a number of possible formats and contents of individual and group accounts. The legislative requirements attempt to assist users to understand and evaluate company progress and the standardisation of presentation aims to facilitate inter-company comparisons. Schedule 4 also sets out the accounting principles and rules according to which amounts

---

[5] Companies Act 1985, s. 221.
[6] Section 226. Section 227 requires directors of a parent company to prepare group accounts.
[7] Section 234.
[8] Section 234B.
[9] Section 235.
[10] Section 238.
[11] In accordance with s. 241.
[12] Section 242.
[13] Section 226(2).
[14] Fourth Company Law Directive on the annual accounts of certain types of companies (EEC) 78/660 [1978] OJ L222, p. 11, since amended. See for more detail ch. 7.
[15] Seventh Company Law Directive on consolidated or group accounts (EEC) 83/349 [1983] OJ L193, p. 1. See for more detail ch. 7.

shown in the company's accounts are to be determined. For example, paragraph 10 states that the company shall be presumed to be carrying on business as a going concern, paragraph 11 states that accounting policies shall be applied consistently within the same accounts and from one financial year to the next, and paragraph 12 states that the amount of any item shall be determined on a prudent basis.

Whilst the Companies Act 1985 contains significant detail on financial disclosure requirements there are also many other provisions in the Act that are relevant to disclosure more broadly. For example, the Act contains a few provisions on disclosure relating to employees.[16] The Act also contains provisions relating to directors' duties, such as the requirement for directors to disclose interests in contracts with the company[17] and the requirement for directors' service contracts to be open to inspection.[18] The Act also contains provisions relating to the role and duties of auditors in the company.[19] The Act covers, additionally, procedures for company meetings at which many of the required disclosures will be discussed with the company's shareholders.[20]

The Financial Services and Markets Act 2000 sets out the principle that listing rules may provide that certain specified securities may not be admitted to the official list unless listing particulars have been submitted to and approved by the competent authority and published.[21] The Act sets out the general duty to disclose in listing particulars all such information as investors and their professional advisers would reasonably require and expect for the purpose of making informed assessments.[22] The Act also requires publication of a prospectus approved by the competent authority for new securities to be offered to the public for the first time before admission to the official list.[23] Issuers of securities to the public should prepare and publish a prospectus. These rules are supplemented by detailed rules as to the contents and format of the prospectus set out by the Financial Services Authority, the UK's competent authority for listing arrangements.

---

[16] For example, Sch. 7 concerns matters to be dealt with in the directors' report and includes provisions requiring disclosure of company policies on employment of disabled people (para. 9) and on action taken for the purposes of employee involvement in company decisions and performance (para. 11).

[17] Section 317.

[18] Section 318.

[19] E.g., ss. 235–237.

[20] Part XI, Chapter IV.

[21] Section 79. See further ch. 8 for more detail.

[22] Section 80. See further ch. 8 for more detail.

[23] Section 84. See further ch. 8 for more detail.

Within the legislation distinctions are made in the requirements relating to different types of company; public and private companies are treated differently as are companies of different size and, further, there are distinctions made between listed and unlisted public companies. Listed companies clearly have the most extensive disclosure burdens whilst small private companies benefit from a range of exemptions.

The statutory provisions outlined above act as a foundation for the overall regulatory framework for disclosure. Whilst they are significantly detailed to the extent that those relating to company accounts may be described as 'lengthy and complex'[24] they are really only a starting point. They are supplemented in greater detail by further mandatory rules and requirements issued by authoritative bodies such as the Financial Services Authority and the Accounting Standards Board.

Non-statutory mandatory requirements

Following the Dearing Committee Report on *The Making of Accounting Standards*[25] which had stated that the lack of a conceptual framework is a handicap to those applying accounting standards, a new accounting regime was created in parallel with amendments to the Companies Act 1985 introduced by the Companies Act 1989. The Financial Reporting Council was established as a company limited by guarantee together with two subsidiaries, the Accounting Standards Board and the Financial Reporting Review Panel. The Financial Reporting Council was designed to provide support to its two subsidiaries and to encourage good financial reporting generally. A later *Review of the Regulatory Regime of the Accountancy Profession*, published in 2002,[26] persuaded the Government to expand the scope of the Financial Reporting Council's responsibilities and powers. Thus since 1 April 2004 under the provisions of the Companies (Audit, Investigations and Community Enterprise) Act 2004 the Financial Reporting Council became a unified regulator with a wide range of functions. The Financial Reporting Council assumed the functions of the Accountancy Foundation relating to accountancy and audit regulation. The 2004 Act provided for the Financial Reporting Council's remit to be expanded to cover three broad

---

[24] As described by Brenda Hannigan in *Company Law* (Lexis Nexis, London, 2003), at p. 502.

[25] Report of the Review Committee, September 1988.

[26] DTI, *Review of the Regulatory Regime of the Accountancy Profession* (October 2002), URN 02/1340 and see also *Review of the Regulatory Regime of the Accountancy Profession: Report to the Secretary of State for Trade and Industry* (January 2003), URN 03/589.

areas of responsibility: the setting of accounting and audit standards; their enforcement or monitoring; and oversight of the major professional accountancy bodies. This expansion of remit is intended to enable the Financial Reporting Council to play a greater role in enhancing investor confidence in the reliability of the financial information of listed companies. The Financial Reporting Council has five key objectives: high quality corporate reporting; high quality auditing; high standards of corporate governance; the integrity, competence and transparency of the accountancy profession; and effectiveness as a unified independent regulator.[27]

The 2004 Act complements this strengthening of the Financial Reporting Council's regulatory functions in a number of ways. The Act requires the professional bodies that supervise auditors to observe independent standard setting, audit monitoring and disciplinary processes. Under the Act the Secretary of State may delegate powers in respect of audit supervision to the Professional Oversight Board for Accountancy of the Financial Reporting Council.

The operating bodies[28] and the Council exercise the FRC's functions. The Committee on Corporate Governance, whose members are drawn from the Council, assists the Financial Reporting Council in its work on corporate governance.

In its document on regulatory strategy[29] the Financial Reporting Council summarises its activities relating to promotion of high quality corporate reporting. The Financial Reporting Council states that it seeks to achieve this objective by contributing to the development and implementation of international financial reporting standards. The Financial Reporting Council also seeks to influence EU policy on accounting standards, including the endorsement of international standards as well as seeking to make progress on the convergence of UK accounting standards with international financial reporting standards. The Financial Reporting Council works also to improve other aspects of UK accounting standards as well as to improve communications between companies and investors. The Financial Reporting Council has a role in proactively enforcing accounting and other corporate reporting standards including influencing EU policy and practice on the enforcement of accounting standards.

---

[27] See Financial Reporting Council, *Regulatory Strategy*, December 2004 (available at www.frc.org.uk).

[28] The Accounting Standards Board, the Auditing Practices Board, the Professional Oversight Board for Accountancy, the Financial Reporting Review Panel and the Accountancy Investigation and Discipline Board.

[29] December 2004 available at www.frc.org.uk.

One of the Financial Reporting Council's operating bodies is the Accounting Standards Board. The Accounting Standards Board (ASB) took over the task of setting accounting standards from the Accounting Standards Committee in 1990 and is recognised for that purpose under the Companies Act 1985.[30] The role of the ASB is to contribute to confidence in corporate reporting and governance by establishing and improving standards of financial accounting and corporate reporting. The ASB develops principles to guide standards and to provide a framework within which others can exercise judgement in resolving financial accounting and corporate reporting issues. The ASB issues reporting standards under section 257 of the Companies Act 1985 as amended by section 13 of the Companies (Audit, Investigations and Community Enterprises) Act 2004 (C(AICE) Act 2004). New accounting standards, and amendments to existing standards, are designed to respond to evolving business practices, new economic developments and deficiencies identified in current practice.

The ASB also collaborates with the International Accounting Standards Board (IASB) and with accounting standard setters from other countries in order to influence the development of international standards and in order to ensure that its standards are developed with due regard to international developments. The Board states in its Foreword to Accounting Standards that financial reporting standards:

> are formulated with due regard to international developments. The Board supports the IASC[31] in its aim to harmonise international financial reporting. As part of this support a financial reporting standard contains a section explaining how it relates to the IAS[32] dealing with the same topic. In most cases, compliance with an FRS automatically ensures compliance with the relevant IAS

In its Convergence Handbook, the Accounting Standards Board seeks to highlight the differences between UK Generally Accepted Accounting Principles and international standards. The Board also considers the preferred treatment so that the outcome should be the best quality

---

[30] The Accounting Standards Board Limited is prescribed as a standard setting body for the purposes of s. 256(1) of the Companies Act 1985 with effect from 20 August 1990 by the Accounting Standards (Prescribed Body) Regulations 1990, SI 1990/1667. The Accounting Standards Board Limited is prescribed as a standard setting body for Northern Ireland for the purposes of Art. 264(1) of the Companies (Northern Ireland) Order 1986 with effect from 15 October 1990, by the Accounting Standards (Prescribed Body) Regulations (Northern Ireland) 1990, SR 1990/338.

[31] International Accounting Standards Committee, now the International Accounting Standards Board. See ch. 7.

[32] International Accounting Standards, now International Financial Reporting Standards, see ch. 7.

standard being chosen rather than the UK simply adopting the IAS. The aim is to achieve a global set of best standards.

A *Statement of Principles for Financial Reporting*[33] produced by the ASB provides a framework within which consistent accounting standards can be formulated. It aims to provide a conceptual framework for the development and review of accounting standards and the views set out in the Statement are implemented in the accounting standard concerned with the reporting of financial performance.[34] The FRS 3 relating to reporting of financial performance requires entities to highlight a range of important components of financial performance to aid users in understanding the performance achieved in the period and to assist them in forming a basis for their assessment of future results and cash flows. Statements of Standard Accounting Practice are binding on all members of the accountancy bodies. These aim to define the presentation of accounting numbers in financial statements with a view to reducing the potentially subjective nature of presentation of financial accounts.

The accounting standards issued by the ASB have both statutory recognition and judicial recognition.[35] Indeed, in an Opinion appended to the ASB's Foreword to Accounting Standards, Mary Arden noted that the status of accounting standards in legal proceedings was enhanced by the changes in the standard-setting process since 1989:

[P]rior to the Companies Act 1989 accounting standards were developed by the ASC, which was a committee established by the six professional accountancy bodies who form the Consultative Committee of Accountancy Bodies ('the CCAB') and funded by them. The standard-setting process was reviewed by a committee established by the CCAB under the chairmanship of Sir Ron Dearing CB. The report of that Committee (the Dearing Report), which was published in 1988 and is entitled *The Making of Accounting Standards*, contained a number of recommendations, including recommendations leading to what are now paragraph 36A and section 245B and the further recommendation that the standard-setting body should be funded on a wider basis. As a result of the implementation of these recommendations the standard-setting body no longer represents simply the views of the accountancy profession. Its members are appointed by a committee drawn from the Council of the Financial Reporting Council Limited ('the

---

[33] Final Statement published by the ASB in December 1999.

[34] FRS 3, Reporting Financial Performance (1993).

[35] Section 256, Companies Act 1985; Accounting Standards (Prescribed Body) Regulations 1990, SI 1990/256; *Lloyd Cheyam & Co* v. *Littlejohn & Co* [1987] BCLC 303. See also conclusion of then Mary Arden QC in the ASB's *Foreward to Accounting Standards*, (1993) that accounting standards may be regarded as a 'source of law in itself in the widest sense of that term' at para. 15. See, however, Andrew McGee, 'The True and Fair View Debate: A Study in the Legal Regulation of Accounting' (1991) 54 *MLR* 874, who argues forcefully that the SSAPs have no more than persuasive force.

FRC'). The Council includes representatives of the Government, representatives of the business and financial community and members of the accountancy profession. Moreover, the Board is now funded, via the FRC, jointly by the Government, the financial community and the accountancy profession[36]

The ASB created the Urgent Issues Task Force (UITF), a Committee that assists the ASB where unsatisfactory or conflicting interpretations have developed or are likely to develop about a requirement of an accounting standard or provision in the Companies Act 1985. The UITF then seeks to arrive at a consensus on the accounting treatment that should be adopted, based on principles rather than on prescription of detail. A consensus is then published as an Abstract and is recognised sufficiently enough to require compliance with it in order for a company's financial statements to provide a true and fair view.

The Financial Reporting Review Panel (FRRP) contributes to confidence in corporate reporting and governance by seeking to ensure that the provision by public and large private companies of financial information and other information falling within its remit complies with relevant reporting requirements. The FRRP examines departures from the requirements of the Companies Act 1985 and applicable accounting standards. If necessary the FRRP may seek an order from the court to remedy such accounts. Its ambit covers listed companies and large companies. The FRRP also develops and operates a selective programme of proactive review of annual accounts and other documents falling within its remit based primarily on risk assessment. The Panel brings its findings to the attention of relevant regulatory bodies so that they can determine whether disciplinary or other sanctions should be applied. The Panel liaises with the Financial Services Authority and other enforcement agencies in the UK and internationally to foster consistent application of accounting requirements and generally to improve the compliance of financial information with relevant reporting requirements.[37]

The Professional Oversight Board for Accountancy (POBA) was created under the 2004 Act and its role is to contribute to confidence in corporate reporting and governance by strengthening the independence and transparency of the regulatory regime for auditing and for the accountancy profession. The POBA's functions are to discharge the statutory responsibilities to be delegated by the Secretary of State for

---

[36] See Appendix to Foreword to Accounting Standards, Opinion of Mary Arden QC, 1993, available at www.frc.org.uk/asb.
[37] Section 245C of the Companies Act 1985 as amended by s. 10 of the C(AICE) Act 2004. See also s. 257 of the Companies Act 1985 as amended by ss. 13 and 14 of the C(AICE) Act 2004.

authorising professional accountancy bodies to act as supervisory bodies and/or to offer a recognised professional qualification and to monitor the audit quality of economically significant entities through the new Audit Inspection Unit.[38]

The Accountancy Investigation and Discipline Board (AIDB) contributes to confidence in corporate reporting and governance by providing an independent body to investigate the conduct of members or member firms of the professional accountancy bodies and to take disciplinary action in public interest cases.[39]

The ASB also passes to other bodies the role of establishing Statements of Recommended Accounting Practice and these are given formal recognition by the ASB. Such Statements are produced for specialised industries or sectors by specified bodies including the British Bankers' Association, the Association of British Insurers, and the National Housing Federation among others. These bodies must satisfy criteria laid down by the Accounting Standards Board and they must also show a need for the SORP. Statements of Recommended Practice supplement the general standards and requirements. The ASB also publishes voluntary statements of best practice. These are not mandatory but their adoption is recommended by the London Stock Exchange and the Financial Reporting Council as well as the One Hundred Group of Finance Directors. In particular the ASB has provided such statements in relation to the contents of the preliminary announcements[40] and interim reports[41] that are required by the London Stock Exchange for listed companies. The statements cover content, basis of presentation, timescale, reliability and distribution.

The ASB also set up a Committee on Accounting for Smaller Entities in 1997 to review accounting standards and UITF Abstracts and to make proposals for the revision or withdrawal of standards and abstracts as well as to recommend how they might apply to smaller entities and also to advise the ASB generally on matters relating to smaller entities. That Committee published in 1997 the Financial Reporting Standard for Smaller Entities[42] and this brings together the relevant accounting

---

[38] Section 46 of the Companies Act 1989, as amended by s. 3 of the C(AICE) Supervisory and Qualifying Bodies Act 2004 and para. 10A of Sch. 11 to the Companies Act 1989, as inserted by s. 1 of the C(AICE) Act 2004.

[39] Paragraph 12A of Sch. 11 of the Companies Act 1989 as inserted by s. 1 of the C(AICE) Act 2004.

[40] Published in July 1998.

[41] Published in July 1997.

[42] This was updated in December 1999.

and disclosure requirements for small entities which are exempted from those other abstracts and standards not included.

The 2004 Act strengthens the system of regulating auditors by imposing independent auditing standards and monitoring and disciplinary procedures on the professional accountancy bodies. The Act extends the Secretary of State's power to require more detailed disclosure of non-audit services provided by auditors to companies. The Act gives additional powers to auditors to obtain information from companies and requires directors to state that they have not withheld relevant information from their auditors. The independent regulation and review of audit is strengthened through the FRC's new role in setting independence standards for auditors through the Auditing Practices Board and monitoring the audit of listed companies and other significant entities through the new Audit Inspection Unit of the Professional Oversight Board for Accountancy. In accordance with these objectives, under the auspices of the FRC the Auditing Practices Board (APB) sets standards and gives guidance: for the performance of external audit and other activities undertaken by accountants that result in reports or other output that is published, required by law or otherwise relied upon in the operation of the financial markets; and in relation to the independence, objectivity and integrity of external auditors and the providers of assurance services. According to the FRC, the APB's functions are to: establish Auditing Standards which set out the basic principles and essential procedures with which external auditors in the UK and the Republic of Ireland are required to comply; issue guidance on the application of Auditing Standards in particular circumstances and industries and timely guidance on new and emerging issues; establish standards and related guidance for accountants providing assurance services; establish Ethical Standards in relation to the independence, objectivity and integrity of external auditors and those providing assurance services; take an active role in the development of statutes, regulations and accounting standards which affect the conduct of auditing and assurance services, both domestically and internationally; contribute to efforts to advance public understanding of the roles and responsibilities of external auditors and the providers of assurance services, including the sponsorship of research; work with the IAASB to encourage the development of high quality international auditing standards and their adoption in the UK.[43]

---

[43] Paragraphs 7(1A) and 8(2) of Sch. 11 to the Companies Act 1989, as inserted by s. 1 of the C(AICE) Act 2004.

The Committee on Corporate Governance leads the FRC's work on corporate governance. The Committee's terms of reference are: to keep under review developments in corporate governance generally, reflecting the FRC's objective of fostering high standards of corporate governance; to undertake reviews, either directly or by overseeing the work of others, and then to consider whether any actions by the FRC would be desirable; and to put proposals to the Council where appropriate. The Committee also monitors the operation of the Combined Code on Corporate Governance and its implementation by listed companies and shareholders. The Committee may issue a clarification where there are doubts about the interpretation of the Code.

With regard to financial reporting relating to securities the Financial Services Authority has a major role in issuing rules to supplement the statutory provisions of the Financial Services and Markets Act 2000. The Financial Services Authority is designated by the Financial Services and Markets Act 2000 as the UK's competent authority for the purposes of the official listing of securities.[44] In this capacity the Financial Services Authority may make listing rules.[45] Indeed chapter 6 of the Listing Rules currently applicable sets out detailed requirements relating to the contents and form of listing particulars and prospectuses relevant to listed securities or to securities being offered to the public for the first time before admission to the Official List. In summary the information required by chapter 6 concerns information relating to the persons responsible for the particulars, the auditors and other advisers, information on the securities for which an application for listing is being made, information about the company and its capital, information about the company's activities and those of its subsidiaries, information about the financial position of the company and its subsidiaries, details about the company's management and information about the company's recent business developments as well as its prospects.

In addition to the requirements of the Financial Services and Markets Act 2000, as well as those of the Financial Services Authority, the London Stock Exchange has its own rules relating to admission and disclosure. Continuing obligations imposed by the London Stock Exchange require a company to control the flow of information if it could be reasonably expected to have an immediate impact on the company's share price. Such information includes profit and dividend announcements as well as more exceptional matters such as the appointment or

---

[44] Section 72(1), the Financial Services Authority already having been defined as 'the Authority' in s. 1(1) of the Financial Services and Markets Act 2000.
[45] Section 74(4).

resignation of directors. Strict observance of the obligations is required. Companies must follow the guiding principle that they should release price sensitive information in a way that ensures all users have simultaneous access to the same information.

Non-mandatory provisions

To supplement the mandatory requirements relating to disclosure provided by statute and rules issued by authoritative and professional bodies, a broad range of non-mandatory provisions has been developed. These offer guidance to those responsible for providing corporate information and whilst they are not compulsory these non-mandatory provisions carry significant authoritative weight not least because they are issued by professionally experienced committees and bodies. The Combined Code on Corporate Governance, for example, contains several 'comply or explain' rules on different aspects of corporate governance. The Accounting Standards Board has published various Statements and guidance documents, as have also bodies such as the Institute of Chartered Accountants in England and Wales.

These non-mandatory provisions contribute to the sophisticated system of regulation of financial reporting. In the area of social and environmental reporting the non-mandatory provisions are the predominant measures for improving the quality and quantity of corporate reporting. Indeed, in this area very few mandatory rules exist. Such provisions in the social and environmental reporting domain take the form of recommendations, guidance, codes and process frameworks and are developed by a variety of different organisations, including international bodies such as the Organisation for Economic Cooperation and Development and multi-sector alliances such as Social Accountability International and SA8000. The European Commission document, *Mapping Instruments for Corporate Social Responsibility*, groups the various instruments in the following manner: aspirational principles and codes of practice; guidelines for management systems and certification schemes; rating indices typically used by socially responsible investment agencies; and accountability and reporting frameworks.[46] In addition, initiatives that present awards for good practice are designed to encourage and provide incentives to companies and other organisations to engage themselves in good corporate practices and reporting activities such as the

---

[46] European Commission, *Mapping Instruments for Corporate Social Responsibility* (European Commission, Directorate-General for Employment and Social Affairs, 2003), at p. 12.

Investors in People Award Scheme for good employment and training practices and reporting on their activities.

A number of problems exist with such schemes and voluntary reporting provisions. First, they lack a clear structure and the relationships between them and with other provisions are not obvious. Secondly, the fact that they are predominantly voluntary means that they are not enforceable and so it is difficult to challenge companies that do not follow them. This has the result of them being potentially manipulated or followed with a degree of insincerity and used for the purpose of market gain rather than for protecting those affected by corporate activities. Thirdly, their voluntary nature presents opportunities for diverse treatments by different companies so that reports that purport to follow their guidance are not easily comparable, making assessments difficult to accomplish. The variety of different provisions and schemes also makes it difficult to have a clear impression of their main features. The document published by the European Commission, *Mapping Instruments for Corporate Social Responsibility*, highlights the diversity of corporate social responsibility tools and the resulting difficulty in identifying which are relevant to a particular company and or situation: 'For many people, CSR-related instruments are a confusing subject' and there is 'no clear direction or authoritative guidance as to what all the instruments are, how they help to improve CSR performance or why and when they should be used'.[47]

Despite the difficulties such instruments do contribute to improvements in the corporate social and environmental reporting process. For example, even if there are no formal sanctions for failure to follow them the market may effectively punish those companies that fail to meet their standards of good practice. The publicity surrounding the achievement of a Benchmark Award or Quality Award for good disclosure has obvious market benefits for the companies concerned. Eventually they may encourage the creation of mandatory provisions. For example, the Operating and Financial Review, which has only recently become compulsory in legislation, has been in existence as a concept for well over a decade. The Accounting Standards Board published a Practice Statement on the OFR in 1993 and has recently published a Reporting Standard to complement the new Regulations.[48]

---

[47] *Ibid.*, at p. 8.
[48] However, the legislation has since been repealed! See speech by Gordon Brown, Chancellor of the Exchequer, at the CBI Annual Conference in London, 28 November 2005, 99/05, available at www.hm-treasury.gov.uk.

Conclusion

The regulatory structure of disclosure and reporting obligations is broadly weighted in favour of financial reporting, which is of particular importance to shareholders who are interested in the profit-making abilities of their companies. In this way, the disclosure system supports the traditional approach of company law that is concerned primarily with the relationship between managers and shareholders. The disclosure regime reflects closely the Anglo-Saxon system of accounting. Legislative provisions are supported by standards created by professional bodies who are themselves closely regulated. The financial reporting requirements of companies are sophisticated, comprising several layers of regulatory demands.

In contrast, narrative, social and environmental reports are directed by a large range of voluntary, non-binding schemes and programmes. Whilst some aspects of narrative reporting – those that connect more obviously to a company's future financial prospects – are increasingly becoming the subject of mandatory provisions, on the whole social and environmental reporting is not supported by formal requirements of the professional bodies and sanctions are a matter of market reactions to what companies do and how they report on what they do. Indeed, it is possible to observe a reluctance to turn narrative and social and environmental reporting into a compulsory activity that can be challenged in the courts by stakeholders. Regulation of such reports remains predominantly at the level of recommendations and guidance statements. Stakeholders, who are more likely to be interested in the social and environmental performance of the company, must make do with a cluster of mostly non-mandatory reporting provisions with the result that it is difficult to challenge managers and companies through legal channels for reporting failures and poor performances.

Notably also, the regulatory structure concentrates on the provision of information in accordance with agreed standards. Little attention is paid to what happens once the information is presented. Dialogue is left to the internal arrangements of the company. The legislation provides for general meetings, but access is limited to shareholders. The professional bodies such as the Financial Reporting Council are not involved in what happens after the presentation of information. They are concerned only with the first stage of corporate governance. In any event, effective disclosure regulation depends on the participants in the process – the providers of the information and the recipients. A network of actors is involved in the collection and dissemination of company information. The next chapter will explore the roles of those responsible for contributing to the disclosure process in this regard.

3 Persons responsible for presenting corporate reports and information

Introduction

The DTI's consultation process on directors and auditors' liability[1] underlined the importance of their role in the reporting process. Indeed, the consultation was expressly stated to be mainly about the directors' duty of care 'both in relation to the conduct and supervision of the company's affairs, and, specifically, the preparation of its accounts'.[2] In addition the consultation was concerned to consider the extent of the auditors' liability since they can be held liable in relation to their audit of the company's accounts. The collapse of Enron led also to the demise of the auditing firm Arthur Andersen, as well as criminal proceedings against some of the auditing firm's partners and the senior directors of the company.[3] Other recent company disasters such as Parmalat, Ahold, Worldcom, Marconi and, most recently, MG Rover, have also resulted in the spotlight being placed on the financial accounts and those responsible for producing and verifying them.[4]

The DTI's consultation was also concerned with getting the right solution for establishing the civil liability of directors and auditors and 'balancing the interests of stakeholders'.[5] The interests to be balanced, according to the DTI are:

---

[1] DTI, *Director and Auditor Liability: A Consultative Document* (DTI, London, December 2003).

[2] DTI, *Director and Auditor Liability: A Consultative Document*, para. 2.1, at p. 8.

[3] Note, however, that the auditors were recently cleared of a conviction of obstruction of justice for shedding documents: see David Teather, 'Andersen cleared by Supreme Court over Enron', *The Guardian*, 1 June 2005, at p. 18.

[4] The Financial Reporting Review Panel examined the accounts and produced a secret report for the DTI: see Simon Bowers, 'Rover questions must be answered' *The Guardian*, 1 June 2005, at p. 18. See also Ian Griffiths, 'Breaking Down the mechanics of the money', *The Guardian*, 15 April 2005 and Ian Griffiths, 'Rover's £400 million accounting puzzle', *The Guardian*, 15 April 2005.

[5] DTI, *Director and Auditor Liability: A Consultative Document*, para. 1.3, at p. 6.

investors, who wish to maintain the supply of competent, appropriately qualified individuals who are willing and able to lead companies; other users of accounts, who want to maintain and, where possible, enhance the quality of the audit; directors, who want to be clear about their responsibilities and liabilities; auditors, who wish to ensure that the risks and reward associated with their professional work are appropriately balanced; and regulators, who are anxious to maintain efficient, well-ordered and transparent markets.[6]

Does the disclosure and reporting regime achieve this balance? The role of those providing information about a company's activities and financial position and their legal responsibilities in this process are of primary importance to this debate.

The key players are the company secretary who is responsible for keeping the company's records and facilitating the flow of information; the directors who are collectively responsible for preparing and presenting the company's reports and accounts together with the company's accountants; the non-executive directors who have a monitoring role of that process, in larger companies through an audit committee; and the auditors who report their professional opinion as to whether the accounts presented to the members show a true and fair view. This chapter will consider the roles of those involved in the reporting process and to what extent they are required to meet the interests of the company, its shareholders and other users of the information they provide.

Those who provide the information: the company secretary and the directors

The company secretary

All companies are required to have a company secretary.[7] In small companies with two or more directors one of the directors often acts as the company secretary. In public companies, however, the company secretary has a more professional status. In part this arises from section 286, Companies Act 1985 which imposes upon the directors a duty to take all reasonable steps to secure that the secretary appears to them to have requisite knowledge and experience to discharge the functions of secretary of the company and also has previous experience or membership of specified professions or professional bodies such as an accountant, chartered secretary, solicitor or barrister.

---

[6] DTI, *Director and Auditor Liability: A Consultative Document*, para. 1.3, at p. 6.
[7] CA 1985, s. 283(1), (2).

The company secretary 'is an officer with a central role in the govern-ance and administration' of the company's affairs.[8] The company secretary's primary administrative role is to ensure that the company complies with applicable legislation and other regulations. As well as procedural requirements, this role includes a responsibility to ensure compliance with disclosure and information requirements. The secre-tary is thus responsible for maintaining the company's registers and documents required to be kept at the company's registered office. Davies summarises the role of the company secretary as follows:

> it is that person who will be charged with the primary responsibility of ensuring that the documentation of the company is in order, that the requisite returns are made to Companies House and that the company's registers are properly main-tained. Moreover, it is the secretary who will in practice be referred to in order to obtain authenticated copies of contracts and resolutions decided upon by the board, and the articles will generally provide that he is one of those in whose presence the company's seal (if it has one) is to be affixed to documents.[9]

The importance of the company secretary's role is clearly recognised in the courts. For example, in the case of *Panorama Developments (Guild-ford) Ltd* v. *Fidelis Furnishing Fabrics Ltd*[10] Lord Denning stated:

> A company secretary is a much more important person nowadays than he was in 1887. He is an officer of the company with extensive duties and responsibilities. This appears not only in the modern Companies Acts, but also by the role which he plays in the day-to-day business of companies. He is no longer a mere clerk. He regularly makes representations on behalf of the company and enters into contracts on its behalf which come within the day-to-day running of the com-pany's business. So much so that he may be held out as having authority to do such things on behalf of the company.

Lord Denning's statement in *Panorama Developments* indicates that the company secretary is important not only within the company but also to third parties. Third parties are likely to rely upon the information provided and be kept up to date by the secretary since that is his actual function. In addition, his ostensible authority as an officer of the com-pany will, according to Lord Denning, most likely entitle third parties to rely upon dealings with the secretary.

The secretary is responsible not for the contents of the information but for ensuring that the formal requirements and deadlines have been

---

[8] For an authoritative guide to the duties of company secretaries see Institute of Chartered Secretaries and Administrators, Guidance document on the *Role of the Company Secretary* (1998) available at www.icsa.org.uk.

[9] Paul L. Davies, *Gower and Davies' Principles of Modern Company Law* (7th edn, Sweet & Maxwell, London, 2003) 297. See also Table A, art. 101.

[10] [1971] 2 QB 711, CA, at p. 160.

complied with. On the other hand, ensuring that records are kept up to date could itself imply a necessity for accurate and correct details. If a secretary fails to keep the company's records up to date or does not comply with specific statutory requirements he is, as an officer of the company alongside the directors,[11] liable to a criminal offence.[12] Indeed, if the company's documents lodged with the Registrar are inaccurate, the liability to a fine is, according to Boyle and Birds 'almost invariably incurred by the secretary'.[13]

In public companies the increasingly professional status of the secretary has arguably contributed to the elevated importance granted to the secretary's role or at least is a reflection of that importance. The Cadbury Report, for example, emphasised the importance of the company secretary by highlighting his responsibilities for making sure that board procedures are followed and that directors have access to his advice and services.[14] This requirement is retained in the Combined Code on Corporate Governance.[15] Thus under main principle A.5, by which 'the board should be supplied in a timely manner with information in a form and of a quality appropriate to enable it to discharge its duties', the supporting principles state that 'the company secretary's responsibilities include ensuring good information flows within the board and its committees and between senior management and non-executive directors, as well as facilitating induction and assisting with professional development as required'. In addition, the company secretary 'should be responsible for advising the board through the chairman on all governance matters'. Then Code Provision A.5.3 states that: '[A]ll directors should have access to the advice and services of the company secretary, who is responsible to the board for ensuring that board procedures are complied with.'

The Higgs review of the role and effectiveness of non-executive directors highlights the importance of company secretaries to the effective performance of non-executive directors. In the research conducted by Higgs consultees highlighted the value of a good company secretary.[16] Thus, as Higgs notes: 'At their best, as a provider of independent

---

[11] See s. 744, Companies Act 1985.

[12] See for example, s. 349, Companies Act 1985.

[13] John Birds (et al), *Boyle and Birds' Company Law* (5th edn, Jordans, Bristol, 2004), at p. 466.

[14] Cadbury Committee, *Report on the Financial Aspects of Corporate Governance* (Gee Publishing, London, 1992), paras. 4.23–4.27.

[15] July 2003, available at www.frc.org.

[16] Derek Higgs, *Review of the role and effectiveness of non-executive directors* (DTI, London, January 2003), para. 11.29, at p. 51.

impartial guidance and advice, a good company secretary is uniquely well placed to assist a non-executive director and to support the chairman in ensuring good use is made of the non-executive directors.'[17] Higgs continues by stating that the company secretary 'has a wide range of responsibilities but among those most central to enhancing non-executive director performance are the facilitation of good information flows, provision of impartial information and guidance on board procedures, legal requirements and corporate governance together with best practice developments.'[18] From this observation it can be easily concluded that a key aspect of good quality information flows and dialogues is a strong and cooperative relationship between the company secretary and the non-executive directors. Non-executive directors rely upon the company secretary for the information required in order to make effective judgements about the performance of the executive directors.

The company secretary may be appointed and removed from office by the board. It is also possible for a secretary, as an officer, to be disqualified by the court in the course of the winding up of a company if it appears that he has been guilty of any fraud in relation to the company or of any breach of his duty as an officer of the company.[19]

The Company Law Review has recommended that in order to reduce the regulatory burden on small private companies such companies will no longer be required to appoint a company secretary leaving them with the option of appointing one or not.[20]

Directors

Whereas the company secretary has administrative and compliance functions, the directors' role in the disclosure process is much more fundamental. The directors will decide how to present information and, although some information requirements are prescribed by statute and other regulatory provisions, the directors still have a lot of control over the information process. The general company law duties of directors are important in this respect and they also have a number of specific statutory duties as company officers with respect to disclosure of information.

---

[17] *Ibid.*   [18] *Ibid.*, para. 11.30, at p. 51.
[19] Company Directors Disqualification Act 1986, s. 4.
[20] White Paper, *Modernising Company Law* (July 2002), Cmnd. 5553-I para. 6.6. See also *Developing the Framework*, paras. 7.34–36 and *Completing the Framework*, paras. 2.18–22. See further White Paper, *Company Law Reform* (DTI, March 2005).

Statutory provisions relating to the role of directors in company reporting and disclosure

The primary purpose of the annual accounts of companies recognised in the companies legislation is to provide an account of the stewardship of the directors to the shareholders and creditors and they must give a true and fair view of a company's financial position. Under section 226 of the Companies Act 1985, the directors are responsible for the preparation of the accounts which are presumably prepared using the accounting records that the company is required to keep under section 221 of that Act. Under section 227, if at the end of a financial year a company is a parent company the directors shall, as well as preparing individual accounts for the year, provide group accounts. Section 233 provides that a company's annual accounts shall be approved by the board of directors and signed on behalf of the board by a director of the company. Subsection (5) also states that if annual accounts are approved which do not comply with the requirements of the Act,

> every director of the company who is party to their approval and who knows that they do not comply or is reckless as to whether they comply is guilty of an offence and liable to a fine. For this purpose every director of the company at the time the accounts are approved shall be taken to be a party to their approval unless he shows that he took all reasonable steps to prevent their being approved.

The directors must also prepare a directors' report under section 234 which also provides for collective responsibility of directors and for a defence to be available for a director to prove that he took all reasonable steps for securing compliance with the requirements. Directors of quoted companies must also prepare for each financial year a directors' remuneration report containing information specified in Schedule 7A of the Act. Section 241 provides that the directors are collectively responsible for laying before the company in general meeting copies of the company's annual accounts, the directors' report and where relevant the directors' remuneration report, as well as the auditors' report on those accounts. The directors are also collectively responsible, under section 242, for delivering copies of the accounts documents to the registrar.

This brief summary of the statutory requirements regarding the financial accounts demonstrates that the directors have collective responsibility for complying with the provisions. The Combined Code on Corporate Governance[21] also makes clear that the board is collectively responsible for the financial reporting. This Code, together with the

---

[21] July 2003, available at www.frc.org.

Turnbull Guidance on Internal Controls, gives to directors guidance on the practical steps they ought to take in order to fulfil their statutory duties effectively. Whilst neither the Code nor the Turnbull Guidance are legally binding, quoted companies under the London Stock Exchange Listing Rules must report in a narrative statement how they have applied the Code's principles and whether or not they have complied with the Code provisions. If the company has not complied with the Code the Listing Rules also require an explanation for this lack of compliance.[22]

Main Principle C.1 states that 'the board should present a balanced and understandable assessment of the company's position and prospects'. In addition, Main Principle C.2 covers internal control and states that the board 'should maintain a sound system of internal control to safeguard shareholders' investments and the company's assets'. The Code incorporates and makes reference to the Turnbull Guidance on Internal Control[23] and this suggests means of applying the Code's main principle. Notably, paragraph 12 of the Guidance states:

Effective financial controls, including the maintenance of proper accounting records, are an important element of internal control. They help ensure that the company is not unnecessarily exposed to avoidable financial risks and that financial information used within the business and for publication is reliable. They also contribute to the safeguarding of assets, including the prevention and detection of fraud.

The internal control system should help ensure the quality of internal and external reporting. This requires the maintenance of proper records and processes that generate a flow of timely, relevant and reliable information from within and outside the organisation. The system will include information and communications processes. At paragraph 26 the Turnbull guidance states: 'The board takes responsibility for the disclosures on internal control in the annual report and accounts.'

Paragraph 3 of the Appendix to the Turnbull Guidance highlights the need for effective information and communication for the purpose of an internal control of risk management. The paragraph sets out a series of questions designed to prompt the directors as they carry out their information and reporting duties: Do management and the board receive timely, relevant and reliable reports on progress against business objectives and the related risks that provide them with the information, from inside and outside the company, needed for decision-making and

---

[22] Paragraph 12.43A, Listing Rules.
[23] The Turnbull Guidance is appended to the Combined Code.

management review purposes? This could include performance reports and indicators of change, together with qualitative information such as on customer satisfaction, employee attitudes etc. Are information needs and related information systems reassessed as objectives and related risks change or as reporting deficiencies are identified? Are periodic reporting procedures, including half-yearly and annual reporting, effective in communicating a balanced and understandable account of the company's position and prospects? Are there established channels of communication for individuals to report suspected breaches of laws and regulations or other improprieties?

The statutory provisions and the corporate governance provisions underline the importance of the directors' role in the company reporting process. They also highlight the procedural requirements for ensuring that directors meet their reporting responsibilities. The case law also demonstrates the relevance of this role in the exercise of the directors' more general legal duties to the company. Indeed, a significant number of cases centre on the disclosure obligations of directors and if they fail to meet those obligations directors risk criminal and civil penalties, including disqualification.

Directors' general duties and how these relate to the disclosure process Any company lawyer knows that directors owe fiduciary duties to the company, including the need to act *bona fide* for the benefit of the company and to prevent a conflict between their personal interests and the interests of the company as well as a duty not to profit from their position as director. Alongside these duties the director owes a degree of skill and care in the manner in which he conducts his functions on the company's behalf. Beside the specific duties relating to disclosure these general duties may indeed also be relevant in controlling the director's disclosure activities.

THE DUTY TO ACT IN GOOD FAITH IN THE INTERESTS OF THE COMPANY The duty to act in good faith in what the director believes to be the best interests of the company has been described by Davies as the 'core duty' of directors because it applies to every decision which the directors take.[24] Generally, the case law concerns directors entering into transactions in which they have not considered the interests of the company or its members or in which they appear to have acted dishonestly. In the arena of disclosure there are a number of possible

---

[24] Paul Davies, *Gower and Davies' Principles of Modern Company Law* (7th edn Sweet & Maxwell, London, 2003) at p. 387.

ways in which the directors could come to be in breach of the duty of good faith. One is where they enter into a transaction without disclosing their own interests or in which they are acting beyond their authority so that the company and its members are put at risk of liability for a transaction with a third party which was not in the company's best interests. The directors might withhold information from a third party entering into a transaction with the company to the effect that the contract is not negotiated fully for the benefit of the company thus leading also to a breach of the duty of good faith. Another possible situation in which the directors could breach the duty of good faith is by presenting inaccurate information about the company or its activities to the shareholders or to others. This could lead the company into problems if the recipients then act upon the incorrect information.

Another related duty is the duty not to act for an improper purpose. This could include directors failing to give sufficient information about their actions when required to do so. It is most likely to occur in the context of a transaction or action rather than just as a matter of disclosure *per se*. Thus, for example, a decision to issue more shares or to raise the share capital might be made without the directors having revealed their own interest in the particular action.

These two rules have a close relationship with the obligation of directors not to place themselves in a position in which there is a conflict between their duties to the company and their personal interests. Davies describes this as 'probably the most important of the directors' fiduciary duties'.[25] There are clearly easily imaginable situations in which directors could find themselves within such a conflict of interests since they have access to the company's property, information and opportunities. Indeed, the law has developed in such a way as to make disclosure integral to the no conflict rule. Thus in order to exonerate himself of the problem of a conflict a director must disclose his interest to the company. At common law this requires a disclosure to the shareholders in general meeting, but a company's articles will generally release the director from this requirement if he discloses to the directors the nature of any material interest that he has. For example, in Table A, articles 85 and 86 allow for a director to have an interest in a transaction provided he has disclosed that interest to the board and he does not vote upon any board resolution by which the contract or his having an interest therein is approved. In any event, the director is required under section 317 of the Companies Act 1985 to disclose his interest to the board of directors. The

---

[25] Davies, at p. 392.

common law duty to inform the shareholders of an interest in a transaction still applies if the articles do not give permission for disclosure to the board.

The directors have easy access to the company's property, information and opportunities. This fact gives rise to the disclosure duties placed upon directors and, indeed, a substantial body of case law has developed in this area. The case of *Regal (Hastings) Ltd* v. *Gulliver*[26] illustrates the strict approach of the courts to this kind of situation. In order to purchase long leases of two cinemas for Regal (Hastings) Ltd, a subsidiary was set up to buy the long leases of the two cinemas. The owner of the cinemas refused to grant the leases unless the subsidiary's share capital was fully paid up or the directors granted personal guarantees. The directors were not willing to provide personal guarantees but instead opted to subscribe for shares in the subsidiary. When the shares were later sold at a profit the new controllers of Regal (Hastings) Ltd caused the company to bring an action against the directors. They were held to be liable to account for the profits they had made even though they had not acted dishonestly. The view of Lord Russell was that the directors stood in a fiduciary relationship to Regal in regard to the exercise of their powers as directors. Having obtained the shares only by reason of the fact that they were the company's directors and in the course of the execution of their office they would be accountable for the profits which they had made. Lord Russell made the point that for someone in a fiduciary position, being liable to account for any profit made does not depend on fraud or absence of *bona fides*. Where a fiduciary is concerned, the 'profiteer, however honest and well-intentioned, cannot escape the risk of being called upon to account'.[27] Similarly, in *Industrial Developments* v. *Cooley*[28] liability was based on misuse of information which the managing director had obtained in his position as director. In that case the director had deliberately concealed the knowledge that he had obtained and turned it to his own advantage by obtaining a construction contract from the Eastern Gas Board. The fact that the company for which Cooley was a managing director had failed to obtain the contract previously did not dissuade the court from holding Cooley liable to account, since he had obtained the information in his position as a director and thus in his fiduciary position to the company he had a duty to pass that information on to the company.[29]

---

[26] [1967] 2 AC 134n, [1942] 1 All ER 378, HL.
[27] *Ibid.*, at p. 144, and p. 386.
[28] [1972] 2 All ER 162, [1972] 2 WLR 443.
[29] See the similar approach adopted by the Court of Appeal in *Bhullar* v. *Bhullar, Re Bhullar Bros Ltd* [2003] EWCA 424, CA.

THE COMMON LAW DUTIES OF SKILL AND CARE   In this branch of directors duties a different aspect of disclosure is relevant. A breach of the duty of skill and care is likely to manifest itself in a failure to provide relevant or sufficient or accurate information within the general information publicity requirements imposed on company directors. In such circumstances the director's level of competence will influence his ability to comply with his duties. As the general consensus of opinion supports the view that section 214 of the Insolvency Act 1986 currently represents the degree of skill and care required of a director[30] it is worth setting out the provisions as it is also likely to be relevant in the context of disclosure and reporting obligations. Moreover, section 214 generally applies in the case of wrongful trading. This point is relevant since, as Hannigan observes, directors are rarely sued for negligence in the management of a company's affairs. Rather, it is usually at the liquidation stage when a liquidator may pursue a director for wrongful trading or disqualification proceedings are brought against a director of an insolvent company on the ground that his conduct has shown him to have fallen below the standards of probity and competence expected of a director.[31] Thus, relevant to the discussion will also be the circumstances in which the Company Directors Disqualification Act 1986 will be invoked, in particular how frequently a director's disclosure obligation failures will be relevant to disclosure proceedings.

Section 214(4) states:

The facts which a director of a company ought to know or ascertain, the conclusions which he ought to reach and the steps which he ought to take are those which would be known or ascertained, or reached or taken, by a reasonably diligent person having both-

(a) the general knowledge, skill and experience that may reasonably be expected of a person carrying out the same functions as are carried out by that director in relation to the company, and

(b) the general knowledge, skill and experience that that director has.

This section came under review in *Re Barings Plc (No. 5), Secretary of State for Trade and Industry* v. *Baker (No. 5)*.[32] At first instance Parker J made it clear that the competence of the director is to be judged in accordance with how the business is organised and what particular role the respondent has been given in the management of the company.

---

[30] *Norman* v. *Theodore Goddard* [1991] BCLC 1028 at 1030–1, per Hoffmann J; *Re D'Jan of London Ltd* [1993] BCC 646 at 658 per Hoffmann LJ.

[31] Brenda Hannigan, *Company Law* (Lexis Nexis, London, 2003), at p. 298.

[32] [1999] 1 BCLC 433, endorsed on appeal [2000] 1 BCLC 523, CA.

Reference will be made to the duties and responsibilities he has assumed in that particular role.[33] A consequence of this approach is, for example, that if the director is an executive director, his conduct is to be evaluated against what could be expected of a reasonably diligent person carrying out his duties and responsibilities as an executive director in that company. As Hannigan observes, the objective standard 'will apply with regard to the functions which an individual undertakes or which are entrusted to him, so permitting a scaling up or down of the content of the duty in the light of the size and complexity of the business and the position of the individual director'.[34] However, whilst some recognition of particular circumstances is granted by the courts, there appear, nevertheless, to exist a minimum number of functions that a director of any size or type of company might have. In *Re Brian D Pierson (Contractors) Ltd*[35] the point was made that:

> The office of director has certain minimum responsibilities and functions, which are not simply discharged by leaving all management functions, and consideration of the company's affairs to another director without question, even in the case of a family company. . . One cannot be a 'sleeping' director; the function of 'directing' on its own requires some consideration of the company's affairs to be exercised.[36]

Hannigan makes specific reference to the maintenance of proper accounting records and the preparation of accounts as one of these minimum requirements, as well as maintaining a minimum knowledge of the nature and conduct of the company's business and its financial position.[37] Indeed, late preparation and delivery of a company's accounts might cause extra difficulties for the directors, since they will be imputed with the knowledge that timely delivery of the accounts would have given them, as happened in *Re Produce Marketing Consortium Ltd (No. 2)*.[38] This case illustrates the point made by Boyle and Birds that section 214 of the Insolvency Act 1986 covers the whole area of a company's financial affairs and attaches liability for omission as well as commission: 'the section imposes a potentially limitless duty on the director to pay constant attention to all aspects of his company's affairs,

---

[33] [1999] 1 BCLC 433, at 483–4, endorsed on appeal [2000] 1 BCLC 523, at 535, CA.
[34] Hannigan, *Company Law*, at p. 301.
[35] [2001] 1 BCLC 275.
[36] *Ibid.*, at p. 309.
[37] Hannigan, *Company Law*, at pp. 301–2. See also *Re Produce Marketing Consortium Ltd (No. 2)* [1989] BCLC 520 at p. 550 and *Re Kaytech International plc, Secretary of State for Trade and Industry* v. *Kaczer* [1999] 2 BCLC 351 at 407; and *Re Landhurst Leasing plc, Secretary of State for Trade and Industry* v. *Ball* [1999] 1 BCLC 286 at 346.
[38] [1989] BCLC 520.

for fear that with hindsight a court may find a reasonably diligent person in his position would have been able to evaluate the company's performance and prospects'.[39] Boyle and Birds note further that in *Re Produce Marketing Consortium Ltd (No. 2)* the judge stressed in making the order under section 214 that the case was not one of deliberate wrongdoing but of 'failure to appreciate what should have been clear'.[40] Similarly, in *Re Westmid Packing Services Ltd, Secretary of State for Trade and Industry v. Griffiths*[41] Lord Woolf stated[42] that: 'Each individual director owes duties to the company to inform himself about its affairs and to join with his co-directors in supervising and controlling them.' In that case two directors were deceived by another director. They were disqualified for two years because they did not satisfy their personal responsibilities for ensuring the company's accounts were properly prepared and keeping themselves properly informed as to the company's financial position.[43]

What does knowledge of the company's affairs entail in this context? Some guidance might be obtained from the case of *Re Continental Assurance Co of London plc*.[44] In that case a small insurance company had collapsed, partly because the company had applied inappropriate accounting policies. The company appeared from its accounts to be solvent in July 1991 when, had an appropriate accounting policy been applied, the directors would have established that the company was insolvent and that they should have taken steps to stop trading. Interestingly, in this case Parke J found that section 214(4) would not impose on the directors a standard so unrealistically high as to require them to have knowledge of accounting concepts of a particularly sophisticated nature:

> In my view the directors would have been expected to be intelligent laymen. They would need to have a knowledge of what the basic accounting principles for an insurance company were. . . They would be expected to be able to look at the company's accounts and with the guidance which they could reasonably expect to be available from the finance director and the auditors, to understand them. They would be expected to be able to participate in a discussion of the accounts, and to ask intelligent questions of the finance director and the auditors. What I do not accept is that they could have been expected to show the sort of intricate appreciation of recondite accounting details possessed by a specialist in the field.[45]

---

[39] Boyle and Birds, *Company Law*, at p. 478.
[40] *Ibid.*, at footnote 2.
[41] [1998] 2 BCLC 646.
[42] *Ibid.*, at 653.
[43] See also *Re Landhurst Leasing plc, Secretary of State for Trade and Industry v Ball* [1999] 1 BCLC 286.
[44] [2001] All ER (D) 229 (Apr), Ch. D.
[45] *Ibid.*, at para. 258.

This opinion of Parke J sets the limits of the directors' duty; if they are not finance directors then they do not need to have a highly sophisticated and specialised knowledge of the technical accounting principles. The level of knowledge needs to be compatible with the need to supervise and monitor the conduct of the company's business enough so as not to accept blindly documents before them and to be able to discuss the documents in depth and to ask challenging questions.[46]

Re Park House Properties Ltd[47] illustrates that the grounds for disqualification for unfitness to direct can include the non-filing of company accounts. If the directors are not active during their directorships they will be guilty of conduct that makes them unfit. In that case the directors could not rely on the fact that one of them only was active: 'Their complete inactivity in relation to, and complete uninvolvement with, the running of the company, the financial problems of the company, the preparation and filing of the accounts, and the decision to spend a substantial sum [on the construction of the extension] seems to me to lead to the conclusion that they are unfit.'[48] The principle was reiterated in *Re Galeforce Pleating Co Ltd.*[49] So long as an individual continues to hold office as a director and, in particular, to receive remuneration from the company, that person must inform himself as to the financial affairs of the company and play an appropriate role in the management of its business.

Is the responsibility for overseeing the accounts an individual or a collective responsibility? Generally, this is a collective responsibility. The Combined Code on Corporate Governance, for example, provides in Main Principle C.1 that the board should present a balanced and understandable assessment of the company's position and prospects. A collective duty would probably prevent directors from being able to say that they had delegated such a responsibility. This point is illustrated in *Re Westmid Packing Services Ltd, Secretary of State for Trade and Industry* v. *Griffiths*[50] in which it was held that by allowing a dominant director to use the company's assets to fund his other businesses by way of interest free unsecured loans which were later unrecoverable, the other directors had failed to keep themselves informed as to the company's' financial position. Lord Woolf MR also made clear in that case that collegiate or collective responsibility must be based on individual

---

[46] Hannigan, *Company Law*, at p. 305.
[47] [1997] 2 BCLC 530.
[48] *Ibid.*, per Neuberger J at 555–6.
[49] [1999] 2 BCLC 704.
[50] [1998] 2 BCLC 646, [1998] 2 All ER 124.

responsibility: 'Each individual director owes duties to the company to inform himself about its affairs and to join with his co-directors in supervising and controlling them.'[51]

As has already been noted above, the Company Directors Disqualification Act 1986 has a close link with the directors' duty of skill and care in so far as the duty is frequently raised in allegations of unfitness to direct. Moreover, Hannigan observes that in situations involving unfitness in insolvency, invariably, the directors will not have maintained proper accounting records and so will usually have failed to prepare and file annual accounts and returns with the registrar of companies.[52] Hannigan cites *Re Howglen Ltd*[53] as a typical set of allegations which include among them the director's failure to ensure that the company maintained adequate accounting records. In cases concerning incompetence, without any dishonesty, the burden is on the Secretary of State to satisfy the court that the conduct complained of demonstrates incompetence of a high degree.

Failure of skill and care and a director's probity are relevant when he fails to keep proper accounting records. Indeed, by failing to keep proper accounting records, the director also fails to act in the interests of the company.

As Hannigan argues, while the directors are running the company in circumstances of mounting financial and other difficulties,

they either deliberately or inadvertently fail to maintain adequate accounting records as they are required to do. Consequently they also fail to comply with their statutory obligations regarding the filing of annual accounts and returns with the registrar of companies. Such failures are viewed seriously by the courts for disclosure is part of the price to be paid for the privilege of trading through a limited liability company. A failure to maintain proper accounting records means that the directors do not know the company's financial position with accuracy and so cannot appreciate the need to take steps to protect their creditors while a failure to file information with the registrar deprives creditors of information which would influence their behaviour.[54]

The above account of directors' duties and their relevance to the directors' role in company reporting to shareholders and creditors, shows that

---

[51] [1998] 2 BCLC 646 at 653, [1998] 2 All ER 124 at 130. See also *Re Barings Plc (No. 5)*, *Secretary of State for Trade and Industry* v. *Baker (No. 5)* [1999] 1 BCLC 433, endorsed on appeal [2000] 1 BCLC 523, CA; *Re Landhurst Leasing plc, Secretary of State for Trade and Industry* v. *Ball* [1999] 1 BCLC 286; *Re Kaytech International plc, Secretary of State for Trade and Industry* v. *Kaczer* [1999] 2 BCLC 351.
[52] Hannigan, *Company Law*, at p. 327.
[53] [2001] 2 BCLC 695.
[54] Hannigan, *Company Law*, at p. 334.

directors face an onerous task. They must take steps to familiarise themselves with a company's financial position and comply with filing requirements laid out in the Companies Acts. One important question is whether a distinction can be made between executive directors and non-executive directors in terms of both their legal duties and their practical position with regard to providing reports and accounts.

The gatekeepers: non-executive directors and auditors

Non-executive directors

The companies legislation makes no distinction between executive directors and non-executive directors. The statutory provisions concerning reporting requirements lay down a collective responsibility f.r all directors. Consequently, non-executive directors are ostensibly treated in the same way as executives with regard to potential liabilities for reporting failures. However, the approach of the courts and their interpretation of section 214 of the Insolvency Act 1986 when considering whether a director has satisfied his duty of skill and care suggests that a distinction might be made to reflect the position of each director and what might be expected of him in his particular role. This point is made clearly in *Re Barings plc (No. 5), Secretary of State for Trade and Industry* v. *Baker*[55] in which Parker J stated that 'the existence and extent of any particular duty will depend upon how the particular business is organised and upon what part in the management of that business the respondent could reasonably be expected to play'.[56] Thus, in *Re Continental Assurance Co of London plc, Secretary of State for Trade and Industry* v. *Burrows*[57] a non-executive director was declared to be unfit because he had failed to see from the parent company's accounts that there had been a financial assistance in breach of section 151 Companies Act 1985. The court took note of the fact that the defendant was a corporate financier and it was held that his failure to know what was in the accounts displayed serious incompetence or neglect justifying a declaration of unfitness. The Combined Code also contains guidance on how to assess the knowledge, skill and experience that may reasonably be expected of a non-executive director, and this notes that the time devoted to the company's affairs is 'likely to be significantly less for a non-executive director than for an executive director' and his 'detailed knowledge and

---

[55] [1999] 1 BCLC 433, endorsed on appeal [2000] 1 BCLC 523 at 535, CA.
[56] [1999] 1 BCLC 433 at 483–4, endorsed on appeal [2000] 1 BCLC 523 at 535, CA.
[57] [1997] 1 BCLC 48.

experience of a company's affairs' will also 'generally be less'.[58] The question then becomes that of what might be expected of a non-executive director?

What is the typical role of a non-executive director? Until the Higgs Review there was no available authoritative guidance on the role of the non-executive director and this resulted in a lack of clarity regarding their role except to observe that the non-executive monitors the activities of the executive board and contributes to the development of strategy.[59] Essentially, the role of the non-executive director, according to Higgs, is 'both to support executives in their leadership of the business and to monitor and supervise their conduct'.[60] Higgs suggested a more complete description of their role to be inserted into the Combined Code on Corporate Governance. Thus published with the Combined Code is Higgs' Guidance on the Role of the Non-Executive Director which describes the key elements of this role.

Strategy: Non-executive directors should constructively challenge and help develop proposals on strategy.

Performance: Non-executive directors should scrutinise the performance of management in meeting agreed goals and objectives and monitor the reporting of performance.

Risk: Non-executive directors should satisfy themselves on the integrity of financial information and that financial controls and systems of risk management are robust and defensible.

People: Non-executive directors are responsible for determining appropriate levels of remuneration of executive directors, and have a prime role in appointing, and where necessary removing, senior management and in succession planning.[61]

This description underlines the importance for the non-executive director of the company's accounts and requires him to be capable not only of understanding them but also to assess them in terms of their integrity and relevance to the company's risk management. It is also clear from this description that a non-executive director would experience considerable difficulty if in defending himself against a claim of negligence or a breach of his duty of skill and care he sought to argue that he had not

---

[58] Combined Code on Corporate Governance (July 2003), Sch. B, para. 1.

[59] Derek Higgs, *Review of the role and effectiveness of non-executive directors* (DTI, January 2003), para. 6.1, at p. 27.

[60] Higgs Review, para. 6.6, at p. 28.

[61] Derek Higgs, *Guidance on the Role of the Non-Executive Director*, published with the Combined Code on Corporate Governance, July 2003, available at www.frc.org; see the original suggestion in Derek Higgs, *Review of the role and effectiveness of non-executive directors* (DTI, January 2003), suggested Code para. A. 1.4, at pp. 27 and 28.

seen the accounts or that he did not have sufficient knowledge to understand them. This point is reinforced by the fact that membership of audit
committees should consist of non-executive directors. Indeed, the audit
committee has an especially important function in the realm of company
reporting.

Following the publication of the Smith Report on Audit Committees[62] and the support given to its recommendations by Higgs in his
own Review, the suggestions were incorporated into the Combined
Code on Corporate Governance. Thus Main Principle C.3 states that
the board 'should establish formal and transparent arrangements for
considering how they should apply the financial reporting and internal
control principles and for maintaining an appropriate relationship with
the company's auditors'. This Main Principle is supplemented by code
provisions which state that the audit committee should contain at least
two members for companies below the FTSE 350 or three for larger
companies all of whom should be independent non-executive directors
and at least one member should have 'recent and relevant financial
experience'. The main role and responsibilities of the audit committee
include monitoring the integrity of the financial statements, reviewing
internal financial controls and internal control and risk management
systems, monitoring and reviewing the effectiveness of the company's
internal audit function, making recommendations on the appointment,
re-appointment and removal of the external auditor, reviewing and
monitoring the external auditor's independence and objectivity and the
effectiveness of the audit process, and developing and implementing
policy on the engagement of the external auditor to supply non-audit
services.[63] This extensive description of the role of the audit committee
is supplemented by the incorporation into the Code of the guidance
provided by the Smith Group. This guidance anticipates a robust audit
committee that should protect the interests of the shareholders in relation to financial reporting and internal control.[64] In addition, the
ICAEW published guidance for audit committees in March 2004 with
the intention of assisting them to monitor the integrity of financial
statements.[65] The guidance directs the audit committee to focus on
the integrity of processes and in this respect provides advice to non-
executive directors about some key reporting principles. In particular the

[62] FRC, *Audit Committees – Combined Code Guidance* (January 2003).
[63] Code provision C.3.2.
[64] See for example, paras. 1.4, 1.6, 1.7, 1.10, 1.11.
[65] Institute of Chartered Accountants in England and Wales, *Guidance for audit committees:
Monitoring the integrity of financial statements*, March 2004, available at www.icaew.co.uk.

guidance highlights the principle of substance over form in accounting treatments of transactions reported in the financial statements.

The relevance of non-executive directors to the company reporting process is undeniable. However, their level of effectiveness might be open to question. In large companies, especially those operating across different geographical locations, it will be difficult for non-executive directors to monitor what the company and its directors are doing. Internal communications with executives may be limited. Higgs remarks that non-executive directors only rarely hear at first hand the views of major shareholders and the majority of respondents in Higgs' survey never discuss company business with their investors.[66] In normal circumstances, according to Higgs, non-executive directors and shareholders have only minimal direct contact.[67] Executive directors are reluctant to allow non-executive directors and shareholders to get closer because non-executive directors would not have enough detail available to them to present an accurate picture of company performance.[68] Higgs recommends increasing opportunities for contact between non-executive directors and major investors, including attendance at meetings between the management board and the major investors. The key is to develop an understanding of the themes and issues and concerns of the major shareholders. By understanding the shareholders' concerns the non-executives can more easily evaluate the managing board's performance from their perspective.[69]

If the company suffers a crisis as a result of a failure to monitor effectively the activities of the board or to evaluate correctly the integrity of the accounts the non-executive directors are likely to find themselves under the spotlight for such failures, especially since there appears to be an increased risk of litigation, including class actions in the US against directors of British companies.[70] The length of such litigation is also problematic.[71] At the same time the cost of directors' and officers' insurance is increasing while its coverage seems to be becoming less

---

[66] Higgs Review, para. 15.5, at p. 67.
[67] Higgs Review, para. 15.6, at p. 67.
[68] Higgs Review, para. 15.8, at p. 68.
[69] Higgs Review, paras. 15.10–15.19, at pp. 68–9.
[70] See, DTI, *Director and Auditor Liability, Summary of responses to the Government's consultation*, available at www.dti.gov.uk response to question 11 at p. 10.
[71] A good example of these difficulties is provided by the Equitable Life litigation against former directors, including non-executive directors. See for a chronology of the events, 'Litigation against former directors and Ernst &Young' available at www.equitable.co.uk/content/content_11.htm.

comprehensive.[72] This situation means that non-executive directors risk liabilities significant enough perhaps to deter people from putting themselves forward as non-executives. Responses to the DTI's consultation on director and auditor liability indicated, at least anecdotally, that potential liability poses a problem for recruitment of non-executive directors.[73] One solution to this problem might be to allow companies to indemnify their non-executive directors, even in cases where this is not permissible for executive directors. However, such a solution could undermine the unitary board structure so cherished in the UK.[74] The Government decided to resolve the problem with a compromise by introducing sections 19 and 20 of the Companies (Audit, Investigations and Community Enterprise) Act 2004. Under these provisions a company may indemnify directors against some liabilities to third parties and may purchase directors' and officers' liability insurance. On the other hand a company may not exempt directors from liability to the company or limit a directors' liability to the company and a company may not indemnify directors against liabilities to the company.[75]

In 2004 the European Commission issued a proposed directive to amend the existing accounting directives with new Articles 50a and 60a establishing collective responsibility of members of the administrative, management and supervisory bodies towards the company for the drawing up and publication of the accounts and annual reports.[76] The proposal includes a suggestion that Member States might extend board responsibility directly to shareholders and other stakeholders. The proposed directive would also require Member States to establish appropriate, effective, proportionate and dissuasive sanctions for breach of such responsibility. Sanctions should not be limited to individual board members. Courts and other enforcement bodies might still however also impose sanctions on individual members. The aim is to increase confidence in the accounts and annual reports on which investors base their decisions in the light of revelations of board misbehaviour in recent corporate scandals. Such a measure would also heighten the importance of and the risks involved in the role of non-executive directors.

[72] See, DTI, *Director and Auditor Liability, Summary of responses to the Government's consultation*, available at www.dti.gov.uk, response to question 11 at p. 10.
[73] *Ibid.*, response to question 13 at p. 11.
[74] *Ibid.*, response to question 14 at p. 12.
[75] See new ss. 309A and 309B, Companies Act 1985.
[76] Proposal for a Directive of the European Parliament and of the Council amending Council Directives 78/660/EEC and 83/349/EEC concerning the annual accounts of certain types of companies and consolidated accounts COM/2004/0725 final – COD 2004/0250, Brussels 27.10.2004, not yet published in Official Journal but available at http://europa.eu.int/scadplus/leg/en/lvb/126009.htm.

In the US the possibility of a disclosure committee for public disclosures in the context of capital formation has been mooted to supplement the regulatory processes relating to securities and disclosures to the investment community. In this context, the audit committee oversees and reviews processes for preparing and reviewing the financial statements, and the disclosure committee would oversee the system of disclosure preparation. The role of the disclosure committee would be to conduct periodic reviews of the corporation's public disclosures. Potential problems include the company's loss of the benefit of the full range of business and leadership experience represented on the board; the company could incur significant expenses; and friction between the full board and the disclosure committee could develop.[77]

Auditors

Elliott and Elliot state that the accountant must be a skilled communicator who is able to instil confidence in the user that the information is: relevant to the user's needs, measured objectively, presented within a timescale that permits decisions to be made with appropriate information, verifiable in that it can be confirmed that the report represents the transactions that have taken place, reliable in that it is as free from bias as possible, a complete picture of material items and a fair representation of the business transactions and events that have occurred or are being planned.[78] Thus the role of the accountant is to interface with the user and establish exactly what financial information is relevant to the decision that is to be made. The Enron disaster, among other corporate failures on both sides of the Atlantic Ocean, brought home the importance of the role of the auditor and the risks involved in the auditor's work. Indeed, some would argue that the 'wave of accounting and financial reporting failures' of 2001–2002 was caused by gatekeepers' acquiescence in managerial fraud.[79] The collapse of Arthur Andersen following Enron's demise shows the extent to which auditors will be penalised if they fail in their duties.

---

[77] See Warren F. Grienberger and Michael C. Lee, 'Should the Board of Directors Have a Disclosure Committee?' available at www.lawhost.com/lawjournal/98spring/committee.html.

[78] Barry Elliott and Jamie Elliott *Financial Accounting and Reporting* (8th edn, FT Prentice Hall, 2004) at p. 5.

[79] For an interesting analysis see John C. Coffee, Jr, 'Gatekeeper Failure and Reform: The Challenge of fashioning Relevant Reforms' in Guido Ferrarini et al (eds.), *Reforming Company and Takeover Law in Europe* (Oxford University Press, Oxford, 2004) 455–505.

The role of the auditor generally   In general, all companies are required to appoint an auditor at each general meeting before which accounts are laid. The auditor must hold office from that meeting until the next general meeting is concluded.[80] A small private company may be exempted from the requirement to appoint an auditor if it meets the conditions to qualify for small company status, is not part of a group, does not have a turnover of more than £5.6 million and does not have a balance sheet total of more than £2.8 million.[81]

The role of the auditor is to assess the accounts and to report to the members on the accounts and reports. The report must state whether in the auditor's opinion the annual accounts have been prepared properly in accordance with the Companies Act 1985 and whether a true and fair view is given in the balance sheet of the state of affairs of the company at the end of the financial year, in the profit and loss account of the profit or loss of the company for the financial year, and if the group accounts, where relevant, give a true and fair view of the state of affairs and profits or losses of the consolidated group.[82] If the auditor is not of the opinion that the accounts satisfy the Companies Act or show a true and fair view of the company's profit or loss or of its state of affairs the auditor must refer to those matters explicitly in his report.[83] The objective of the audit is to provide reasonable reassurance that material misstatements in the accounts will be detected. The auditor must therefore carry out such investigations as will enable him to form an opinion as to whether proper accounting records have been kept by the company and proper returns adequate for the audit have been received from branches not visited by him, and whether the company's individual accounts are in agreement with the accounting records and returns.[84] In short the auditor provides the company's members with an opinion on the quality of stewardship they get from management. As was stated in the Cadbury Report: 'the audit provides an external and objective check on the way in which financial statements have been prepared and presented, and it is an essential part of the checks and balances required.'[85]

---

[80] Companies Act 1985, s. 384(1).
[81] Companies Act 1985 (Audit Exemptions) Regulations 1994, SI 1994/1935; Companies Act 1985 (Audit Exemptions) Regulations 1997, SI 1997/936; Companies Act 1985 (Audit Exemptions) Regulations 2000, SI 2000/1430; Companies Act 1985 (Accounts of Small and Medium-sized Enterprises and Audit Exemptions) (Amendment) Regulations 2004, SI 2004/16.
[82] Companies Act 1985, s. 235(2).
[83] *Newton* v. *BSA* [1906] 2 Ch. 378.
[84] Companies Act 1985, s. 237(1).
[85] Cadbury Committee, *Report on the Financial Aspects of Corporate Governance* (Gee Publishing, London, 1992) para. 5.1.

The judiciary has also described what it regards as the role of the auditor. In *Caparo plc* v. *Dickman*[86] Bingham LJ in the Court of Appeal stated that the auditor 'is employed by the company to exercise his professional skill and judgment for the purpose of giving the shareholders an independent report on the reliability of the company's accounts and thus on their investment.' Then in the House of Lords[87] Lord Oliver of Aylmerton stated that

it is the auditor's function to ensure, so far as possible, that the financial information as to the company's affairs prepared by the directors accurately reflects the company's position in order, first, to protect the company itself from the consequences of undetected errors or, possibly, wrongdoing (by, for instance, declaring dividends out of capital) and, secondly, to provide shareholders with reliable intelligence for the purpose of enabling them to scrutinise the conduct of the company's affairs and to exercise their collective powers to reward or control or remove those to whom that conduct has been confided. . .

In short, the purpose of the statutory audit is to enable shareholders to review the past management of the company and to exercise their rights to influence future management.

The audit aims to provide reasonable reassurance that financial documents are free from material misstatements so the audit should ensure that any misstatements would in fact be detected. The auditor cannot guarantee to detect fraud and is not required to approach his work with suspicion but rather with a spirit of inquiry. If he does discover fraud then the auditor should either report this to the management body or, if the management body is implicated, the auditor should inform a third party of that fact.

The Auditing Practices Board published in 1993 SAS 600 Auditors' Reports on Financial Statements which provides guidance on the content of the auditors' report. This requires the report to be addressed to the members because the audit is undertaken on their behalf. The report must state that the preparation of the financial statements is the responsibility of the directors while the auditors are responsible for auditing those statements. The report must also state that the audit has been planned and performed so as to obtain reasonable assurance that the financial statements are free from material misstatement whether caused by fraud, or other irregularity, or error. In addition to SAS 600, a recent EC Directive amending the first and second directives[88] also prescribes

---

[86] [1990] 2 AC 605.　　　[87] [1990] 1 All ER 568.

[88] Directive 2003/51/EC of the European Parliament and of the Council of 18 June 2003 amending Directives 78/660/EEC, 83/349/EEC, 86/635/EEC and 91/674/EEC on the annual and consolidated accounts of certain types of companies, banks and other financial institutions and insurance undertakings OJ L 178, 17.7.2003, at p. 16.

the detail of auditors' reports at EU level in order to achieve comparability. These should include the following: an introduction identifying the accounts which are the subject of the statutory audit together with the financial reporting framework that has been applied in their preparation; a description of the scope of the audit identifying the auditing standards in accordance with which the audit was conducted; an audit opinion stating whether or not the accounts give a true and fair view; a reference to any matters to which the statutory auditors draw attention by way of emphasis without qualifying the audit opinion; an opinion concerning the consistency of the annual report with the accounts for the same year; and the report shall be signed and dated by the statutory auditors.[89]

Auditors have a right of access to the company's accounting records and they are entitled to inquire of the company's officers any information and explanations they consider necessary.[90] They also have a right to attend a general meeting and to speak at the general meeting on any aspect of the business with which they are concerned.[91]

AUDITORS' LIABILITY   The potential liability of auditors for their audit reports remains a contentious issue. The courts have managed to limit the scope of their liability for negligence but in contractual liability, whilst the range of claimants is limited, the sums they may claim are potentially enormous. If the auditor assumes responsibility for the advice sought or the task he or she does is through a contractual arrangement or an 'almost contractual' arrangement this gives rise to a duty under *Hedley Byrne & Co Ltd* v. *Heller & Partners Ltd*.[92] *Caparo plc* v. *Dickman* however highlights other possible situations in which the test is of a relationship of sufficient proximity between the party owing the duty and the party to whom that duty is allegedly owed. *Caparo* limited the scope of the auditors' duty of care so that third parties were essentially blocked from relying on the audit report for the purposes of investing in the company. Thus the auditors owe their duty to the company and to the shareholders collectively but they are not responsible for protecting investments in the company. The court's view was that statutory duties of an auditor are not intended to protect the interests of the public at large or investors in the market. Essentially, it must be proven that the auditor knew that his statement would be relied upon by the plaintiff in deciding whether or not to enter upon a particular transaction. Even if

---

[89] *Ibid.*, arts. 1 and 2.   [90] Companies Act 1985, s. 389A.
[91] Companies Act 1985, s. 390.
[92] [1963] 2 All ER 575.

reliance was foreseeable, it is also necessary to have regard to the trans-action for the purpose of which the statement was made.

Caparo adds two further dimensions to the establishment of a duty of care and these are reasonable foreseeability of damage as well as the imposition of a duty of care being just and reasonable in all the circum-stances. The latter dimension arises from the aim to prevent 'liability in an indeterminate amount for an indeterminate time to an indeterminate class'. In other words the approach of the House of Lords was to seek to prevent a flood of litigation against auditors. How is proximity assessed following *Caparo*? In short the test is whether the auditor knows actually or by inference that his report will be communicated to a person either individually or as a member of a class of persons for a particular purpose and that such person will rely on that report. If as was established in *Caparo* the objective of the report is to enable shareholders to exercise collectively informed control of the company then this does not entail a duty of care to the public who might use the report for other purposes or even to individual investors making a decision about a potential invest-ment. The purpose of the report in a formal sense will be restricted to assisting shareholders to make informed decisions about the stewardship role of the managers and so will not give rise to a duty of care if used for other purposes.[93] The Government in its Company Law Review indicated an intention to maintain this limited scope of liability of auditors.[94]

Whilst *Caparo* limits the scope of auditors' liability it does not protect auditors from enormous claims arising out of the losses of their corpor-ate clients. The claim for £5.2 billion brought by the liquidators of the Bank of Credit and Commerce International against Price Waterhouse and Ernst & Whinney illustrates the potential severity of the problem for auditors.[95] Such financial risk is, according to the auditing profession, 'making the statutory audit unattractive as a business activity'.[96] The

---

[93] However, see the recent Scottish case of *Royal Bank of Scotland* v. *Bannerman Johnstone Maclay* 2003 SLT 181 which would appear to extend the scope of liability to creditors in circumstances in which the auditor did not issue a disclaimer of liability with the accounts, noted in Paul Davies, 'Post-Enron Developments in the United Kingdom' in Guido Ferrarini et al (ed.), *Reforming Company and Takeover Law in Europe* (Oxford University Press, Oxford, 2004) 185–223 at note 199, p. 221.

[94] See Company Law Review Steering Group, *Modern Company Law for a Competitive Economy:Final Report* (DTI, London, 2001) paras. 8.128–8.144.

[95] Referred to by Pettet, who notes that the claim was eventually scaled down to around £250 million and settled: see Ben Pettet, *Company Law* (2nd edn, Longman, London, 2005) at p. 189, noting *Financial Times* report, 5 August 1994.

[96] See DTI, *Director and Auditor Liability – A Consultative Document* (DTI, London, December 2003) URN 03/1638, para. 6.8.

potential consequence is a 'risk of a move towards negative, defensive auditing' and 'the trend to exit from high-risk companies will accelerate' and 'some of the big firms might decide to cease providing audit services'.[97] This problem of 'bottomless pit' liability has been addressed periodically at governmental level. For example this was a major factor leading to the creation of the Limited Liability Partnerships Act 2000. More recently, the Government consulted on the issue of auditor liability and asked whether it would be appropriate to allow auditors to limit their liability contractually.[98] The Companies (Audit, Investigations and Community Enterprise) Act 2004 retains the prohibition in section 310, Companies Act 1985, of companies exempting or indemnifying auditors against liability for breach of duty or breach of trust in relation to the company.

The Company Law Reform Bill contains proposals for partial protection for auditors against multi-million pound negligence claims. Under the proposals, shareholders would be able to agree a limit to the auditor's liability for damage incurred by a company to such an amount that is determined by the courts to be just and equitable, having regard to the relative extent of responsibility of the auditor for the damage incurred. The Government proposes that any such limitation would apply in situations where damage to the company has been caused through the misconduct of an audit and the company could recover separately the loss suffered as a result of another defendant's actions. The auditor would be fully liable for any fraudulent acts. The company would not be permitted to agree in advance a monetary limit to the auditors' liability.[99] However, the proposals were recently stalled as a result of interventions by a shareholder alliance of the Investment Management Association, the Association of British Insurers and Morley Fund Management, worried by the impact of international auditing standards upon the quality of auditing. The likely outcome remains unclear at the time of writing.[100]

The Government proposes also to make it a criminal offence knowingly or recklessly to give an incorrect audit opinion.[101] This proposal echoes some of the provisions in the US Sarbanes Oxley Act 2002, introduced in the wake of the Enron collapse. Notably, the Act, which introduced a new government accounting board to oversee the

---

[97] *Ibid.*, at para. 6.9.

[98] *Ibid.*, at para. 7.4 and q28.

[99] White Paper, *Company Law Reform* (DTI, March 2005) para. 3.5.

[100] See Barney Jopson, 'Accountants put champagne on ice as party loses its fizz', *Financial Times*, 21 June 2005, at p. 3.

[101] White Paper, *Company Law Reform* (DTI, March 2005) para. 3.5.

work of auditors with power to impose civil and criminal sanctions against auditors who fail to discharge their duties to provide independent and accurate assessments of the financial health of public companies, has extra-territorial effect and so could affect auditors responsible for verifying the accounts of British or European companies that have a listing on a US Stock Exchange.

Making the audit effective

A number of steps have been taken to improve the process and quality of company audits. For example, recently, the Companies (Audit, Investigations and Community Enterprise) Act 2004 introduced provisions for the auditors to obtain information from a wider group of people. The duty will fall upon directors to supply the information necessary for a successful audit.[102] In public companies and large private companies, the Financial Reporting Review Panel can, under the 2004 Act, require auditors, or former auditors, to produce documents or to provide information and explanations.[103] In the Company Law Reform Bill the Government proposes shareholders' rights to question auditors in advance of AGMs or by writing to the auditor via the company with reasonable questions relating to the auditors' report or conduct of the audit. Lead audit partners will also be required to sign the report as an encouragement of further personal responsibility for the actions taken by the audit team.[104]

The APB has made clear that the primary objective of the audit is for the auditors to provide independent assurance to the shareholders that the directors have prepared the financial statements properly and in this way they assist the shareholders to exercise their proprietary powers as shareholders in the annual general meeting. The APB adds that:

public confidence in the operation of the capital markets and in the conduct of public interest entities depends in part upon the credibility of the opinions and reports issued by the auditors in connection with the audit of the financial statements. *Such credibility depends on beliefs concerning the integrity, objectivity and independence of the auditors and the quality of audit work they perform.*[105]

---

[102] Companies (Audit, Investigations and Community Enterprise) Act 2004, s. 8.
[103] *Ibid.*, ss. 12 and 15.
[104] White Paper, *Company Law Reform* (DTI, March 2005) para. 3.5.
[105] APB Ethical Standard 1, *Integrity, Objectivity and Independence*, October 2004, at paras. 3 and 4. Emphasis added.

Similarly, the ICAEW has stated:

The quality of the audit opinion is a vital element in maintaining confidence in financial reporting. A key element is that the audit opinion should be free from bias. If the auditors are to achieve this, they must be objective in reaching their opinion. This requires independence of mind from the company being audited. In addition, particularly in respect of listed and other public interest companies, they need to consider external perception of independence.[106]

Despite these claims of the importance of independence of auditors to the credibility and quality of their reports, the Enron debacle gave rise to serious doubts about the level of their independence.[107] The potential conflict of interests created by the provision of non-audit services for an audit client leads to suspicions about the value of the audit report. The Enron disaster pushed the Government, together with the Financial Services Authority and the accounting professions, to review accounting and auditing issues.[108] The DTI also undertook a review of the regulatory regime of the accountancy profession.[109] These responses resulted in a number of changes. The CGAA Report proposed that some non-audit services should not be provided if they would involve the audit firm performing management functions for their client or if it would mean auditing its own work. The CGAA Report also recommended stronger disclosure requirements for non-audit services[110] and it recommended also regular rotation of auditor partners. The ICAEW has put these recommendations into effect.[111]

The 'Swift Report'[112] also resulted in significant changes to the regulatory structure of the accounting and auditing professions bringing the regulation of both under a single body, the independent Financial Reporting Council. This now presides over a number of subsidiary bodies: the Accounting Standards Board, the Financial Reporting Review Panel, the Auditing Practices Board, the Investigation and

---

[106] ICAEW, *Reviewing Auditor Independence: Guidance for Audit Committees* (ICAEW, London, 2003), at p. 3.

[107] See Davies (2004), above, at p. 207. Cf. Coffee (2004), above, at pp. 471–3.

[108] The Co-ordinating Group on Audit and Accounting Issues – Interim Report, URN 02/1092 (July 2002) and Final Report, URN 03/567 (January 2003).

[109] Review Group – *Review of the Regulatory Regime of the Accountancy Profession: A Consultative Document*, URN 02/1340 (October 2002).

[110] See the draft Regulations under the Companies (Audit, Investigations and Community Enterprise) Act 2004: Consultation Paper (November 2004).

[111] See for example, ICAEW, *Reviewing Auditor Independence: Guidance for Audit Committees* (ICAEW, London, 2003) and *Additional Guidance on Independence for Auditors* which is additional to the *Guide to Professional Ethics*.

[112] Review Group – *Review of the Regulatory Regime of the Accountancy Profession: A Consultative Document*, URN 02/1340 (October 2002).

Discipline Board, and the Professional Oversight Board. The Accounting Standards Board is assisted by an Urgent Issues Task Force and the Professional Oversight Board is assisted by the Audit Inspection Unit.[113] The important feature of this new structure is that it has installed outside control into what was previously a largely self-regulated profession.[114] The Financial Reporting Council has put some of its powers into practice already by warning of commercial conflicts of interests and poor legal compliance putting the quality of company audits at risk following recent inspection of twenty-seven audits of leading companies in the UK.[115]

A number of proposals relating to auditing have been made at the European level, partly as a continuation of the reorientation of EU policy on the statutory audit that started in 1996 with a Green Paper on the role and responsibility of the statutory auditor.[116] The collapse of Enron, Parmalat and other companies have added another dimension to the work that is continuing at the EU level.[117] The European Commission's Communication on *Reinforcing the statutory audit in the EU* sees audit as an important part of good corporate governance practice.[118] The Communication proposed modernising the Eighth Directive to create a shorter, more comprehensive piece of legislation with sufficiently clear principles that will underpin all statutory audits within the EU. The original, unamended Eighth Directive did not refer to auditing standards, independence requirements or ethical codes. The Communication recommends use of clear principles in EU legislation flanked with implementing measures and detailed guidance and best practice recommendations. The 1998 Communication on statutory audit supported monitored self-regulation so that the audit profession itself carries out the regulatory process.[119] The 2003 Communication seeks instead to

---

[113] See ch. 2, above.

[114] Further provisions relating to the regulatory structure are laid down in the Companies (Audit, Investigations and Community Enterprise) Act 2004. See also Davies (2004), above.

[115] See Barney Jopson, 'Warning on threat to quality of auditing', *Financial Times*, 21 June 2005, at p. 1.

[116] European Commission, Green Paper on *The Role, Position and Liability of the Statutory Auditor in the EU* OJ C 321, 28.10.1996, p. 1.

[117] See e.g., Commission Communication, *Reinforcing the statutory audit in the EU* (2003/C 236/02) for a description of earlier work and initial reaction to Enron and the US Sarbanes Oxley Act 2002; and Proposal on statutory audit of annual accounts and consolidated accounts and amending Council Directives 78/660/EEC and 83/349/EEC, March 2004, available at http://europa.eu.int/comm/internal_market/en/company/audit/index.htm.

[118] Commission Communication, *Reinforcing the statutory audit in the EU* (2003/C 236/02).

[119] Commission Communication, *The Statutory Audit in the European Union, the way forward* OJ C 143, 8.5.1998, p. 12.

shift the balance between representatives of the public interest and those of the audit profession to ensure that the public interest remains the overriding principle. The Communication also expresses support for use of International Standards on Auditing as a requirement for all EU statutory audits from 2005 onwards. The Communication suggests that the overarching governance structure needs to be more public interest led rather than profession oriented. The Communication recommends harmonising public oversight and use of an audit committee for assisting the statutory auditors to stay at arm's length from management as well as to ensure high quality financial reporting and statutory audit and well-functioning effective internal control including audit practices.[120] Endorsing the Recommendation of 2002 on auditor independence, the Communication suggests incorporation of the principles expressed in the earlier Recommendation into the modernised Eighth Directive.

Then in March 2004 the Commission published a Proposal for a Directive of the European Parliament and of the Council on statutory audit of annual accounts and consolidated accounts and amending Council Directives 78/660/EEC and 83/349/EEC.[121] The proposal aims to bring about the policy direction set out in reinforcing the statutory audit communication and also to provide a basis for effective and balanced international regulatory cooperation with oversight bodies of third countries such as the US Public Company Accounting Oversight Board. The proposal concentrates on independence and restricts the non-audit work of auditors. It requires publicity about the structure of the audit including details of which companies it has audited over the previous year and all non-audit work details and if it is part of a group structure. The proposal adopts the policy of a public oversight body so that monitoring of auditors and their work and independence is not just carried out by the professional body but by a government-appointed body of experts who are not members of the profession. An audit regulatory committee at EU level would allow for swift regulatory responses via the adoption of implementing measures. Public interest entities – those that are large enough and those listed on securities exchanges – would be required to appoint an independent audit committee. The proposal is part of a wider corporate governance programme.

---

[120] The European Parliament recently supported a relaxation of the proposals on audit committees, agreeing that the provisions should only apply where no national rules exist. See Tobias Buck and Barney Jopson, 'Europe softens line on audit committees', *Financial Times*, 22 June 2005, at p. 1.
[121] COM (2004) 177 final, Brussels, 16.3.2004.

Conclusion

The roles of those responsible for presenting company reports and information are fundamental to the quality of the reporting regime. The
company secretary is increasingly regarded as a compliance *professional*
with control over the information and record-keeping functions of the
company. Directors have the primary responsibility for reporting and
filing requirements and their legal duties are closely tied to their
reporting responsibilities. Non-executive directors are important internal monitors of the activities of the management board. They are
required to be familiar with the reports presented by the executive
directors and to evaluate those reports from the perspective of the
investors' interests. Their role on the audit committee is of particular
relevance. Auditors act as external monitors of the reports and accounts
presented by the directors and they must also provide a report stating
whether or not in their judgement those accounts and reports present a
true and fair view of the company's profit or loss or state of affairs at the
end of the financial year. The auditors' report is presented to the company's members and it is clear that their main legal relationship is with
the shareholders rather than with the board of directors. However, the
problems relating to lack of independence suggest that the board of
directors has the capacity to intrude on that relationship at the expense
of the shareholders' interests.

The emphasis in these different roles is broadly the same: protection of
the members and the financial security of the company. One observation
is that there appears to be no concerted effort to coordinate the roles.
Indeed, the chapter describes distinct functions of the various persons
involved in presenting information to the company's members. To an
extent the separation between the directors and the non-executives and
auditors is a necessary element of the independence required to evaluate
effectively the reports of the executives. Yet the failure to consider how
these groups interact leaves the possibility of that independence being
lost.

The emphasis on procedural requirements reflects the difficulty inherent in judging the substantive decisions of the relevant actors. Multiple
factors will lead to specific decisions and in reality one can only judge
those decisions by investigating whether or not they have been reached
by following an appropriate or prescribed process. This point might also
go some way to addressing the continuing problem of large liability risks.
If a non-executive director or an auditor has at least pursued the correct
steps towards making their decisions, then even if that decision turns out
to be incorrect, they will be less likely to be regarded as negligent in their

actions and will thereby avoid exposure to a large compensation claim. Similarly, if their independence can be achieved and maintained they will be less susceptible to suspicion of fraud or negligence or influence. Nevertheless, the self-regulatory stance of the 1990s appears gradually to be giving way to regulation and monitoring by outside bodies, such as the Financial Reporting Council and its subsidiary bodies.

Whilst these reforms may improve the disclosure system internally, the increasing level of international activity of auditors, the Big Four in particular, leads to the question of whether it would be more appropriate to seek the development of international regulation by an organisation such as the OECD. In Alexander's view, the OECD should take the lead in reforming auditing standards which should not be purely Anglo-American based. A truly international code of practice for auditors from the OECD would be most appropriate for adopting international accounting standards rather than the industry-financed and controlled IASC.[122]

---

[122] Kern Alexander, 'The Need for International Regulation of Auditors and Public Companies' (2002) 23 *Company Lawyer* 341–3.

4   Users of corporate reports

One of the most important questions in any discussion about disclosure and corporate reporting is that of to whom must companies report? Financial reports detail the company's financial position including its profit achievement and forecasts, making such reports especially relevant to the company's shareholders, whose concern is with profit figures which largely determine the value of their shares and the likelihood of dividend payments. However, in reality a variety of potential users are interested in seeing financial and other information relating to the company. Indeed, the number of possible users with different interests presents a significant challenge for disclosure regulation. A particular difficulty is how best to balance the different and competing needs of the various user groups and how to prioritise them, if necessary, for the purpose of presenting and delivering corporate reports.

This discussion could be regarded as a subheading within the broader shareholder–stakeholder debate that raises the question of for whom should managers run companies. The answer to this question depends on which theory of company law one adopts and in turn such theory will determine who should be entitled to receive information from the directors or the company. This chapter will first list the potential user groups and will describe their main information needs. Secondly, the chapter will outline the predicament of legislators and policy-makers when faced with the broad range of possible information recipients and their different interests. The third section will outline the choice of legal and theoretical models that might inform the debate on how to deal with the range of possible users, and will consider whether to view the users as a broad but coherent group or as competitors for information. If they are considered as having compatible needs how might those needs be accommodated in the presentation and content of a company's information? If their needs are considered to be different but equal how are all such needs to be satisfied? Alternatively, how are users to be placed in a hierarchy if their different needs are competing and viewed as unequal?

Different potential recipients of company information

Corporate information is needed both internally within the company and externally. Internally, the use of information depends on the company's size and type. For example, a small, closely-held or family run company may require very little exchange and use of information since those running the company will effectively have several identities as managers, employees and shareholders of the company. In such companies the need for information structures is not really necessary. However, in larger companies information will have several functions and its use may be both vertical and horizontal. For example, information will be used for decision-making, resource allocation and governance purposes. Vertically, information may be exchanged and used by superiors and subordinates, as well as owner/senior management, senior management and business unit managers, and business unit managers and functional managers.[1]

External use of company information gives rise to a potentially broad set of users with different ways of using information provided by the company. There are some overlaps that may be observed in the identities of the internal and external users. For example, it could be argued that employees are concerned with internal information sharing activities but it is also possible to regard them as being engaged in external reporting. In 1975, the Accounting Standards Steering Committee's document *The Corporate Report*[2] listed the following users having a reasonable right to receive information on the company: equity investors, loan creditors, employees, analyst-advisers, business contacts, government and the public. More recently, the Accounting Standards Board identified present and potential investors, lenders, suppliers and other trade creditors, employees, customers, government and agencies, and the public.[3] The Institute of Chartered Accountants in England and Wales identifies external users as actual and potential investors, employees, lenders, suppliers and other trade creditors, governments and their agencies and members of the public.[4] The Department of Trade and Industry

---

[1] This set of internal uses and users of information has been identified by Johansson and Östman in Sven-Erik Johansson and Lars Östman, *Accounting Theory: Integrating Behaviour and Measurement* (Pitman, London, 1995), at p. 17.

[2] Accounting Standards Steering Committee, *The Corporate Report* (ASSC, London, 1975) (hereinafter 'ASSC').

[3] Accounting Standards Board, *Statement of Principles for Financial Reporting* (December London, 1999) circulated in *Accountancy* (March 2000) 109.

[4] Institute of Chartered Accountants in England and Wales, *The 21st Century Annual Report* (ICAEW, London, 1999).

identifies the following users as relevant: shareholders in exercising governance functions; creditors who need to have a clear picture of the position and prospects of their debtor; investors (shareholders and creditors) both actual and potential, who wish to know whether to acquire, retain or sell, a stake in the business; and other stakeholders (including employees) and the wider public, who have a variety of relationships with the business.[5]

These lists are, in fact, very similar, suggesting that it is possible to identify a finite and exhaustive set of user groups. The DTI's list is the least specific, making reference to 'other stakeholders'. It is appropriate at this stage to consider each identified group and their potential information needs and uses in a little more detail.

Equity investors

The equity investor group includes existing and potential shareholders and holders of convertible securities, options or warrants. The equity investor group requires information to assist in reaching share-trading decisions on whether or not to subscribe to new share issues or to sell shares. Investors may wish to make judgements about likely movements in share prices, likely levels of future dividend payments and management efficiency. They may require information concerning a company's present position, and future prospects and management performance will be relevant. Investors also require information to help them reach voting decisions at general meetings. Present and potential investors will be interested in information that helps them to assess how effectively management has fulfilled its stewardship role. They also require information to help them in taking decisions about investment or potential investment so they will be concerned with the risk inherent in, and return provided by, their investments. For this they require information on the entity's financial performance and financial position in order effectively to assess its cash generation abilities and its financial adaptability.[6] It is worth noting that investors do not necessarily form a homogenous group but, instead, comprise different interests and requirements. For example, a private shareholder is not likely to focus on all the same issues as an institutional investor. Likewise, certain specialist investors such as 'ethical investors' may have more specific information

---

[5] DTI, *Modern Company Law for a Competitive Economy: Developing the Framework* (March 2000) para. 5.4, at p. 152.
[6] ASB (1999), at p. 112.

requirements than the general financial figures usually associated with shareholder interests.

Loan creditors

The loan creditor group includes existing and potential holders of debentures and loan stock providers of short-term secured and unsecured loans and finance. The ASSC expressed the view that the information needs of the loan creditors would be similar in many respects to the needs of equity investors. More specifically, short-term creditors will want to know how much cash a business has got as well as appraise the net realisable value by knowing the priority of and amount of other various claims. Long-term creditors may have similar interests to shareholders, such as their interest in estimating the overall strength and position of the business some way into the future. The ASSC also noted that there were some distinctions to be made between the interests of loan creditors and equity investors. For example, unlike equity investors, loan creditors are primarily concerned with the risk and consequences of default.[7] The ASB stated that lenders require information which helps them to decide whether to lend and on what terms to lend; to assess whether their loans and any related interest will be repaid.[8]

Business contacts

The business contact group is broad ranging, covering suppliers, trade creditors, customers, competitors and business rivals and managers, investors and employees connected with firms involved in mergers and takeovers. Some such contacts will only be able to demand information where it coincides with the information needs of the other identified groups. Suppliers and other trade creditors require information that helps them to decide whether to sell goods to the company and to assess the likelihood that they will be paid. They need similar information to that required by short-term loan creditors. But long-standing suppliers may also wish to assess the company's future in terms of financial viability and in terms of sales volume and market share. Customers require information regarding the entity's continued existence for matters such as maintaining warranties and obtaining continued supplies. Such customers may wish to assess the reliability of the business in the short term as well as the long term in order to assess the possible quality of after-sales service and an effective guarantee.

---

[7] ASSC (1975), at pp. 26–7.   [8] ASB (1999), para. 1.3(b), at p. 112.

Analysts

The analyst adviser group includes financial analysts, journalists, economists, statisticians, researchers, trade unions, stockbrokers and other providers of advisory services, such as credit rating agencies. This group of users comprises essentially a collection of experts who advise other groups. For example, trade unions advise employee members based partly on information they have obtained from the company, whilst stockbrokers and investment analysts use company information to advise existing and potential investors.

Employees

The employee group includes existing, potential and past employees. Employees require information for assessing the security and prospects of employment and information for the purpose of collective bargaining including the ability of the employer to meet wage demands, working conditions etc. They also need to assess present and future job security based on information concerning economic stability of the business into the future. Therefore employees need information, sometimes at plant and local level, on the employer's stability and profitability as well as the employer's ability to provide remuneration, employment opportunities, retirement and other benefits. The ASSC suggested that the 'general purpose' report might provide this information. Special purpose reports might also be required to cover specific information needs of employee groups. Indeed, they need information in a clear and simple, non-technical way and they may require non-financial information such as management attitudes to staff involvement in decision-making and promotion policies.

Employee recipients might also have different requirements and interests. For example, employee representatives may seek information to equip them for negotiations on matters such as pay and conditions, whereas some individual employees may be interested in information limited to matters affecting them personally. Some employees and their representatives will hold long-term views and seek information allowing them to make decisions about their future based on information obtained from the company, whilst other employees may only be interested in short-term issues, perhaps because they are temporary workers for the company.

Competitors

Competitors and business rivals will seek information about what gives the company a competitive advantage. They might seek a merger or amalgamation and would therefore need to assess what they could do with the business. Some of their information needs would overlap with those of the equity group but they would also need to consider, with the help of relevant information, how their own takeover or merger might take effect.

Government and related agencies

Government includes tax authorities, departments and agencies concerned with the supervision of commerce and industry and local authorities. A government's needs will largely coincide with those of the investors, creditors and employees but some special needs will require separate specific reports such as information for tax collection, statistical surveys and other purposes such as regulation of corporate activities. Policy-making activities mean also that a government requires future-oriented information.

The public

The public includes taxpayers, consumers and other community and special interest groups such as political parties, consumer and environmental protection societies and regional pressure groups. According to the ASB, the public requires information 'to assess trends and recent developments in the entity's prosperity and the range of its activities.'[9] More specifically, local concerns include employment, pollution and health and safety. Wider concerns might include energy use, use of subsidies, dealings with foreign governments and contributions to charities in money or kind. The public will be able to gain information from 'general purpose' reports where their interests coincide with the interests of the other user groups and perhaps more of their interests could be met if there were developed generally acceptable measurement techniques. Much of this information is non-financial and might not even be measurable.

From the above description of the different user groups it is possible to see that their concerns have aspects in common. Indeed, the ASB expressed the view in its Statement of Principles, that the interests of different users with a variety of purposes are served by the publication of financial statements and general purpose financial reports that allow them to take informed decisions.[10] In this light the ASB adopts a

[9] ASB (1999), para. 1.3(g), at p. 112.
[10] ASB (1999), paras. 1.3–1.7, at p. 112.

rebuttable assumption that financial statements that focus on the interests that investors have will, in effect, also be focussing on the common
interest that all users have in the entity's financial performance and
financial position.[11] Similarly, Barton argues that 'to satisfy the basic
functions of decision making, control and accountability, users require
information about financial position and profitability and a summary
record of past operations, or of some aspects of these items. From this
information they must be able to ascertain the firm's solvency and
earning power, and the risks associated with investment in it.' Barton
suggests that the specific information needs reduce to five matters:

1. information on cash position and cash flows;
2. information on the financing of operations and on funds flows;
3. information on the earning power of the firm as this indicates its
   success in achieving a major goal – the earning of profits;
4. information on the financial position of the firm as this indicates the
   investment in the firm's assets, its resources and financial capacity to
   do things in the future, and it is the denominator in the return on
   investment calculation;
5. information on the financial risk incurred in investing funds in the
   firm.

Barton observes that there is considerable overlap in these information
requirements but that they are so closely related that these overlaps are
inevitable. Additionally the major variables being measured are all based
on the transactions of the firm and these involve cash or a cash substi-
tute. The basic functions of decision-making and accountability and
control are also interrelated.[12]

However, despite such observations, it is possible to note that
each group also has interests specific only to that group. Furthermore,
within each group there may be 'sub-groups' with yet more specific
interests, adding a further layer of complexity to the process of corporate
information sharing.

The predicament involved in recognising a variety of users

This broad range of potential information recipients gives rise to several
questions relevant to a disclosure regime: is it appropriate to regard all

---

[11] ASB (1999), para. 1.11, at p. 112.
[12] A. D. Barton, *Objectives and Basic Concepts of Accounting* (Australian Accounting
Research Foundation, Melbourne, 1982), at pp. 27–8.

the groups as having an equal claim to information from the company? If the answer to this question is affirmative, then should information be disseminated for a general purpose or should information be delivered in different forms to cater for the needs of each recognised group of users? Alternatively, should the users be placed in a hierarchical order that gives priority to one or more groups over others? If so, should the information be presented to meet the prioritised group's specific needs whilst still being available to the others? All of these questions have organisational, cost and communication implications for a company. They also have implications for the effectiveness of the corporate disclosure regime. The theoretical and legal models adopted for the company might help to answer such questions since they would provide some direction as to how a disclosure system should be operated and which users are to be granted rights to company information.

Possible theoretical and legal models for the company

Debates about the nature and objectives of companies have tended to focus on three broad theoretical models during the twentieth and early twenty-first centuries. These are the shareholder-centred model, the stakeholder or pluralist model and, more recently in the UK, the 'enlightened shareholder value' model.[13] Each such model would have consequences for a disclosure system, and would define the character of such a disclosure system in specific ways. In reality, it is possible to observe the influence of all three broad models in existing company law, including also in the disclosure system as it has developed although it is also clear to see that the dominant model has traditionally been, and remains, the shareholder-centred model.

The traditional legal model of the company, at least in the UK, centres on the shareholders as owners of the company. According to this 'traditional legal model' power within the company is divided between the directors and the shareholders. As Stokes observes, '[T]he object is to organise the internal structure of the company so that, whilst the directors as the managers of the company are given ample discretionary power

---

[13] It is not my intention to rehearse these well-developed theories in this book. My reference to the theories is to demonstrate how they might influence the disclosure system. The reader is referred to the following works for fuller expositions of the relevant theories: J. E. Parkinson, *Corporate Power and Responsibility: Issues in the Theory of Company Law* (OUP, Oxford, 1993); Ben Pettet, *Company Law* (Longman, London 2001) especially ch. 3; Mary Stokes, 'Company Law and Legal Theory' in W. Twining (ed.), *Legal Theory and Common Law* (Blackwell, Oxford, 1986) 155; David Millon, 'Theories of the Corporation' (1990) *Duke Law Journal* 201.

to operate the company effectively, they are nevertheless obliged to exercise that power in the interests of the owners of the company.'[14] Standard textbooks in the UK typically portray shareholders in this light. For example, Hannigan explains the separation of ownership and control in the following way:

> As the number of shareholders in a company increases, it is obviously impossible for all to be involved in the management and control of the company's affairs so a separation will develop between those who own the company (the shareholders) and those who manage it (the directors).[15]

Parkinson explains this attribution of ownership to shareholders as follows:

> the focus on shareholder interests results from a private conception of the company and company law. The underlying theory views the shareholders as having an entitlement that the company be operated for their benefit (or for whatever other purposes they may choose) by virtue of their position as members or owners. The law respects the right of the shareholders to determine the objectives of their association through contract and accepts that by virtue of their capital contributions they should be regarded as the owners of the company. By reason of their ownership rights, and given the traditional logic of ownership, it is taken that the shareholders are entitled to have the company run in their interests: it is *their* company.[16]

According to this explanation, the shareholders gain the status of owners of the company from the fact that they have made capital contributions; a link then is made between ownership of shares and the right to have the company run in their interests as owners.[17] Coupled with the rise of 'managerialism' which involves a separation of ownership and control, entailing a dispersed ownership and passive shareholders,[18] the need to ensure that managers run the company in the interests of the shareholders gives rise to a search for ways to align the objectives of the owners and the managers. The requirement for managers to run the company with a shareholder-oriented focus has also been justified on the basis that the shareholders are residual claimants to the firm's income.[19] From this

---

[14] Stokes, *ibid.*, at p. 166.

[15] Brenda Hannigan, *Company Law* (LexisNexis, London, 2003), at p. 144.

[16] J. E. Parkinson, *Corporate Power and Responsibility: Issues in the Theory of Company Law* (OUP, Oxford, 1993) pp. 75–6, emphasis retained.

[17] Fiona Macmillan Patfield, 'Challenges for Company Law' in Fiona Macmillan Patfield (ed.), *Perspectives on Company Law:1* (Kluwer, London, 1995) 1, at p. 12.

[18] The classic exposition of this company law phenomenon is Adolf Berle and Gardiner Means, *The Modern Corporation and Private Property* (rev. edn 1968, first published 1932, Harcourt, New York).

[19] Exponents of this position are numerous. For example see F. H. Easterbrook and D. R. Fischel, *The Economic Structure of Corporate Law* (Harvard University Press,

perspective, derived from the nexus of contracts theories, their claim stands last in line after the claims of creditors and employees, because, it might be argued, creditors have fixed claims and employees generally negotiate compensation schedules in advance of performance. This position as residual claimants gives to the shareholders an incentive to monitor the activities of managers. Since, as residual claimants, the shareholders effectively bear the risks, they are treated as the principals for whom the managers are to act as agents.[20] Market forces, supplemented by legal rules, create incentives for managers to minimise agency costs by acting for the benefit of the shareholders.

These shareholder-centred approaches to company law lead conclusively to privileging the shareholders with a priority claim to information if not an exclusive claim. As owners (literally or metaphorically) or as residual claimants who have no day-to-day control over the management of the business, shareholders need to monitor what the managers are doing on their behalf and with their investment. This means that shareholders require to be informed in order to hold directors to account and to evaluate and take decisions based on what they have learned about the directors' actions. From this position the company's accounts and reports should be tailored to the investment and stewardship decisions of its shareholders. Financial reporting lends itself quite readily to such a perspective since its main objective is to provide a true and fair view of the company's financial position and future prospects, focussing in particular on the profits and losses of the company and its financial balance sheet.

The traditional legal model of the company corresponds in many ways to this shareholder-centred perspective. For example, the fiduciary duties of directors require them to act *bona fide* in the interest of the company[21] a phrase that is translated generally to mean that directors must act for the benefit of the existing and future shareholders.[22] At least

---

1991); E. F. Fama and M. C. Jensen, 'Separation of Ownership and Control' (1983) 26 *Journal of Law and Economics* 301.

20 See especially, Alchian and Demzetz, 'Production, Information Costs, and Economic Organization' (1972) 62 *American Economic Review* 777; Jensen and Meckling, 'Theory of the Firm: Managerial Behavior, Agency Costs and Ownership Structure' (1976) 3 *Journal of Financial Economics* 305.

21 *Re Smith & Fawcett Ltd* [1942] Ch 304, CA, per Lord Greene MR, at p. 306.

22 *Greenhalgh* v. *Arderne Cinemas Ltd* [1951] Ch 286. Lord Evershed MR referred to the corporators as a general body, at p. 291. *The Savoy Hotel Ltd, and the Berkeley Hotel Co., Ltd, Report of an Investigation under section 165(6) of the Companies Act 1948* (HM Stationery Office, 1954) introduced the need to take account of the long-term interests of the company so that the interests of future shareholders as well as present shareholders should be considered.

technically, shareholders in general meeting have residual control by being granted the power to remove directors.[23] More specifically, with regard to disclosure, the investors' information needs are given primacy in the formal requirements for financial reports. Thus, for example, the Companies Act requires directors to prepare *for their shareholders*[24] for each financial year, annual accounts[25] and a directors' report.[26]

An alternative approach is to adopt the stakeholder – or pluralist – approach which does not necessarily prioritise the needs of the shareholders but, instead, seeks to balance their interests with the interests of other groups affected by the company's activities. This approach gives recognition to the claims of other groups beyond the shareholders because they 'can be affected by an organisation or may in turn bring influence to bear'.[27] Wheeler and Sillanpää's list of stakeholders includes customers, employees and investors as key stakeholders, together with local communities, suppliers and other business partners to make up the 'primary social stakeholders'.[28] 'Secondary social stakeholders' include civil society, business at large and various interest groups.[29] The 'non-social stakeholders'[30] include the natural environment, non-human species, future generations and their defenders in pressure groups.

This stakeholder view[31] rests on the argument that, as a citizen,[32] a company has a social responsibility and should recognise the community of interests which are affected by its behaviour.[33] This view of the company means that the interests of shareholders are placed alongside, and perhaps in competition with, the other stakeholder interest groups. Some of these interest groups have closer contact with the company on a daily basis than do their shareholders, providing a normative justification

---

[23] Section 303, Companies Act, 1985.   [24] Emphasis added.
[25] Section 226.
[26] Section 234.
[27] This definition is provided by David Wheeler and Maria Sillanpää, in 'Including the Stakeholders: the Business Case' (1998) 31 *Long Range Planning* 201 at p. 205.
[28] They are 'primary social stakeholders' because the impacts of relationships are direct and they involve human entities: Wheeler and Sillanpää, *ibid.*, at p. 205.
[29] 'Secondary social stakeholders' have less direct involvement but are sometimes extremely influential: Wheeler and Sillanpää, *ibid.*, at p. 205.
[30] 'Non-social stakeholders' do not have human relationships but they may be direct or indirect: Wheeler and Sillanpää, *ibid.*, at p. 205.
[31] The stakeholder literature is vast but readers are referred to the following examples: Will Hutton, *The State We're In* (Vintage, London, 1996, first published by Jonathan Cape, 1995); Royal Society of Arts, *Tomorrow's Company* (1995); J. Kay and A. Silberstone, 'Corporate Governance' (1995, August) *NIESR* 84.
[32] For a view of the corporation as a citizen see James Boyd White, 'How Should We Talk About Corporations? The Languages of Economics and of Citizenship' (1985) 94 *Yale LJ* 1416.
[33] Patfield, above, at p. 11.

for their recognition. For example, there is the employee who works every day in and for the company; the neighbourhood in which the company is located experiences direct contact with the company and its employees – including noise, traffic and maybe pollution; some customers might regularly purchase the goods of a particular company and develop a reliance on them – such as mothers who have a preference for particular nappies or baby foods. All such constituents may arguably be regarded as having a closer relationship with the company than many of its shareholders who remain passive and distant. There is little in present company law that shows recognition of this viewpoint on companies. Section 309 of the Companies Act 1985 does require the managers to consider the interests of the employees when carrying out their duties for the company and they have a duty to act in the collective interests of the creditors when the company goes into insolvency. However, these requirements are very limited in their application. In the disclosure arena the rising popularity of environmental and social reporting lends at least some credence to this pluralist perspective. However, as will be observed later in this book, the social and environmental reporting aspects of corporate disclosure requirements are considerably less developed than are the financial reporting requirements that tend to address more readily the interests of the shareholders.

A major problem for the stakeholder vision is that it fails to explain how to accommodate and balance all the potential interests that may arise in connection with a company's activities. With regard to disclosure, this problem is particularly acute since the requirement to meet the needs of all potential information interests gives rise to significant cost implications for the company.

The third, more recent, model of the company was presented by the Company Law Review Steering Group during the consultations for the company law review as an answer to the problems encountered by the pluralist vision. This is the so-called 'enlightened shareholder value' approach which seeks to bridge the interests of shareholders and stakeholders by connecting environmental sustainability and social responsibility to long-term shareholder value. The enlightened shareholder recognises that a short-term profit maximisation approach will ultimately reduce the quality and success of the company. The Steering Group was clearly influenced by the problem inherent in a pluralist approach of finding a practicable means to balance the interests of relevant parties without necessarily giving priority to those of members.[34]

---

[34] *Modern Company Law for a Competitive Economy: Completing the Structure*, November 2000, at para. 3.5.

The Company Law Review Steering Group also introduced the possibility of the Operating and Financial Review which symbolises the 'enlightened shareholder value' model.[35] The CLR had this to say:

Our approach is that the document is not financial in the narrow sense; as the title indicates, it is a qualitative, as well as a financial, evaluation of performance and trends and intentions. On the other hand it is an analysis and description of the business as an operational and commercial entity prepared by the directors from their perspective as managers of the business. This does not of course mean it is to be a mere marketing document – they are required to give a good faith objective assessment from their perspective. As to the matter of the target audience, the issue is resolved by the fact that the document is to be published like financial accounts. The directors will need to consider in accordance with their general duties how best to perform their function of preparing this document so as, subject to the law, to promote the success of the company for the benefit of its members.[36]

The OFR would still be, then, a financial document addressed to the shareholders, but with qualitative, as well as quantitative, contents.

The Institute of Chartered Accountants in England and Wales expressed a preference for the enlightened shareholder value approach introduced by the DTI. However, in doing so, the ICAEW also indicated the potentially limited scope of such a principle. In their view the creation of shareholder value 'is, in principle, also the best way of securing overall prosperity through economic growth and international competitiveness'.[37] The Institute was keen to state also that this objective does not mean that the needs of other stakeholders can be ignored and stressed the fact that by meeting the needs of stakeholders a company will create the greatest shareholder value.[38] However, this justified for the Institute a focus on investors' information needs in the company's external reporting. Immediately the Institute went on to say that such an approach was consistent with the fact that the investors take the greatest risk and that information designed to meet their needs is also likely to meet many of the needs of other stakeholders.[39] One could argue that this interpretation essentially treats the stakeholders as instrumental to the furtherance of the shareholders or investors' needs. The only genuine

---

[35] For a justification of the enlightened shareholder value concept, see *Modern Company Law for a Competitive Economy: Strategic Framework* (DTI, 1999) paras. 5.1.10–5.1.12.

[36] *Modern Company Law for a Competitive Economy: Completing the Structure*, November 2000, para 3.33. The White Paper, *Company Law Reform* (DTI, March 2005) confirms this.

[37] The Institute of Chartered Accountants in England and Wales, *Inside Out: Reporting on Shareholder Value* (ICAEW, 1999), at p. 14.

[38] *Ibid.* See also I. Cornelius and M. Davies, *Shareholder Value* (FT Financial Publishing, 1997), esp. at pp. 199–204.   [39] *Ibid.*

link between the shareholder and stakeholder interests is a forward-looking strategy. This itself presents a problem since, as is acknowledged by the ICAEW and the ASB, the annual report's main limitation is that it tends to give an historical perspective rather than present the company's strategic direction.

Competing or companion claims to information?

The current position in the UK relating to disclosure does not appear to follow any of the above theoretical positions exclusively. Whilst the traditional legal model is arguably the more conservative and gives primacy to shareholders the accounting standards debates indicate at least a recognition of the existence, if not relevance, of other groups' interests. However, accounting standards setters, such as the Accounting Standards Board, have sought to avoid the argument about competing claims or how all the claims might be balanced by asserting that the shareholders' interest in a company's financial performance and position represents and reflects also the interest of the other groups. For example, as noted above, the ASB adopts the view that the shareholders' needs will broadly represent also the interests of the other groups, particularly in the area of financial reporting. The ASB assumes a common interest among users in the entity's financial performance and financial position.[40] The ASB claims that,

in determining which information to include in the financial statements and how to present that information, it can usually be presumed that: a) information that is needed by investors will be given in either the financial statements or some other general purpose financial report; and b) information that is not needed by investors need not be given in the financial statements.[41]

This approach appears to identify investors' interests as financial and regards their financial interest as being comprehensive enough to satisfy also the financial interests of other constituent groups. Therefore, addressing the interests of investors would also give a sufficient degree of financial information to the other groups. Any other information that is not of a financial nature, it would appear, is unlikely to be of interest to the shareholders. That information would therefore not be relevant in the financial statements.

The ASB suggests that the purposes of all users involve taking informed economic decisions, including stewardship decisions.[42] This

---

[40] Accounting Standards Board, *Statement of Principles for Financial Reporting*, December 1999, paras. 1.10–12.
[41] *Ibid.*
[42] ASB, December 1999, para. 1.3, at p. 112.

coincidence of interests might justify the provision of general purpose financial statements. However, the ASB also acknowledges that there are limitations since financial reports are usually based on conventionalised representation of transactions and focus on financial effects but not on the non-financial issues and they tend to be historically directed.[43] Often the financial statements require accompanying information and supplementary special reports.[44] These observations lead the ASB to admit that the assumption of similarity of needs is rebuttable.[45]

Meier-Schatz presents an argument that could indeed be used to rebut the ASB's presumption that the shareholders' interests in financial reports might also satisfy the interests of other stakeholders. Indeed, Meier-Schatz expresses scepticism about the utility of financial reports. For example, where shareholders are to vote on issues such as board elections financial information is less relevant than information on individual members, composition, structure and functioning of the board.[46] Financial information might deter self-dealing but shareholders also need specific information on management's integrity and loyalty.[47] Meier-Schatz also has doubts regarding the ability of financial information to enable the public to control corporate management activity. He suggests that a reliable feedback mechanism is required.[48] Furthermore, financial information pertains to the economic performance of the company which, according to Meier-Schatz, is not usually the area where the social pressure of public opinion is likely to be generated.[49]

In any event, while there may be some similarities in the informational needs of the different users, research has shown that there may also be important differences in the informational needs of the users. Some information items are considered to be more important for certain users than for others. For example, Benjamin and Stanga found that bankers would attribute more importance to forecasted information such as projected earnings information than would analysts.[50] Of course, the reasons for different attributions of importance may be relevant. Thus, for example, Benjamin and Stanga suggest that differences may be the result of differences in sophistication levels between the groups

---

[43] ASB, December 1999, para. 1.8, at p. 112.
[44] ASB, December 1999, para. 1.9, at p. 112.
[45] ASB, December 1999, para. 1.11, at p. 113.
[46] Christian J. Meier-Schatz, 'Objectives of Financial Disclosure Regulation' (1986) 8 *Journal of Comparative Business and Capital Market Law* 219, at p. 227.
[47] *Ibid.*, at p. 228.
[48] *Ibid.*, at p. 231.
[49] *Ibid.*, at p. 231.
[50] James J. Benjamin and Keith G. Stanga, 'Differences in Disclosure Needs of Major Users of Financial Statements' (1977) *Accounting and Business Research* 187, at p. 191.

surveyed.[51] However, the general result of these findings might provide justification for different information to be provided to each relevant group that would satisfy their interests and requirements.[52]

These research findings, together with the argument expressed by Meier Schatz, suggest that the information needs of shareholders and stakeholders do not necessarily coincide. The consequence of this suggestion is that there may occur a need to inform all user groups separately, tailoring information to meet their specific needs. This was the suggestion made by the ASSC in *The Corporate Report* in 1975. Alternatively, a hierarchy of users might be established.

Problems arise with all possible strategies. For example, the shareholder vision that prioritises the shareholders as recipients of information could be misguided partly by the theoretical model and the approach itself contains contradictions. The separation of ownership and control theory that theoretically underlines the need for corporate governance and disclosure, may be challenged in a number of ways. In the smallest companies often shareholders and managers are not separated but are the same persons so that the shareholders are obviously aware of the management's activities! Thus to focus on the shareholders as recipients of information in such companies is a fruitless exercise. Indeed, this is recognised in the Companies Act 1985, which allows for abbreviated reports to be laid before the general meeting and imposes less restrictive reporting obligations on small companies.[53] Private shareholders in larger companies may still be dispersed. Yet this fact of their small and dispersed shareholdings gives to private shareholders little incentive to monitor the activities of the directors and they become, instead, rationally apathetic, choosing to show little interest in the annual reports for monitoring purposes. Indeed, there is mixed evidence about the extent to which private shareholders read their companies' annual reports.[54] The introduction of summary financial statements demonstrates recognition of the problems individual shareholders have with complex and detailed financial accounts.

Perhaps the strongest challenge to the claims of the separation of ownership and control theory is the concentration of shares held by institutional shareholders. This fact gives to such shareholders the weight and authority that individually dispersed shareholders with diversified portfolios lack. This then offers a reason for providing the institutional shareholders with information in order for them to be able to

---

[51] *Ibid.*, at p. 192.   [52] *Ibid.*, at p. 192.
[53] See ch. 6
[54] See ch. 6 for more details.

monitor effectively the directors' activities. Yet research suggests either that institutional investors prefer to use the 'exit strategy' and leave an ailing company or that they prefer to monitor the directors more informally through negotiations in private. From this viewpoint, formal information requirements may not be appropriate in this regard. For all shareholders the fact that litigation is discouraged in company law[55] and that shareholders are expected to cooperate with company decisions gives them little incentive but to use 'exit' and invest elsewhere. Thus to focus on them with information for corporate governance purposes seems pointless. Their investment decisions will determine whether they stay or escape and not whether they will challenge the board.

If a company were to adopt a stakeholder model, the main problem becomes that of how to meet all user groups' information needs. A stakeholder approach could expose the company to a potentially unlimited number of information recipients with significant cost implications for the company. The ASSC's proposal to create special separate reports for each group was not received with any enthusiasm back in the 1970s. One possible solution might be that suggested by Janice Dean who highlights the possibility of creating stakeholder networks through which there are interconnections between different stakeholder groups. Where groups clash Dean's suggestion is for managers to decide the balance as one that serves the continuing prosperity and development of the corporation as an entity. In this way, even if stakeholder claims are refused, their special interests must be set in the context of an overall framework of responsibilities for the company. In this way, reputation and trust go beyond self-interest making it necessary to arrange an integrated system of communications for insiders and outsiders.[56]

A stakeholder approach might also add to the difficulty in holding directors to account. The Hampel Committee, for example, expressed this problem as follows:

to redefine the directors' responsibilities in terms of the stakeholders would mean identifying all the various stakeholder groups and deciding the nature and extent of the directors' responsibilities to each. The result would be that the directors were not effectively accountable to anyone since there would be no clear yardstick for judging their performance.[57]

Yet this rejection of an adoption of a stakeholder perspective ignores the reality of the increasing importance of intangible assets such as

---

[55] Consistent with the ruling in *Foss* v. *Harbottle* (1843) 2 Hare 461.
[56] See further Janice Dean, *Directing Public Companies: Company Law and the Stakeholder Society* (Cavendish, London, 2001) at pp. 106–7ff.
[57] Hampel Committee, *Report on Corporate Governance* (Gee, London, 1998), para. 1.7.

employee knowledge and expertise. Some commentators argue that the stakeholder approach is both a moral imperative and a commercial necessity,[58] which in turn would require a redirection of the disclosure regime. One possible way forward is to view stakeholders not as discrete and unconnected groups but as an integrated network of interests that can be aligned with the company's interests and strategies through structured communication.[59] Alternatively, the company could be viewed as positioned at the centre of a circle of interest groups in which the outermost layers are more entitled to information from the company. Thus, arguably, among those closer to or more involved in a company's activities the common interest will be the continued existence of the company. The further removed a constituent group remains from the company's activities and decisions the less such constituents will be interested in the company's existence. Profit is likely to be of little interest as a goal for such constituents and they will not necessarily wish to ensure that the company continues. Instead that group will seek more careful control of the company's activities, creating for them a greater need for information to make possible that control. Additionally, one might argue that the users least connected to the company are the users most in need of information. For example, analysts and advisers require information in order to advise the company's shareholders and offer opinions based on comparative analysis which shareholders within the company may not find so easily. Another example is that of employees who might prefer to obtain advice from their representatives or trade unions, which, again, will be qualified to read the information and perhaps also be better placed to make comparisons with other companies.

External bodies such as NGOs with expertise on good behaviour and best practice, could, based on information gained, provide companies with guidance and assistance for improving processes etc. One problem is that debate on disclosure tends to carry with it notions of antagonism or conflict and could in this way encourage a negative or defensive approach by those being monitored or required to deliver the information.

It might at first be thought that the law and regulation of disclosure recognises the whole potential variety of users. After all as is stated by Freedman and Power: 'Statute requires companies not only to have their

---

[58] Thomas Clarke, 'The Stakeholder Corporation: A Business Philosophy for the Information Age' (1998) 31 *Long Range Planning* 182.
[59] See Eileen Scholes and David Clutterbuck, 'Communication with Stakeholders: An Integrated Approach' (1998) 31 *Long Range Planning* 227.

accounts audited but also to file these audited details in a public register at Companies House. This "disclosure philosophy" has frequently been projected as providing public protection." Yet in reality, as Freedman and Power observe, the courts have limited dramatically the body of interested users who are actually entitled to a duty of care by the auditors.[60] Even in doing this, in the case of *Caparo Industries plc* v. *Dickman*,[61] the House of Lords shied of making a crude distinction between the shareholders and others, Lord Oliver stating that that would be 'so unreasonable a distinction', thus leading him instead to distinguish between shareholders as a collective body and shareholders as individuals making investment decisions. This seems ironic considering that the general consensus in the accounting literature is that a primary objective of the accounts is to assist the users in making economic decisions[62] as well as controlling and making the managers accountable. The legal approach thus appears to be at odds with the accounting approach. Surely if the objectives are to be recognised the law should also provide mechanisms for enforcing the recognised purposes and functions of the accounts. The dilemma for the regulation of the financial disclosure is that the legal approach gives rise to a severe expectation gap, which is unlikely to generate the trust and cooperation that are vital to effective communication. It should also be noted that the directors, who have responsibility for preparing the accounts, will also be liable to investors if they have been fraudulent and so users who rely on dishonestly misleading accounts are not entirely denied access to remedies.

Conclusion

Currently, disclosure regulation emphasises shareholder interest in profit maximisation. This has resulted in the provision of complex financial information. Yet increasingly, such an approach is considered to be limited. The financial accounts, as will be seen in ch. 6, do not meet the interests or decision-making needs of shareholders and neither institutional nor individual shareholders appear universally to read the full accounts. Additionally, a broader range of assets that have gained relevance, such as the intangible assets of employee expertise and knowledge, provides a commercial incentive to recognise and address the interests of

---

[60] Judith Freedman and Michael Power, 'Law and Accounting: Transition and Transformation' (1991) 54 *MLR* 769 at pp. 778–781.
[61] [1990] 1 All ER 568.
[62] As is claimed by the ASB in its *Statement of Principles of Financial Reporting* (December 1999).

the company's stakeholders. From this viewpoint the company's reports and communications should not be addressed to shareholders alone.

Even within each group there are different needs, not least among the shareholders. Thus to identify their needs and interests is not an easy task. Some of their interests do overlap, as is recognised by the ASB. However, that point should not be overemphasised. There is indeed an argument to suggest that employees, rather than shareholders, represent the heart of the company.[63] The failure of company law to recognise this fact so far, and the current fashion in the UK for favouring the enlightened shareholder view, serves to retain the emphasis on financial reporting and in those financial reports to continue to produce complex accounts, now to be accompanied by a more complete directors' report. A more appropriate approach would be to tackle the issue of communication with an integrated group of constituents relevant to the company.

---

[63] See e.g., Robert M. Grant, 'The Knowledge-Based View of the Firm's Implications for Management Practice (1997) 30 *Long Range Planning* 450. See also Scholes and Clutterbuck above.

5   The Companies Register

The role of Companies House

A key participant in the corporate information process in the UK is the Companies Registrar at Companies House, an executive agency of the Department of Trade and Industry. Indeed, a system of registration has existed in the UK since 1844. As well as incorporating and dissolving limited companies, Companies House describes its main functions as being to examine and store company information delivered under the Companies Act 1985 and related legislation and to make this information available to the public.[1] Indeed, the role of Companies House is to meet one of the fundamental justifications for a disclosure regime, as is expressed by the DTI:

> Corporate status confers privileges on companies, in particular in relation to taxation and, in the case of limited companies, limiting the liability to creditors of the members of the company (shareholders) to the amount of capital subscribed. In return for these privileges, third parties such as potential creditors (customers, suppliers, lenders, public authorities etc), shareholders and employees are entitled to access to basic information about the company, its directors and its assets to enable them to make informed judgements about its affairs, and the risk of entering into any dealings with the company.[2]

Companies House is active in the receipt and processing of information for public access in three broad categories connected with the company's life. Certain disclosures are required on a company's incorporation; continuing disclosure is required on an annual basis or on the occurrence of specific changes such as change of company name or of directors; and disclosure requirements also arise relating to the dissolution of a company.

In the Final Report of its quinquennial review of Companies House the Department of Trade and Industry observed that the core business

---

[1] See www.companies-house.gov.uk.
[2] DTI, *Final Report of the Review of Companies House* (July 2000), executive summary, para. 6.

of Companies House is to discharge the regulatory function laid down in UK and EU Company Law, in particular 'to register new limited liability companies, ensure that registered companies provide the information required by statute, chase up and where necessary prosecute companies in default and ensure that the information collected is made available to all'.[3] The essential functions of Companies House identified by the DTI include reception of statutory information, basic data validation, processing of data and input, making information public, system design and management, ensuring compliance by chasing and prosecuting defaulters and owning the database. As the DTI states, customers 'look to Companies House as a reliable source of accurate and up-to-date information'.[4]

One aspect of the work of Companies House in relation to disclosure is that it seeks to make the process of disclosing and obtaining information relatively easy as this facilitates transparency and effective decision-making within and concerning companies. In this way, the gradual move towards electronic filing aims not only to improve accessibility to the information but also to reduce costs and increase efficiency of the information process. Thus, for example, the electronic annual return requires a company with fewer than twenty members only to check the information that is pre-printed and to make any necessary amendments. This reduces costs in time and effort for companies in preparing their annual returns. The availability of electronic data also makes the information more accessible for the public. From this perspective Companies House has an important contribution to make in improving the flow of information and its accessibility with the objective of making decisions more informed and easily based on accurate information about a company. Companies House also has to deal with the broadest range of companies from the smallest two-member companies to companies with billions of shares. Its system needs to accommodate the information needs of that broad range of companies too. The use of web filing and electronic filing facilitates this process.

Information required by Companies House when a company is formed

Information disclosure is necessary from the earliest point of a company's existence. The Companies Act 1985 lays down the information requirements when a company is being founded. In order for a company

---

[3] DTI, *Final Report of the Review of Companies House* (July 2000), para. 5.3.
[4] DTI, *Final Report of the Review of Companies House* (July 2000), executive summary, para. 9.

to be established those founding the company must submit to Companies House a number of documents: Memorandum of Association, Articles of Association if Table A is not adopted, section 10 statement[5], and statement of compliance[6].

The Memorandum of Association sets out: the company's name, where the registered office of the company is situated (in England, Wales or Scotland); and the company's objects.[7] Other clauses to be included in the memorandum depend on the type of company being incorporated.

The Articles of Association contain the rules for the running of the company's internal affairs. A company may adopt the whole of Table A as its articles or any part of it. A company limited by shares for which the whole of Table A has been adopted without modification does not need to deliver a copy for registration. However, in these circumstances a letter must be attached to the application saying this. If Table A is adopted with modifications, the modified version must be delivered for registration and must be signed by each subscriber in front of a witness who must attest the signature.

In accordance with section 10, Companies Act 1985, Companies House requires the delivery of 'Form 10'. This gives details of the first director(s) and secretary and the intended address of the registered office. As well as their names and addresses, the company's directors must give their date of birth, occupation and details of other directorships they have held within the last five years. Each officer appointed and each subscriber (or their agent) must sign and date the form.

Companies House requires the delivery of 'Form 12' in accordance with section 12, Companies Act 1985. Form 12 is a statutory declaration of compliance with all the legal requirements relating to the incorporation of a company. It must be signed by a solicitor who is forming the company, or by one of the people named as a director or company secretary on Form 10. It must be signed in the presence of a commissioner for oaths, a notary public, a justice of the peace or a solicitor.

After the documents have been inspected, the registrar keeps them and makes them available for public inspection.

The White Paper on *Modernising Company Law* contains proposals relating to company formation and the documents and information to be delivered to the registrar of companies. Clause 5 of the draft Bill sets out the information requirements for a proposal to form a company, which must be delivered to the registrar. These include notification of the name of the company, notification of the type of company,

---

[5] Companies Act 1985, s. 10.   [6] Companies Act 1985, s. 12.
[7] Companies Act 1985, s. 2.

notification of whether its registered office will be in England and Wales, in Wales, or in Scotland, notification of the intended address of its first registered office, notification of the name of each founder member, the share capital or guarantee notification, notification of the fact, if relevant, that a private company is to be subject to the new 'mandatory scheme',[8] the names of the intended first directors and secretary and a statement by each such person that he consents to act in that capacity, and the text of the constitution authenticated by each founder member if the company is to differ from the relevant model constitution.[9] In addition to this information the first director or secretary are required to deliver to the registrar a statement of compliance confirming that the purpose for which the company is intended is lawful and that the information given relating to its foundation is correct and complete.[10]

It is possible to observe from these proposals that the documentation and information to be delivered to the registrar will remain largely the same. The most significant changes appear to be the proposal for one constitutional document instead of separate memorandum and articles of association and the proposal to reverse the default position for private companies so that they may choose to opt into the mandatory scheme rather than start with the position of having to comply with the requirements of the mandatory scheme before positively opting out.

However, the registrar at this stage is arguably merely concerned with formalities. If the actors succeed in getting the correct documentation to the registrar then the registrar is likely to grant the certificate of incorporation. This certificate provides conclusive evidence that the legislative requirements in respect of registration have been complied with and that the association is a company authorised to be registered, and is duly registered.[11]

Information required to be sent to the registrar during a company's life

Companies House is not only relevant upon incorporation, but during the company's life various documents must be sent to the registrar.

---

[8] The 'mandatory scheme' as established by cl. 127(1) of the draft Companies Bill, is the scheme under which companies will be required to lay financial statements and reports, hold AGMs and to have automatic retirement of auditors. The intended default position will be that private companies will not be subject to the scheme and that public companies will be subject to the scheme. Private and public companies will be able to opt in and out of the scheme under the proposed legislation.

[9] Clause 5, Companies Bill, Cm.5553-II (July 2002).

[10] Clause 7, Companies Bill, Cm.5553-II (July 2002).

[11] Companies Act 1985, s. 13(7)(a).

Arguably the most important of these documents are the Annual Return and the Accounts.

The Annual Return provides a 'snapshot of certain company information'[12] at the made-up date. An annual return, made up to the company's return date, must be delivered to the registrar within 28 days of that date.[13] It must contain the following information: the name of the company; its registered number; the type of company it is, for example, private or public; the registered office address of the company; the address where certain company registers are kept if not at the registered office; the principal business activities of the company; the name and address of the company secretary; the name, usual residential address, date of birth, nationality and business occupation of all the company's directors; the date to which the annual return is made up.[14] If the company has share capital, the annual return must also contain: the nominal value of total issued share capital; the names and addresses of every member and the number and type of shares each such member holds or transfers from other shareholders.[15]

Whether trading or not, all limited companies are required to keep accounting records[16] and the directors of a company must file accounts for each accounting period with the registrar.[17] The accounts will normally include a balance sheet, a profit and loss account, a directors' report, an auditors' report, notes to the accounts and, where relevant, group accounts.[18]

The other more common documents to be provided to the registrar include forms relating to change of accounting reference date,[19] change of situation or address of registered office,[20] changes relating to directors and secretary including appointment or termination of appointment and changes to the company's register of directors and secretaries,[21] as well as information concerning allotment of shares,[22] notice of increase in

---

[12] Companies House, Guidance Booklet, *Annual Return*, available at www.companies house.gov.uk/.
[13] Companies Act 1985, s. 363.
[14] Companies Act 1985, s. 364.
[15] Companies Act 1985, s. 364A.
[16] Companies Act 1985, s. 221.
[17] Companies Act 1985, s. 242.
[18] See ch. 6 for a more complete discussion of the accounts.
[19] Form 225, pursuant to Companies Act 1985, s. 225.
[20] Form 287, pursuant to Companies Act 1985, s. 287(3).
[21] Form 288, pursuant to Companies Act 1985, s. 288. Form 288(a) is used for the appointment of an officer. Form 288(b) is used for an officer ceasing to act as a result of, for example, resignation, removal or death. Form 288(c) is used for a change in details of an officer such as a change of name or new residential address.
[22] Form 88, pursuant to Companies Act 1985, s. 88.

nominal capital,[23] particulars of mortgages and charges and declaration of satisfaction of mortgages or charges[24] and company resolutions.[25]

All of this information is again connected to the identity of the company and its actors. The information is filed with the registrar so that it can then be made accessible to the public who may be interested in the company.

The Department of Trade and Industry and the Company Law Steering Group have made recommendations for modifying the information provision requirements relating to the registrar. The key objective of the review in this respect was to 'minimise the regulatory burden on companies insofar as is possible while ensuring that sufficient is known about each company for its actual and potential members, creditors, suppliers, and others to make decisions over their relationship with that company'.[26] The Steering Group stated that consultations had confirmed that the features of central registration are much valued, with the consequence that they recommended only minor changes to the system. They suggested the addition of the requirements to register the appointment of a judicial factor, to file all former names of directors so that women could not exclude maiden names or former married names and to file the company registration number and place of registration for corporate directors. Almost all the existing requirements were considered to be essential with some minor reviews such as reducing the period for keeping details of former members on a company's register from twenty years to twelve years and companies should have statutory immunity from claims relating to entries after the expiry of twelve years.

Some controversy remains over the requirement to file information relating to directors' and secretaries' residential addresses. The Steering Group recommended in its Final Report that directors' residential addresses should continue to be filed with the central register in order for enforcement and regulatory bodies as well as liquidators and also creditors and shareholders to be able to discover the individual's residential address. However, it suggested also that directors should be given the option in the future of either supplying their residential address to be kept on the public record or filing both a service address and their residential address which would be placed on a separate register with restricted access. The enactment of the Criminal Justice and Police Act

---

[23] Form 123, pursuant to Companies Act 1985, s. 123.

[24] See Companies Act 1985, ss. 395–424.

[25] Copies of all special and extraordinary resolutions and some ordinary resolutions must be delivered to the registrar within fifteen days of them being passed by the company (see Companies Act 1985, ss. 380, 111, 123, and 367).

[26] Final Report, para. 11.38, p. 235.

2001 introduced the possibility of directors and secretaries obtaining confidentiality orders to disapply the requirement for the supply of their home address where the public availability of their residential address exposes them to a serious risk of intimidation or violence. In its White Paper, *Modernising Company Law*,[27] the Government expressed a preference for assessing how the confidentiality order provisions operate in practice before forming a final view on the issue of publicity of directors' and secretaries' residential addresses. In the latest White Paper, *Company Law Reform*,[28] the Government proposes to remove the requirement on most directors to disclose publicly their home address.

Documents to be delivered to the registrar upon the company's liquidation or insolvency

When a voluntary arrangement is agreed upon, the supervisor must send to the registrar a copy of the chairman's report of the meeting at which the voluntary arrangement was approved[29] and at least once every twelve months the supervisor is required to send to the registrar and other interested parties an account of receipts and payments and a progress report.[30] When the arrangement is completed the supervisor must notify the registrar of this fact within twenty-eight days of its completion,[31] and he or she must also notify the registrar within seven days of an order to revoke or suspend the arrangement.[32]

Where an administration order is made the administrator appointed by the order must notify the registrar of the order[33] and send to the registrar a copy of the court order.[34] He or she must also send copies of proposals made in respect of the administration order[35] as well as notice of the results of meetings of creditors relating to such proposals.[36] Every six months thereafter the administrator must send to the registrar an account of payments and receipts.[37] After the court discharges or varies the terms

---

[27] July 2002, Cm. 553–I.   [28] March 2005.

[29] Insolvency Rules 1986, SI 1986/1925, r.1.24(5). See also Insolvency Act 1986, s. 4(5). Companies House Form 1.1.

[30] Insolvency Rules, 1986, r.1.26(2). Companies House Form 1.3.

[31] Insolvency Rules, 1986, r.1.29(3).

[32] Insolvency Rules, 1986, r.1.25(5). Companies House Form 1.2.

[33] Insolvency Rules, 1986, r.2.10(3). Companies House Form 2.6.

[34] Insolvency Act 1986, section 21(2); Insolvency Rules, 1986, r.2.10(5). Companies House Form 2.7.

[35] Insolvency Act 1986, s. 23(1); Insolvency Rules 1986, r.2.16(1).

[36] Insolvency Act, 1986, s. 25(6).

[37] Insolvency Rules, 1986, r.2.52(1). Companies House Form 2.15.

of the order the administrator must notify the registrar of such changes within fourteen days.[38]

The person who appoints an administrative receiver, a receiver or manager is responsible for notifying the registrar within seven days of the appointment.[39] The administrative receiver must publish his or her appointment in the Gazette and in an appropriate newspaper[40] and when an administrative receiver, receiver or manager ceases to act they must also notify the registrar.[41] An administrative receiver is responsible for making a report to the registrar and creditors within three months of appointment explaining the circumstances of the appointment and the actions he or she is taking together with a summary of any statement of affairs prepared for him or her by officers or employees of the company.[42] An account of receipts and payments must be sent to the registrar each twelve months by the administrative receiver,[43] after twelve months of his or her appointment and every subsequent six months, as well as within one month of ceasing to act as a receiver or manager.[44]

Any resolutions for the voluntary winding up of the company must be copied to the registrar, together with a statutory declaration of solvency from a majority of the company's directors,[45] within fifteen days of the meeting[46] and published in the Gazette within fourteen days.[47] The liquidator then appointed to wind up the company's affairs must within 14 days of his or her appointment notify the registrar and publish the appointment in the Gazette as well as in the local newspaper.[48] Within seven days of the creditors' meeting the liquidator must send a statement of affairs[49] and Form 4.20 to the registrar as well as a statement of the company's payments and receipts for the first twelve months of the liquidation and thereafter every six months.[50] Within one week of the final meetings of the creditors and members the receiver must send to the registrar an account and a return of the final meeting.[51]

---

[38] Insolvency Act 1986, s. 27(6).
[39] Companies Act 1985, s. 405. Companies House Form 405.
[40] Insolvency Rules 1986, r.3.2(3).
[41] Companies Act 1985, s. 405, Insolvency Act 1986, s. 45(4).
[42] Insolvency Act 1986, s. 48(1) and s. 48(5).
[43] Insolvency Rules 1986, r.3.32.
[44] Insolvency Act 1986, s. 38.
[45] Insolvency Act 1986, s. 89.
[46] Insolvency Act 1986, s. 84(3).
[47] Insolvency Act 1986, s. 85(1).
[48] Insolvency Act 1986, s. 109(1).
[49] Insolvency Rules 1986, r.4.34.
[50] Insolvency Act 1986, s. 192 and Insolvency Rules 1986, r.4.223. Companies House Form 4.68
[51] Insolvency Act 1986, ss. 94(3) and 106(3).

Where the court orders the company to be wound up the company must send to the registrar a copy of the winding-up order.[52]

It is possible for a director to apply to the registrar to strike off the company under section 652A of the Companies Act 1985. This must be done on the prescribed form[53] and conditions apply such as the requirement that the company has not traded, changed its name or become subject to insolvency proceedings during the previous three months. The registrar will place a copy of the application on the company's public record and will advertise and invite objections by placing a notification of the application in the London Gazette. After three months the registrar will strike off the company and the company is dissolved when the registrar publishes a notice to that effect in the Gazette.[54]

The registrar may also decide to strike off companies that appear to be defunct, for example because he has not received documents that should have been sent to him or because he has had mail returned from a registered office undelivered.[55] A notice will be placed on the company's public record and in the Gazette of the registrar's intention to strike it off[56] and after three months a further notice that the company will be dissolved ends the company's life.[57]

Information relating to oversea companies

A range of information must be delivered to the registrar when a company incorporated outside Great Britain establishes a place of business in Great Britain. Section 691 of the Companies Act 1985 requires that in such circumstances the company shall deliver within one month to the registrar a certified copy of the charter, statutes or memorandum and articles of association or other constitutional document of the company with a certified translation in English where relevant as well as a return in the prescribed form which contains details about the company directors, the company secretary, and when the company began trading in Great Britain. Any changes to this information or to the status of the oversea company must also be notified on the relevant forms to the companies registrar.[58]

---

[52] Insolvency Act 1986, s. 130(1).
[53] Companies House Form 652a. See generally Companies Act 1985, ss. 652 and 652A to 652F.
[54] Companies Act 1985, s. 652A(4).
[55] Companies Act 1985, s. 652.
[56] Companies Act 1985, s. 652(3).
[57] Companies Act 1985, s. 652(5).
[58] For further details see Part XXIII Companies Act 1985, and the Guidance Booklet by Companies House on Oversea Companies available at www.companieshouse.gov.uk/.

The importance of the companies registrar for disclosure

It is clear from this outline that the companies registrar receives and handles an enormous store of information concerning companies. Indeed, Companies House states on its own website that there are over 200 forms that companies could file. The above outline also gives an indication of the general character of the information with which the registrar is concerned. Essentially the information covers the location of the company, the identity of its officers, the nature of the company defined by its objects and constitutional arrangements, its share structure and identity of its membership and the financial status and capacity of the company as well as its continued existence or otherwise. These aspects of the company are important to persons considering whether or not to enter into dealings with the company as potential creditors or investors or business partners. Should things go wrong or should they need to seek further information they are provided by the public records created by the registrar with addresses and contact points for the company. In short, the information available at Companies House is relevant to the role of company law as facilitating 'the exercise of effective business choices through the availability of information so that those choices can be properly informed and based on an assessment of the risks involved'.[59] The key feature of Companies House is that it provides 'anonymous access to a mass of information maintained at central locations for all companies. Members of the public can thus obtain information with minimal inconvenience and expense both to themselves and to the companies concerned, and without alerting the company to their interest'.[60]

The registrar has a number of functions in connection with the information delivered. The registrar acts as an inspector, a gatekeeper and as an enforcer. For example, when a company is being formed the registrar checks the information presented before deciding whether or not to grant a certificate of incorporation. The registrar checks that the required formalities have been complied with. The registrar as gatekeeper places information on the public register and is therefore responsible for ensuring that the public have access to essential information about the company. As a law enforcer the registrar is empowered to impose fines on company officers for non-compliance with information requirements

---

[59] DTI, *Modern Company Law for a Competitive Economy: Developing the Framework* (DTI, March 2000) para. 10.3, at p. 310.
[60] *Ibid.*, para. 10.34, at p. 321.

as well as request information to be given with the ultimate threat of his or her power to strike a company's name from the register. It is also within the registrar's discretion to dissolve a company on the basis of its apparent defunct status.

There are a number of positive benefits that may be identified with the role of the registrar. He may act as a restraint upon potentially illegal activity or potential non-compliance. Company officers may be deterred from illegal behaviour if they are aware of its potential negative publicity and equally such publicity could encourage compliance with information requirements. The regular cycle of information delivery requirements also provides company officers with a genuine opportunity to review the financial status of their company as well as its internal structures. This could have the effect of improving strategic decision-making for a company's future activities. Additionally, if the information is available and it has been checked by the registrar at least for formal correctness, this may have the effect of improving the level of trust between a company and its potential business partners as well as between the company officers and its members. Additionally, the use of prescribed and standardised forms assists with making reference and comparisons between companies.

One of the current problems with the information handled and distributed by the registrar is that the publication of such information in the London and Edinburgh Gazettes limits its accessibility. This problem was noted by the Steering Group in the Final Report to the Company Law Review.[61] In *Developing the Framework* the Steering Group elaborated upon the problem highlighting the fact that the Gazette is little known by the public and that the Gazette does not ensure sufficient coverage or access to the information published therein. The Steering Group suggested numerous other ways of publishing the information such as a custom-built publication produced by the registrar and published in a number of ways such as via the offices of Companies House and via its website as well as supplying it direct to customers who requested it. The Directive amending the First Company Law Directive,[62] which comes into force no later than 31 December 2006, provides that the national gazette may be kept in electronic form or replaced fully by an electronic system that will fulfil the same role.

Another problem with the system identified by the Steering Group is that of false or incorrect information, some of which could be supplied

---

[61] At p. 240, para. 11.48.
[62] Directive 2003/58/EC amending Council Directive 68/151/EEC as regards disclosure requirements in respect of certain types of companies OJ L 221/13.

by vexatious or fictitious directors. The steering group recommended that it should be an offence knowingly or recklessly to deliver information which is misleading, false or deceptive in a material to the registrar. This was supported by the consultees,[63] and has been inserted in the new Company Law Reform Bill.[64]

A number of features have developed which may be criticised. For example the variation in the time periods within which changes to company details must be notified arguably creates confusion for company officers charged with delivering that information. There is a valid argument for rationalising these time periods in order to reduce the potential confusion. In addition there continues to exist a problem with late filing of accounts[65] which indicates perhaps a lack of understanding by companies of what is required by Companies House. One suggestion is that the penalties that can be administered against late filing of accounts are only of modest amounts providing a key to the problem.[66] The reduction of failure by companies to meet their filing deadlines may require an increase in fines so that they have an incentive to file on time.[67]

Another problem identified during the Company Law Review is the overlap between information required to be filed with the companies registrar and other information that companies themselves are required to make available. Arguably two methods of disclosure have different purposes justifying the maintenance of a distinction between them.[68] The specific role of Companies House, in the view of the Company Law Review Steering Group, is to provide anonymous access to a mass of information that will enable members of the public to obtain information with minimal inconvenience and expense both to themselves and to the companies concerned.[69]

A number of balances need to be struck. For example a balance is needed between the interests of those wanting information and the burdens which filing requirements impose on companies. A balance also needs to be achieved between having more information and the register

---

[63] Developing the Framework, para. 10.60, at p. 329; question 10.12, at p. 330; and Completing the Framework, para. 8.27, at p. 164.

[64] See White Paper, *Company Law Reform* (March 2005), para. 4.9.

[65] Cross estimates that around 124,000 companies fail to provide their annual accounts and returns in time, based on the compliance figures produced by Companies House in its annual report July 2002.

[66] See Simon Cross, 'Companies House', *International Accountant*, October 2002, 24, at p. 25.

[67] *Ibid.*

[68] *Modern Company Law for a Competitive Economy: Developing the Framework* (DTI, March 2000) para. 10.34, p. 321.   [69] *Ibid.*

being too cluttered. Ideally the information available needs actually to be useful and the salient facts need to be easily obtained without them being obscured by too much other information. The Company Law Reform Bill introduces a provision by which the Registrar will have ability to remove items from the public register which have been erroneously placed there or which are 'surplus' and unnecessary.[70]

Companies House also recognises that the range of those searching the register is broad. Thus approximately 40 per cent of those accessing the register to use the information are banks, lawyers and other commercial parties. 10 per cent of this group are individuals. 60 per cent percent of users also provide information in other ways by researching on the register and presenting it in other ways such as within sectors. Or they use the information on the register to provide financial analysis or credit rating services.[71]

Modernising the First Company Law Directive

Many of the information registration requirements are a fundamental part of European Company Law. The First Company Law Directive laid down specific details requiring to be delivered to the companies registrar on incorporation and during the lifetime of a company.

The First Directive has arguably resulted in what are perceived as burdens on business and Companies House has devoted itself to reducing those burdens. As time has passed some suggest that these requirements are, to an extent, obsolete since they have been overtaken by technological developments and international corporate activities which impose different needs and demands. The Conference on Company Law and the Single Market held in December 1997 was,

devoted to three important themes, among which was the impact of modern methods of communication on company law. One of the conclusions of the Conference was that the compulsory disclosure system organised by the First Directive might benefit significantly from the introduction of modern technology, which could help to meet the important objective of making company information more easily and rapidly accessible.[72]

These points were recognised clearly by the steering group in its document *Developing the Framework*:

---

[70] White Paper, *Company Law Reform* (March 2004), para. 4.9.

[71] Brenda Hannigan, *Company Law* (LexisNexis, London, 2003) pp. 9–10, citing Companies House, *Development Plan 2001–2004*, para. 1.13

[72] Explanatory Memorandum to the proposal for amending the First Directive as regards disclosure aspects of certain types of companies (COM 2002, 279, Brussels, 3.6. 2002).

One general reason for looking afresh at information registration is that, whilst the central principle underlying registration and disclosure may be unchanging, the conditions in which the principle has to operate have been subject to quite notable changes. In particular the revolution in information technology has changed not only how information is stored, recovered, transferred and copied but also the uses to which it can be put. Those who first proposed that companies should make publicly available the names and addresses of all their shareholders could not have envisaged that these lists would be used to target advertising. And, whilst electronic transmission has greatly reduced the burden involved in the provision, storage and sorting of information, if it leads to a large increase in the amount of information available this may paradoxically make it harder for people to find the information they need.[73]

Directive 2003/58/EC of the European Parliament and of the Council of 15 July 2003 amending Council Directive 68/151/EEC as regards disclosure requirements in respect of certain types of companies[74] responds to the SLIM Simplification of the Legislation on the Internal Market process and thereby seeks to modernise the First Company Law Directive. Its primary objectives are to make company information more easily and rapidly accessible to interested parties and to simplify the disclosure formalities imposed upon companies. The new Directive aims to enable companies to file their compulsory documents electronically or by paper means, to ease cross-border access to company information and to allow for voluntary registration in additional languages. The new Directive also requires that company registers shall, by 2007, retain electronic versions of company documents and particulars filed electronically or on paper. This Directive will enter into force on 1 January 2007.

Companies House has already developed an electronic filing and disclosure system. In its Annual Report for 2003–2004, Companies House reported that electronic incorporations by the year-end of 2003–4 accounted for 67 per cent of total incorporations with Companies House. It is also now possible for companies to file their annual return online by using an electronic shuttle and according to the Annual Report, the web-filing service now caters for 65 per cent of companies' filing needs including registered office address changes and appointments or resignations of directors and secretaries.[75] Companies House is also working towards a system for electronic filing of accounts by 2006 and so should be able to comply with the amending Directive.[76] The public targets for 2004–5 as stated in the Annual Report[77] are to achieve a 15 per cent take up for

---

[73] At p. 310, para. 10.4.   [74] OJ L 221/13.
[75] Companies House, *Annual Report 2003–2004*, at p. 14.
[76] Strategic Direction 2003–2006 – The Future of Companies House.
[77] Companies House, *Annual Report 2003–2004*, at p. 23.

electronic submission of documents by the end of 2004–5, 35 per cent by the end of 2005–6 and 55 per cent by the end of 2006–7. In any event, as Hannigan suggests, even at this stage, 'Companies House is one of the most advanced electronic registries in the world.'[78]

The Company Law Review highlighted the advantages of electronic technology in information provision by companies stating that electronic technology 'offers the basis of a better dialogue with shareholders and others'.[79] From this perspective the Steering Group argued that electronic filing of company information at Companies House should be encouraged and developed. In addition, electronic filing makes possible standardisation of information on a standard form 'which could assist the transfer of financial information onto the registry database and aid searching or interpretation'.[80] Later, the Steering Group, on the basis of responses to its earlier opinion, suggested providing the registrar with a power to instruct on the form and manner of delivery of information and that this power should be sufficiently broad as to enable the registrar in the future to require electronic filing.[81] As it currently operates, the electronic registration service falls into two broad categories: web filing and electronic filing. The web-filing service is designed for the benefit of occasional presenters allowing them to submit their information via the Companies House website. The electronic filing service is designed for frequent filing of information via email with the aid of approved software. The annual return may be submitted in this way and Companies House plans that in the long term it will be possible to submit accounts in this way. Occasional searchers may use WebCheck which enables customers to buy information about a company such as its most recently filed accounts and its annual return. More frequent users are able to subscribe to Companies House Direct for online access to information contained in the public databases.

European and international developments on the role of the Companies Registrar

In European law the principle of mutual recognition is of fundamental importance and this has implications for the different commercial registries across Europe. The case of *Centros Ltd*[82] involved a Danish couple

---

[78] Brenda Hannigan, *Company Law* (LexisNexis, London, 2003) at p. 7.
[79] *Modern Company Law for a Competitive Economy: Developing the Framework* (DTI, March 2000), para. 5.114, at p. 195.
[80] *Ibid.*, para. 5.121, at p. 197.
[81] *Modern Company Law for a Competitive Economy: Completing the Structure* (DTI, November 2000), paras. 6.63–64, at p. 134.
[82] C-212/97: *Centros Ltd* v. *Erhvervs-Og Selskabsstyresen* [1999] ECR I-1459, ECJ.

who had set up and registered their company in England but did not trade in England and later applied to the Danish authorities for permission to set up a branch in Denmark. That would enable them to avoid the stricter capital requirement rule in Denmark. The ECJ ruled that the freedom of establishment should enable a company to be established in one member state and to set up a branch in another member state. It did not matter that the actors chose to set up their company in a member state with more lenient rules. The ruling means that it would be contrary to the EC Treaty for a member state to refuse to register a branch of a company formed in accordance with the law of another member state in which it has a registered office. Moreover, in the context of registration of companies, the ruling also demonstrates a lack of harmonised provisions and the need for cooperation between commercial registries in the EU. At the very least each registry has to accept and take on trust that what has been done by another registry has been done correctly.[83] The problem is, however, that without sufficient harmonisation in the area of incorporation it is arguably difficult to accept the principle of mutual recognition if only because of the problem of lack of trust that this would create in the system by potential creditors and shareholders.[84] In addition, where there is international corporate activity this also requires acceptance of the control exerted by foreign authorities which may require equivalence of functions.[85] Such problems point to a need to establish some common principles of register disclosure in Europe beyond those set out in the First Directive and Second Company Law Directives.[86]

Conclusion

Companies House has an essential role in balancing the 'need to minimise the regulatory burden on companies insofar as is possible' and 'ensuring that sufficient is known about each company for its actual and potential members, creditors, suppliers and others to make decisions over their relationship with that company'. As the Steering Group stated in the Company Law Review, 'Companies House uniquely

---

[83] See Rafael Arenas Garcia, 'Registry Disclosure in Europe. Towards a European Registry Space' available at www.ecrforum.org/sevilla last accessed 25 August 2004.

[84] *Ibid.*

[85] *Ibid.*

[86] The Second Company Law Directive imposes a minimum capital requirement for public companies but not for private companies but some member states do themselves insist on a minimum capital for private companies. This gave rise to the problem in *Centros.*

provides anonymous and easy access to key information for all companies' and 'these features of central registration are much valued'.[87] The move towards a complete electronic filing system is intended to improve the possibility of dialogue within a company as well as between the company and members of the public by making the provision of information easier and cheaper as well as by making that information easier to find and interpret. The recent annual reports of Companies House demonstrate a real commitment to using electronic facilities not least because of the increasing international influences on business. Electronic technology enables information to be delivered faster and further thereby meeting the demands imposed by such broader corporate activity.

A number of issues remain problematic such as the type of information required to be filed on the public register, the time limits for providing such information, and also how the registrar publicises certain information. Section 744 of the Companies Act 1985 currently restricts the registrar to publishing in the London or Edinburgh Gazettes such information as the proposed or planned dissolution of a company. The London and Edinburgh Gazettes are not well-known publications thus denying to the public access to important information. The Company Law Review recommended a change in the law to allow the registrar to approve the method of publication of documents. This recommendation was supported by the consultees in the Company Law Review process, as were the recommendations that it should be an offence knowingly or recklessly to deliver false information to the registrar and that the registrar should have a discretionary power to add information to the public record in order to rectify previously filed incorrect information.[88]

---

[87] *Modern Company Law for a Competitive Economy: Final Report* (DTI, June 2001), para. 11.38, at pp. 235–6.

[88] See *Modern Company Law for a Competitive Economy: Final Report* (DTI, June 2001), para. 11.48, at pp. 240–1.

Part II

Financial reporting

6   Financial reporting

Introduction

It has been argued that the need to consider the objectives of audited accounts 'is not purely the task of the accounting profession; it is central to company law'.[1] The relevance o5f audited financial accounts to company law lies in their contribution to corporate governance by providing a facility for judging the stewardship of the managers at least from the perspective of their effect on the company's financial position. Indeed, a major feature of the 'disclosure philosophy' is the requirement for companies to produce audited accounts and to make these available to their members and debenture holders and also to the public by delivering them to the registrar of companies. The most recognised purposes of these accounts are to enable shareholders and others to make economic decisions and to judge the managers' use of resources.

The financial reporting aspects of disclosure also comprise the most developed area of disclosure obligations. The chapter on the regulatory structure demonstrated that financial reporting requirements exist in a combination of statutory provisions, shaped by European Directives, and professional accounting standards issued by the Accounting Standards Board. This chapter will provide a brief outline of the financial reporting requirements before considering their effectiveness in the light of their objectives and communication quality.

Statutory reporting requirements

Duty to keep accounting records

Section 221 of the Companies Act 1985 requires companies to keep at their registered office (or at any other place as the directors see fit)

---

[1] Judith Freedman and Michael Power, 'Law and Accounting: Transition and Transformation' (1991) 54 *MLR* 769, at p. 780.

accounting records which should be sufficient to show and explain the company's transactions, should enable the directors to ensure that the profit and loss and balance sheets they prepare will comply with the statutory requirements, and should disclose with reasonable accuracy at any time the financial position of the company. Such accounting records should consist of entries from day to day of all sums of moneys received and spent by the company and the matters in respect of which the receipt and expenditure takes place, a record of the company's assets and liabilities and statements relating to the holding of stock, records of stock-takings and statements of all goods sold and purchased (except by ordinary retail trade) in sufficient detail to enable the identification of the goods and the buyers and sellers. An officer of a company who knowingly and wilfully authorises or permits it to keep accounting records that do not conform with section 221 is guilty of an offence punishable by a fine or imprisonment for up to two years or both, unless it can be shown that the officer acted honestly and that such inadequacies were excusable in the circumstances. Such records must be kept for a minimum of three years by a private company and a minimum of six years by a public company.[2] Failure to keep such accounting records will result in a criminal offence, unless the company officers can show that they acted honestly, and that the default was excusable in the circumstances.

The accounting records must be open to inspection by the company's officers at all times. In this context the term officers includes the directors, secretary and managers.[3] An auditor might also be included since under a separate provision he is also given a right of access.[4] Members of the company do not have a right to inspect the accounting records[5] but, under article 109 of Table A, they may gain such right by ordinary resolution or through authorisation by a director.

---

[2] Section 222(5) Companies Act 1985. VAT records must be kept for six years and records relating to the manufacture of consumer goods must be kept for twenty years.

[3] See D. Prentice, 'A Director's Right of Access to Corporate Books of Account' (1978) 94 LQR 184. Noting the case of Conway v. Petronius Clothing Co Ltd [1978] 1 WLR 72 in which Slade J held that the section (then similar to s. 221, though not exactly the same) did not entitle directors to a right of access but was aimed at grounding criminal penalties for failure to keep the records. Yet, as Prentice notes, it is difficult to see how without such a right directors could ensure that any accounts prepared by them comply with the statutory and other requirements.

[4] Section 398A(1), Companies Act 1985.

[5] See Lonrho Ltd v. Shell Petroleum Co Ltd [1980] 1 WLR 627, per Lord Diplock noting that the board has control of the documents on behalf of the company and that if the shareholders request inspection the directors have a duty to consider whether to grant such access to the documents would be in the best interests of the company, which, Lord Diplock points out, are not exclusively those of the company's shareholders but may include those of its creditors: at p. 634; see also Murray's Judicial Factor v. Thomas Murray and Sons (Ice Merchants) Ltd [1993] BCLC 1437.

Accounting reference period and accounting reference date

Accounting requirements focus upon certainty and comparability from one year to the next. This is achieved partly by a requirement that the company has an accounting reference period and an accounting reference date established with the Registrar of Companies. The accounting reference date is the end date of the accounting reference period and the date to which the accounts must be prepared. If a company which was incorporated before 1 April 1996 did not within nine months from the date of its incorporation notify the registrar of its reference date then a date is applied automatically. For companies incorporated before 1 April 1990, the date is 31 March and for companies incorporated after 1 April 1990 the date is the last day of the month in which the anniversary of the company's incorporation falls.[6] The accounting reference date of a company incorporated on or after 1 April 1996 is the last day of the month in which the anniversary of its incorporation falls.[7] The directors of a parent company also have a duty to ensure that the financial years of their company and its subsidiaries coincide, unless they consider that there are good reasons to have different dates.[8] Any change of accounting reference period must be notified to the Registrar of Companies.[9]

Duty to prepare accounts

Under section 226 of the Companies Act 1985, the directors of a company are required to prepare the individual accounts for each financial year for presentation to the shareholders. The individual accounts consist of a balance sheet as at the last day of the year and a profit and loss account.[10] If the company is a parent company the directors, under section 227, must also prepare group accounts unless they are exempt under section 228 because they are included in the accounts of a larger group.[11] Group accounts comprise a consolidated balance sheet dealing with the state of affairs of the parent company and its subsidiary

---

[6] Section 224(3)(a)(b), Companies Act 1985. For example, if the company is incorporated on 8 May the correct accounting reference date will be 31 May from the following year.

[7] Section 224(3A), Companies Act 1985, inserted by the Companies Act 1985 (Miscellaneous Accounting Amendments) Regulations 1996, SI 1996/189.

[8] Section 223(5), Companies Act 1985.

[9] Section 225, Companies Act 1985.

[10] Section 226(1), Companies Act 1985.

[11] See also s. 229 which deals with exclusions for subsidiary undertakings. Sections 228 and 229 were inserted by the Companies Act 1989, s. 5(3).

undertakings, and a consolidated profit and loss account dealing with the profit or loss of the parent company and its subsidiary undertakings.[12] Where accounts are prepared they must show a true and fair view of the company's or the group's state of affairs as at the end of the financial year and the profit and loss for the financial year and they must each comply with the relevant Schedules.[13]

The directors of a company are also required to prepare a directors' report[14] containing a fair review of the development of the business of the company and its subsidiary undertakings during the financial year and of their position at the end of it.[15] In addition to the accounts and the directors' report there must generally also be prepared an auditors' report.[16] All except small companies must also provide cash flow statements.

Laying and delivering of accounts and reports

Every company must send a copy of its accounts and directors' and auditors' reports to its members and debenture holders and to anyone else entitled to receive notices of general meetings such as the company's auditors.[17] These shall be sent to such persons not less than twenty-one days before the date of the meeting at which copies of the documents must also be laid. If such copies are sent less than twenty-one days before the date of the meeting they shall, notwithstanding that fact, be deemed to have been duly sent if it is so agreed by all the members entitled to attend and vote at the meeting.[18] Companies are not bound to send copies of the accounts and reports to those who are not entitled to receive notices of general meetings and of whose address the company is unaware.[19]

Additionally, members and debenture holders are entitled to demand, at any time and without any charge, a copy of the company's last annual accounts and directors' report and a copy of the auditors' report on those accounts.[20] If such a demand is not complied with within seven days, then

---

[12] Section 227(2), Companies Act 1985.

[13] Schedule 4 for individual accounts and Sch. 4A for consolidated accounts. See respectively s. 226 and s. 227, Companies Act 1985.

[14] Section 234, inserted by the Companies Act 1989, s. 8(1).

[15] Details are provided below.

[16] Section 235, inserted by the Companies Act 1989, s. 9. See below for further details.

[17] Section 238(1), Companies Act 1985.

[18] Section 238(4), Companies Act 1985.

[19] Section 238(2)(3), Companies Act 1985.

[20] Section 239, Companies Act 1985.

that default renders the company and its officers guilty of an offence and liable to a fine and, for continued contravention, a daily default fine.[21]

Listed companies, if they comply with conditions laid down by the Secretary of State, may send to their shareholders a summary financial statement instead of the full accounts and reports.[22] Every such summary financial statement shall state that it is only a summary of information in the company's annual accounts and the directors' report, contain a statement by the company's auditors of their opinion as to whether the summary financial statement is consistent with those accounts and report and complies with the Act's and relevant Regulations' requirements, state whether the auditors' report on the annual accounts was qualified or unqualified and, if it was qualified, set out the report in full together with any further material needed to understand the qualification, state whether the auditors' report on the annual accounts contained a statement under section 237(2)[23] or 237(3)[24] and, if so, set out the statement in full. The summary financial statement should include a statement that members and debenture holders have the right to demand free of charge a copy of the company's last full accounts and reports. The Companies Act 1985 (Summary Financial Statements) Regulations 1995[25] also require the summary statement to disclose the name of the person who signed the statement on behalf of the board of directors and, if the company does not have to prepare groups accounts, a statement that the summary financial statement does not provide sufficient information to allow for a full understanding of the results and state of affairs of the company, and that for further information the full annual accounts, the auditors' report and the directors' report should be consulted.[26] The summary statement should comprise the directors' report or a summary with details of matters relating to the review of the business, matters relating to important post balance sheet events, matters relating to likely future developments in the business, and a whole list of directors.[27] The summary statement should provide a summary profit and loss account, and a summary balance sheet.[28]

As well as sending copies to members and debenture holders and to those entitled to notices of general meetings, directors of a company are

---

[21] Section 239(3), Companies Act 1985.
[22] Section 251, Companies Act 1985.
[23] Accounting records or returns inadequate or accounts not agreeing with records and returns.
[24] Failure to obtain necessary information and explanations.
[25] SI 1995/2092.
[26] *Ibid.*, para. 7.
[27] *Ibid.*, Sch. I.   [28] *Ibid.*, Sch. I.

also required, generally, to lay before the company in general meeting copies of the accounts and the directors' and auditors' reports.[29] Usually directors of public companies are allowed a period of seven months after the end of the accounting reference period and directors of private companies are allowed ten months in order to lay the accounts before the company in general meeting. If notice is given to the Registrar stating that the company is carrying on business or has interests abroad and claims a three-month extension of the period for laying and delivering the accounts and reports, then such a time extension may be granted. The Secretary of State may also extend the time allowed for laying and delivering the accounts and this requires written notice.[30] A private company may also dispense with the requirement to lay the accounts before the general meeting by elective resolution and, instead, the written resolution procedures may be applied.[31]

Company directors are also required to deliver a copy of the company's annual accounts and directors' and auditors' reports to the Registrar of Companies.[32] Delivery of the accounts to the registrar must take place within the period for laying the accounts before the general meeting. Failure to deliver within this period will render the company and the directors guilty of an offence and liable to a fine and a daily default fine for continued contravention unless they can prove that they took all reasonable steps for securing compliance. Civil penalties may also be recovered by the registrar from the company for failure to deliver within the required time period. Certain unlimited companies are not required to deliver accounts to the registrar if they comply with the relevant requirements laid down in section 254 of the Companies Act 1985 and small and medium sized companies may deliver abbreviated accounts.[33]

A small company is defined as having at least two of the following characteristics: a turnover of not more than £2.8 million, a balance sheet total of not more than £1.4 million and an average number of employees of not more than 50. A medium-sized company is defined as having at least two of the following characteristics: a turnover not more than £11.2 million, a balance sheet total not more than £5.6 million and an average number of employees not more than 250.[34] In these cases the companies

[29] Companies Act 1985, s. 241(1).
[30] Companies Act 1985, s. 244.
[31] Companies Act 1985, s. 252.
[32] Section 242(1).
[33] Section 246(1). The Government plans to retain this option but that small and medium-sized companies should be required to disclose the amount of turnover for the relevant financial year: see White Paper, *Company Law Reform* (March 2005), para. 4.10.
[34] Section 247(3)–(6), Companies Act 1985.

do not have to disclose in their financial statements whether the accounts have been prepared in accordance with applicable accounting standards, particulars of any material departure from those standards and the reason for it, and the amount of remuneration payable to the auditors for non-audit work. Small companies do not have to publish a cash flow statement or accompanying information in the notes.

A small company must, however, disclose the following information: an abbreviated balance sheet; a special auditors' report; notes covering: accounting policies; share capital and details of allotments; fixed asset movements; debtors due after more than one year; secured creditors; creditors due after more than one year; aggregate creditors due after five years; loans to directors and officers; corresponding amounts for the previous year; name of ultimate parent company; transactions concerning directors.[35]

Form and content of the accounts

The individual accounts (the profit and loss statement and the balance sheet) must generally comply with Schedule 4 of the Companies Act 1985.[36] Consolidated or group accounts must comply with Schedule 4A of the Companies Act 1985.[37]

As well as specifying the required details, Schedule 4 lays down the requirement that accounts must be drawn up in accordance with five principles unless the directors consider that there are special reasons for departing from those principles. The five principles are that the company shall be presumed to be carrying on business as a going concern; that accounting policies shall be applied consistently within the same accounts and from one financial year to the next; the amount of any item shall be determined on a prudent basis; all income and charges relating to the relevant financial year shall be taken into account, without regard to the date of receipt or payment; and in determining the aggregate amount of any item, the amount of each individual asset or liability that falls to be taken into account shall be determined separately.[38]

The balance sheet must give a true and fair view of the company's state of affairs at the end of its financial year and the profit and loss account must give a true and fair view of its profits or loss for the financial year.[39]

---

[35] See Companies Act 1985, s. 246 and Sch. 8.
[36] As amended by the Companies Act 1989.
[37] Introduced by Sch. 2 of the Companies Act 1989.
[38] Schedule 4, paras. 10–14. See also FRS 18 'Accounting Policies', effective since 22 June 2001.
[39] Section 226(2).

These accounts must contain sufficient information to provide a true and fair view and particulars of any departure from the Act's requirements must be given with the reasons for such departure and its effect in the notes to the accounts.

There are four possible formats for the profit and loss account.[40] Their differences relate to the classification of expenditure, formats 1 and 3 requiring a functional analysis of expenditure and formats 2 and 4 requiring a subjective analysis of the type of expenditure. Directors may choose which format to apply in the company's first financial year but must use the same format in the following years unless they consider there to exist special reasons for a change in format.[41] If such a change is made they must state the reasons for the change in the notes to the accounts in which the format is first adopted. Factors that might be relevant in choosing the format include the type of business and the commercial significance of the format. The corresponding amount for each item for the previous year must also be shown with reasons given for any adjustment.

Details of disclosure requirements include[42] turnover: the amount of turnover attributable to each described class of business, the amount of profit or loss before taxation attributable to each class of business, the amount of turnover attributable to each geographical market, where the markets differ substantially from each other. Expenditure relating to the remuneration of auditors must be disclosed in the notes as well as fees for non-audit work.[43] The profit and loss account should also disclose details of the average number of persons employed in the year, the average number of persons employed in the year within each category; the aggregate wages and salaries paid and payable; social security costs; other pension costs; hire of plant and machinery; directors' emoluments; pensions of directors and past directors; and compensation for loss of office of directors and past directors. Profit and loss accounts require details of research and development costs, and extraordinary and exceptional items such as profits or losses on the sale or termination of an operation; costs of a fundamental reorganisation or restructuring having a material effect on the nature and focus of the reporting entities operations and amounts which are no more than marginal adjustments to depreciation previously charged. Earnings per share should also be shown, which is defined as the profit in pence attributable to each equity share, based on the profit of the period after tax, minority interests and extraordinary items and after deducting

[40] Provided in Sch. 4.   [41] Schedule 4, para. 2.   [42] See generally, Sch. 4.
[43] This requirement is made of all companies except small and medium-sized companies: see s. 390A, Companies Act 1985.

preference dividends and other appropriations in respect of preference shares, divided by the number of equity shares at issue and ranking for dividend in respect of the period.[44] A primary statement showing the total of recognised gains and losses and its components should also be shown. Companies are required to prepare their accounts in accordance with the order prescribed in the format chosen. This requirement presumably aims to ease comparability.

There are two formats to choose from regarding the balance sheet.[45] Again consistency of choice is required unless the directors see special reasons for choosing the other format later. The balance sheet contains details about the assets and liabilities of the company. Assets may be tangible or intangible, the latter including goodwill. Tangible fixed assets include investment properties, land and buildings. Investments must be shown with the distinction between fixed and current assets. Fixed assets are those intended for use on a continuing basis in the company's activities. The balance sheet also contains details of stocks and long-term contracts. Current assets include debtors with debts due within one year or more the two categories being distinguished, cash in hand or at bank. Creditors should also be shown, again distinguishing those with credits due within one year and those due after one year. Dividends are to be shown as liabilities.

Companies, with certain exceptions, are required to show cash flow statements that reveal their cash generation and their cash absorption for the relevant period. This disclosure is broken down into the following headings: operating activities; returns on investments and servicing of finance; taxation; investing activities; financing. Comparative figures for the previous year are also required.

The notes to the accounts must contain details of accounting policies, staff details and where relevant the amount charged to revenue for the hire of plant and machinery.[46] Other disclosure requirements relate to the corporate governance developments during the 1990s and companies must state whether or not they comply with the Combined Code of Corporate Governance.

The directors' report

The directors' report is required annually[47] and contains a business review and, if relevant, a statement as to disclosure of information

---

[44] FRS 3.   [45] Schedule 4.   [46] Schedule 4.
[47] Section 234. See also Companies Act 1985 (Operating and Financial Review and Directors' Report etc.) Regulations 2005, SI 2005/1011, especially Part 2 now repealed.

to auditors required by section 234ZA, Companies Act 1985. If the company is a parent company and the directors of the company prepare group accounts the directors' report must be a consolidated report. Sections 234ZZA and 234ZZB set out the required contents of the directors' report. Under the general requirements the directors' report must state the names of the persons who, at any time during the financial year, were directors of the company, the principal activities of the company in the course of the year, and the amount (if any) that the directors recommend should be paid by way of dividend. The Schedule 7 requirements include information on changes in asset values, directors' shareholdings and other interests and contributions for political and charitable purposes; information relating to the acquisition by a company of its own shares or charges on them; information relating to the employment, training and advancement of disabled persons; information relating to the involvement of employees in the affairs, policy and performance of the company; and information relating to the policy and practice on the payment of creditors. Section 234ZZB requires that the business review must contain a fair review of the business of the company; and a description of the principal risks and uncertainties facing the company. The review must be a balanced and comprehensive analysis of the development and performance of the business of the company during the financial year and the position of the company at the end of that year, consistent with the size and complexity of the business. The analysis must use key financial performance indicators and where appropriate other key performance indicators such as information relating to environmental and employment matters, if such indicators are necessary for an understanding of the development, performance or position of the business of the company. Most small companies do not need to provide a business review or information relating to the amount to be paid as dividend and most medium-sized companies do not need to use the non-financial key performance indicators for their business review.[48] The report must be approved by the board of directors and signed by a director or the secretary on behalf of the board and the copy delivered to the registrar must contain an original signature.

---

[48] Such exceptions do not apply to public companies, companies carrying out regulated financial services market activities, or companies carrying out insurance market activities: see s. 247A (1B) inserted by reg. 6.

The directors' remuneration report

Quoted companies must provide a directors' remuneration report that explains in detail the company's policy on directors' service contracts, including their notice periods, termination arrangements and remuneration of each individual director.[49] The report must also contain details of the membership and role of the remuneration committee. The company is also required to provide details of the performance conditions relating to each director's entitlement to share options or long-term incentive plan details, and the report must show a performance graph for the last five financial years. The information required by Part 3 of Schedule 7A is subject to audit and this information covers remuneration details and compensation for loss of office for individual directors.

The auditors' report

Audit reports should contain a clear statement of opinion on whether the annual accounts have been prepared properly in accordance with the Companies Act 1985. The report must state whether the accounts give a true and fair view of the company's state of affairs and of its profit or loss. The auditors' report must also state whether the directors' report or operating and financial review is consistent with the accounts and, where relevant, whether a directors' remuneration report has been properly prepared.[50] The auditors' opinion is based on review and assessment of the conclusions drawn from evidence obtained in the course of the audit. The report must contain a title identifying those to whom the report is addressed; an introductory paragraph identifying the financial statements audited; respective responsibilities of the directors and auditors; the basis of the auditor's opinion; the opinion itself; the manuscript or printed signature of the auditor; the date of the report. The auditor should provide an explanation of the basis of opinion including a statement of compliance with auditing standards (or otherwise, with reason), a statement that the auditing process includes the examination of relevant evidence on a test basis, an assessment of significant estimates and judgements made by the directors and consideration of whether the accounting policies are appropriate, consistent and adequately disclosed, a statement that the audit was planned and performed so as to obtain reasonable assurance that the financial statements are free from material

---

[49] Section 234B, Companies Act 1985 and Sch. 7A. See also Directors' Remuneration Report Regulations 2002, SI 2002/1986.
[50] Section 235.

misstatements. The auditors' report shall be made to the company's members on all annual accounts of the company.[51] Certain small companies may be exempt from the audit requirements.[52]

Recognition of the needs of small companies

The Government clearly recognises that the needs and characteristics of small companies are different from those of large companies. The separation of ownership and control concept has little relevance in the small company in which usually the shareholders and the directors are the same individuals thereby eradicating the need for disclosure for accountability purposes. However, those dealing with the company from the outside still require information and so disclosure is still necessary but the subjects emphasised and the amount of disclosure necessary are quite different. Throughout the 1990s successive governments sought to address more closely the needs of small companies.

As part of the Conservative Governments' Deregulation Initiative consultations were published with the purpose of seeking to relax the disclosure and accounting and auditing requirements for small companies. For example, there was a review of the audit and accounting requirements for very small companies. It was considered that the smaller the company the higher the proportionate cost of audit and the greater the level of dissatisfaction with the cost of and need for audit.[53] The DTI Consultative Document, *Accounting Simplifications*, set out clearly the balances that need to be made with respect to disclosure requirements relating to small companies. For example, a small company is not defined

---

[51] Section 235(1), Companies Act 1985.

[52] See s. 249A, inserted by the Companies Act 1985 (Audit Exemption) Regulations 1994, SI 1994/1935, reg. 2. See also s. 247B which provides for a special auditors' report to be prepared for certain companies that have delivered abbreviated accounts but which are not exempt from the obligation to appoint auditors, inserted by the Companies Act 1985 (Accounts of Small and Medium-sized Companies and Minor Accounting Amendments) Regulations 1997, SI 1997/220, regs. 1(3) and 5. See also Companies Act 1985 (Audit Exemption) Regulations 1997, SI 1997/936; Companies Act 1985 (Audit Exemption) Regulations 2000, SI 2000/1403; and Companies Act 1985 (Accounts of Small and Medium Sized Enterprises and the Audit Exemptions) (Amendment) Regulations 2004, SI 2004/16.

[53] See DTI, *Audit and Accounting Requirements for Very Small Companies: A Consultative Document* (DTI, London, April 1993). See also: DTI, *Accounting Simplifications: A Consultative Document* (DTI, London, May 1995); DTI, *Accounting Simplifications: Re-arrangements to Companies Act Schedule on Small Company Accounts: A Consultative Document* (DTI, London, July 1996); DTI, *Small Company Accounts: A Possible Standard Format: A Consultative Document* (DTI, London, September 1996); DTI, *Small Companies Audit Exemption: Consultation on Proposed Amendments: A Consultative Document* (DTI, London, January 1997).

by the number of shareholders so that even if the company is small it may have a large number of shareholders and the costs of distributing accounts to all such shareholders may be expensive. On the other hand those shareholders ought to be entitled to receive accounts of a company in which they have made an investment. A balance might be struck by giving the shareholders an opportunity to opt out of receiving the accounts.[54] Filing accounts for the public record may also continue to be necessary since statistics from Companies House, according to the DTI, show that the records of companies of all sizes are used by enquirers.[55]

Small and medium-sized companies are relieved of many of the reporting requirements imposed on larger companies and are permitted to publish or deliver to the registrar abbreviated accounts under section 246(1) of the Companies Act 1985. The requirements for the contents of small company accounts are set out in Schedule 8, and accounts delivered to the registrar are not required compulsorily to provide the profit and loss account or the directors' report. Nor are small private companies obliged to have their accounts audited unless requested by a member or members holding at least 10 per cent in the aggregate in nominal value of the company's issued share capital or any class thereof.[56]

These statutory requirements cover the broad aspects of financial reporting. However, as was stated above, the legislative provisions are supplemented in detail by standards issued by the Accounting Standards Board.[57] Accounting Standards are not legally binding but a court is likely to infer that accounts that provide a true and fair view of the company's position and profit and loss comply with the accounting standards. Thus they gain indirect legal authority.[58]

Professional standards

Accounting Standards developed by the ASB are contained in 'Financial Reporting Standards' (FRSs). The ASB also adopted the standards issued by the ASC, so that they too fall within the legal definition of Accounting Standards under Part VII of the Companies Act 1985. These are designated 'Statements of Standard Accounting Practice' (SSAPs).

---

[54] DTI, 1995 *Accounting Simplifications*, at p. 11.

[55] DTI, 1995 *Accounting Simplifications*, at p. 12.

[56] Companies Act 1985 (Audit Exemption) Regulations 1994, SI 1994/1935, inserting new ss. 249A to 249E into the Companies Act 1985. See also SI 1997/936; SI 2000/1403 and SI 2004/16 amending ss. 249A and 249B.

[57] References to accounting standards in the Act are contained in para. 36A of Sch. 4, para. 49 of Part 1 of Sch. 9 and para. 18B of Part 1 of Sch. 9A.

[58] See ch. 2 above.

Some of the SSAPs have been superseded by FRSs. Others remain in force and continue to be known as SSAPs. FRSs are based on the *Statement of Principles for Financial Reporting*,[59] which seeks to provide a framework for the consistent and logical formulation of individual accounting standards and addresses the concepts underlying the information presented in financial statements.

The ASB's Statement of Principles for Financial Reporting

The ASB published its *Statement of Principles for Financial Reporting* in December 1999. This Statement was a response to the report entitled *The Making of Accounting Standards* which was published in September 1988 under the Chairmanship of Sir Ron Dearing CB. The report observed:

a lack of a conceptual framework is a handicap to those involved in setting standards as well as to those applying them. . . . We believe that work in this area will assist standard-setters in formulating their thinking on particular accounting issues, facilitate judgements on the sufficiency of the disclosures required to give a true and fair view, and assist preparers and auditors in interpreting accounting standards and in resolving accounting issues not dealt with by specific standards.

What is a conceptual framework? The US Financial Accounting Standards Board stated in its Scope and Implications of the Conceptual Framework Project 1967 that:

a conceptual framework is a constitution, a coherent system of interrelated objectives and fundamentals that can lead to consistent standards and that prescribes the nature, function and limits of financial accounting and financial statements.

Elliott and Elliott describe a conceptual framework as a basic structure for organising one's thinking about what one is trying to do and how to go about it. It can answer questions such as: for whom and by whom are the accounts to be prepared? For what purposes are they wanted? What kind of accounting reports are suitable for these purposes? How do present accounts fit the bill? How could accounting practices be improved to make them more suitable?[60] They refer to MacVe whose view is that a conceptual framework 'would provide a consistent approach for making decisions about choices of accounting practice and for setting

---

[59] The current statement, December 1999.
[60] Barry Elliott and Jamie Elliott, *Financial Accounting and Reporting* (8th edn, FT, Prentice Hall, London, 2004), at p. 139.

standards'.[61] Stamp highlights the following elements: general agreement on the overall objectives of financial reporting and general agreement on the nature and needs of the various users of financial reports and identification of a set of criteria to be used in choosing between alternative solutions to standard setting problems and in assessing the quality and utility of financial reports.[62]

The *Statement of Principles for Financial Reporting* is a framework document intended to provide conceptual input into the ASB's work on the development and review of accounting standards. The *Statement* is not, therefore, an accounting standard nor does it contain any requirements on how financial statements are to be prepared. However, a number of the principles in the *Statement* are of fundamental importance to existing accounting standards. For example, several standards are developed in accordance with definitions contained in the *Statement* such as its definitions of assets and liabilities. FRS 3 'Reporting Financial Performance' gives effect to the *Statement's* details on the presentation of information about financial performance.

The *Statement of Principles* covers objectives, qualitative characteristics of financial information, the elements of financial statements, recognition principles, measurement principles and presentation guidance. The aim is for the statement to provide clarification of the conceptual underpinnings of proposed accounting standards and to enable standards to be developed in a consistent manner as well as to assist preparers and users of financial statements. The *Statement of Principles* therefore plays a very important role in the standard-setting process, although it is only one of the factors that the ASB takes into account when setting standards. Other factors include legal requirements, cost-benefit considerations, industry-specific issues, the desirability of evolutionary change and implementation issues.

Arguably, the *Statement* is not sufficient to act as a conceptual framework. This is likely to cause problems for the quality of the regulation and the reports produced by companies. Indeed, as Elliott and Elliott suggest: 'standard setters in the UK have been operating in a professional environment where there has been no unique, agreed conceptual framework upon which to base new standards'.[63] Although there are no

---

[61] Barry Elliott and Jamie Elliott, *Financial Accounting and Reporting* (8th edn, FT Prentice Hall, London, 2004), at p. 139, citing R. MacVe, *A Conceptual Framework for Financial Accounting and Reporting* (ICAEW, London, 1981).

[62] Edward Stamp, 'First steps towards a British conceptual framework' (1982) *Accountancy* (March 1982) 123, at p. 124.

[63] Barry Elliott and Jamie Elliott, *Financial Accounting and Reporting* (8th edn, FT Prentice Hall, London, 2004), at p. 138.

fixed plans for a future review, the ASB expects the *Statement* to be revised periodically to reflect evolving accounting objectives.

Creating accounting standards[64]

The ASB identifies topics in need of FRSs either from its own research or from external sources, including submissions from interested parties. The ASB then gives instructions to its staff to undertake a programme of research and consultation. This programme involves 'consideration of and consultation on the relevant conceptual issues, existing pronouncements and practice in the UK, the Republic of Ireland and overseas and the economic, legal and practical implications of the introduction of particular accounting requirements'. After the ASB has discussed the issues it produces a discussion draft which it then circulates to parties who have registered their interest with the ASB. Alternatively, the ASB will publish a discussion paper. The purpose of either of the draft or discussion paper is to form a basis for discussion with those parties who will be affected by, or who have knowledge of, the issues raised in the proposals. After such discussions the ASB publishes a Financial Reporting Exposure Draft. The aim of this draft is to allow all interested parties to comment on the proposals and to enable the ASB to assess if the proposal is appropriate and the likelihood of its being accepted. Following feedback, the exposure draft is refined and may be followed by another period of public or selective exposure prior to the issue of an FRS. Although the ASB takes into account the views of interested parties, the ASB determines the content of an FRS based on the results of its research, public consultation and weighing up of the benefits and costs of providing the resulting information. FRSs are also drafted in the context of current UK and Republic of Ireland legislation and European Community directives. The ASB aims to ensure consistency between accounting standards and the legislative requirements. Similarly, FRSs are normally designed to comply with international accounting standards.

Accounting standards apply to financial statements that are intended to give a true and fair view of a company's state of affairs at the balance sheet date and of its profit or loss (or income and expenditure) for the financial period ending on that date. According to the ASB's *Foreword to Accounting Standards*: '[A]ccounting standards are authoritative statements of how particular types of transaction and other events should

---

[64] The information in this following paragraph is taken from the ASB's *Foreword to Accounting Standards*, available at www.frc.org.uk/asb.

be reflected in financial statements and accordingly compliance with accounting standards will normally be necessary for financial statements to give a true and fair view.'[65] Additionally, in applying accounting standards it is important to be guided by the spirit and reasoning behind them.[66] Individual FRSs set out the spirit and reasoning and these are based on the ASB's *Statement of Principles for Financial Reporting*. The ASB's Foreword adds that it may, in special circumstances, be necessary to depart from accounting standards in order to give a true and fair view. However, because accounting standards are 'formulated with the objective of ensuring that the information resulting from their application faithfully represents the underlying commercial activity', the ASB envisages that any such departure will be rare.[67] In such cases, it will be necessary to disclose, in the financial statements, 'particulars of any material departure from an accounting standard, the reasons for it and its financial effects'.[68]

Legal status of accounting standards

Statements of Standard Accounting Practice and Financial Reporting Standards define how particular types of transactions and other events are to be reflected in the financial statements.[69] The Companies Act

---

[65] ASB, *Foreword to Accounting Standards*, para 16. available at www.frc.org.uk.

[66] *Ibid.*, para. 17.

[67] *Ibid.*, para. 18.

[68] *Ibid.*, para. 19.

[69] Current applicable standards include: FRS 1 (Revised 1996) – Cash Flow Statements; FRS 2 – Accounting for Subsidiary Undertakings; FRS 3 – Reporting Financial Performance; FRS 4 – Capital Instruments; FRS 5 – Reporting the Substance of Transactions; FRS 6 – Acquisitions and Mergers; FRS 7 – Fair Values in Acquisition Accounting; FRS 8 – Related Party Disclosures; FRS 9 – Associates and Joint Ventures; FRS 10 – Goodwill and Intangible Assets; FRS 11 – Impairment of Fixed Assets and Goodwill; FRS 12 – Provisions, Contingent Liabilities and Contingent Assets; FRS 13 – Derivatives and other Financial Instruments: Disclosures; FRS 14 – Earnings per Share; FRS 15 - Tangible Fixed Assets; FRS 16 – Current Tax; FRS 17 – Retirement Benefits; FRS 18 – Accounting Policies; FRS 19 – Deferred Tax; FRS 20 (IFRS2) – Share-based Payment; FRS 21 (IAS 10) – Events after the Balance Sheet Date; FRS 22 (IAS 33) – Earnings per Share; FRS 23 (IAS 21) – The Effects of Changes in Foreign Exchange Rates; FRS 24 (IAS 29) – Financial Reporting in Hyperinflationary Economies; FRS 25 (IAS 32) – Financial Instruments: Disclosure and Presentation; FRS 26 (IAS 39) – Financial Instruments: Measurement; FRS 27 – Life Assurance. SSAP 4 – Accounting for government grants; SSAP 5 – Accounting for value added tax; SSAP 9 – Stocks and long-term contracts; SSAP 13 – Accounting for research and development; SSAP 15 – Status of SSAP 15; SSAP 17 – Accounting for post balance sheet events; SSAP 19 – Accounting for investment properties; SSAP 20 – Foreign currency translation; SSAP 21 – Accounting for leases and hire purchase contracts; SSAP 24 – Accounting for pension costs; SSAP 25 – Segmental reporting. FRSSE (Effective June 2002) – Financial Reporting Standard for Smaller Entities. For further details see ASB's website at www.frc.org.uk.

1985 gives statutory recognition to the existence of accounting standards and by implication to their beneficial role in financial reporting.[70]

The FRSs are particularly relevant to the legal requirement that accounts provide a true and fair view of the company's financial position. Thus according to an opinion written by Mary Arden, and appended to the ASB's Foreword,[71] 'while the true and fair view which the law requires to be given is not qualified in any way, the task of interpreting the true and fair requirement cannot be performed by the Court without evidence as to the practices and views of accountants'. In Mary Arden's view, the court will infer from section 256 that statutory policy favours both the issue of accounting standards (by a body prescribed by regulation) and compliance with them: indeed section 256(3)(c) additionally contemplates the investigation of departures from them and confers power to provide public funding for such purpose. The court will also, according to Arden, infer from paragraph 36A of Schedule 4 that accounts meeting the true and fair requirement will, in general, follow, rather than depart from, standards and that departure is sufficiently abnormal to require to be justified. Additionally, if a particular standard is generally followed, the court is likely to find that accounts must comply with it in order to show a true and fair view. In support of her opinion, Mary Arden refers to the case of *Lloyd Cheyham* v. *Littlejohn*[72] in which Woolf J held that standards of the then ASC were 'very strong evidence as to what is the proper standard which should be adopted'.[73]

The relevance of the true and fair view override

As is clearly expressed in the ASB's *Statement of Principles* the requirement that accounts provide a true and fair view of the company's financial position is a fundamental aspect of the regulation of company reporting. The basic statutory requirement of the profit and loss account and the balance sheet is to provide a true and fair view of the company's financial position during the financial year and at the time the accounts are presented.[74] As has been noted above, the true and fair view concept also lends weight to the accounting standards published by the ASB.

The expression is not defined in the Companies Act. Nor is it defined in the ASB's *Statement of Principles for Financial Reporting* even though it

---

[70] Section 256, Companies Act 1985; see also Sch. 4, para. 36A.
[71] Opinion written 21 April 1993, and appended to ASB's Foreword to FRS.
[72] [1987] BCLC 303.
[73] *Ibid.*, at p. 313.
[74] Section 226(2), Companies Act 1985.

is at the foundation of the statement. One possible result of this lack of a definition is that 'it is commonly agreed that there can be more than one true and fair view of a given situation'.[75] McGee notes three different views: one, that it simply requires compliance with all the prescribed rules; two, that there must be adherence to generally accepted accounting principles; and three, that the requirement is superimposed on the basic procedures and formats laid down in the Act.[76] The consensus appears at least to be that 'compliance with all the specific requirements of the Companies Acts does not guarantee that a true and fair view will be given, nor does compliance with all the relevant SSAPs'.[77] In this respect McGee argues that if all that was necessary were to comply with the detailed rules of the Act then there would be no need to make the true and fair view requirement a separate provision in the Act.[78] The true and fair view concept is partly designed to eradicate the creative accounting that can arise from the existence of rigid rules. Indeed, the term 'true and fair view' replaced 'true and correct' in order to encourage observance of the spirit as well as the letter of the law.

An opinion of counsel, published in 1983, came only to offer a negative statement: 'accounts will not be true and fair unless the information they contain is sufficient in quantity and quality to satisfy the reasonable expectations of the readers to whom they are addressed.'[79] Bird suggests that 'the effect of this meaning will change as readers' reasonable expectations change'.[80] From this perspective, a true and fair view override arguably responds to the evolutionary nature of accounting and reporting objectives by allowing for greater adaptability to changed circumstances than would more rigid legislative provisions or standards. Furthermore, the content of an internationally agreed meaning could vary among countries as well as among times. Indeed, the legislative provisions in many other countries refer to '*a* faithful picture' indicating that there may be more than one view of what is true and fair.[81] In the Companies Act 1985 reference is also to *a* rather than to *the* true and fair view, thus reinforcing the possibility that there may be more than one true and fair view. Moreover, the increasing moves towards

---

[75] Peter Bird, 'Group Accounts and the True and Fair View' (1982) *JBL* 364, at p. 365.
[76] Andrew McGee, 'The "True and Fair View" Debate: A Study in the Legal Regulation of Accounting' (1991) 54 *MLR* 874, at pp. 877–8.
[77] Bird, 'Group Accounts. . .', at p. 367.
[78] McGee, at p. 878.
[79] Leonard Hoffman QC and Mary H. Arden, 'The Accounting Standards Committee Joint Opinion', *Accountancy*, November 1983, 154, para. 8.
[80] Peter Bird, 'What is a "True and Fair View"?' (1984) *JBL* 480, at p. 483.
[81] Bird (1984), at p. 484.

European level harmonisation and further, globalisation and the adoption of international accounting standards, present a further challenge to the objective of achieving comparability and equivalence of information required of annual accounts.[82]

Whilst the true and fair view concept may have the ability to accommodate different or changing needs, its downside is that such a vague standard might conflict with the policy goal of producing comparable accounts. The concept could also encourage disclosure *short* of creative accounting. This can potentially result in uncertainty and rather opaque disclosure presentation.

Characteristics of annual financial reports

The Company Law Review identified some of the key problems and limitations of the annual accounts and reports of many listed companies. For example, reports have become more complex and technical.[83] One consequence is that reports have grown in size leading to an 'overload of information' that 'obscures the clear presentation of performance.'[84] Additionally, the current annual statutory reporting cycle, which allows listed companies seven months from the financial year end to delivery of the accounts to the registrar, does not provide timely information.[85] Another common criticism is directed at the fact that accounting and reporting remains essentially backward looking and concentrates on financial indicators.[86] Indeed, Charkham and Simpson, observing that numbers have prevailed over words in information published to shareholders, suggest that numbers tend to look backwards whilst investors are looking instead for information about the present state of the company and its future.[87] Other problems also result from an emphasis on

---

[82] See K. P. E. Lasok and Edmond Grace, 'Fair Accounting' (1988) *JBL* 235. It is notable that in the case of *Tomberger* v. *Gebrüder von der Wettern GmbH* Case C – 234/94) [1996] All ER (EC) 805, the European Court of Justice made no attempt to define the term 'true and fair' view even though this is the primary objective of the Fourth Directive and the case turned upon the question of its meaning. The Court held that guidance upon the principle was to be found in Arts. 31 and 59 of the Directive and that a true and fair view would be ensured by taking account of all elements (i.e., profits made, liabilities and losses, charges, income) which actually related to the financial year in question: see para. 22 of the judgement, at p. 815.

[83] DTI, *Modern Company Law for a Competitive Economy: Developing the Framework* (DTI, London, March 2000), p. 157, para. 5.19.

[84] *Ibid.*

[85] *Ibid.*

[86] *Ibid.*, p. 158, para 5.19.

[87] Jonathan Charkham and Anne Simpson, *Fair Shares: The Future of Shareholder Power and Responsibility* (Oxford University Press, Oxford, 1998), at pp. 198–9.

numbers. For example, the profit figure is the 'key note' of financial reports, encouraging short-termism and the audited profit figure is itself subject to uncertainties.[88] Lowenstein also notes 'enormous emphasis' upon earnings per share represented by a single number, urging managers to manage for the measured outcome rather than the economically better outcome. He further argues that reliance on numbers enables financial reports to be manipulated.[89] In addition, the balance sheet 'is a hotch potch of costs, valuations and adjusted figures which indicate neither the worth of an entity as a whole nor the separate worths of its individual components'.[90] Concepts upon which financial statements are based are not consistent or logical and do not lead to a portrayal of economic reality.[91] Finally, whilst there is some recognition of small companies' needs, the overall character of reporting requirements is that 'one size fits all.'[92] It is hardly surprising, in the light of these criticisms, that one commentator described annual accounts and reports as 'unintelligible'.[93] According to the Institute of Chartered Accountants in Scotland, terminology used in the accounts has 'outgrown common sense'.

Another observation that has been made which arguably reflects the quality of financial reports is that they do not address adequately their users' needs. Often there is poor access to the information required and when provided it is not always timely. In short, according to Charkham and Simpson, 'standards are patchy and access is poor'.[94] In addition, Bartlett and Chandler claim that the typical annual report is hardly user friendly, especially if a broad definition of users is to be adopted.[95] The Institute of Chartered Accountants of Scotland also stated in 1988 that the accounts have 'almost invariably lagged behind the current needs of their users'.[96]

Chapter 4 provided an overview of users and their needs. Even if one accepts the ASB's narrow view described in that chapter – that users

---

[88] ASSC, *The Corporate Report* (1975), at p. 47.

[89] Louis Lowenstein, 'Financial Transparency and Corporate Governance: The United States as a Model?' in Ross Grantham and Charles Rickett, *Corporate Personality in the 20th Century* (Hart, Oxford, 1998) 279, at p. 289 (hereinafter 'Lowenstein').

[90] Research Committee of the Institute of Chartered Accountants of Scotland, *Making Corporate Reports Valuable* (ICAS, Kogan Page, 1988), at p. 34

[91] *Ibid.*, p. 20 and also ch. 4.

[92] *Ibid.*

[93] R. Turner, 'Clear and Simple', *Accountancy*, October 2000, vol. 126, No. 1286, 156, at p. 156.

[94] Charkham and Simpson, at p. 200.

[95] Susan A. Bartlett and Roy A. Chandler, 'The Private Shareholder, Corporate Governance and the Role of the Annual Report' (1999) *JBL* 415, at p. 417.

[96] Research Committee of the Institute of Chartered Accountants of Scotland, *Making Corporate Reports Valuable* (ICAS, Kogan Page, London, 1988), at p. 34.

have an overall common interest in using information for making economic decisions and judging the stewardship of the directors – the above criticisms would suggest that users' needs are not met in financial reports. Empirical evidence in the UK and in the US has frequently revealed that annual reports are neither useful nor of interest to many shareholders. Lee and Tweedie during the 1970s revealed that many private shareholders did little more than skim the annual report and shareholders also rated the financial press as being slightly more useful in investment decision-making than the profit and loss account.[97] Shareholders then also indicated the view that the economic prospects of the company were the most important item of information but the information about the future would not necessarily be provided by the company.[98] The shareholders also did not appear to have the technical know-how that was demanded of them in the reporting system. Lee and Tweedie concluded that private shareholders had an insufficient understanding of the financial reports with which they were presented.

Bartlett and Chandler followed up Lee and Tweedie's research at the end of the 1990s.[99] They found that the annual report was still not widely read and that despite significant changes in financial reporting there was little change since the Lee and Tweedie studies. Bartlett and Chandler provide evidence of little interest by private shareholders in the financial data provided in the annual report. While 38 per cent of shareholders claim to read the chairman's statement thoroughly,[100] the figures for reading of other sections in the annual report provide less

---

[97] T. A. Lee and D. P. Tweedie, 'Accounting Information: An Investigation of Private Shareholder Understanding' (1975) *Accounting and Business Research* 3; 'Accounting Information: An Investigation of Private Shareholder Usage' (1975) *Accounting and Business Research* 280; 'The Private Shareholder: his Sources of Financial Information and his Understanding of Reporting Practices' (1976) *Accounting and Business Research* 304.

[98] Arnold suggests also that shareholders 'have two main, interdependent, information requirements forecasts of future dividends and relative risk, and regular reports explaining both differences between forecast and actual dividends, and changes in forecasts if expectations have changed.' He observes that traditionally, reports to shareholders generally cover only past performance and the current position of the business: see John Arnold, 'The Information Requirements of Shareholders' in Bryan Carsberg and Tony Hope (eds.), *Current Issues in Accounting* (Phillip Allan, Oxford, 1977) 107, at p. 115.

[99] Susan A. Bartlett and Roy A. Chandler, 'The Corporate Report and the Private Shareholder: Lee and Tweedie Twenty Years On' (1997) 29 *British Accounting Review* 245.

[100] Hines confirms that the chairman's report appears to be the most popular section of the annual report and that for decision-making the profit and loss statement is the most popular: R. D. Hines, 'The Usefulness of Annual Reports: the Anomaly between the Efficient Markets Hypothesis and Shareholder Surveys' (1982) *Accounting and Business Research* 296, at p. 297.

optimism with regard to its usefulness, with only around 23 per cent claiming to read the profit and loss account thoroughly, fewer than 16 per cent claiming to read the balance sheet thoroughly, only 11 per cent claiming to read the cash flow statement thoroughly, fewer than 15 per cent claiming to read the statement of total recognised gains and losses thoroughly, only 5 per cent reading thoroughly the directors' statement of responsibility, and only 8 per cent reading the auditors' report thoroughly. Some sections of the annual report were 'largely ignored', including information on board and corporate matters, as well as additional financial data and information on a company's subsidiaries and associated undertakings. The majority also more or less ignored statements on cash flow and total recognised gains and losses. More concern is expressed than appears to be credited for in corporate environmental spending and product safety and that pure personal gain is not the only interest of shareholders.[101] Brown and De Tore cite surveys indicating that less than five minutes is spent by 40 per cent of stakeholders on reading the annual reports and that 37 per cent of shareholders do not read or even look at it.[102] Miller and Young make the point that:

A common theme of modern financial analysis is that traditional financial statements do not tell you enough. Some assert that financial statements focus too much on the past and not enough on the future. Some assert that financial statements do not adequately focus on critical factors that create long-term value. Some assert that financial statements need to focus more on the separate segments of the enterprise. In the broadest sense, many assert that traditional financial statements simply do not sufficiently focus on just what users need.[103]

To deal with the problem of information overload and shareholder requests for less information, Lee and Tweedie and Bartlett and Chandler all suggested the use of summary financial statements which shareholders would find easier to understand. This has since been made possible for public companies.[104]

Another problem is that the varied user needs make it difficult for all such needs and interests to be satisfied in a general purpose report. As is

---

[101] Marc J. Epstein and Martin Freedman, 'Social Disclosure and the Individual Investor' (1994) 7 *Accounting, Auditing and Accountability Journal* 94–109, at p. 107.

[102] J. Robert Brown, Jr and Stephen M. De Tore, 'Rationalizing the Disclosure Process: The Summary Annual Report' (1988–89) 39 *Case Western Reserve Law Review* 39 at p. 56 and footnote 77.

[103] Richard I. Miller and Michael R. Young, 'Financial Reporting and Risk Management in the 21st Century' (1997) 65 *Fordham Law Review* 1987, at p. 1988; see also their footnote 1 for further references to such criticisms, at pp. 1988–9.

[104] Section 251, Companies Act 1985 and Companies Act 1985 (Summary Financial Statements) Regulations 1995, SI 1995/2092.

stated by Bartlett and Chandler: 'In the end, it is unlikely that general purpose annual reports are ever going to satisfy the widely differing information needs of a large body of shareholders.'[105]

The annual report does have some benefits.[106] Hines suggests it might be more useful for long-term decision-making than for short-term decision-making and acts as a confirmer or disconfirmer of information which investors have previously received and as a convenient summary of operations, results and financial position.[107] As the 'voice of management'[108] its main use seems to be to enhance for managers their relations with shareholders. It may contribute to shareholder loyalty and satisfaction, and thereby help to maintain share prices, long-term ownership, and loyalty of shareholders in contests for control. It also serves as an important promotional piece for distribution to investors throughout the year.[109] As Whitney describes it: 'quite apart from its utilization as a report of results of operations for the preceding year, the document has been used, among other things, as a showcase for a company's products or services, and as a vehicle for an expression of management's opinion respecting business and economic affairs which have relevance to the company's business.'[110] It is not surprising that the annual report has been described by at least one commentator as more akin to public relations than to public disclosure.[111]

What explains the apparent failure of financial reports to meet their users' needs?

A number of factors explain these apparent failures of financial reports. One factor is the regulatory framework in which financial reports are drafted and published. Accounting procedures, for example, might be regarded as too flexible, permitting companies to hide problems for too long. Accounting methods also tend to reveal a preference by auditors for conservative accounting practices such as reporting actual

---

[105] Bartlett and Chandler, at p. 259. See also James J. Benjamin and Keith G. Stanga, 'Differences in Disclosure Needs of Major Users of Financial Statements' (1977) *Accounting and Business Research* 187, at p. 192.

[106] See generally, A. A. Sommer, Jr, 'The Annual Report: A Prime Disclosure Document' (1972) *Duke LJ* 1093.

[107] Hines, at p. 309.

[108] This term is used frequently, since management is generally free to design the annual report in any way it wants to.

[109] Brown and De Tore, at p. 75.

[110] Jack M. Whitney II, 'Disclosure in the Annual Report to Shareholders' (1974) *Fifth Annual Institute on Securities Regulation*, Vol. 5, 103, at pp. 103–4.

[111] Robert S. Kant, 'The New Annual Report to Shareholders' (1974–75) 20 *Villanova Law Review* 273, at p. 277.

expenditures, but again this provides a poor guide to decisions about future investments.[112] In contrast, the legal requirements have been described as a 'legislative straightjacket',[113] with the result that managers, 'for fear of giving hostages to fortune, stick to what the existing regulations require'.[114] The legislative requirements, as noted above, also lean towards historical information rather than forward-looking information.[115] Whilst historic cost financial reporting has some benefits it has become clear that 'accountants have long known that historical cost financial reports do not attempt to meet the information needs of all users of accounts'.[116] Statutory requirements barely make demands for qualitative information so that accounting for stewardship is poor.[117] Another problem may be over-regulation of some corporate information. For example, as Brown and De Tore have suggested, the net effect of a regulatory encroachment may be to 'deny management the flexibility to determine the appropriate format for communicating information to its shareholders'.[118] The piecemeal development of reporting regulation has also led to a 'hotch-potch' of requirements with a lack of structure.[119]

A number of commentators have referred to the 'territorial' contest between lawyers and accountants with regard to controlling access to particular areas of work and to the process of financial reporting.[120] This 'battle' between the two professions may also contribute to communication problems in the presentation of the accounts. Freedman and Power, for example, note that lawyers tend to be more concerned with 'preserving the integrity of legal form' and the accountants are 'promoters of substance'. This tension has led to accusations by the accountants that legal form may inhibit their ability to present useful

---

[112] *Ibid.*, at pp. 86–7.
[113] DTI, *Modern Company Law for a Competitive Economy: Developing the Framework* (2000), para. 5.20, at p. 160.
[114] ICAS, *Making Corporate Reports Valuable* (1988), at p. 19.
[115] DTI, *Developing the Framework* (2000), para 5.19, at p. 158.
[116] Statement by Chris Swinson in ICAEW, *The 21st Century Annual Report* (ICAEW, London, 1998), p. 5. At p. 4 Swinson suggests that in the past we were served well by historical financial reporting, allowing shareholders to judge the performance of their company and its directors, and ensuring the avoidance of some of the excesses of imprudent dividend declaration. On the other hand, as Swinson observes at p. 5, historic cost financial reporting does not enable the measuring of human capital or intellectual capital or of the nature and possible extent of a company's environmental obligations.
[117] *Ibid.*
[118] Brown and De Tore, at p. 56.
[119] *Ibid.*
[120] Freedman and Power, at p. 770; Yves Dezalay, 'Territorial Battles and Tribal Disputes' (1991) 54 *MLR* 792.

information and legal rules may constrain their freedom to require new approaches, while the lawyers suggest that the accountants' judgements of substance are too idiosyncratic and subjective. The formats and specific details requirements in Schedules 4 and 4A of the Companies Act 1985 could impose constraints upon accountants when seeking to disclose more relevant material to their users that are more in line with their needs.

Another problem is that contexts change and needs evolve so that rules which remain static become outdated. They can be changed but the process of changing statutes is renowned for its delays and cumbersome processes. Indeed, Dearing suggested that the incorporation of standards into law would require a legalistic approach and reduce the ability of the financial community to respond quickly to adapt to new developments.[121]

There is also a need to consider the requirement of certainty, and so a balance between flexibility and certainty has to be struck. Inevitably there will be tensions between relevance in a changing environment and consistency that allows for comparability and trust. Ultimately, as is suggested by Macdonald, the communication of useful information means for lawyers, objective information and for accountants relevant information.

The formalistic approach of the law has led to many communicative problems. For example, McBarnet and Whelan have chronicled the phenomenon of creative accounting, which they define as 'using the law to escape legal control without actually violating legal rules'.[122] This definition is elaborated upon by McBarnet and Whelan in their later work so that creative compliance is described essentially as 'advantageous interpretations of grey areas, seeking out loopholes in specific rules, or dreaming up devices which regulators had not even thought of, let alone regulated'.[123] Thus the accounts would be in accordance with the letter but not the spirit of the law and standards. McBarnet and Whelan suggest that the formalistic conception of law underlies its structural manipulability and creative compliance.[124] In the system

---

[121] Dearing Committee, *The Making of Accounting Standards* (ICAEW, London, 1988) para. 10.3, at p. 23.

[122] Doreen McBarnet and Christopher Whelan, 'The Elusive Spirit of the Law: Formalism and the Struggle for Legal Control' (1991) 54 *MLR* 848; Doreen McBarnet and Christopher Whelan, *Creative Accounting and the Cross-Eyed Javelin Thrower* (Wiley, Chichester, 1999). See also T. Pijper, *Creative Accounting: The Effectiveness of Financial Reporting in the UK* (MacMillan, London, 1993).

[123] McBarnet and Whelan (1999), at p. 6.

[124] McBarnet and Whelan (1999), at p. 848.

created to combat creative accounting following the recommendations of the Dearing Report, a greater emphasis was placed upon the use of principles rather than specific rules. In part this is explained by McBarnet and Whelan: 'specific rules with very precise definitions and criteria invite creative compliance – complying with the specific letter of the law but not its spirit'.[125] In formalism there is an emphasis on uniformity, consistency and predictability; formalism assumes that there is consistency, predictability, logical coherence and ultimately autonomy and closure.[126] McBarnet and Whelan observe that an anti-formalistic response to the rigid rules was developing that indicated a shift towards 'openness and flexibility, extra-legal regulation and a recognition of economic and commercial realities'.[127] The move towards substance over form led to the adoption of more flexible concepts.

The nature of the true and fair override might also be questioned. McBarnet and Whelan, for example, consider the use of the notes to the accounts for presenting a true and fair view where the numbers do not.[128] They provide an example of Rosehaugh, a property development company, which supplied details of its subsidiaries in over seven pages of notes.[129] McBarnet and Whelan, suggest that this could be seen as 'non-disclosing disclosure' because it obscures sensitive information, tucking it away in masses of detailed small print.[130] It might be argued that to obscure material information in the notes is actually misleading. Yet this tactic would almost seem to be justified by the Companies Act itself, since sections 226(4) and 227(5) state that the necessary information shall be given in the accounts *or in a note to them*.[131] Additionally, under the efficient capital markets hypothesis economists would argue that if the information appears in the financial statements or in the footnotes it would have little effect on the market price of a company's stock since the market is allegedly capable of absorbing information and reflects that information in market prices.[132] The jury appears still to be out as far as the regime created to control creative accounting is concerned.[133]

---

[125] *Ibid.*, at p. 28 they cite the Financial Reporting Council who argue that this approach 'will remain relevant to innovations in business and finance and which are most likley to discourage ingenious standards avoidance practices': FRC, *The State of Financial Reporting* (FRC, London, 1991), at para. 5.5.

[126] McBarnet and Whelan (1991), at p. 849.

[127] *Ibid.*, at p. 851.

[128] McBarnet and Whelan (1999), at pp. 206–8.

[129] *Ibid.*, at p. 207.

[130] *Ibid.*, at p. 207.

[131] *Ibid.*, at p. 208.

[132] Charles C. Cox, 'Accounting Standards from an Economist's Perspective' (1985) 7 *Journal of Comparative Business and Capital Market Law* 349, at p. 355.

[133] McBarnet and Whelan (1999), part V, at pp. 255–75.

It is not just the true and fair view concept that causes so many difficulties of interpretation. The Companies Act contains terminology that is capable of being construed in several alternative ways. For example, references to assets, liabilities, surplus, even when defined, may be difficult actually to interpret. Indeed, Siegel, pointing to similar terminology and definitions in the American legislation, states that 'the absence of any substantial decisional gloss on these ambiguous terms leaves the corporate planner in a quandary'.[134] Yet at the same time, to put rigid definitions into the legislation would be problematic since such terminology and concepts are constantly under review by the accounting professions. As is stated by the American Committee on Corporate Laws,

In the view of the Committee, the widespread controversy concerning various accounting principles, and their constant reevaluation, requires a statutory standard of reasonableness, as a matter of law, recognizing that there may be equally acceptable alternative solutions to specific issues as well as areas requiring judgment in interpreting such principles.[135]

One problem is that legislation tends to use terms that have not even been clearly articulated by the accountants. This may have the consequence of creating difficulty for advisers in conclusively stating whether proposed or completed transactions meet the statutory standards and for those preparing the accounts to know whether they meet the statutory requirements.

What makes financial information useful?

In its *Statement of Principles for Financial Reporting* the ASB provides that '[T]he objective of financial statements is to provide information about the financial position, performance and financial adaptability of an enterprise that is useful to a wide range of users for assessing the stewardship of management and for making economic decisions.'[136] It would appear that from this perspective, the key question is whether or not financial reports provide users with adequate information to enable them to make rational economic decisions and to hold the managers to account. In order to meet this objective the ASB suggests in its

---

[134] Stanley Siegel, 'A Critical Examination of State Regulation of Accounting Principles' (1985) 7 *Journal of Comparative Business and Capital Market Law* 317, at p. 321.

[135] Committee on Corporate Laws, 'Changes in the Model Business Corporation Act – Amendments to Financial Provisions' (1979) 34 *Business Law* 1867 at p. 1884, cited by Siegel, at p. 322.

[136] ASB, *Statement of Principles for Financial Reporting* (ASB, London, 1999) para. 1.1.

Statement that certain qualitative characteristics are required of financial information. The key qualities for making such information useful are, according to the ASB: relevance, reliability, comparability and understandability. In addition, materiality is a threshold quality for all information given. The ASB provides its advice in the following diagram:

Threshold Quality	MATERIALITY	Giving information that is not material may impair the usefulness of the other information given	
RELEVANCE	RELIABILITY	COMPARABILITY	UNDERST-ANDABILITY
Information that has the ability to influence economic decisions	Information that is a complete and faithful representation	Similarities and differences can be discerned and evaluated	The significance of the information can be perceived
Predictive value	Faithful representation	Consistency	Users' abilities
Confirmatory value	Neutral Free from material error Complete Prudence	Disclosure	Aggregation and classification

The quality characteristics of relevance, reliability, comparability and understandability are repeatedly identified[137] as part of the evaluation of the usefulness or appropriateness of the financial information presented to the various users. Other criteria identified, which are closely related or part of these criteria, are timeliness and accuracy. In the guidance to its *Statement of Principles*, the ASB provides, effectively summarising chapter 3:

In deciding what information should be included in financial statements, when it should be included and how it should be presented, the aim is to ensure that financial statements yield useful information. Financial information is useful if it

---

[137] See also Barry Elliott and Jamie Elliott, *Financial Accounting and Reporting* (8th edn, FT Prentice Hall, London, 2004), at p. 5.

is: relevant – in other words if it has the ability to influence the economic decisions of users and is provided in time to influence those decisions; reliable – in other words, if it can be depended upon to represent faithfully what it either purports to represent or could reasonably be expected to represent and therefore reflects the substance of the transactions and other events that have taken place; it is complete and is free from deliberate or systematic bias and material error; and in its preparation under conditions of uncertainty, a degree of caution has been applied in exercising the necessary judgements; comparable – in other words, if it enables users to discern and evaluate similarities in, and differences between, the nature and effects of transactions and other events over time and across different reporting entities; understandable – in other words, if its signifi-cance can be perceived by users that have a reasonable knowledge of business and economic activities and accounting and a willingness to study with reasonable diligence the information provided.[138]

What are the main features of each of the qualities of usefulness?

Relevance   Relevance must be considered from the perspective of the user rather than from the sender's perspective. Barton suggests that in order to be relevant the information must materially bear upon the matter being considered and influence the decision or appraisal made.[139] It must also reduce the degree of uncertainty about the result of a decision already taken. The information must therefore be complete and material. Timeliness is also connected to or is a part of relevance so that the information must be presented when it is needed by the user. The longer the time period after the need is established the less relevant the awaited information will become. As Barton argues, timeliness in-volves both frequency and time lag for the presentation of information. Timeliness may be achieved by the issue of interim, quarterly reports with enough details to be able to make frequent judgements. That way the information is not so outdated.[140] However, this could lead to overload and to an increasing emphasis on short-term results. This is likely to be exacerbated by the growing reliance upon internet and electronic networks for the release of information.

---

[138] See ASB website, providing guidance on the *Statement of Principles of Financial Reporting*, para. 7, www.asb.org.uk.

[139] A. D. Barton, *The Objectives and Basic Concepts of Accounting* (Australia Accounting Research foundation, Melbourne, 1982), at p. 32.

[140] Barton, *ibid.*, at p. 32. See also Robert Mims, 'The SEC and Corporate Financial Disclosure: A View from the Press' (1985) 7 *Journal of Comparative Business and Capital Markets Law* 387, at p. 390.

Reliability   Reliability of information is necessary for the purposes of prediction and control and accountability. The information must be accurate, faithfully reflecting the financial conditions or events it is purporting to represent. In order to be reliable it must be verifiable, neutral and complete. It must be free from bias and it must not omit relevant information. If the information is an estimate, that should be made clear so that the user can identify and distinguish it from information denoted as factual truth.

Comparability   In order to make decisions and to evaluate the managerial activity it is necessary to be able to compare the company's performance with previous similar time periods such as the previous financial year and also with other similar enterprises as well as within separate divisions within a company. Comparability requires consistency in that the methods of accounting are uniformly applied and a universally similar accounting system is applied. Any changes should be disclosed to the users so that they are not making false comparisons. One step towards achieving comparability is by adopting a regulatory approach. The existence of formal rules that specify a standardised basic list of required data makes comparisons among financial reports possible.[141]

Understandability   Users need to be able to understand the information with which they are supplied. The information should therefore be expressed as simply as the material or subject matter will allow. All potential users – and not just the more sophisticated users – should be able to understand the information, otherwise a bias occurs. One way of distinguishing the different users is to present the material to each of them in accordance with their levels of understanding so that, for example, summarised accounts can be provided to less sophisticated users. However, this could lead to different information being provided that could again give rise to accusations of bias and unfair discrimination. This potential problem is reinforced by the empirical findings of Lee and Tweedie that indicate less reliance by private shareholders on professional advisers such as stockbrokers, even though the majority of

---

[141] See in this respect, Joel Seligman, 'The SEC and Accounting: A Historical Perspective' (1985) 7 *Journal of Comparative Business and Capital Market Law* 241, at pp. 242–52, discussing the role of the SEC in the standardisation of items to be disclosed in corporate financial reports. See also Joel Seligman, 'The Historical Need for a Mandatory Disclosure System' (1983) 9 *Journal of Corporate Law* 1.

such shareholders claim to have no training in finance or accounting.[142] To be understandable the information format should be clear with headings, explanations of concepts and accounting methods.

As described by the ASB, these qualitative criteria appear deceptively straightforward. However, their application in reality may be more complex. Indeed, some observers have conducted empirical surveys on users' needs and also on the definitions or characteristics of the qualitative criteria. Such surveys reveal difficulties in identifying the needs and their order of relevance for users. For example, Stamp reported on a survey he conducted of the Accounting Standards Committee members in the early 1980s which revealed that among six possible measurement bases the members could not agree upon one single measurement basis that could be regarded as superior to all the others. From this he concluded that the process of meeting the needs of users is treated as one of optimisation, in which trade-offs must be made between various criteria such as between objectivity and relevance.[143] He also highlighted the fact that there are considerable semantic problems concerned with what is meant by words such as objectivity, relevance, materiality, freedom from bias, rationality etc. Thus, although accounting deals with figures, many of its most important problems arise because of accountants' uncertainty about the meaning of the words they use. Additionally the criteria could overlap or they could also be in conflict.[144]

In the US, the American Institute of Certified Public Accountants ('AICPA') formed the Jenkins Special Committee on Financial Reporting to assess the needs of users of financial information and to recommend improvements in financial reporting. This Committee suggested that to meet users' needs the business reports should contain more information with a forward-looking perspective; focus more on the facts that create long-term value, including non-financial measures; and better align the information reported externally with the information reported to senior management.[145]

As has been noted above, a major criticism of financial accounts is that they are generally based upon historical information and do not provide

---

[142] Lee and Tweedie, 'The Private Shareholder: his Sources of Financial Information and his Understanding of Reporting Practices' (1976) *Accounting and Business Research* 304, at p. 314.

[143] Edward Stamp, 'First Steps towards a British Conceptual Framework' (1982) *Accountancy* (March 1982) 123, at p.124.

[144] *Ibid.*

[145] See AICPA, Special Committee on Financial Reporting, *Improving Business Reporting – A Customer Focus: Meeting the Information Needs of Investors and Creditors* (1994).

the user with an indication of the company's future earnings, a major factor in the investor's decision to invest or stay with the company, and therefore also a major factor in determining the usefulness of the accounts. Indeed, there are frequent calls for the disclosure of projected earnings.[146] However, this type of disclosure is itself likely to have some difficulties. For example, over how long a period should the projection be made? What assumptions will underlie the projection and to what extent will the forecast be affected by a change of conditions? What about verification of those projections? What liability should they carry if any? How should such verification be realised? At the very least investigation of the internal procedures and methodology used in making the forecasts are required, ensuring that the appropriate persons from the company were involved in making the forecast and establishing whether or not the assumptions were reasonable.

Forecasts are potentially problematic because they may inaccurately rely upon assumptions regarding the continuance of underlying factors over time without change. Aspects which may be relevant include changes in money rates, labour contracts, wage rates, environmental controls, costs of materials, marketing expenses, administrative costs, cost of transportation, governmental policies, tax rates, labour unrest. Any of these could make reasonable forecasts later unreliable. It is also necessary to disclose the assumptions upon which forecasts are made, but sometimes the statements may be difficult to express with any degree of clarity. If there are lots of underlying assumptions it might be impracticable to disclose all of them. Forecasts could give rise to undesirable behaviour by management. For example, forecasts might be set very low to try to ensure that they will be met. Or earnings figures might be manipulated in order to indicate achievement of the forecasts. Those companies in more stable sectors may not have difficulties but those in more volatile and competitive sectors may not be able to predict so easily.

Again, use of forecasts raises many questions: How should a company present forecasts? Should the company use a range of forecast figures or a single figure? If it adopts a range should it say if it the middle figure is the most reliable? How far should company disclaimers be taken into account? How frequently should projections be updated? When is there

---

[146] See e.g., David S. Ruder, 'Disclosure of Financial Projections – Developments, Problems and Techniques' (1974) *Fifth Annual Institute on Securities Regulation*, vol. 5, 5; Carl W. Schneider, 'Financial Projections – Practical Problems of Disclosure' (1974) *Fifth Annual Institute on Securities Regulation*, vol. 5, 47.

a material change in the circumstances that will affect the forecasted figure? What then is a material change? What about businesses with different divisions – should forecasts be made for each division?

One problem that might grow as a result of the use of forecasts is that of increasing litigation. For example, in relation to the provision of data providing forecasts of future earnings, Mims asks, 'No doubt the SEC believes that the public should have access to the informal forecasts that have always been available to securities analysts, but what happens when those forecasts begin to go awry?' This concern is also raised by Brown and De Tore, noting that 'disclosure of projections is fraught with risk. Attempts to forecast the future often prove incorrect. Disgruntled shareholders often attempt to use incorrect projections to obtain damages under the antifraud provisions.'[147] One response is that management may be tempted to manipulate the financial figures and to conduct the company's business in more risky ways in order to try and meet those forecasts.[148] More helpful is the SEC's adoption of a 'safe harbour' rule designed to reduce management's exposure to liability for projections that ultimately prove incorrect, so that projections will not be considered fraudulent unless produced in bad faith or without a reasonable basis.[149] Miller and Young summarise the problem in the following way:

> The basic problem is that improvement in the systems of financial reporting will largely involve a trend away from objectively verifiable data into data that is more subjective and therefore based on judgement. This increases the litigation risk, insofar as a trend to subjective data increases the opportunity for second guessing, particularly when things do not turn out as planned. . . Any change in the direction of improving financial reporting will where the profession has given assurance as to more modern presentations of data, potentially increase its exposure to litigation.[150]

Conclusion

Financial reporting is a fundamental aspect of the disclosure regime for companies. In the UK the regulation of financial reporting is multi-layered, detailed and complex. However, those features do not guarantee an entirely effective system. Indeed, many problems exist with the financial reporting activities of companies. Recent corporate collapses such as Enron and MG Rover highlighted problems with the accounts.

---

[147] Brown and De Tore, at p. 88.
[148] Robert Mims, 'The SEC and Corporate Financial Disclosure: A View from the Press' (1985) 7 *Journal of Comparative Business and Capital Market Law* 387, at p. 389.
[149] Brown and De Tore, at p. 88.
[150] Miller and Young, at p. 1990.

One deficiency in the regulatory regime is the lack of a sufficient conceptual framework that guides clearly those involved in the accounting process. This results in arguably over-complex rules and processes and ultimately in a failure to meet the needs of those using the accounts. Whilst their basic needs are identified as requiring reports that are reliable, relevant, comparable and understandable, these characteristics require further definition for them to have practical value. There is controversy about the extent to which investors are interested in all aspects of the accounts and increasingly there is concern about the amount of information that investors are expected to read. Information overload is potentially as much a problem as insufficient information. The use of summary financial statements might go some way towards alleviating this problem. The complexity of the accounts and the use of certain accounting principles such as the true and fair view override also contribute to the uncertainty and lack of enthusiasm for such information by the investors. In addition the continuing problem of the historical focus of financial accounts reduces their relevance for investors who are more likely to be interested in the future prospects of the company.

General rules and general purpose reports fail to address the specific needs of different companies and different users. The company law reform process has sought to resolve the problems experienced by small companies. The new Company Law Reform Bill proposes to separate and clarify the rules for smaller companies in its 'think small first' policy. General purpose reports are also unlikely to meet all user needs. Indeed as noted in chapter 4, even within specific categories there may be conflict and competition and these need to be prioritised appropriately. One solution would be to provide separate reports for each different group but this would not only increase costs but could lead to accusations of bias and favourable treatment of certain groups over others.

This chapter has highlighted the complexity of the multi-layered system of financial reporting regulation. Recent changes to the accounting regime may help to streamline the arrangements but it is also necessary to encourage coordination between the different regulatory bodies.

The financial reporting rules and principles are directed predominantly at meeting the shareholders' interests. The assumption is that their needs are representative of the other stakeholder users. However, private shareholders, at least, have revealed an overall lack of interest in the financial reports of their companies despite changes made in the system to encourage their participation. This continued problem might require more attention being paid to the place of reporting within the whole communication and decision-making process. How companies engage with their shareholders is important if the financial reports are to have a purpose. Alternatively communication with other user groups may be more appropriate if they take a more genuine interest in the company's finances and position.

Some of the challenges to the financial reporting regime come from the fact that many of the rules are shaped by the need to implement European provisions, and are influenced too by global trading activities. The next chapter will consider those aspects of financial reporting.

7   International aspects of financial reporting

Introduction

The previous chapter considered the general position in the UK with regard to financial reporting by companies. The regulatory structure and the financial reporting and accounting environment in the UK are largely guided and regulated by private and professional bodies such as the Accounting Standards Board and the Institutes of Chartered Accountants in England and Wales and in Scotland. The UK has had a long tradition of accounting and therefore has a well-developed system. Nevertheless the UK's membership of the European Union, together with globalisation of capital markets and international trade, has had a significant impact on financial reporting in the UK. In January 2005 new international standards came into force in the UK as a result of European measures to adopt standards created by the International Accounting Standards Board. This new accounting and reporting regime will have a significant impact upon business reporting in the UK and within the accounting environment there has been scepticism about the level of preparedness of companies for the new standards. This chapter will explore the European and international financial reporting rules and will consider also the impact upon companies based in the UK.

The development of an international financial reporting regime

Historically, accounting and reporting processes developed independently and have national characteristics different from those in other countries. However, an increasingly globalised economy and instant communication facilities have made necessary an international level of control of financial accounting. One potential obstacle to the success of international trade is lack of transparency owing to different ways of providing information, leading to insufficient understanding of accounts produced by companies in other jurisdictions and little opportunity for comparability of different accounts and reports. From this position the globalisation of accounting standards aims to improve transparency and make for better comparison of accounts between companies internationally with the objective of making cross-border trade easier. Attempts to converge different accounting and reporting systems have laid the foundations for an international financial reporting regulatory environment.

This ambition for an internationally focused approach to financial accounting and reporting has developed against a background comprising of different legal and cultural traditions. The differences among national accounting rules and practices reflect cultural and economic distinctions, in particular in the provision of finance, the existing legal systems, the link between accounting and taxation and cultural differences between societies.[1] Thus, for example, in Germany banks have traditionally been the major supplier of extra funds leading companies to rely more on loan capital. By contrast shareholders have been the major provider of extra funds in the UK and the US encouraging companies to rely on equity capital to finance their activities, thus leading to active stock exchanges. In addition, different legal systems result in different regulatory forms for accounting. Common law countries are more likely to have relatively minimalist company laws, leaving rule setting to private standard setters, whereas code systems are more likely to include accounting rules in their laws and so the state has a bigger role in shaping accounting practices. The link between accounting and taxation is also relevant. Taxation may influence how transactions are recognised and measured whereas in countries with a weaker link between accounting and taxation the rules for valuation may be quite distinct.

In the UK, shareholders are recognised as the main providers of capital. From this perspective they are considered to have a great interest in the way in which companies communicate their financial information. They therefore rely on the expertise of accountants who check on their behalf the communication process and its outcome within a company. Consequently accountants play a major role in the standard-setting process.[2]

In contrast, where debt finance prevails those jurisdictions tend to be more protective of creditors. Large creditors such as banks are able to obtain inside information from the companies to whom they provide

---

[1] For a description of the different types of accounting system see David Alexander, Anne Britton and Ann Jorissen, *International Financial Reporting and Analysis* (Thomson, London, 2003), ch. 2.

[2] Alexander, Britton and Jorissen, at p. 29.

loans and they are less in need of public financial information published by these companies. Often governments make use of financial information for their own purposes, such as taxation or policy setting. An example may be found in the Belgian system where social balance accounts are required as an aid to the government in setting employment policy. In these jurisdictions financial statements serve the interests of a range of different stakeholders including creditors and government. They are interested in the underlying assets of the company and the determination of taxable income. Indeed, in France and Germany, taxation rules provide a basis upon which accounting rules are to be developed. Valuation rules and accounting practices will be more conservative or prudent than in countries with a shareholder orientation. Codified countries also tend to be more concerned with uniformity and compliance with prescribed accounting plans leading to detailed formats for balance sheet and profit and loss accounts.[3]

The cultural differences present a picture of diametrically opposed systems highlighting individualism versus collectivism, large versus small power distance, strong versus weak level of certainty, professionalism versus statutory control, uniformity versus flexibility, conservatism versus optimism, secrecy versus transparency. These differences in approach make comparability more difficult to achieve so that users of company accounts are less able to evaluate the reported transactions and events.[4]

Globalisation has reduced the differences in approach to business and investment observed above. This has encouraged moves towards convergence of accounting and reporting systems also. Thus, some companies in debt financed and codified legal systems countries have adopted International Accounting Standards and principles. Such companies may seek to gain investments from the international capital markets. By adopting and following international standards their location is less of an influence. It is also possible to observe that certain industries or sectors tend to follow specific patterns or trends with regard to their choice of accounting regime. For example, software companies generally use US GAAP.[5]

European steps towards international standards

Membership of the European Union has had enormously important consequences for the UK, not least in the area of accounting and financial reporting. Financial reporting has traditionally been regulated

[3] *Ibid.*, ch. 2.   [4] *Ibid.*, ch. 2.   [5] *Ibid.*, at p. 36.

within the framework of the EU's company law harmonisation programme. For a long period the most significant regulatory measures
were the Accounting Directives of 1978[6] and 1983[7]. A key characteristic
of those Directives is their flexibility, particularly in the broad range of
options they afford to Member States and to companies in the way
accounts are regulated and presented. Increasingly in the company law
programme Member States have been granted greater freedom and in
part that is the very essence of Directives as a legal instrument, since they
leave to Member States discretion in the manner in which their provisions will be implemented. The Accounting Directives have indeed
been described as 'second generation Directives' that marked a move
away from the more prescriptive 'first generation Directives' within the
company law programme at least.[8]

However, at the same time, alongside these development: within the
EU, internationally a process of convergence has been emerging. The
International Accounting Standards Committee was founded in 1973
and today, as the International Accounting Standards Board, one of its
stated objectives is:

To develop, in the public interest, a single set of high quality, understandable
and enforceable global accounting standards that require high quality, transparent and comparable information in financial statements and other financial
reporting to help participants in the world's capital markets and other users
make economic decisions.[9]

These measures are considered essential to the increasingly important
international activities of those businesses which look beyond their own

---

[6] Council Directive 78/660/EEC of 25 July 1978 on the annual accounts of certain types of
companies OJ L 222, 14.8.1978, 11 (amended by Directive 2001/65/EC (OJ L 283,
27.10.2001, 28)).

[7] Council Directive 83/349/EEC of 13 June 1983 on consolidated accounts, OJ L 193,
18.7.1983, 1 (amended by Directive 2001/65/EC (OJ L 283, 27.10.2001, 28). See also
Council Directive 86/635/EEC of 8 December 1986 on the annual accounts and consolidated accounts of banks and other financial institutions, OJ L 372, 31.12.1986, 1
(amended by Directive 2001/65/EC (OJ l 283, 27.10.2001, 28)) and Council Directive
91/674/EEC on the annual accounts and consolidated accounts of insurance companies
OJ L 374, 31.12.1991, 7.

[8] See e.g., Rafael Guasch Martorell, 'La Armonización en el Marco del Derecho Europeo de
Sociedades: La Obligación de Resultado Exigida por las Directivas Societarias a los
Estados Miembros' (1994) 596 Revista General De Derecho 5651 at p. 5663. See also
Charlotte Villiers, European Company Law – Towards Democracy? (Ashgate, Aldershot,
1998). See also Lorna Woods and Charlotte Villiers, 'The Legislative Process and the
Institutions of the European Union: A Case Study of the Development of European
Company Law' in Paul Craig and Carole Harlow (eds.), Lawmaking in the European Union
- Proceedings of W G Hart Legal Workshop 1996 (Sweet and Maxwell, London, 1998).

[9] IASC, Foundation Constitution, Part A, para 2, last revised on 8 July 2002, available at
www.iasc.org.uk.

national markets for capital investment. Yet the capacity for international trade and investment is limited if financial reporting is substantially different across trading borders. Such differences make comparisons between the financial statements of different businesses more difficult. The existence of such differences increases costs of producing and analysing financial statements. Ernst & Young describe the position in the following way:

A deep, accessible and liquid capital market in Europe is important for the development of new businesses in Europe. The growth and entrepreneurial culture essential to development will thrive better with a clear route to market for equity. This is particularly important to an enlarged community as new businesses will grow more strongly with the help of equity capital. Conversely, without an integrated capital market these potential macro-economic benefits will not be realised, economic growth will be lower and the opportunity of achieving competitive advantage in the global capital markets will be lost … Without high quality, reliable, comparable and transparent financial information, even if all other barriers are removed, investors will remain sceptical and demand a premium for their capital.[10]

In 1990 a conference took place within the EU organised by the Commission. It was concluded there that the EU needed to take into account the harmonisation efforts at a broader international level and to cooperate with the international accounting standard setters.[11] In 1995 the Commission published a Communication indicating its recognition of a need to alter and modernise its accounting regime.[12] Its own Directives were not as demanding as the rules of the Securities and Exchange Commission in the United States of America with the consequence that European companies would have to prepare a second set of accounts if they were seeking capital on international markets.[13] Such a situation may be confusing. The same information presented in different ways could lead to different interpretations and comparability would be difficult to achieve and expensive.[14] The Commission also recognised that the options provided within the Directives caused a lack of a common position on accounts in Europe with the consequence of weakening the EU's role on the international accounting standards setting scene.[15] The Commission therefore decided to seek a more

---

[10] See Ernst & Young, 'IAS – Case for a Single Financial Reporting Framework' at www. ey.com/global/content.nsf/International/Assurance, last visited 10 September 2003.
[11] See Com. 95(508), at para. 2.6.
[12] Com. 95 (508), above note 5.
[13] Com. 95 (508), paras. 1.2, 1.3 and 3.3.
[14] Com. 95 (508), at para. 3.3.
[15] Com. 95 (508), para. 3.4.

positive role and at the same time preserve its own accounting regulation achievements.[16]

In 2000 another Communication was published focusing on financial reporting strategy.[17] This Communication stated that 'globalisation and information technology developments have created a unique momentum to realise a single, efficient and competitive EU securities market'.[18] Member States' securities markets were consolidated by new technologies, globalisation, the introduction of the Euro and information and communication technologies as well as electronic trading platforms.[19] In the 2000 Communication document the Commission also noted that there had been strong pressure towards convergence of accounting standards.[20] The Commission saw the need for a single set of comparable financial statements by a European company. Thus the Commission stated:

Relevant, timely, reliable and comparable information about the performance and financial position of an enterprise continues to be of central importance in safeguarding the interests of investors, creditors and other stakeholders to ensure a level playing field between competitors.[21]

The European Commission adopted the strategy of supporting the core set of standards created by the International Organization of Securities Commission and the IASC and the 2000 Communication document proposed the endorsement of the international standards by the EU. The policy was to make the international standards effective by 2005 in order to comply with the conclusions of the Lisbon European Council which set the goal of a fully-integrated financial services market by then.[22]

The new accounting legislation

The result of the Commission's policy in legislative terms is a Regulation for the endorsement and enforcement of the international accounting standards created by the IASB[23] together with a Directive to

[16] Com. 95 (508), paras. 1.4 and 1.5.
[17] Communication from the Commission, *EU Financial Reporting Strategy: the way forward*, Com. (2000) 359 final, Brussels 13.6.2000.
[18] Com. 2000 (359), Executive Summary.
[19] Com. 2000 (359), para. 3.
[20] Com. 2000 (359), para. 5.
[21] Com. 2000 (359), para. 8.
[22] Com. 2000 (359), para. 13.
[23] Regulation (EC) no. 1606/2002 of the European Parliament and of the Council of 19 July 2002 on the application of international accounting standards OJ L 243, 11.09.2002, 1.

modernise the existing Fourth and Seventh Directives to enable them to be compatible with the international accounting standards that are to be endorsed.[24]

The Regulation

The Regulation states the need to supplement the legal framework applicable to publicly traded companies in their financial reporting activities. Thus Article 3 provides for the Commission to decide, under the Committee procedure set out in Decision 1999/468/EC,[25] on the applicability within the Community of international standards provided they: are not contrary to the true and fair view principle, are conducive to the European public good, and meet the criteria of understandability, relevance, reliability and comparability required of the financial information needed for making economic decisions and assessing the stewardship of management. Adopted international standards shall be published in the Official Journal as a Commission Regulation and since January 2005 companies are required to prepare consolidated accounts in conformity with those international standards if at their balance sheet date their securities are admitted to trading on a regulated market of any Member State.[26]

The Modernising Directive

The existing Directives still have a role since they apply to non-publicly traded companies and to those areas not touched by the international accounting standards and they continue to apply to the annual accounts of all companies. The Modernising Directive brings the original Accounting Directives into line with the international standards[27] with the additional requirements also of financial reports containing analyses of environmental, social and other aspects relevant to an understanding of the company's development and position. The aim is to provide a level playing field between companies which apply international accounting standards and those which do not.[28]

---

[24] Directive of the European Parliament and of the Council of 18 June 2003 amending Council Directives 78/660/EEC, 83/349/EEC and 91/674/EEC on the annual and consolidated accounts of certain types of companies and insurance undertakings OJ L 178/16, 17.7.2003.

[25] Article 6 refers to Decision 1999/468/EC as laying down the relevant procedure.

[26] Article 4.

[27] See IP/02/799.

[28] Preamble, para. 5.

The new accounting regime

The new legislation and the European Commission's commitment to the adoption of the international accounting standards has significantly altered the accounting regime in the EU. A number of observations can be made:

A two-tier accounting system

A two-tier accounting regime has possibly been created, at least in the short term. One level will apply to publicly traded companies for whose consolidated accounts the international accounting standards will be applicable. Another level will apply to other businesses and to the annual accounts of all limited companies. It should be noted, however, that Member States have been given the option of extending the application of the international standards to annual accounts and to non-publicly traded companies.[29] If the Member States take up these options that would reduce the extent of the two-tier system. The potential impact is further reduced (at least in the short term prior to any revision of the international accounting standards) by the modernisation of the existing Directives so that they operate in a broadly similar way to the international accounting standards.

Priority to International Accounting Standards

If, despite modernising the Directives, any incompatibility between an adopted international accounting standard and the Directives should arise, the Regulation has the effect of the international accounting standards taking precedence. This is acknowledged specifically by the Commission in its 1995 Communication document.[30] The IASB has also adopted a cooperative stance and expressed a willingness in such circumstances to re-examine any international accounting standards which are found not to be in conformity with the Directives.[31]

Mandatory standards

The Regulation has the effect of making the international accounting standards mandatory. This is an interesting result since the IASB itself

---

[29] Article 5 of the Regulation.
[30] See para. 5.3 of the 1995 Document, Com. (1995) 508.
[31] *Ibid.*

does not endow the standards with this status because the IASB would not have authority to enforce them. The IASB acknowledges that Member States have the option of giving them legally binding status. The Regulation itself is, of course, directly applicable and any endorsed international standard would become directly applicable as it would be given effect by way of a Regulation. As is known, under Article 249 EU Treaty, a Regulation, being directly applicable, becomes part of the domestic law of the Member States without needing transposition, with the effect that, so long as their provisions are sufficiently clear, precise and relevant to the situation of an individual litigant, it is capable of being relied upon and enforced by individuals in their national courts.

The Committee of European Securities Regulators published a proposed statement of principles in October 2002,[32] suggesting the establishment by Member States of Competent Independent Administrative Authorities that would have ultimate responsibility for enforcement of compliance and such enforcement would be predominantly risk based combined with rotation and or sampling of the financial information of selected companies. It would comprise a range of formal checks to indepth substantive checking of the information provided by the selected companies. In the case of a material misstatement enforcers should take appropriate action to achieve disclosure and if relevant a correction of the misstatement.

Importance of committees in the endorsement process

The endorsement process, like the Commission's proposed enforcement negotiations, makes heavy use of committees. As has already been noted above, the Regulation refers to Decision 1999/468/EC which sets out the committee procedure. The Communication documents also refer to the comitology procedure, justified on the basis of the subsidiarity and proportionality principles for the purpose of amending the Directives. Yet what exists in reality is an extremely complex arrangement with the involvement of several committees whose precise roles and status are not entirely clear. As was proposed in the 2000 Communication document the endorsement mechanism requires a two-tiered structure comprising a technical level and a political level.

---

[32] Committee of European Securities Regulators, Proposed Statement of Principles of Enforcement of Accounting Standards in Europe, Consultation Paper, October 2002, CESR/02 – 188b, available at www.europefesco.org.

The technical level   The technical level consists of the European Financial Reporting Advisory Group (hereinafter 'EFRAG'), a committee of independent experts from the private sector,[33] to advise the Commission on the suitability of international accounting standards and their compatibility with the Directives. A supervisory board ascertains that individual members of the technical group work in the European interest.

The political level   Following advice from EFRAG the Commission then puts forward its proposal to the Accounting Regulatory Committee consisting of official representatives from the Member States and chaired by the Commission. The Accounting Regulatory Committee votes by qualified majority voting whether or not to accept the proposal to adopt the international accounting standards. If the Committee votes against the proposal the Commission may submit it to the Council of Ministers. The Council of Ministers is then given three months to adopt or block the proposal, also by qualified majority voting. If it blocks the proposal the Commission can resubmit it. The European Parliament also has a right to comment but not to veto.[34]

Alongside these committees, the Contact Committee, which was set up under the Fourth Directive, is to check the compatibility of the international accounting standards and the Directives and any amendments to the Directives considered to be necessary will be effected by the Committee. The aim is to achieve a common position internationally and between Europe and the relevant international bodies, in particular the IASB. Thus, a technical subcommittee of the Contact Committee has a role of 'meeting regularly to discuss matters particularly relating to international accounting standards' and also seeks common positions on exposure drafts.[35] It appears that EFRAG plays this role as the Contact Committee's technical subcommittee. Through this arrangement the Commission seeks effective participation in the IASB's standard setting process.[36]

The Accounting Advisory Forum, which represents users and preparers of accounts, meets with the Contact Committee but it is not clear

---

[33] For further information about EFRAG see www.iasplus.com/efrag/ efrag.htm.

[34] This interpretation of the procedure is offered in the Consultation Document issued by the Department of Trade and Industry: *International Accounting Standards: A Consultation Document on the Possible Extension of the European Regulation on International Accounting Standards*, URN 02/1158 (30 August 2002), at pp. 35–6, paras. 7–11.

[35] See www.europa.eu.int/comm/internal_market/en/company/account/committ/contact/ index.htm.

[36] See Com. 95 (508), at para. 5.4 in which the Commission states: 'In order to ensure an appropriate European input into the continuing work of the IASC, the Contact Committee will examine and seek to establish an agreed position on future Exposure Drafts (or draft standards) published by the IASC. An agreed Union position on Exposure Drafts can thus be conveyed to the IASC.'

at which stage this is consulted. Indeed, the Commission, in 1995, noted the weakness of this Forum since 'in the absence of a clear mandate, the results of its work do not carry enough weight to exercise a real influence on accounting developments'.[37]

What it is possible to conclude is that the endorsement process comprises a rather messy arrangement. There are several committees involved, some more official than others, and with overlapping roles. It is not clear precisely who make up the committees. For example, who are the official representatives of the Member States in the Accounting Regulatory Committee?[38] The EFRAG members come from the private sector from bodies such as the Union des Confédérations de l'Industries et des Employeurs d'Europe (UNICE) and the Fédération des Experts Comptables Européens (FEE) but there is no indication that they must come from specified bodies and it claims also to operate independently of each of the European organisations involved.

The justification for the use of committees is acceptable when reference is made to the principles of subsidiarity and proportionality but the usual criticisms of the committee process can also be levelled against the arrangements that are apparent in the field of financial reporting. Gráinne de Búrca set out the better-known criticisms in her essay in the edited collection *The Evolution of EU Law*.[39] She included lack of transparency; the complexity and opaque nature of the system; the marginalisation of the European Parliament leading to claims of democratic deficit; and the haphazard nature of the process. All of these criticisms are valid in the example of committee usage within the field of financial reporting. Indeed, with so many committees involved the arrangement arguably distances the European Parliament even further as well as the companies and investors who are directly affected by the regulations that emerge from the process. On the other hand Zeff expresses concern about the possibility of political lobbying at EC level through use of EFRAG, the Technical Expert Group and the Accounting Regulatory Committee by European multinationals to avoid competitive disadvantage gained by companies applying US GAAP. Members of Congress have similar experience in the US of self-interested lobbying by companies and governments.[40]

---

[37] *Ibid.*
[38] This is a common question raised about the so-called official representatives within the committee process: see for example, De Búrca below.
[39] Gráinne de Búrca, 'The Institutional Development of the EU: A Constitutional Analysis' in Paul Craig and Gráinne de Búrca (eds.), *The Evolution of EU Law* (Oxford University Press, Oxford, 1999) pp. 55–81, esp. at pp. 71–5.
[40] Stephen A. Zeff, 'US GAAP confronts the IASB: Roles of the SEC and the European Commission' (2003) 28 *North Carolina Journal of International Law and Commercial Regulation* 879.

Role of the IASB

The role of the IASB is fundamental to the effectiveness of international regulation of financial accounting and reporting. Yet this body is also open to criticism. First, there is evidence that the IASB is open to lobbying which can stand in the way of a democratic result.[41] Indeed, it has been suggested that Sir David Tweedie, chairman of the IASB, 'underestimated the potential for political interference once businesses started lobbying'. The potential for lobbying has been demonstrated by reactions to the IAS 39 concerned with showing the impact of derivatives on accounts. Lobbying, in particular from French banks, forced the European Parliament to allow carve-outs and exemptions, with the result that 'the ability to compare companies across borders has been diluted and a dangerous precedent has been set that political pressure can force changes to standards that are supposed to be set independently'.[42] The potential result is that, as Scholte observes, the IASB has no provisions for public participation or consultation.[43] Currently the European Commission has an observer role with the IASB and EFRAG seeks to influence its decisions by submitting opinions on exposure drafts and consultations but none of this gives a clear formal role to the EU in the decision-making process leading to the eventual standards created. The membership of the IASB is based on technical expertise[44] and its own Constitution states specifically that selection of members shall not be based on geographical representation.[45] The role of the IASB's members is 'to act in the public interest and to have regard to the IASB framework'.[46] A small – albeit geographically wide – number of jurisdictions has dominated the IASB since its beginnings. In 1973 the IASC was founded as a result of an agreement by the accounting bodies in Australia, Canada, France, Germany, Japan, Mexico, the Netherlands, the United Kingdom and Ireland and the United States of America. Today, based in London, the Board members come from nine countries.[47] According to Fuller, eight board members come from

[41] See Stephen A. Zeff, '"Political" Lobbying of Proposed Standards: A Challenge to the IASB', *Accounting Horizons*, Vol. 16, March 2002. Zeff notes a campaign by US industry to oppose any attempt by the IASB to develop a standard on employee stock options that goes further than the disclosure requirement in the FASB statement no. 123.

[42] Jane Fuller, 'Setting the standard: does Europe's accounts overhaul add up for business?' *Financial Times*, 23 November 2004, 17.

[43] See J. A. Scholte, 'Civil Society and Democracy in Global Governance', CSGR working paper N-65/01, available at www.warwick.ac.uk/fac/soc/CSGR/wpapers/wp6501.pdf, at p. 16.

[44] IASC Constitution, para. 20.

[45] IASC Constitution, para. 21.

[46] IASC Constitution, para. 24.

[47] See www.iasc.org.uk/cmt.

Britain or North America, and one each from Australia and South Africa, countries that also have Anglo-Saxon accounting traditions. There is one board member from Japan and three from the rest of Europe. This shows an imbalance of representation in the IASB, especially considering the fact that more than 90 countries require or permit the use of IFRS since 2005.[48] Additionally, the IASB has been accused of not consulting widely enough in Europe and taking insufficient account of differing national practices.[49]

International Financial Reporting Standards

In its *Preface to International Financial Reporting Standards*[50] the IASB sets out its objectives. These are: to develop, in the public interest, a single set of high quality, understandable and enforceable global accounting standards that require high quality, transparent and comparable information in financial statements and other financial reporting to help participants in the world's capital markets and other users make economic decisions; to promote the use and rigorous application of those standards; and to work actively with national standard-setters to bring about convergence of national accounting standards and IFRS to high quality solutions.

The Preface also sets out the scope of International Financial Reporting Standards (IFRS), due process for developing IFRS and Interpretations, and policies on effective dates, format, and language for IFRS. The due process steps for a Standard will involve consultation with an advisory group, as well as invitations to the public to comment. Field tests and meetings are also open to public observation. Similarly, due process for interpretations involves studies of national standards and practices, as well as invitations to comment and public meetings.

IAS 1 is concerned with presentation of financial statements and prescribes the basis for presentation of general purpose financial statements, to ensure comparability both with the entity's financial statements of previous periods and with the financial statements of other entities. Under IAS 1 a complete set of financial statements comprises a balance sheet; an income statement; a statement of changes in equity; a cash flow statement; and notes, comprising a summary of significant accounting policies and other explanatory notes. Financial statements present fairly the financial position, financial performance and cash flows of an entity. Fair presentation requires faithful representation of the effects of

---

[48] Fuller, at p. 17.   [49] Fuller, at p. 17.
[50] Available at www.iasc.org.uk.

transactions, events and conditions in accordance with the definitions and recognition criteria for assets, liabilities, income and expenses set out in the Framework for the Preparation and Presentation of Financial Statements. The application of IFRSs, with additional disclosure when necessary, is presumed to result in financial statements that achieve a fair presentation. An entity makes an explicit and unreserved statement of compliance with IFRSs in the notes to the financial statements. Such a statement is only made on compliance with all the requirements of IFRSs. A departure from IFRSs is acceptable only where compliance with IFRSs conflicts with providing information useful to users in making economic decisions.

IAS 1 specifies the following about the preparation and presentation of financial statements. Financial statements are prepared on a going-concern basis unless management either intends to liquidate the entity or to cease trading, or has no realistic alternative but to do so. Financial statements, except for cash flow information, are prepared using the accrual basis of accounting. The presentation and classification of items in the financial statements are usually retained from one period to the next. Each material class of similar items is presented separately. Dissimilar items are presented separately unless they are immaterial. Omissions or misstatements of items are material if they could, individually or collectively, influence the economic decisions of users taken on the basis of the financial statements. Assets and liabilities, and income and expenses, are not offset unless required or permitted by an IFRS. Comparative information is disclosed for all amounts reported in the financial statements, unless an IFRS requires or permits otherwise. Financial statements are presented at least annually.

IFRS 1 covers first-time adoption of international financial reporting standards and provides guidance on how companies should implement IFRS.

The Framework for the Preparation and Presentation of Financial Statements was adopted by the IASB in April 2001. The Framework focuses on financial statements that are prepared for the purpose of providing information that is useful in making economic decisions:

The Board of the IASC believes that financial statements prepared for this purpose meet the common needs of most users. This is because nearly all users are making economic decisions, for example, to:

a. decide when to buy, hold or sell an equity investment;
b. assess the stewardship or accountability of management;
c. assess the ability of the enterprise to pay and provide other benefits to its employees;

d. assess the security for amounts lent to the enterprise;
e. determine taxation policies;
f. determine distributable profits and dividends;
g. prepare and use national income statistics; or
h. regulate the activities of enterprises

The Framework emphasises the wide range of users but suggests they have a common interest in economic information: present and potential investors, employees, lenders, suppliers and other trade creditors, customers, governments and their agencies and the public.

Observers note that the new accounting regime with the introduction of the IFRS 'is now horrendously complex; it is now as if the rules are designed for financial regulators rather than investors'.[51] For example, early difficulties with 'confusion and volatile share price' were predicted. It was also stated that investors would be 'likely to struggle for a while deciphering what is pure accounting noise versus new information relevant for valuation purposes'.[52] 'Hard work will be needed in distinguishing, particularly at first, between what is accounting-induced [artificial] volatility and what is genuine information about economic volatility.'[53]

Other problems arise from potential language difficulties. The IASB operates and publishes its standards in English, but there are approved translations in several languages. The IASB uses a mixture of UK and US terms even though technically UK and US terms are 'extensively different'. As is shown by Alexander Britton and Jorrisen:

UK	US	IASB
Stock	Inventory	Inventory
Shares	Stock	Shares
Own shares	Treasury stock	Treasury shares
Debtors	Receivables	Receivables
Creditors	Payables	Payables
Finance lease	Capital lease	Finance lease
Turnover	Sales (or revenue)	Sales (or revenue)
Acquisition	Purchase	Acquisition
Merger	Pooling of interests	Uniting of interests
Fixed assets	Non-current assets	Non-current assets
Profit and loss	Income statement	Income statement

(Source: Alexander, Britton and Jorissen, at p. 18.)

---

[51] Nils Pratley, 'Fears over new "fair value" accounts', *The Guardian*, 3 January 2005, 18.
[52] *Ibid.*, quoting Jeanot Blanchet of Morgan Stanley.
[53] *Ibid.*

Implementation

In the UK the IAS have been adopted under the Companies Act 1985 (Amendment of Accounting Rules and IAS) Regulations 2004.[54] These Regulations amend sections 226 and 227 of the 1985 Act. Companies must now present accounts according to section 226A and consolidated accounts according to section 227A or according to IAS. Schedule 2 of the Regulations alter Schedule 4 of the Companies Act 1985 on the form and content of company accounts to reflect the changes introduced by adoption of the IAS and the Modernisation Directive. The DTI has decided to extend the use of IAS to single plcs and other companies and LLPs if they wish to use them. A review of the impact of the Regulation will be conducted around 2008 and the DTI will then decide if the time is right to move to mandatory use of IAS.

The process is one of a gradual development towards universal application of IFRS. This is illustrated by the response of the ICAEW to the DTI's consultation.[55] The ICAEW stated that unlisted companies require time to prepare for a radical change in accounting. In response to the international standards the ASB will converge UK accounting standards as closely as possible with the IAS. The ASB's programme of convergence is likely to mean that in the near future UK standards will be almost identical to IASB standards. The decision of a reporting entity at that stage to migrate from UK GAAP to IAS would not involve substantial changes to its financial statements. The ICAEW advocates a principles-based approach and also a continued and constructive dialogue between the ASB and the IASB that will allow UK views and experience to carry weight in the new financial reporting framework.

US standards come closer

The European Commission made a positive choice of the IASB's standards in preference to the Generally Accepted Accounting Principles in the United States of America. Primarily this was because the international accounting standards of the IASB are drawn up with an international perspective rather than being tailored to the US environment. Additionally, the US GAAP are very detailed and technically demanding. Furthermore, the EU has no influence on the elaboration of US GAAP. In any event, the recent Memorandum of Agreement between the IASB and the US Financial Accounting Standards Board

---

[54] SI 2004/2947.   [55] See Tech. 29/02.

to achieve real convergence between their respective accounting standards[56] will bring the US GAAP closer to the EU and its Member States and the companies operating within the EU. The external reach of the Sarbanes Oxley Act 2002 also requires knowledge of the US GAAP by those companies trading on US exchanges.

Conclusion

It remains to be seen to what extent international standards will affect company financial reports in the UK. Recent indications suggest that international financial reporting standards will have an impact, not least on the ability of companies to pay dividends to their shareholders. For example, British Airways was recently reported to have claimed that recognising its £1.4 billion pension fund deficit on the balance sheet to meet international financial reporting standards would push its distributable reserves down to minus £100 million, thereby taking away the company's right to pay a dividend.[57] This report suggests that IFRS are indeed having an impact on the presentation of earnings figures. They could also affect tax liabilities, borrowing agreements, use of financial instruments and stock market valuations.[58]

The new international standards raise questions of accountability of the standard-setters, particularly since what originated as technical changes have become increasingly political measures,[59] in which the International Accounting Standards Board is subject to political pressure.[60]

One could argue that the implementation of these standards adds yet another layer to an already complex financial reporting and accounting system. However, their existence is necessary as an aid to cross-border trade and steps to converge with the US GAAP will also mean that companies are not forced to reconcile their accounts when trading in the US. However, since the IFRS have been framed in general terms this may lead to varied interpretations and standard-setters in different countries may each issue their own interpretive rulings. Over time this

---

[56] See the announcement at www.iasc.org.uk/cmt/ 0001.asp. 29 October 2002.
[57] Barney Jopson, 'Stringent rules now squeeze shareholders', *Financial Times*, 9/10 July 2005, at p. M3.
[58] Barney Jopson, 'Mid-cap groups at risk from IFRS', *Financial Times*, 9/10 July 2005, at p. M3.
[59] Deborah Hargreaves and Henry Tricks, 'New accounting rules raise questions of accountability', *Financial Times*, 9 December 2004, at p. 20.
[60] Henry Tricks and Deborah Hargreaves, 'Accounting watchdog sees trouble', *Financial Times*, 10 November 2004.

would lead to a fragmentation of the single standard.[61] The standards also operate on the same principles with which the UK accounting environment is familiar, such as reliability, relevance, comparability and understandability of accounts. Notably also, the standards emphasise the assumed common economic decision-making interests of investors and other potential users.

---

[61] Robert E. Litan, *et al, The Enron Failure and the State of Corporate Disclosure* (The Brookings Institute, Washington DC, 2002) extract from book, available at www.brookings.edu.

8 Disclosure in securities markets regulation

Introduction

Disclosure has recently been described as 'a powerful tool' for market efficiency and investor protection.[1] Indeed, disclosure requirements form a key regulatory device in the securities markets. Theoretically at least, as was noted in chapter 1, disclosure regulation serves to prevent fraud and to protect investors by allowing them to make informed decisions. This protection increases investor confidence and lays the foundations for a more efficient capital market. At the same time European Union efforts to create a fully integrated capital market have depended on the development of a harmonised regime of minimum disclosure requirements coupled with a policy of mutual recognition. The legislation created at European level has also played a large role in shaping the UK's regulation of financial services and securities markets. Intervention by government and public bodies in this area, resulting in a complex and detailed regulatory framework, has led one observer to note a shift away from company law and private law into a public law of securities regulation.[2] Thus, whilst arguably this chapter is not concerned with company law in its purest sense, its relevance arises, first, from the fact that much of the theoretical debate on disclosure has arisen in the context of securities regulation and, secondly, because trading in securities is an important activity for those companies wishing to raise capital from the public.

This chapter will consider briefly the objectives of disclosure in the area of securities markets. The current disclosure rules operating in the UK will then be considered by reference to the previous generation of European Directives. This will be followed by a discussion of the Financial Services Action Plan and the Lamfalussy Process and how these are

---

[1] Niamh Moloney, 'Time to take stock on the markets: the financial services action plan concludes as the company law action plan rolls out' (2004) 53 *ICLQ*, 999–1023, at p. 1002.
[2] Ben Pettet, *Company Law* (2nd edn, Pearson, London, 2005), at pp. 313–14.

likely to influence securities regulation in the UK. The impact of developments in the US will also be considered. The chapter will explore the role and potential effectiveness of the disclosure regime in this context before concluding.

Reasons for mandatory disclosure in the securities markets

Many of the theoretical arguments surrounding disclosure that were outlined in the first chapter of this book were developed within the context of regulation of the securities markets. In short, disclosure aims to address the problems of information asymmetry between issuers and investors. According to Lannoo, the combination of information asymmetry and managerial misappropriation demands that statutory disclosure regulation 'can facilitate more informed investment decision-making by differentiating between efficient and inefficient firms if the markets fail to do so'. Good performing firms will be distinguished from bad performing firms and this, in turn, 'prevents resources ending up in the "lemons" market where good and bad performing firms on average get the same pricing'.[3] A sufficient amount of credible information must be provided and issuers must receive a correct price for their securities.[4]

This allocative efficiency should result from a combination of the ability of an effective disclosure regime to prevent fraud and protect investors by giving them sufficient information to make informed decisions. Whilst an efficient capital market might not, theoretically, require control of available information because securities prices in such a market reflect all available information and adjust quickly in response to new information, it might also be argued that an unregulated market would not provide sufficient information for the efficient pricing of securities. A more general view is arguably that investor protection induces investor confidence in the capital markets and encourages participation in such markets. Disclosure regulation might also provide the fairness and transparency required for market integrity. Kraakman provides a summary of the reasons for a mandatory disclosure regime by highlighting the deficiencies of a voluntary disclosure framework. First, the agency problem between shareholders and corporate insiders creates disincentives for dissemination of bad news. Managers will be tempted

---

[3] Karel Lannoo, 'The Emerging Framework for Disclosure in the EU' (2003) 3 *JCLS* 329–58, at p. 332 and referring also to G. Akerlof, 'The Market for "Lemons": Quality, Uncertainty and the Market Mechanism' (1970) 90 *Quarterly Journal of Economics* 629.
[4] *Ibid.*

to misrepresent the company's finances and shareholders will not wish to reduce the value of their shareholdings with the release of bad news. Secondly, mandatory disclosure could avoid the problem of bonding agreements that do not guarantee the credibility of information provided. Thirdly, a voluntary regime does not necessarily address the disincentives to provide information such as the private costs incurred in disclosure and the problem of releasing sensitive information to competitors and hostile acquirers. Fourthly, a voluntary framework leads to less valuable information because it is not standardised and therefore is unlikely to be either comprehensive or comparable.[5]

Within the European Union there has been an increasing level of support for disclosure as a regulatory technique in company law generally. For example, the High Level Group of Company Law Experts claimed recently that disclosure may be more efficient than substantive regulation through more or less detailed rules. It creates a lighter regulatory environment and allows for greater flexibility and adaptability.[6] In the securities markets such attributes give disclosure a potential advantage over more substantive attempts to create a deeper and more integrated capital market. Reference to disclosure makes possible harmonisation and standardisation with mutual recognition. The European developments have also shaped securities regulation in the UK during the last two decades to the extent that current securities law in the UK is largely designed to implement the European Directives relevant in this area.

Disclosure requirements in the securities market in the UK

Mandatory disclosure has long been accepted as an appropriate method of regulating the securities markets in the UK. Indeed, disclosure was a key basis of the Gladstone reforms of company law in 1844 and 1845. The Companies Act 1844, for example, introduced a requirement for registration of a prospectus when shares were issued to the public.[7]

---

[5] Reinier Kraakman, 'Disclosure and Corporate Governance: An Overview Essay' in Guido Ferrarini, et al (eds.), *Reforming Company and Takeover Law in Europe* (OUP, Oxford, 2004), 95–113, at pp. 99–101. For a comprehensive summary of the debate on mandatory versus voluntary disclosure, see Hanno Merkt, 'Disclosing Disclosure: Europe's Winding Road to Competitive Standards of Publication of Company-Related Information' in the same volume, 115–44.

[6] *Report of the High Level Group of Company Law Experts on a Modern Regulatory Framework for Company Law in Europe*, Brussels, 4 November 2002, at p. 34.

[7] Joint Stock Companies Act 1844, s. 4.

Public issues of securities continued to be regulated by the companies legislation until the 1980s when it became necessary to implement three EC directives on listed securities. The regulations that transposed those directives into UK law disapplied the provisions in the companies legislation relating to listed securities, although unlisted securities were still governed by Part IV of the Companies Act 1985. At the same time as this process of implementation of the EC Directives the DTI had embarked upon a fundamental review of securities law.[8] This led to the creation of a comprehensive system of securities regulation under the Financial Services Act 1986. This Act was intended to support a largely self-regulatory system, introducing the Securities and Investments Board ('SIB') to oversee the carrying on of investment business in the UK. A two-tier system developed in which the SIB effectively regulated the self-regulatory organisations that were themselves intended to regulate certain sectors of financial services. By the mid-1990s there were new calls for change to this two-tier system of regulation which would widen the scope of the powers of the regulatory authority and reduce the self-regulatory emphasis. The SIB changed its name to the Financial Services Authority and amalgamated with the self-regulatory organisations. The Financial Services Authority was then given statutory functions in the Financial Services and Markets Act 2000 which altered securities regulation by directing it away from the private law domain of company law towards a state-controlled area that requires the Financial Services Authority, as the UK's financial regulator, to be subject to checks and balances.[9]

The objectives of securities regulation are set out in the Financial Services and Markets Act 2000. These include market confidence, public awareness, protection of consumers and reduction of financial crime. More specifically with regard to the public awareness and consumer protection objectives, provision of information is clearly relevant. Indeed, public awareness is described in the Act as 'promoting public understanding of the financial system' and includes '(a) promoting awareness of the benefits and risks associated with different kinds of investment or other financial dealing; and (b) the provision of appropriate information and advice'.[10] In providing protection for consumers the Act refers the Financial Services Authority to 'the needs that consumers may have for advice and accurate information'.[11] The Financial Services

---

[8] Professor L.C.B. Gower, *Review of Investor Protection* (Cmnd. 9125) 1984.

[9] See Pettet, *Company Law*, for an account of the development of securities regulation in the UK, ch. 17.

[10] FSMA 2000, s. 2(2)(b).   [11] *Ibid.*, s. 5(2)(c).

and Markets Act 2000, having set out these objectives for securities regulation, provides the framework for publicity relating to listed and unlisted securities.[12]

Section 79 of the Financial Services and Markets Act 2000 sets out the principle that where an offer of securities is made to the public for the first time prior to their admission to the Official List a prospectus must be produced and published. The Financial Services Authority is given power to require a prospectus as a condition of admission to listing. Detailed requirements concerning the contents of the prospectus are contained in Chapters 5 and 6 of the Listing Rules. Currently, the contents are largely determined by the Listing Particulars Directive[13] as consolidated in the Consolidated Admissions and Reporting Directive,[14] and in accordance with Article 7 of the Public Offers Directive.[15] The new Prospectus Directive[16] will regulate the contents of listing particulars when it is implemented. The contents required for listing particulars or for a prospectus are virtually identical. The difference between the two types of document becomes apparent with regard to potential liability for inaccurate or incomplete information. In both cases the issuer, directors, any person who accepts responsibility, and any person who has authorised its contents face potential liability. With regard to a prospectus, an offeror may also be held liable even if had no control over the preparation of the prospectus, such as an employee.

The overriding duty when preparing a prospectus or listing particulars is that of disclosure. Thus under sections 80 and 84 of the Financial Services and Markets Act 2000 (FSMA 2000), the listing particulars or the prospectus must contain 'all such information' as investors and their professional advisers would reasonably require, and would reasonably expect to find there, for the purpose of making an informed assessment of the assets and liabilities and the rights attached to the securities involved in the issue. The information required is whatever is within the knowledge of the person responsible for the prospectus or listing

---

[12] See in particular, Part VI, ss. 72–103, which now contain the relevant sections for listed and unlisted securities publicity, and Schs. 9 and 11.

[13] Directive co-ordinating the requirements for the drawing up, scrutiny and distribution of the listing particulars to be published for the admission of securities to official stock exchange listing (80/390/EEC) OJ L 100, 17.4.1980, p. 1.

[14] Directive 2001/34/EC on the admission of securities to official stock exchange listing and on information to be published on those securities, OJ L 184, 06.7.2001, p. 1.

[15] Council Directive co-ordinating the requirements for the drawing up, scrutiny and distribution of the prospectus to be published when transferable securities are offered to the public (89/298/EEC) OJ l 124, 5.5.1989, p. 8.

[16] Directive on the Prospectus to be published when securities are offered to the public or admitted to trading 2003/71/EC, OJ L 345, 31.12.2003, p. 64.

particulars or such knowledge as it would be reasonable to expect to find by making inquiries. Regard must also be had to the following factors: the nature of the securities and of the issuer, the nature of the persons likely to consider their acquisition; the fact that certain matters may reasonably be expected to be within the knowledge of professional advisers which potential investors might be expected to consult. The FSA may exempt information that would be contrary to the public interest or seriously detrimental to the issuer.[17] A supplementary prospectus or particulars must be issued before the commencement of dealings (i.e., after their admission to the Official List) if a significant change or a significant new matter has emerged.[18] The FSA carries out a vetting role so that documents must be submitted to the FSA in draft for formal approval prior to publication.[19] The prospectus or listing particulars must be filed with the companies registrar on or before the date of publication.[20]

Unlisted securities are regulated by the Public Offers of Securities Regulations 1995[21] which implement the Public Offers Directive. Regulation 4 provides that when securities are offered to the public in the UK for the first time the offeror shall publish a prospectus by making it available to the public, free of charge, at an address in the UK, from the time he first offers the securities until the end of the period during which the offer remains open. The Regulations may apply to companies and large investors offering their shareholdings if the offer is significant enough to constitute an offer to the public. The prospectus must be filed with the registrar but there are no vetting provisions. Schedule 1 of the Regulations sets out the requirements relating to the form and content of the prospectus: information relating to the issuer and its capital, financial position, activities and organisation, the offeror, the persons responsible for the prospectus, the securities and the offer. The information must be presented in as easily analysable and comprehensible form as possible. Within the Regulation there is an overriding duty of disclosure similar to that in section 80 of the FSMA 2000. Thus under Regulation 9 a prospectus relating to unlisted securities must contain all such information as investors would reasonably require and reasonably expect to find there, for the purpose of making an informed assessment of the assets and liabilities, financial position, profits and losses and prospects of the issuer and of the rights attaching to the securities. Regard must be had to the nature of the securities and of the issuer. The requirement is to disclose only information within the knowledge of the persons responsible for the

---

[17] Section 82, FSMA 2000.   [18] Section 81, FSMA 2000.
[19] Section 75, FSMA 2000.   [20] Section 83, FSMA 2000.
[21] SI 1995/1537.

prospectus or which it would be reasonable for them to obtain by making enquiries. It is possible for secondary prospectuses to be published without the necessity to create a whole new prospectus if more than one offering is made in a year. This must be accompanied by the earlier prospectus.

A new Prospectuses Directive will regulate this area when implemented in the near future. This specifies that if significant changes occur or there is a significant inaccuracy in the prospectus one or more supplementary prospectuses may have to be published and any such prospectuses would also have to be delivered to the registrar.

Mutual recognition provisions

Mutual recognition provisions allow for securities to be offered or admitted to listing on the basis of a prospectus or set of listing particulars which has satisfied the requirements imposed by one of the Member States and act as a passport for the offering or listing of securities in other Member States.[22] Implementation of the new Prospectus Directive will result in changes to the provisions of Schedule 4 as the Directive will, in most circumstances, require the FSA to recognise prospectuses or listing particulars approved in other Member States and remove the power to require additional information in the document. Section 87 of the FSMA 2000 makes provision for the submission to and approval of the FSA of prospectuses relating to unlisted securities.

Developments under the European Financial Services Action Plan 1999

A major influence on the development of the UK provisions described above was the attempt at European level to create a single market and, in particular, a deep and integrated capital market. Thus many of the UK's provisions sought to implement the Directives created at European level. The first Directives created at European level included: the Admissions Directive[23] which set out minimum conditions to be met by a company when seeking to get its securities admitted to listing on a stock exchange in a Member State; the Listing Particulars Directive[24] which laid down the

---

[22] See, for example, Art. 21 Public Offers Directive, arts. 38–40 of the Consolidated Admissions and Reporting Directive, Sch. 4 Public Offers of Securities Regulations.

[23] Directive co-ordinating the conditions for the admission of securities to official stock exchange listing (79/279/EEC) OJ L 66, 16.3.1979, p. 21.

[24] Directive co-ordinating the requirements for the drawing up, scrutiny and distribution of the listing particulars to be published for the admission of securities to official stock exchange listing (80/390/EEC) OJ L 100, 17.4.1980, p. 1.

requirements as to the contents and format of the listing particulars and the need for their approval by a competent authority; and the Interim Reports Directive[25] which laid down continuing disclosure obligations on issuers after securities were admitted to listing. These Directives were consolidated in the Consolidated Admissions and Reporting Directive (CARD)[26] in 2001. Public offers of unlisted securities were dealt with in the Prospectus Directive 1989.[27] This Directive laid down the requirements as to the content, scrutiny and distribution of prospectuses when transferable securities are offered to the public. Two mutual recognition Directives were adopted: in 1987[28] – amending the Listing Particulars Directive – and in 1990[29] to provide mutual recognition of prospectuses. Together, these Directives were intended to harmonise the disclosure requirements relating to public offers of listed and unlisted securities. Whilst the Directives did achieve a level of harmonisation and mutual recognition, the achievement of a truly European securities market was limited by obstacles such as language differences, investment cultures and tax barriers.[30] Indeed, Kraakman suggests that there was too low a degree of harmonisation,

which did not allow mutual recognition to work, bad enforcement of rules, and insufficient cooperation among authorities. More generally, the regulatory framework was unclear, complex and overlapping. It was a reflection of the low levels of development and a high degree of state-protection and fragmentation that characterised Europe's capital markets.[31]

In an attempt to improve its progress in 'ensuring a single market for wholesale financial services; developing open and secure retail markets; and implementing state-of-the art prudential rules and supervision to

---

[25] Directive on information to be published on a regular basis by companies the shares of which have been admitted to official stock exchange listing (82/121/EEC) OJ L 48, 20.2.1982, p. 26.

[26] Directive 2001/34/EC on the admission of securities to official stock exchange listing and on information to be published on those securities: OJ L 184, 06.7.2001, p. 1.

[27] Council Directive co-ordinating the requirements for the drawing up, scrutiny and distribution of the prospectus to be published when transferable securities are offered to the public (89/298/EEC) OJ l 124, 5.5.1989, p. 8.

[28] Directive 87/345/EEC amending Directive 80/390/EEC co-ordinating the requirement for the drawing up, scrutiny, and distribution of the listing particulars to be published for the admission of securities to official stock exchange listing: OJ L 185, 4.7.1987, p. 81.

[29] Directive 90/211/EEC amending Directive 89/298/EEC co-ordinating the requirements for the drawing up, scrutiny and distribution of the prospectus to be published when transferable securities are offered to the public: OJ L 112, 3.5.1990, p. 24.

[30] Brenda Hannigan, *Company Law* (LexisNexis, London, 2003) at p. 56.

[31] Kraakman, 'The Emerging Framework for Disclosure in the EU' (2003) 3 *JCLS* 329–58, at p. 38.

enhance the stability of the European Union's financial markets'[32] the European Commission adopted a Financial Services Action Plan on 11 May 1999.[33] The plan contained more than forty proposals which would include new Directives on securities regulation. The Action Plan has been assisted by the 'Lamfalussy Process' which was designed to accelerate the legislative process in order to make possible the realisation of the measures proposed. This was especially important given the 2005 deadline for completion of the measures laid down in the Action Plan.

The Lamfalussy Process was proposed by the 'Committee of Wise Men' chaired by Baron Alexandre Lamfalussy, who recognised that the legislative process was too slow, too detailed and too rigid, which had the effect of reducing the quality of the legislation.[34] The Committee found that there was insufficient consultation and transparency in the legislative process and that Directives could not be updated easily in order to accommodate market developments. In addition, Member States did not implement Directives sufficiently quickly, and the ambiguous character of many Directives meant also that they were implemented and applied differently. The Committee of Wise Men suggested a process designed to solve these problems, consisting of four separate levels. At Level 1 legislation would contain framework principles and power would be delegated to the Commission to define implementing measures. At Level 2 the Commission would adopt implementing measures following advice from the new European Securities Committee, and the new Committee of European Securities Regulators would also advise the Commission on the preparation of technical implementing measures. At Level 3 national regulators implement the legislation at national level and they may follow guidelines and common standards issued by the Committee of European Securities Regulators. Finally, at Level 4 enforcement of Community law would be strengthened by a requirement for the Commission to check Member State compliance with the legislation and to take legal action for failure to comply. At each level consultation is built into the process to aid transparency and ensure that the legislation is workable. Whilst criticisms might be made of the Lamfalussy process, such as its failure to deal with 'national

---

[32] Joe Coffee and Jonathan Overett Somnier, 'The Market Abuse Directive – The First Use of the Lamfalussy Process' (2003) 18 *Journal of International Banking Law and Regulation* 370–6, at p. 370.

[33] Commission of the European Union, *Financial Services: Implementing the Framework for Financial Markets: Action Plan*, Communication of the Commission COM (1999) 232.

[34] Committee of Wise Men, *Final Report of the Committee of Wise Men on the Regulation of European Capital Markets* (Lamfalussy Report, Brussels, 2001) available at http://europa.eu.int/comm/internal-market.

protectionism and bureaucratic inertia',[35] it has made a contribution to the development of new Directives concerning disclosure in the field of securities law, not least by making the process more transparent and leading to legislation which is more informed by encouraging dialogue between market participants, regulators and the EU institutions.[36]

Under the Financial Services Action Plan a number of Directives have been adopted or are being developed that will replace the older Directives relating to securities market disclosures. The most important of these include: the new Prospectus Directive, the Market Abuse Directive, the Transparency Directive and the Investment Services Directive.

The Prospectus Directive

The new Prospectus Directive[37] replaces the provisions in CARD deriving from the old Listing Particulars Directive and the old Prospectus Directive. This Directive came into force on 30 June 2005 and provides a framework applicable to securities offered to the public or admitted to listing on an official stock exchange. The Directive is designed to provide issuers with a passport prospectus that enables them to raise finance on competitive terms on an EU-wide basis by having their securities admitted to listing on a regulated market in other EU jurisdictions without having to obtain approval from the competent authority of those other jurisdictions and to provide investors and intermediaries with access to all markets from a single point of entry. Thus, as a maximum harmonisation Directive, it does not permit Member States to impose any super equivalent requirements and issuers are only permitted to omit information in very limited circumstances. The Directive sets out the initial information and disclosure requirements for issues of securities that are offered to the public or are admitted to trading on a regulated market in the EU. The Directive determines the content of the prospectus to be approved by a competent authority of the Member State. The Prospectus Directive applies to prospectuses for securities being admitted to trading on any regulated market in the UK including Virt-x and AIM.

---

[35] For an interesting description of the process and strong criticisms see Gérard Hertig and Ruben Lee, 'Four Predictions About the Future of EU Securities Regulation' (2003) 3 *JCLS* 359–77. See especially pp. 364–70.

[36] Michael McKee, 'The Unpredictable Future of European Securities Regulation: A Response to Four Predictions About the Future of EU Securities Regulation by Gerard Hertig and Ruben Lee' (2003) 18 *Journal of International Banking Law and Regulation* 277–83, especially at p. 283. See also John F. Mogg, 'Regulating Financial Services in Europe: A New Approach' (2002) 26 *Fordham International Law Journal* 58–82.

[37] Directive on the prospectus to be published when securities are offered to the public or admitted to trading 2003/71/EC, OJ L 345, 31.12.2003, p. 64.

The European Commission has, under Level 2 of the Lamfalussy Process, adopted a Regulation to implement the framework principles laid down in the Directive.[38] This Regulation provides details on the information to be given in prospectuses, the format and aspects of any such prospectus and the information to be incorporated by reference in the prospectus.

The Market Abuse Directive

The Directive on insider dealing and market manipulation[39] of 28 January 2003 came into force on 12 October 2004 and was the first to be implemented under the Lamfalussy Process.[40] The Directive is designed to ensure the integrity of EU financial markets, to establish common standards against market abuse throughout the EU and to enhance investor confidence in these markets. The Directive harmonises rules on insider dealing and market manipulation in securities markets. The Directive contains provisions relating *inter alia* to disclosures to be made by those producing and disseminating research and safe harbour provisions. Price-sensitive information must be released as soon as possible, and selective disclosure of price-sensitive information may be made to persons owing a duty of confidentiality, disclosure of dealings in own securities by persons with managerial responsibility; and issuers to maintain insider lists.

The Transparency Directive

The Transparency Directive[41] seeks to improve and harmonise disclosure requirements relating to issuers whose securities are admitted to

---

[38] Commission Regulation (EC) 809/2004 of 2 April 2004 implementing Directive 2003/71/EC of the European Parliament and of the Council as regards information contained in prospectuses as well as the format, incorporation by reference and publication of such prospectuses and dissemination of advertisements: OJ L 215, 16.6.2004, p. 3.

[39] Directive on insider dealing and market manipulation 2003/6/EC OJ L 96, 12.4.2003, p. 1.

[40] See EC Commission Mandate of 27 March 2002 and EC Commission Mandate of 31 January 2003 (MARKT/G2 D (2003)). Advice from CESR on Level 2 Implementing Measures for the proposed Market Abuse Directive (Ref: CESR/02.089d). This process led the Commission to adopt three separate measures for implementing the Directive: Commission Directive 2003/124/EC on defining and disclosing inside information and market abuse OJ 2003 L 339/70; Commission Directive 2003/125/EC on presentation of investment recommendations and disclosure of conflicts of interest OJ 2003 L 339/73; Commission Regulation (EC) 2273/2003 on exemptions for buy-back programmes and stabilisation of financial instruments OJ 2003 L 336/33.

[41] Directive on the harmonisation of transparency requirements in relation to information on issuers whose securities are admitted to trading on a regulated market 2004/109EC, OJ l 390, 31.12.2004, at p. 38.

listing with the objective of setting higher standards and increasing the frequency of disclosure. The Directive contains provisions regarding disclosure of significant holdings in public companies. The Directive contains rules on periodic financial reports and sets out the mechanism through which information is to be disseminated. Annual and half-yearly financial reports and interim financial statements for shares are required and an interim management statement must be provided unless the share issuer already provides quarterly reports. The Directive sets out the content of the information required and makes reference to inter-national accounting standards as the standard applicable for annual and half-yearly reports. Similar to the Prospectus Directive, the Transpar-ency Directive prohibits other Member States from imposing more stringent disclosure requirements on an issuer than those already im-posed in its home Member State. As a framework directive the Directive sets out general high-level obligations to be enforced by competent authorities in the Member States. The Directive seeks speedy, pan-European dissemination of regulated information. In favour of quarterly reporting it could be argued that it reduces information asymmetries and eases access to financial information since it gives to shareholders a more regular and standardised information flow.[42] It also reduces the oppor-tunities for insider trading by directors.[43] However, quarterly reports could be argued to favour a static model of disclosure whereas continu-ous disclosure would offer more to investors. Transparency covers how as well as what information is disclosed.

The success of the Transparency Directive depends on improving mechanisms to distribute information. According to a position paper published by the London Stock Exchange,[44] real-time electronic push distribution of news would be more beneficial than quarterly reports and the use of corporate websites which increase the costs of producing information and require investors to pull the information and actively search for it. One problem is that investors do not always know where to look for the information they need and there may be thousands of websites to consider. Mandating quarterly reporting is unlikely to deliver higher standards of disclosure. Relevant immediate disclosure is more likely to achieve greater transparency than periodic disclosures, whatever the intervals between them. A quarterly reporting requirement arguably shifts the focus from transparency and continuity, towards

---

[42] Lannoo, 'The Emerging Framework', at p. 348.
[43] Ibid.
[44] London Stock Exchange et al, *News Dissemination and the EU Transparency Directive* (October 2003), available at www.londonstockexchange.com.

greater emphasis on short-term performance. Such an approach, in the view of the London Stock Exchange, creates an incentive to save up bad news and release it through a periodic statement. This also implies that information is static rather than dynamic when in reality the information may be stale by the time it reaches the investor. The London Stock Exchange group argues that the requirements should concentrate on current disclosure by using modern technology. In this way, real-time electronic push reduces scope for market abuse and is more efficient and equitable since it entails dissemination to news agencies and investor websites. This may help to remove information asymmetries that disproportionately affect retail investors. Indeed, the Transparency Directive provides for Member States' authorities to publish filed information on their websites and to ensure timely access to disclosed information. Article 21 states that the issuer is required 'to use such media as may reasonably be relied upon for effective dissemination of information to the public throughout the Community'. This is interpreted by Lannoo to mean that the use of the internet for publishing significant corporate events becomes mandatory.[45] Effective electronic information dissemination may ensure a level playing field, encourage cross-border share trading, reduce scope for market abuse and harmonise access across the EU to company information.

The Directive on Markets and Financial Instruments

The Directive on Markets and Financial Instruments[46] replaces the Investment Services Directive 93/22/EEC regulating the authorisation, behaviour and conduct of business of securities firms and markets. The Directive carries forward the passport principle by enabling firms to carry on business in other Member States without further requirements being imposed on them by the regulatory authorities of those host states. The Directive aims to provide for an integrated securities market in the EU and for the cross-border provision of investment services, whilst enhancing the protection of investors and market integrity. The Directive will require operators of regulated markets to have effective arrangements in place to check that issuers whose securities are traded on regulated markets comply with their disclosure obligations in the Prospectus Directive, the Market Abuse Directive and the Transparency Directive.

---

[45] Lannoo, 'The Emerging Framework', at p. 347.
[46] Directive 2004/39/EC, OJ L 145, 21.4.2004, p. 1

These Directives provide some formidable challenges for the Member States, including the UK. The Treasury Department, together with the Financial Services Authority and the Bank of England, responded by publishing two documents concerned with implementing the Financial Services Action Plan and the UK's approach to the EU's future programme. The Financial Services Authority also commenced a review of the Listing Regime.

The UK authorities' response

The Treasury Department, the Financial Services Authority and the Bank of England published two documents in response to the EU's Financial Services Action Plan including its measures on securities regulation.[47] These documents highlight the challenge that the Financial Services Action Plan presents and discuss potential methods of implementing the Plan in an effective, proportionate and consistent manner. The document on strategy focuses, for the future, on considering better implementation and enforcement of EU measures affecting the financial sector, alternatives to EU regulation through use of competition policy, market-based solutions and initiatives at national level; better regulation in which cost and benefit assessments should be undertaken and financial market participants should be consulted; further development of the Lamfalussy arrangements; and recognition of the global nature of financial services, entailing adoption of a global perspective when considering the impact of EU financial services regulation on the competitiveness of EU-based firms and financial centres. Both documents advocate more open consultation and involvement of business and market participants and an integrated approach to the individual measures that recognises how they interact. The Financial Services Authority also embarked on a review of the listing regime as part of its response to the new regulatory framework initiated by the EU.[48] The aims of the review were to simplify and modernise the listing regime, to ensure the UK regime provides an appropriate level of regulation and the flexibility and transparency required by those wishing to raise capital in the London markets and to

---

[47] HM Treasury, Financial Services Authority and Bank of England, *The EU Financial Services Action Plan: Delivering the FSAP in the UK* (HMSO, London, May 2004); and *After the EU Financial Services Action Plan: A new strategic approach* (HMSO, London, May 2004).

[48] Financial Services Authority, *Review of the Listing Regime*, Consultation Paper CP203 and see further: *The Listing Review and Implementation of the Prospectus Directive*, Consultation Paper, CP04/16 which contains draft rules for implementing the Prospectus Directive and feedback on CP203.

accommodate EU regulatory changes. It appears from these responses that the regulatory framework for financial services in the UK needs to be made more flexible and transparent and capable of adapting to new measures adopted at EU level. A recognition of the European and global nature of financial services is also required and emphasis is given also to the need for consultation and participation of market participants in the regulatory process.

More specifically with regard to the disclosure requirements laid down in the European measures described above, changes are required in the UK. The Financial Services Authority has implemented the Prospectus Directive by, first, changing the structure of the rule book by dividing it into three parts comprising the Listing Rules, the Disclosure Rules and the Prospectus Rules. The restructure of the rule book is intended to reflect the wider role of the Financial Services Authority in the regulation of primary securities markets under the directives. The new rule book separates the rules derived from the directives and seeks to allow issuers of different securities types to identify clearly the rules applicable to them. Thus the Listing Rules contain rules and guidance for issuers of securities admitted or seeking admission to the Official List. The rules focus on eligibility for listing and the continuing obligations of listed issuers and sponsors. The Disclosure Rules contain rules and guidance relating to the publication and control of 'inside information' and the disclosure of transactions by persons discharging managerial responsibilities and their connected persons. The Prospectus Rules contain the rules, regulations and guidance outlining circumstances in which a prospectus is required and what that prospectus must contain.

The prospectus requirements, in accordance with the Directive, prescribe the contents and format of prospectuses; allowing incorporation by reference and for the use of three-part prospectuses; and they set out the exemptions from the requirement to produce prospectuses. The rules also include provisions relating to passport rights and procedures for approval as well as providing for a requirement for issuers to produce annual information updates and the setting up of a qualified investors register. Most of the detailed rules relating to the contents of prospectuses have already been prescribed by the Prospectus Directive and as a maximum harmonisation Directive the Financial Services Authority has little discretion in making the most of the rule changes. The Prospectus Directive did not require many fundamental changes to the previous rules except that the rules would be extended in scope to cover public offers of securities where no application has been made for admission to listing which were previously governed by the Public Offers of Securities Regulations 1995, and the new rules include the ability to passport prospectuses on a pan-European basis implemented through the introduction of the concept of home/host Member State. The implementation of the Transparency Directive will also require the Financial Services Authority to make revisions to the Listing Rules relating to continuing financial reporting; the disclosure of major shareholdings; information that issuers must provide to holders of their securities; and wider access to information about issuers and their securities.

The prescribed format and contents of the Prospectus following implementation of the Prospectus Directive and Regulation are detailed. Thus a prospectus must consist of three principal components either separately or combined in a single prospectus. These components are: a brief, non-technical summary conveying the essential characteristics and risks associated with the issuer, any guarantor and the securities; a registration document containing information about the issuer; and a securities note providing details of the securities to be offered or admitted to trading. This three-part format is designed to support the shelf-registration system introduced by the Directive. The prospectus relating to shares must include:

- details about risk factors, financial information, three years' accounts; unaudited half-year interim financial statements if the prospectus is dated more than nine months after the end of the last audited financial statements; an operating and financial review or Management's Discussion and Analysis section;
- issuer's capital resources and cash flow including a working capital statement; a description of significant change regarding the financial or trading position of the group since the last financial statements or negative statement; significant recent trends in production, sales and inventory, and costs and selling prices since the last financial year;
- information on known trends, uncertainties, demands or commitments or events that are likely to have a material effect on the issuer's prospects for the current financial year; statement of indebtedness within ninety days of the prospectus; independently audited financial data on any significant transactions; information on shareholders and management; details on members of the management, supervisory and administrative bodies; information on persons holding a notifiable share interest under national law; a description of direct or indirect control and measures taken against potential abuse; a description of the issuer's current principal investments and principal investments within the previous three years; a summary of material contracts entered into by the issuer or a group member in the previous two years outside the ordinary course of business;

- a description of any significant new factors, material mistakes or inaccuracy after the prospectus is approved and before the final closing of the offer to the public or when trading begins must be provided as a supplement to the prospectus.

Under the Transparency Directive the key feature regarding disclosure is the requirement for issuers with securities admitted to trading on a regulated market in any Member State to publish an annual financial report within four months of the end of each of its financial years. Issuers with shares or debt securities must publish half-yearly financial reports covering the first six months of its financial years within two months of the end of that period and issuers of shares admitted to trading on a regulated market will be obliged to publish interim management statements during the first six months and the second six months of its financial years if they do not already publish quarterly financial reports. Such information must be filed with the competent authority of the issuer's home Member State. The Transparency Directive is not a maximum harmonisation Directive and so differs from the Prospectus Directive in that it allows home Member States to lay down more stringent requirements than those laid down in the Directive. Such abilities are limited for a host Member State. The annual report must contain, according to the Directive, the issuer's audited financial statements, a management report and a responsibility statement by which the appropriate persons within the issuer expressly accept responsibility for the annual report.

These Directives are fundamentally concerned with protecting the integrity of the securities markets and protecting the investors. What is the position when a prospectus does not provide investors with correct information?

Remedies for false or misleading information

Part VI of the Financial Services and Markets Act 2000 provides statutory remedies for false or misleading information, failure to disclose the information required to be included in a prospectus or set of listing particulars, or failure to publish when required a supplementary prospectus or set of listing particulars. Under section 90 the person or persons responsible (the issuer or its directors) are liable to pay compensation to any person who has acquired any of the securities in question and suffered a loss in respect of them as a result of any untrue or misleading statement. If the person responsible can show that when the prospectus was submitted to the UK Listing Authority after having made reasonable inquiries, that he reasonably believed that the statement was true and was not misleading or that the omission was properly omitted, he will have a defence.[49] He must also show that he continued in the belief of the truth of the statement at the time when the securities were acquired by the investor. Other defences are also available within the Act such as being able to show that the statement was made by or on the authority of an expert[50] or where the defendant has published or tried to publish a correction.[51] If the person suffering the loss knew that the statement was inaccurate or that there was an omission that would cause such loss he will not be able to claim.[52]

It might be possible to raise a contractual claim against defective prospectuses or listing particulars in which case the claimant would argue for rescission of contract. However, generally, silence is not actionable unless it renders what is said to be false or misleading. The investor must also be able to show reliance on the information to claim rescission. It might alternatively be possible to seek compensation instead of or in addition to rescission. If an investor was induced to enter into a contract by false information he or she could sue in tort for deceit or for breach of duty of care and claim damages for negligence. In such circumstances who could make such a claim?

An investor who has acquired securities and suffered loss in respect of them as a result of an untrue or misleading statement contained in the prospectus or listing particulars relating to those securities or as a result of an omission of information required to be contained in that document may claim compensation. The initial subscribers or subsequent purchasers might also be able to claim if they can show that their loss results from the inaccuracies in or omissions from the prospectus or listing particulars. As time goes on market purchasers will find it increasingly difficult to argue convincingly that the price at which the shares are trading in the market is still distorted by the false information contained in a prospectus and a claim may fail on that ground. Indeed, a claim under the Misrepresentation Act 1967 must show a contractual nexus and is therefore limited to those who purchase the shares initially by way of allotment from the company or who purchase shares from an investment bank which has offered them to the public.

A claim for breach of a duty of care needs to show that the claimant was owed a duty of care. The claimant must therefore show that he or she was a member of the class intended by the maker of the statement to

---

[49] Financial Services and Markets Act 2000, s. 9 and see also Sch. 10.
[50] *Ibid.*, Sch. 10, para. 2.   [51] *Ibid.*, Sch. 10, para. 3.
[52] *Ibid.*, Sch. 10, para. 6.

be induced to act on the basis of the false statement. Thus in *Al Nakib Investments (Jersey) Ltd* v. *Longcroft*[53] an investor who acquired shares in the market could not rely on statements made in a rights issue since that statement was made to encourage shareholders to purchase shares of a subsidiary in a rights issue. The plaintiffs bought the shares on the market and so their purchase was not part of a rights issue. Mervyn Davies J stated that use of a prospectus for a purpose other than that for which it was intended would negate a duty of care for misstatements in that prospectus. The court applied *Caparo Industries* v. *Dickman*[54] to confirm that use of a prospectus for a purpose other than for the transaction intended would not incur a duty of care. In *Possfund Custodian Trustee Ltd* v. *Diamond/ Parr* v. *Diamond*[55] the plaintiffs bought shares on the basis of information in the prospectus in connection with a flotation at a substantial premium on the Unlisted Securities Market. The plaintiffs claimed that the prospectus materially misrepresented the company's financial position by substantially understating its liabilities and that the shares they bought were valueless. The plaintiffs sought to recover damages for negligence against the directors, auditors and financial advisers of the company. The defendants argued that there was no cause of action. However, the court held that the claim merited full consideration at trial since it was arguable that persons responsible for the issue of a prospectus owed a duty of care to purchasers in an aftermarket. The plaintiffs therefore needed to establish that the defendants had assumed such a duty to them either by express communication or by showing that it was reasonable for the plaintiff to rely on the material representation and that he believed the representor intended him to act upon it. Lightman J stated that the main question was whether it is arguable that those responsible for the issue of a company's prospectus owe a duty of care to subsequent purchasers of that company's shares in the market.

When examining the substantive issues relating to the application to strike out, Lightman J went through the history of the prospectus. In the nineteenth century the common law allowed a claim in damages to the investor who incurred a loss after investing in reliance on a false or misleading prospectus only if he could establish the tort of deceit.[56] The prospectus was an invitation issued to the public to subscribe for shares, and not to purchase shares in the market, and the prospectus could only incur liability if relied on for the purpose for which it was

---

[53] [1990] 1 WLR 1390, Ch. D.
[54] [1990] 2 AC 605, [1990] 1 All ER 568, [1990] 2 WLR 358, HL.
[55] [1996] 1 WLR 1351.   [56] *Derry* v. *Peek* (1889) 14 App Cases 337.

issued, namely the making of a decision whether to subscribe, and not if relied on for the purpose of deciding whether or not to make purchases in the market. Reference was made to *Peek* v. *Gurney*[57] in which it was expressed that the representations contained within the prospectus were exhausted upon the allotment being completed. Tracing the history, Lightman noted affidavit evidence from Kleinwort Benson Securities Ltd and Arthur Andersen that commercial practice today has changed the nature of the prospectus so that the established purpose of a prospectus and its contents were no longer confined to inducing investors to become placees, but extended to inducing the public to make aftermarket purchases.

Today, a prospectus is perceived as intended to be acted upon for the purposes of aftermarket purchases and that indeed is the intention of those who prepare and are responsible for them. Having established this, it then would be necessary to consider if there was an intention that the purchaser rely on the prospectus and whether the necessary proximity existed between those responsible for the prospectus and the purchaser. It would be necessary to establish objectively that such an intention existed. Such an intention would be established if the representor expressly communicates intent to the representee or that the representee reasonably relied on the representation and he reasonably believed that the representor intended him to act upon it. Lightman concluded that the starting point in determining the ambit of the duty of care in respect of a prospectus is the statutory purpose of the prospectus. But that is only the beginning: it is not necessarily also the end. It does not necessarily preclude a superadded purpose if a superadded purpose can be shown to exist. The plaintiffs would say the prospectus must be examined in the light of changed market practice and philosophy current at its date of preparation and circulation. If the plaintiffs claim that there has developed and been generally recognised an additional purpose, an additional perceived intention on the part of the issuer and other parties to a prospectus, namely to inform and encourage aftermarket purchasers, this would make arguable the case for a duty of care.

The point at which a prospectus becomes spent has perhaps been extended and left open as a result of judicial acceptance of established commercial practice. As is expressed by Doyle: 'the company and its directors will have every hope of further purchases on the secondary aftermarket since these will support the share price and therefore make it more likely that all rights will be taken up. Commercially speaking it is

---

[57] (1873) LR 6 HL 377.

very difficult to support any contrary view of the function of a public offer document.'[58] This version of reality might also be connected with the other commercial realities such as consumer power and professional indemnities. As Grier responds to his own question of whether these persons have an indeterminate liability to a potentially indeterminate number of claimants, he states that it is a question of consumer power: 'Nowadays the emphasis is on regulation and protection of the unwitting investor. It would be a foolhardy politician who said that investors should look after themselves and that it is not the government's job to provide a framework to protect investors. In any event, some or most of the responsible persons are likely to be backed by professional indemnities.'[59]

Conclusion

Securities regulation depends on disclosure as a facilitator of integrity in the capital markets. The increasing push for an integrated European capital market has led to a major overhaul of securities regulation centred upon the new European Directives that have just come into force or will have done so by the end of 2006. These Directives highlight the importance of disclosure and facilitate the 'synchronisation of information disclosure' in all Member States. Such a development may improve equality of treatment but this will also depend on treatment of prospectuses and market participants by the regulatory authorities in each of the Member States. One might question the apparent inconsistency of approach among the Directives in this respect, the Prospectus Directive being a maximum harmonisation Directive leaving very little discretion to the Member States and their authorities, contrasted with the Transparency Directive which is a minimum harmonisation Directive providing the possibility of different rules and 'super-equivalents'. Is it really possible for maximal harmonisation to co-exist with minimal harmonisation[60] since this could lead to contradictions in approach?

From a disclosure point of view the level of prescription regarding content and format seeks a balance between the possibility of distinguishing between different types of securities transactions and recognising their distinct features and making prospectuses reasonably comparable and understandable, especially for the growing number of retail investors.

---

[58] Louis Doyle, 'Change in the wind on common law defective-prospectus liability?'(1996) 17 *Co. Law* 279–81, at p. 280.
[59] Nicholas Grier, 'Watch out for share-pushers' (1998) 19 *Co. Law* 311–4, at p. 313.
[60] Lannoo, 'The Emerging Framework', at p. 346.

The Prospectus Directive and Regulation will arguably move prospectuses closer to the US style of disclosure requirements, resulting in a 'fairly stylized document, and there is a customary sequence for organizing the material'.[61] This does not necessarily mean that the document is of no value. Indeed it should provide the potential investor with a clear understanding of the business in which he or she might be dealing. Ultimately, as Schneider *et al* remark:

> The prospectus is a somewhat schizophrenic document, having two purposes which often present conflicting pulls. On the one hand, it is a selling document. It is used by the principal underwriters to form the underwriting syndicate and a dealer group, and by the underwriters and dealers to sell the securities to the public. From this point of view, it is desirable to present the best possible image. On the other hand, the prospectus is a disclosure document, an insurance policy against liability.[62]

This area of law, both in Europe and in the UK, has developed into a complex and sophisticated structure of investor protection based largely on the principle of transparency, procedurally and substantively. Procedurally, transparency is a key feature of the regulatory process. The Lamfalussy Process seeks to speed up legislative development but entails consultation with the market participants. Similarly, in the UK the FSA encourages participation by the business actors and those involved in the securities markets. This has the benefit of ironing out technical problems and making the legislation more acceptable to those covered by it.[63] Substantively, transparency is encouraged in the detailed disclosure requirements of issuers as a protection for those investing in their securities. As Lannoo has observed, disclosure may be a cost for issuers, but it would attract more investors.[64] Thus in principle these objectives are to be welcomed. However, in practice they do have problems. For example, the Lamfalussy Process may speed up legislation at Level 1 but at Levels 2 and 3 the consultation exercises lead to numerous documents and further Directives resulting in ambiguity and complexity that reduces the quality of the provisions.[65] The consultation stage also has insufficient

---

[61] Carl W. Schneider, Joseph M. Manko, and Robert S. Kant, 'Going Public: Practice, Procedure and Consequences' (1981) 27 *Villanova Law Review* 1–51, at p. 10.

[62] *Ibid.*, at p. 14.

[63] Burcak Inel, 'Assessing the First Two Years of the New Regulatory Framework for Financial Markets in Europe' (2003) 18 *Journal of International Banking Law and Regulation* 363–9, esp. at p. 368.

[64] Lannoo, 'The Emerging Framework', at p. 344.

[65] See e.g., Coffee and Somnier, esp. at pp. 375–6.

time with the feeling that consultation is rushed which can also damage faith in the quality of the legislation.[66]

Involvement of market participants is a key feature. The opportunity for business to influence the legislative framework is strong. The aim is to achieve a competitive and creditable pan-European securities market that can operate effectively in a globalised world with fast technology and with competition from the US and Asia. Transparency, disclosure, and participation are incentives to draw investors into the integrated capital markets. The general thrust of the recent Directives has been an attempt to balance protection of investors with reduction of regulatory and disclosure burdens. At this early stage it remains to be seen if that balance has been achieved.

[66] Burcak Inel, 'Assessing the First Two Years', at p. 368.

Part III

Narrative reporting

9   The Operating and Financial Review

Introduction

The Operating and Financial Review ('OFR') is one of the most controversial new developments in recent company law history in the UK. The
recent decision to scrap the Regulations before they gained practical effect
has now proved equally controversial, being greeted by a wave of opposition in the financial press.[1] This chapter will explore the regulations
had they continued to apply in the hope of highlighting their relevance to the general disclosure debate. The objective of this narrative
report is to provide a review of the company's activities with an
indication of its future potential. As is expressed by the Explanatory
Memorandum to the Regulations: 'The objective of the OFR is to
achieve good corporate governance by improving the quality, usefulness and relevance of information provided by quoted companies, thus
improving the understanding of the business and its prospects
and encouraging shareholders to exercise effective and responsible
control.'[2] Thus the OFR is a report 'setting out the principal drivers
of a company's performance both in the past and in the future'.[3]

According to the DTI, the OFR should 'cover the issues traditionally
seen as key to a company's performance – an account of its business,
objectives and strategy, a review of developments over the past year, and a
description of the main risks'.[4] The Government adds that the OFR 'will
also cover prospects for the future and, where necessary, information
about the environment, employees, customers or social and community

---

[1] See, for example, letter page in *Financial Times*, 29 November and 1 December 2005.
[2] Explanatory Memorandum to the Regulations for an Operating and Financial Review,
para. 7.3: the Companies Act 1985 (Operating and Financial Review and Directors
Report etc) Regulations 2005, SI 2005/1011.
[3] See Foreword by Patricia Hewitt, Secretary of State for Trade and Industry, in the
Consultation Document, *Draft Regulations on the Operating and Financial Review and
Directors' Report* (DTI, London, May 2004), available at www.dti.gov.uk/.
[4] *Ibid.*

issues where that information is important for an assessment of the company'.[5] The Government regarded this as 'a step change to the quality of reporting by companies'.[6] In this way the OFR might have been a major element of the transparency and accountability aspect of corporate governance contributing to improvements to the quality, timeliness and accessibility of information available for shareholders. The OFR should furnish shareholders with the information necessary for them to exercise effective control and informed influence over companies.

The OFR would have been a new statutory requirement for quoted companies while at the same time unquoted large and medium-sized companies are required to provide a narrative report in their Directors' Report that provides a 'fair review of the business of the company and its subsidiary undertakings'.[7] Small companies have no obligation to provide an OFR or an enhanced business review in their Directors' Report.

Development of the new statutory OFR

The proposal for the statutory OFR was rooted in a 1993 statement of best practice on the OFR published by the Accounting Standards Board. That statement provided a framework for a narrative report produced by directors covering the main factors underlying their company's performance and financial provisions. The statement was regarded as a positive development, giving rise to significant increases in the quality and the quantity of narrative reporting.[8]

The Company Law Review had recommended in its Final Report that 'companies with significant economic power' – UK companies over a certain size threshold – should be required to prepare and publish an OFR.[9] The Government supported this recommendation, adopting the view that companies should provide more qualitative and forward-looking reporting in addition to quantitative, historical or internally relevant information. The Government took forward the Company Law Review's recommendation in its White Paper *Modernising Company Law*[10] proposing the introduction of draft clauses for relevant companies to publish an OFR with the over-arching objective of providing 'a discussion and analysis of the business and the main trends and factors underlying

---

[5] *Ibid.*   [6] *Ibid.*
[7] New s. 234 Companies Act 1985, substituted by reg. 2.
[8] White Paper, *Modernising Company Law*, Cm. 5553 I and II, July 2002, para. 4.28, at p. 38.
[9] Company Law Review Steering Committee, *Modern Company Law for a Competitive Economy: Final Report* (July 2001), para. 8.57, at p. 189.
[10] White Paper, *Modernising Company Law*, Cm. 5553 I and II (July 2002).

the results and financial position and likely to affect performance in the future, so as to enable users to assess the strategies adopted by the business and the potential for successfully achieving them'.[11]

Following the White Paper, the Accounting Standards Board revised its 1993 statement of best practice in January 2003.[12] The original statement published by the ASB in 1993 was built on the foundations of existing best practice by providing a framework within which directors could discuss the main factors underlying the company's performance and financial position. The later version was designed to reflect subsequent improvements in narrative reporting.

In May 2004 the Government published draft regulations for the OFR, which proposed to insert a new section 234 AA into the existing Companies Act 1985. This section would form the basis of a statutory requirement for an OFR. The proposed section was accompanied by a new Schedule containing further details. The Government suggested that the Accounting Standards Board publish a new standard for the OFR, updating its statement and giving it more authoritative force. In addition the Government's Working Group on Materiality published guidance for directors on the materiality issue. This guidance was supplemented by further guidance published independently by the Institute of Chartered Accountants in England and Wales.

In November 2004 the Accounting Standards Board published a draft Exposure Document for a Reporting Standard for the Operating and Financial Review for consultation with the intention that the eventual standard would be an authoritative reporting requirement for the relevant companies. Regulations on the Operating and Financial Review became effective from 1 April 2005. The Accounting Standards Board published its definitive Reporting Standard in May 2005. These provisions were also partly shaped by requirements in the EU Accounts Modernisation Directive[13] which requires an enhanced review of a company's business in the directors' report to be prepared and published for financial years beginning on or after 1 January 2005. In particular, the Regulations implemented Articles 1.4, 1.17 (in part) and 2.10 of the Modernisation Directive which require all large and medium-sized companies to provide a statement of the development and

---

[11] *Ibid.*, see especially the discussion of cl. 73, para. 3, in Annex D, at p. 140.

[12] Note that a statement is intended to have persuasive rather than mandatory force and is not an accounting standard.

[13] Directive 2003/51/EC of the European Parliament and the Council of 18 June 2003 amending Directives 78/660/EEC, 83/349/EEC and 91/674/EEC on the annual and consolidated accounts of certain types of companies, banks and other financial institutions and insurance undertakings, OJ L178, 17.7.2003, p. 16.

performance of the business and an assessment of the principal risks and uncertainties.

Policy and theoretical basis for the OFR

The spirit envisaged by the ASB when it published its 1993 statement was not actually defined but could be deduced from what was said about its essential features. Weetman, for example, refers to a top-down structure, objective discussion, analysis and explanation of the main features of the company, and dynamics of operating activities and of financial position. The top-down structure provides for discussion of individual aspects of the business in the context of a discussion of the business as a whole. This should therefore provide the reader with an overview of the business. The balanced and objective discussion requires an even-handed treatment of both good and bad aspects of the business.[14] According to the Government in its White Paper, the OFR should provide more qualitative and forward-looking reporting, in addition to information that is quantitative, historical, or about internal company matters.

The business environment is being reshaped by various factors such as globalisation, more widespread share ownership, greater significance of intangible assets, more litigation and more emphasis on social responsibility.[15] This requires greater transparency and information in order for confidence to remain in the capital markets. In this context as described in the Explanatory Memorandum a narrative report would reflect the increasing importance of intangible assets such as skills and knowledge of employees, their business relationships and their reputation. Information about future plans, opportunities, risks and strategies would be as important as an historical review of performance. The Government also argues that directors need to consider the success of the company and should take into account relationships with employees, customers and suppliers and the company's impact on the wider community as well as the company's impact on the environment. The OFR should contain details of all these aspects where they are relevant to an assessment of the company's business. The Government considered that

---

[14] Pauline Weetman and Bill Collins, *Operating and Financial Review: Experiences and Exploration* (Edinburgh, Institute of Chartered Accountants of Scotland, 1996), at p. 3.
[15] See Final Regulatory Impact Assessment on the Operating and Financial Review and Directors' Report Regulations, Annex B to the Explanatory Memorandum, which provides the backdrop to the introduction of a statutory operating and financial review in paras. 18–20.

this approach would help to give members the information they require to hold directors to account and that such a reporting requirement would help a wider cross-section of a company's stakeholders. The OFR should be part of a balanced approach to the issue of the scope of company law.[16] It is an analysis and description of the business as an operational and commercial entity prepared by the directors from their perspective as managers of the business.[17] The Working Group Guidelines for directors state that the introduction of the mandatory OFR emphasises the need for directors to look at long-term as well as short-term issues and to take all the factors affecting the company's relationships appropriately into account. The need for directors to think and manage in this broader context, and to report accordingly, should help the company to perform better and bring substantial benefits to shareholders and all other stakeholders.

Regulatory structure

The regulatory structure for the new OFR highlights a tiered approach similar to the regulatory structure relevant to financial reporting. For example, the Companies Act 1985 provided for the basic obligation for quoted companies to provide an OFR and this was supplemented by a Schedule that outlined the main requirements. The Standard published by the ASB adds substance to the statutory provisions for the contents and principles behind the report. Paragraph 8 of the new Schedule 7ZA introduced by regulation 9 made clear that an OFR must comply with the ASB's standard since the review must 'state whether it has been prepared in accordance with relevant reporting standards', and must 'contain particulars of, and reasons for, any departure from such standards'. By complying with this standard, directors are presumed to have complied with the statutory requirements. Similarly, as was observed in the financial reporting chapter, compliance with accounting standards is necessary for financial statements to give a true and fair view. Additionally, directors of relevant companies are provided with implementation guidance which is not legally binding but which directors are advised to consult as a guide for complying with the statutory requirements.

Alongside these legislative provisions, standards and guidance, professional bodies such as the Institute of Chartered Accountants in England

---

[16] Department of Trade and Industry, *Modern Company Law for a Competitive Economy: Completing the Structure* (November 2000) (hereinafter 'DTI, November 2000') para. 3.9, at p. 36.
[17] DTI November 2000, para. 3.33, at p. 46.

and Wales published guidance such as the interim process guidance document *Preparing an Operating and Financial Review*.[18] The ICAEW guidance was intended to assist directors in their preparation of the OFR and the guidance set out good practice principles that directors may wish to follow.

Principles of the OFR

The Regulations and the Reporting Standard made clear the key principles underlying the OFR. The Regulations specified that the OFR would be a 'balanced and comprehensive analysis' of the development, performance and position of the business of the company and the main trends and factors underlying that development, performance and position as well as the main trends and factors that are likely to affect the future development, performance and position of the company's business. The analysis would be prepared so as to assist the members of the company to assess the company's strategies and the potential success of such strategies.[19]

The ASB Reporting Standard outlined the broad high level principles for the content of an OFR. The main principles are that: the OFR would set out an analysis of the business through the eyes of the directors; it would focus on matters that are relevant to the interest of the members; it would have a forward-looking orientation, identifying those trends and factors relevant to the members' assessment of the current and future performance of the business and the progress towards the achievement of long-term business objectives; it would complement as well as supplement the financial statements, in order to enhance the overall corporate disclosure; it would be comprehensive and understandable; it would be balanced and neutral, dealing even-handedly with both good and bad aspects; it would be comparable over time.[20] In summary, the main objective was that the OFR would be a balanced and comprehensive report by the directors that would enable the company's members to assess the current position and future prospects of the business.

Contents of the OFR

The Company Law Review recommended that all OFRs should contain the following three elements: the company's business and business

---

[18] Institute of Chartered Accountants in England and Wales, *Preparing an Operating and Financial Review: interim process guidance for UK directors* (January 2003).
[19] Schedule 7ZA.
[20] ASB Reporting Standard 1, Operating and Financial Review, May 2005, see paras. 5–26.

objectives, strategy and principal drivers of performance; a fair review of the development of the company's and/or group's business over the year and position at the end of it, including material post year-end events, operating performance and material changes; and the dynamics of the business – known events, trends, uncertainties and other factors which may substantially affect future performance, including investment programmes.[21] The main requirement in reporting on these elements would be to meet the objective of the OFR as described in the CLR *Final Report*, and following the *Developing The Framework* document. The objective was 'to provide a discussion and analysis of the performance of the business and the main trends and factors underlying the results and financial position and likely to affect performance in the future, so as to enable users to assess the strategies adopted by the business and the potential for successfully achieving them'.[22]

The Regulations provided for a new Schedule 7ZA on the objective and contents of the OFR. Paragraph 2 lays down the following mandatory content requirements:

The review must include-

a. a statement of the business, objectives and strategies of the company;
b. a description of the resources available to the company;
c. a description of the principal risks and uncertainties facing the company; and
d. a description of the capital structure, the treasury policies and objectives and the liquidity of the company.

The Schedule continued would have to by specifying other contents that would have to be included in the OFR in order to meet the objective and general content requirements. Thus to the extent necessary to meet such requirements the review, according to paragraph 4 must include:

a. information about environmental matters (including the impact of the business of the company on the environment),
b. information about the company's employees, and
c. information about social and community issues.

---

[21] Company Law Review Steering Group, *Modern Company Law for a Competitive Economy: Final Report* (Department of Trade and Industry, June 2001) para. 8.40, at pp. 182–4.

[22] Company Law Review Steering Group, *Modern Company Law for a Competitive Economy: Final Report* (Department of Trade and Industry, June 2001) para. 8.32, at p. 181. See also Company Law Review Steering Group, *Modern Company Law for a Competitive Economy: Developing the Framework* (DTI, March 2000) para. 5.7, at p. 182.

(2) The review would, in particular, include:

a. information about the policies of the company in each area mentioned in sub-paragraph (1), and
b. information about the extent to which those policies have been successfully implemented.

In accordance with paragraph 5, the review would also include:

a. information about persons with whom the company has contractual or other arrangements which are essential to the business of the company; and
b. information about receipts from, and returns to, members of the company in respect of shares held by them.

What appears from these two lists is that the mandatory contents focus upon the business itself and how it is being developed and is performing. The second list, however, is not compulsory but would have to be considered by the directors with regard to its necessity for enabling members of the company to assess the company's operations, financial position and future business strategies and prospects.

Paragraphs 6 and 7 specified that the OFR should include analysis that uses certain performance indicators and the OFR should refer to and explain the company's accounts:

6. (1) The review must include analysis using financial and, where appropriate, other key performance indicators, including information relating to environmental matters and employee matters.
(2) In sub-paragraph (1), 'key performance indicators' means factors by reference to which the development, performance or position of the business of the company can be measured effectively.
7. To the extent necessary to comply with the general requirements of paragraphs 1 and 2, the review must, where appropriate, include references to, and additional explanations of, amounts included in the company's annual accounts.

The ASB Reporting Standard also provided in its disclosure framework details of the contents required to meet the objective of the OFR. The main contents to be included covered: the nature, objectives and strategies of the business; the development and performance of the business, both in the period under review and the future; the resources, risks and uncertainties and relationships that may affect the entity's long-term value; and the position of the business including a description of the structure, treasury policies and objectives and liquidity of the entity, both in the period under review and the future. The ASB Reporting Standard also specified particular information that should be included, to the extent necessary to assist members to assess the strategies adopted by the company and the potential for those strategies to succeed. Such items included: market and competitive environment; regulatory environment; technological change; persons with whom the entity has relations, such as customers and suppliers; employees; environmental matters; social and community issues; receipts from, and returns to, shareholders; and all other relevant matters.

The ASB's Reporting Standard was more detailed than the schedule requirements on the matters to be included in order to meet the objective of enabling investors to make an informed assessment of the company's position. For example, the reporting standard included market and competitive environment, regulatory environment and technological change as potentially relevant to such an assessment by the investors. Environmental matters and employee relations were part of a longer list and whilst there was no suggestion that the list was hierarchical, the extension of the list of particular matters might be interpreted by some observers as watering down or reducing the degree of importance to be attributed to these specific issues.[23]

Despite earlier claims that the OFR would make reporting on non-financial matters mandatory for the first time, the reality was that only financially relevant matters appeared to be compulsory. The mandatory list provided in paragraph 2 of Schedule 7ZA was essentially financial. A statement of the business, objectives and strategies of the company, alongside a description of the resources available to the company; a description of the principal risks and uncertainties facing the company; and a description of the capital structure, the treasury policies and objectives and the liquidity of the company, make clear that the emphasis was on the financial viability of the company's business. The performance indicators identified in the Regulations were also primarily financial. Paragraphs 6 and 7 for example referred to financial and, 'where appropriate', other key performance indicators as well as a need to refer to the annual accounts. Thus 'where appropriate' means that the other possible performance indicators may be omitted if the directors so decide, though this appeared, from the wording of the draft legislation, not to be possible for the financial indicators. The possibility then was that the other matters and indicators, social, environmental, employee etc may be claimed by the directors not to have sufficient impact on the company and its prospects as to merit discussion in the OFR. As CORE suggested: 'This will result in a chaotic reporting environment, where

---

[23] See for example, Andrew Taylor, 'Kingsmill denies review diluted', *Financial Times*, 11 April 2005, at p. 4.

reports will vary hugely in quality, comparability and credibility. In short, it will encourage "business as usual" thinking.'[24]

The CLR clearly regarded the inclusion of 'public interest matters' in the OFR as preferable[25] and the Government itself envisaged also that directors must take into account the company's impact on the environment – as 'first among equals' – as well as the company's relationships with employees, customers and suppliers and the company's impact on the wider community as relevant to achieving the company's objectives.[26] This backdrop suggests that the OFR ought to have been a wide-ranging document covering areas such as environmental impact, employee relations, and social and community impact. Indeed, some respondents to the consultations held the opinion that matters such as employee relations would always be material to an understanding of the business so that, despite their non-mandatory position in the legislation, in reality such matters would have to be covered.[27]

Although the Regulations were relatively concise, the standard that supports and complements the Regulations was quite detailed. One respondent to the draft Statement for example states: 'we are concerned that the length of the Standard and the amount of detail it contains could result in a box ticking approach in preparing an OFR and lengthy reports that are aimed at ensuring compliance with the Regulations'.[28] Later, the same respondent adds: 'A shorter Standard would help ensure that directors produce an OFR, which in accordance with the first principle, reflects the business through their own eyes.'[29] Another problem was that the Regulations and the Reporting Standard were not entirely consistent. For example, the draft reporting standard included additional specific matters in paragraph 27 beyond those listed in paragraphs 4 and 5 of the draft Schedule 7ZA. Some of the terminology used in each of the texts was also inconsistent and could therefore cause confusion to those participating in the process of preparing and receiving

---

[24] *CORE Coalition Response to the UK Government's Draft Regulations on the Operating and Financial Review and Directors' Report Consultation Document* (6 August 2004), p. 2, available at www.corporate-responsibility.org.

[25] Company Law Review Steering Group, *Modern Company Law for a Competitive Economy: Developing the Framework* (March 2000), para. 5.77, at p. 181.

[26] White Paper, para. 4.31, at p. 38.

[27] See CORE, above.

[28] Investment Management Association, Letter to David Loweth, Accounting Standards Board (28 February 2005), p. 2, available at www.investmentuk.org.

[29] Investment Management Association, Letter to David Loweth, Accounting Standards Board (28 February 2005), p. 2, available at www.investmentuk.org.

an OFR. For example, whilst the Regulations referred to the company and its subsidiaries the draft Standard referred to the entity.

A number of more substantive observations can be made in relation to the OFR. The contents of the OFR were open to question, especially since a broad range of matters were for the directors to decide upon with regard to their inclusion. A related concern was that of confidential information, especially since the OFR would have been a document that would address the company's future objectives, strategies and prospects.

Confidentiality

The Government did not agree with the Company Law Review on the issue of confidentiality. The Review's opinion was that companies should be permitted not to disclose information which is, in the directors' judgement, of such confidentiality or commercial sensitivity that to do so would materially prejudice the company's interests.[30] Whilst the Government did not expect companies to disclose matters that would have a damaging effect on their future plans the Government also considered it difficult to see how an OFR could be anything other than misleading if it was completely silent about an issue which, by definition, would have a material impact on the company's interests.[31] If a confidentiality exception were possible there would have to be a way of making clear to readers that information was omitted in order for the OFR not to be misleading.[32]

The consensus of opinion among the public consultees was that the Government's approach was most appropriate since 'by its nature all confidential information is likely to be key to understanding the objectives and strategy of the business'.[33] However it was also noted by some respondents that 'it would be unrealistic to expect companies to be too specific regarding matters affecting their competitive edge. Commercial sensitivity and operational needs may, of necessity, limit how much information a company should properly be expected to divulge.'[34]

---

[30] Company Law Review Steering Group, *Modern Company Law for a Competitive Economy: Final Report*, (DTI, June 2001), vol. I, para. 8.37, at p. 182.

[31] White Paper, *Modernising Company Law*, Cm. 5553-I, App. D, para. 27, at p. 145.

[32] *Ibid.*, para. 28, at p. 145.

[33] Opinion of KPMG reported in the Explanatory Memorandum to the Draft Regulations, para. 2.112. The Government reported that 68 per cent of the 62 responses supported the approach of not including a confidentiality provision in the Regulations: see para. 2.111.

[34] Opinion of National Association of Pension Funds, reported at para. 2.113.

Impact of the OFR requirements on directors' duties

The contents of the OFR were intended to be in the discretion of the directors. The directors were to decide which facts and indicators would be necessary to assist members in assessing the company's business position and strategies and their prospects of success in the future. Indeed, the Trade and Industry Committee Sixth Report noted that the Government intended not to lay down more detailed statutory requirements for OFRs on the ground that a degree of flexibility would ensure that directors think carefully about the content and would encourage the directors to integrate environmental, social and employment factors into their consideration of company policy as a whole, embedding them across the corporate policy arena 'rather than confining them to a corporate social responsibility ghetto'.[35] However, the discretion afforded to the directors could result in the omission of the non-mandatory items listed in Schedule 7ZA and in paragraph 29 of the ASB's Reporting Standard if the directors were of the opinion that they did not affect the company's business and were not necessary to assist the investors' assessment of the company's business.

On the other hand, this discretion granted to the directors in the OFR corresponds to changes to director's duties proposed in the White Paper, *Company Law Reform*, that would encourage them to take account of long-term as well short-term consequences of their actions; and to recognise the importance to the success of the business of relations with all their stakeholders, of maintaining high standards of business conduct, and of the impact of their actions on the community and the environment.[36] This approach also supports the principles approach to company reporting. A flexible framework should allow the OFR to meet the particular circumstances of each company's business and should also avoid a mechanical box-ticking approach that would arise from a detailed checklist of content requirements. Thus, part of the directors' discretion was intended to result in OFRs containing useful forward-looking information that reflects the unique features of each company. However, there was a potential danger that the discretion given to directors to report on certain matters only to the extent necessary to

---

[35] HC 439, para. 60.

[36] White Paper, *Modernising Company Law* (July 2002), Cm. 5553-I, para. 3.6 at pp. 26–7 and para. 4.31, at p. 38, in which the connection between the OFR and the proposed change to the directors' duties is made. See also White Paper, *Company Law Reform* (March 2005) which makes express reference to the OFR reflecting the enlightened shareholder value approach to directors' duties: para. 3.3.

meet the objectives of the OFR might result in a significant variation between reports in comparability and quality.

In order to arrive at a decision about the appropriate content for the OFR responsibly, the importance of process was underlined. Guidance for directors was published in 2004 by the Working Group on Materiality.[37]

The 2004 draft Guidance had two main elements: principles and the process that would be appropriate for directors in making their decisions about what should be included in the OFR. The principles focused on the objective of the OFR which, as noted above, was to enable[38] the members of the company to assess the company's strategies and the potential for those strategies to succeed.[39] This objective was to provide the framework for the directors' decisions as to what to include and how to present such material in the OFR. The directors would also need to consider the users of the OFR and, according to the Working Group, although the Regulations focused on the members, the issues of importance to other users would also be relevant. Others would base decisions on the OFR, and their decisions could then affect a company's performance and its value. From this perspective the directors were advised to take a broad view, taking into account the interests of other stakeholders.[40] The OFR should include a statement about the business objectives and strategies, based on its purpose and values.[41]

---

[37] Set up in December 2002 with the following terms of reference: 'to develop broad principles and practical guidance on how directors can assess whether an item is material to their company and hence whether it must be included in an OFR'. The term 'materiality' was subsequently abandoned and the Guidance issued in 2004 emphasised, instead, information that is necessary for an understanding of the business. Similarly, the Regulations omit the materiality principle. The legislation and guidance are now correspondent to the requirement specified in the EU Accounts Modernisation Directive, that directors provide information that is appropriate *to the extent necessary for an understanding of the business.* (Emphasis added.)

[38] Note the change of position in the explanatory memorandum to the latest draft regulations. In its discussion about the lack of a safe harbour clause the memorandum states that the directors' duties relating to the OFR are to *assist* members rather than the more onerous need to enable members to make an informed assessment of the company's business. See discussion below.

[39] Working Group on Materiality, *The Operating and Financial Review: Practical Guidance for Directors* (DTI, May 2004) (referred to by the ASB in its draft reporting standard as the 'Radcliffe Report') para. i, at p. 9. See also DTI, *Draft Regulations on the Operating and Financial Review and Directors' Report: A Consultative Document* (May 2004), para. 3.2, at p. 16.

[40] Working Group on Materiality, *The Operating and Financial Review: Practical Guidance for Directors* (DTI, May 2004), para. i, at p. 9.

[41] *Ibid.*, para. i, p. 10.

The starting point for directors was to make good faith honest judgements.[42] This required collective action and the knowledge and experience of the board as a whole.[43] The scope of the information in the OFR required a balance between historic review and a focus on the future.[44] This requires a judgement about the appropriate time period for the business and the taking into account of particular objectives and strategies for the future. Information would have been both quantitative and qualitative and would also be financial and non-financial.[45] Information would have covered facts, events, probabilities, risks and opportunities, including anticipated events likely to have an impact on the company.[46] Risk includes reputation of the business.[47] Future potential significance would be a key test of issues that may or may not be included.

Directors also would have needed to measure and describe what was being reported. The Guidance suggested that directors should in addition consider the internal and external relevance of information. The Guidance further highlighted the need for consistency and a balanced approach to disclosure.[48]

With regard to process, the Guidance suggested six criteria for use when assessing the process that the directors might have followed: the process should be planned; it should be transparent; there should be appropriate consultation within the business, with members and other key groups; all relevant existing information and comparators should be taken into account and externally relevant matters should also be considered; the process should be comprehensive and consistent; and it should be subject to review.[49] The Guidance then set out ten questions that were designed to put directors in the right direction in following the process for preparing the OFR.[50] What is clear from this document

---

[42] *Ibid.*, para. ii, at p. 10.
[43] *Ibid.*, para. ii, at pp. 10–11.
[44] *Ibid.*, para. iii, at p. 11.
[45] *Ibid.*, para. iii, at p. 12.
[46] *Ibid.*, para. iii, at pp. 12–13.
[47] *Ibid.*, para. iii, at p. 13.
[48] *Ibid.*, paras. v and vi, at pp. 16–17.
[49] *Ibid.*, at p. 19.
[50] These questions are designed to allow directors to test themselves and to consider carefully the process they have adopted for preparing the OFR: Does the board already have, or does it have ready access to, all the relevant knowledge and skills to make its judgements as to what should or should not be included in the OFR? If not, how will this be addressed? An early task for the board will be to approve the process and satisfy itself that the process is being properly applied before it can exercise its judgements. How will the board work in discharging these key responsibilities? What information should be considered at the outset for possible inclusion in the OFR? What do other sources suggest might be important and should be considered for inclusion? What key

is that the process by which OFRs would be prepared would also be the basis upon which directors would be judged in the fulfilment of their duties. Substantive judgements of the directors were to be a matter for their discretion, but their use of such discretion could be open to challenge if they did not follow an appropriate procedure.

The importance of the process adopted by the directors was recognised widely. For example, the ICAEW's interim guidance document published in January 2003 highlighted the significance of the process of preparing the OFR. The ICAEW underlined the impact of the OFR requirements on directors' duties, noting that directors would be additionally responsible for complying with the requirements of the law on the OFR; complying with any rules as to form or content; complying with any rules about the manner in which the OFR is to be prepared; and approving and signing the OFR.[51] The ICAEW added that the OFR process would not 'be a simple certification or factual statement of information. Directors will have to make a judgement as to what information is useful and would allow shareholders to make an informed assessment of the business.'[52] According to the ICAEW, the process should include drawing up a plan and timetable, providing clear and full instructions to those involved in the preparation process, a review of the process that is put in place, a review of the final contents of the OFR, collating information from various sources, making sure that the OFR is coordinated with other reporting documents, putting in place controls to check the accuracy of the information presented, and continually evaluating the feedback and review of the OFR process.

Directors' liability

The relevance of the OFR to directors' duties and the potential liability of directors for OFRs that do not meet their objective was also an issue of

---

information does the corporate management information systems provide now on these topics? What, in the light of all this, are the information gaps? What should the plans be for filling these gaps? How will the information be put together? How should the information put before the board be validated, and by whom? How, once the information has been put together, does the board decide whether it should be included or not? What processes of challenge, both internal and external, should be used? What sign-off procedures should be in place? How should the information that is to be included be presented in the OFR? And how should the information in the OFR be linked to other information published by the company? What feedback arrangements and review procedures should be in place between one OFR cycle and another?

[51] ICAEW, *Preparing an Operating and Financial Review: Interim process guidance for UK directors* (January 2003), at p. 7.

[52] *Ibid.*, at p. 8.

debate. The White Paper suggested that directors might face legal challenges if they default in their duties relating to the OFR.[53] The possibility of liability for the OFR presented a potential limitation on the information that directors might be prepared to put into the OFR. Such inhibition could be lifted by the inclusion of a safe harbour clause in the legislation that would protect directors from damages claims relating to the OFR. Indeed, most respondents to the Government's consultations on the OFR favoured including such a provision in the legislation, as the Government noted in its explanatory memorandum to the draft Regulations.[54] Arguably a safe harbour provision would encourage the inclusion in the OFR of more quantitative and forward-looking information. However, the Government chose not to include a safe harbour provision, so that all the directors were left with was a rebuttable presumption that following the ASB's Reporting Standard would mean that the law had been complied with. One criticism that could be made of this approach is that it might lead to the boilerplate disclosures that the Government sought to avoid, since these would be safer than a balanced and comprehensive analysis that includes good and bad news. Otherwise, directors might be forced to go to the expense of involving lawyers in the preparation of the OFR, as a protection from liability.[55]

Conscious of these criticisms, the Government's response was to tone down the originally proposed requirements such as, for example, removing the reference to due and careful enquiry as the standard of care for preparing the OFR and for *assisting* the members rather than 'enabling' them to assess the company's strategies.[56] The recent introduction of a permission for companies to indemnify directors in respect of proceedings brought by third parties, and also the permission for companies to pay directors' defence costs as they are incurred, was also, in

---

[53] The White Paper stated: 'It will, of course, be for directors to decide precisely what information is material to their particular business. However, the Bill will make the directors responsible for how these factors are covered in the OFR. The Government believes this will lead to companies providing not only information in the right quantity but also information of the right quality. Any company that fails to do so will risk adverse comparison and questions from shareholders and others. Ultimately the directors may need to defend the process behind their reporting before the courts.' White Paper, *Modernising Company Law*, Cm. 5553 I (July 2002), para. 4.33, at p. 39.

[54] At para. 2.119 of the Explanatory Memorandum, the Government stated that it had received 89 responses to this question of whether there should be a safe harbour clause. Of these 62 per cent disagreed with the Government's proposal to omit a 'safe harbour' provision from the Regulations, with 28 per cent agreeing. The majority of business disagreed with this proposal. Of investors who responded to this question, one-third disagreed with the proposals.

[55] See para. 2.121.

[56] See para. 2.127.

the Government's view, an alternative to the introduction of a safe harbour provision.[57]

Not only did the potential liability of directors arising from the introduction of the OFR pose difficulties, but also the OFR raised issues about the role of the auditor. This will be considered in the next section.

What would the OFR have meant for the role of the auditor?

Regulation 10 inserted section 235(3A) into the Companies Act 1985, and this provided that the auditors of a quoted company must state in their report:

a. whether in their opinion the information given in the operating and financial review for the financial year for which the annual accounts are prepared is consistent with those accounts; and

b. whether any matters have come to their attention, in the performance of their functions as auditors of the company, which in their opinion are inconsistent with the information given in the operating and financial review.

This provision relaxed the earlier proposal for auditors to give an opinion as to whether the directors have prepared the OFR after 'due and careful enquiry'. This relaxation came about as a result of responses to the Government's consultations on the role of the auditor.

The draft regulation 8 presented in May 2004 proposed a requirement that auditors express an opinion on whether the directors have prepared the OFR after 'due and careful enquiry'. The aim of this proposal was not for auditors to second-guess the directors' judgements, but to 'examine the process the directors followed in making their judgements and come to a view as to its adequacy'.[58] The Government explained this by saying that it expected the auditors

to examine whether the directors have taken appropriate steps to satisfy themselves that the OFR presents a balanced and comprehensive analysis of the development and performance of the company. In so doing, the auditors must satisfy themselves that each statement made in the OFR has been made after due consideration and is not inconsistent with the accounts and matters that have come to their attention during the course of the audit.[59]

---

[57] Sections 19 and 20 of the Companies (Audit, Investigations and Community Enterprise) Act 2004.

[58] DTI, *Draft Regulations on the Operating and Financial Review and Directors' Report: A Consultative Document* (May 2004), para. 3.58, at p. 29.

[59] DTI, *Draft Regulations on the Operating and Financial Review and Directors' Report: A Consultative Document* (May 2004), para. 3.59, at p. 29.

Business respondents argued that 'due and careful enquiry' implied a prospectus level standard and they were concerned therefore that this would result in auditors undertaking verification and due diligence exercises, and that this in turn would lead to significant costs both in audit fees and professional advice. Overall, responses from business, investors and professional bodies showed support for the auditors comparing the substance of the OFR with the results from the audit, but were strongly opposed to the auditors making a judgement about the process that the directors followed at preparation stage.

Some argued that the role of auditors should go further and actually look at the outcome of the OFR. For example: the Environment Agency suggested that 'the current emphasis is too much on auditing the "process" and not enough on the "content or quality" of the disclosures which is actually what investors need assurance on. A business can appear to have a good annual governance process but could still be economically and environmentally unsustainable in the medium term.'

The Government's response to these observations was to state that it accepted consultees' concerns that the auditors' role as originally drafted might present directors with unnecessary challenges and hinder the frank and candid reporting which it seeks. On the other hand, information relating to future objectives and strategies which cannot be verified against accounts might justify the requirement of a higher level of assurance than consistency with accounts only. Other sources would therefore need to be considered. The Government also stated that it expects directors to apply the same level of care to preparation of the OFR as all other financial and accounting statements. The Government concluded that the auditors would no longer be required to give an opinion on whether the directors have prepared the OFR after due and careful enquiry. Instead, the auditors would be required to check for consistency with the accounts and to consider whether any other matters have come to their attention in the conduct of the (annual) audit which are inconsistent with the information in the OFR.

The removal of the duty to express an opinion on whether the OFR had been created after due and careful enquiry reduced the emphasis on process, yet the auditor might have found it difficult to assess the content because he or she was not sufficiently knowledgeable about environmental or social factors. The attraction of judging any statements in relation to their financial impact is likely to be significant and this, in the end, simply reinforces the shareholder focus even in this step towards social and environmental reporting. At its worst, the effect could be that suggested by CORE in its response to the OFR proposals:

in areas where business may only use subjective measures, such as for labour standards, or environmental risk, auditors will not be required to examine how these assessments of risk were made, and why business may have chosen to ignore other risks that were not reported on. The lack of any scrutiny of social and environmental data could lead to the worst vagaries of corporate abuse: degradation of environmental resources; the production of harmful products where local governments have weak laws; or supporting regimes where human rights violations occur.[60]

One possible approach to resolve these difficulties would be to create a framework in which the contents of the OFR should be tested for clarity, accuracy and reliability; this could be done through a multi-stakeholder process involving employees, unions, consumer organisations and NGOs as well as auditors.[61]

Users

Under the Regulations, the OFR was to be addressed to the 'members' or shareholders. This approach corresponds with the proposed statement of directors' duties set out in the White Paper stating that the goal for the directors should be the success of the company for the benefit of its members as a whole.[62]

In its response to the consultation on the draft Regulations, in December 2004, the Government stated that the draft Regulations were designed to transform the CLR objective[63] into a legislative requirement that results in useful, relevant reporting that would assist shareholders to assess companies' strategies and their potential to succeed. In acting in the best interests of shareholders, the Government argues that the directors must recognise the company's need to foster relationships with its employees, customers and suppliers, its need to maintain its business reputation and its need to consider the company's impact on the community and the environment. On this basis the OFR Regulations would require information that would also be of interest to stakeholders, such

---

[60] See CORE, *What's wrong with the OFR?* (November 2004), available at www.corporate-responsibility.org.

[61] *CORE Coalition Response to the UK Government's Draft Regulations on the Operating and Financial Review and Directors' Report Consultation Document* (6 August 2004), p. 12, available at www.corporate-responsibility.org.

[62] See White Paper, *Company Law Reform* (March 2005), para 3.3.

[63] 'to provide a discussion and analysis of the performance of the business and the main trends and factors underlying the results and financial position and likely to affect performance in the future, so as to enable users to assess the strategies adopted by the business and the potential for successfully achieving them'.

as employees, suppliers and customers of the company as well as those with an interest in the environment.[64]

When responding to the White Paper, *Modernising Company Law*, the Government also discussed the issue of shareholders and stakeholders in relation to the OFR. The Government noted the views of witnesses such as CORE, the TUC and others and concluded that the OFR 'would be of benefit not only to shareholders and potential investors in companies, but also to all those concerned with wider aspects of company behaviour, whether as employees, local residents, or as interest groups involved in environmental/social issues or general corporate governance'.[65]

Despite the Government's claims that the OFR would contain information that would be of interest to other users, the ASB's Reporting Standard made it clear that the members' needs must determine the contents of the OFR. Thus the principles set out in the Reporting Standard included that the OFR 'shall focus on matters that are relevant to the interests of members'.[66] The Standard explained that the members' needs 'are paramount when directors consider what information shall be contained in the OFR'. The disclosure framework set out in the Standard also stated that the OFR 'shall provide information to assist members to assess the strategies adopted by the entity and the potential for those strategies to succeed'.[67]

The fact that the OFR was only to be addressed to the shareholders would have limited its potential uses. One could argue that stakeholders affected by the company's operations should have an equal right to access to the OFR and also be able to respond to the report by having the opportunity for dialogue with the company. Whilst it appears to be the case that other stakeholder groups would have access to the OFR the focus of the information to be included was the interests of the members. This may have limited the possible responses by other users. Indeed, the extent to which they would be able to communicate with the company about the report remains unclear. This fact explains the response of Amnesty International to the earlier consultation paper on materiality:

---

[64] See DTI, *Draft Regulations on the Operating and Financial Review and Directors' Report, A Consultative Document* (May 2004), paras. 3.5–3.9, at pp. 17–18.

[65] Sixth Report of Session 2002–03, HC 439, para. 69.

[66] Accounting Standards Board, Reporting Standard 1, *Operating and Financial Review* (2005), para. 7.

[67] Accounting Standards Board, Reporting Standard 1, *Operating and Financial Review* (2005), para. 28.

the presumption that the primary users of an operating and financial review are only the members of a company must be redressed for several reasons. Firstly company impacts fall across all stakeholders, not just its members. . . . A more useful view . . . can be derived by considering the views of the wider stakeholder community with which the company interacts. It follows that all stakeholders should be considered equal users of an operating and financial review.[68]

Enforcement of the OFR requirements

In its Consultative Document of 2004, the Government proposed an enforcement regime that would include criminal offences and penalties and administrative enforcement through the Financial Reporting Review Panel. The regime would be similar to the enforcement of financial reporting requirements. That regime comprises: criminal sanctions for directors who are party, knowingly or recklessly to the approval of defective accounts, and for the failure to sign accounts;[69] and an administrative procedure whereby the Secretary of State or a body authorised by the Secretary (in practice, the Financial Reporting Review Panel (FRRP)) may apply to the court for an order obliging a company to prepare revised accounts where it appears that the accounts do not comply with the law.[70] The existing criminal sanctions are rarely invoked. Responses to the consultation made very little comment on this aspect of enforcement, which the Government interpreted as suggesting that the principle is well understood and uncontroversial. The Government therefore stated an intention to implement criminal sanctions for the OFR and directors' report, and for those sanctions to apply to OFRs and directors' reports prepared for financial years beginning on or after 1 April 2005.[71]

With regard to the administrative element of the enforcement regime for the OFR some respondents were concerned that the FRRP would 'second-guess' directors' judgements and be a heavy-handed enforcer, whilst others doubted whether the FRRP would be able to enforce the OFR effectively. As one respondent put it: 'If the auditors have not unearthed a serious problem, it is difficult to imagine that the FRRP will be able to do so.' In order to ease the introduction of the OFR, the Government intended to delay by one year the commencement of the

---

[68] Amnesty International UK Response to the Operating and Financial Review Working Group on Materiality (DTI, September 2003).
[69] Section 233(5), Companies Act 1985.
[70] Sections 245–245C, Companies Act 1985.
[71] Government Explanatory memorandum to the draft regulations, para. 2.100. See reg. 8, inserting new s. 234AA(5) into the Companies Act 1985.

administrative enforcement mechanism.[72] The role of the FRRP would be to consider, both as part of its proactive role of examining the financial statements of larger companies and in response to specific complaints, whether companies' OFRs complied with the legal requirements. The FRRP already looks at any voluntarily prepared OFR when examining a company's accounts. The Government intended that the FRRP would intervene where: the OFR was factually wrong in a material respect, or, if the issue was one of opinion rather than fact, it contained an opinion which no reasonable board could have formed if it had followed a proper process of collecting and evaluating evidence.[73] The Environment Agency was concerned about the impartiality of the FRRP, given its funding by the business that it regulates.

CORE proposed further measures including the creation of an OFR ombudsman and giving '. . . legal standing to all persons affected by a company's activities to challenge its accounts'.

Conclusion

Would the OFR be an appropriate way forward? The OFR as was intended was limited by the fact that the requirements applied only to quoted companies, despite the fact that the original proposals were that 'economically significant companies' would be required to produce an OFR. However, more positively, by endowing the OFR with statutory status, narrative reporting would potentially be elevated to a level comparable to that of audited financial statements. The aim would be to help shareholders participate in decisions on strategy and value creation rather than just to decide on takeover bids, board appointments and remuneration. It would also theoretically resolve the problem of the historical vision of the financial accounts when investors have demonstrated a desire and need for future-oriented reports. The OFR was closely connected to the 'enlightened shareholder value' approach to directors' duties by encouraging reporting on information beyond the financial figures. This would be a significant step beyond the long-criticised financial accounts. However, the information outside the company's financial position was not to be compulsory and only would be required if it was necessary for assisting the members to assess the corporate strategies, that decision being a matter for the directors to decide. The OFR extended the role of the auditor to check that the directors have followed the correct processes, but the vigilance and actions of the FRRP

---

[72] Government Explanatory memorandum to the draft regulations, para. 2.102.
[73] Government Explanatory memorandum to the draft regulations, para. 2.106.

would be essential in establishing the OFR as a document to be taken seriously.

The OFR legislation and reporting standard made clear the intention to assist the members – it was not really about providing more information to 'outsiders' although lip-service is paid to their interests. Stakeholders may have read the information but they were not granted any right to challenge the company legally on what it claimed in its OFR. They would have to rely on the shareholders to take such steps. One question that arises is whether or not the investor is interested in social disclosure. This question has relevance for the next chapter that explores more specifically social and environmental reporting.

The repeal of the OFR legislation was justified by the government as getting rid of gold-plating[74] and as a recalibration of government policy.[75] One could observe this development as testimony to the relatively weak regulatory structure of the narrative reporting elements of disclosure and corporate reporting, compared with the financial reporting aspects. Nevertheless, the EU's Modernisation Directive requires at least a balanced review of a company's business, indicating that the disappearance of the OFR ought not to leave an empty gap on this regulatory front. It remains to be seen how the Government will take this kind of reporting forward.

---

[74] See speech by the Rt Hon Gordon Brown MP, Chancellor of the Exchequer, at the CBI Annual Conference in London, 28 November 2005, 99/05 available at www.hm.treasury.gov.uk.
[75] See Barney Jopson, 'Brown's U-turn on reporting rule defended as a "recalibration"', *Financial Times*, 16 December 2005.

10   Social and environmental reporting

Introduction

Whilst the operating and financial review legislation would not have made
social and environmental reporting compulsory it might have been
regarded as a first step in that direction. Corporate social and environmental reporting has been debated for more than thirty years. The activity
was regarded as an experiment in the 1970s but it fell off the agenda
during the 1980s. Then in the mid-1990s the possibility of a social
accounting requirement returned.[1] Currently, the attention paid to social
and environmental reporting gives an impression that it is a widespread
corporate activity. A substantial body of guidelines and schemes for
effective social and environmental reporting has been developed alongside a wealth of literature and observation of the activity. Yet, despite such
attention this aspect of disclosure remains inadequately developed with
an insufficient number of companies having established it as an integral
part of their reporting agenda. Indeed, there are 'vast swathes of the
economy that have not even begun to disclose information on their social
and environmental impact'.[2] In particular, three areas of business engage
in little or no social reporting: 'behind the scenes companies' without
famous reputations or brand names; state-owned and public sector organisations; and small and medium-sized businesses, which represent the
vast majority of companies registered in the UK at least.[3]

A number of barriers have obstructed the development of social and
environmental reporting. For example, a clear definition of social and environmental reporting has not been established. Nor have the required
contents of social and environmental reports been made clear. The
voluntary nature of such reporting has arguably also slowed down its

---

[1] Rob Gray, 'Thirty years of social accounting, reporting and auditing: what (if anything)
have we learnt?' (2001) 10 *Business Ethics: A European Review* 9–15, at p. 9.
[2] Steve Hilton, 'Identikit bureaucrats or romantic crusaders?' *The Guardian, The Giving
List*, 8 November 2004, 12–13, at p. 12.
[3] Steve Hilton, *ibid.*

development. Without uniform or standardised requirements, reports are not easily comparable. Reports may be used for presenting a positive image of the company rather than necessarily providing an accurate assessment of the company's performance in these fields. Indeed, the limited degree of shareholder interest in such information, coupled with the shareholder-centred focus of company law, has limited the opportunity to use social and environmental reports in any purposeful sense beyond them being used as self-congratulatory public relations documents. Such reports emphasise a company's successes, highlighting good news and ignoring bad news, and present the philanthropic acts of the company, such as its donations to charity or its sponsorship of sporting or educational activities.[4] The quality of the reports is consequently often poor with little worthwhile information presented. The lack of legal intervention also results in an absence of effective enforcement mechanisms against failure to provide social or environmental information. Potential users, in particular the stakeholder recipients, are not empowered to take action against a company they consider to be failing in their social or environmental responsibilities, or for not providing them with the information they seek. In reality, social and economic reporting tends to be controlled by the business actors who indulge in stakeholder management rather than provision of objective reports. Audit of social and environmental information is also underdeveloped, so that the credibility of what is reported is left open to doubt.

Nevertheless, despite the existence of these problems and limitations there is a growing interest in social and environmental reporting from bodies such as Global Reporting Initiative and AccountAbility's AA 1000 Framework. Initiatives by the European Commission also reveal an intention to develop the field formally. To be effective social and environmental reporting activity requires recognition of corporate social responsibility and accountability and an acceptance of the view that the needs and interests of those affected by corporate activity are as relevant as the profit-maximisation interests of shareholders. This approach relies on a social contract perspective. Under this social contract the company is given power to operate and through its activities it must deliver some socially desirable ends to society in general and should give economic, social and political benefits to those groups from which it derives its power.[5] In other words, the 'modern corporation exists to provide

---

[4] M. R. Mathews, 'Social and Environmental Accounting: A Practical Demonstration of Ethical Concern?' (1995) 14 *Journal of Business Ethics* 663–71, at pp. 666–7.
[5] Mathews, at p. 667, quoting A. D. Shocker and S. P. Sethi, 'An Approach to Incorporating Social Preferences in Developing Corporate Action Strategies', in S. P. Sethi (ed.), *The Unstable Ground Corporate Social Policy in a Dynamic Society* (Melville, Calif., 1974).

benefits to society'.[6] As Mathews argues: 'If the social contract argument is accepted . . . then there is a need for data to be collected, analysed and disclosed and verified, to enable society to evaluate the performance of the organisation in areas other than the determination of income and net worth.'[7] This gives a basis upon which to develop social, environmental and ethical reports. Social and environmental reporting has a relationship, according to Gray, with accountability, democracy and sustainability.[8] Yet, despite this possible interpretation of social and environmental reporting, there exists overall a reluctance to develop this area for its own sake, which is reflected in the attempts to connect social and environmental performance to economic success. That approach might be necessary for the time being, giving strength to the triple bottom line approach, but for social and environmental reporting to be fully effective in a way that ultimately improves corporate behaviour it arguably requires to be viewed as important independently and regardless of the financial performance of the company.

This chapter will consider the development of social and environmental reporting. First, it will outline the various possible definitions of social and environmental reporting and the objectives of this form of corporate disclosure. It will then consider the regulatory approach to this activity before describing the features of social and environmental reports. The chapter will speculate on how the role of auditors may change as social and environmental reporting develops. After highlighting the problems with the voluntary approach the chapter will explore the possibility of graduation on to sustainability reporting. The significance of social and environmental reporting to corporate social responsibility and the corporate social contract generally will conclude the chapter.

Definitions

There are several possible definitions of social and environmental reporting ranging from very basic disclosures to 'sustainability reporting'. Put most simply, environmental reporting is 'a voluntary method of communicating environmental performance to all the organisation's stakeholders'.[9] The Accounting Standards Steering

---

[6] Mathews, at p. 668.
[7] Mathews, at p. 668.
[8] Rob Gray, 'Thirty years'.
[9] http://cei.sund.ac.uk/envrep/reports.htm.

Committee's *Corporate Report*, published in 1975, introduced the concept of social reporting as the reporting of those costs and benefits, which may or may not be quantifiable in money terms, arising from economic activities and subsequently borne or received by the community at large or particular groups not holding a direct relationship with the reporting entity.[10] Another definition of social reporting is provided by Gray, Owen and Maunders:

the process of communicating the social and environmental effects of organisations' economic actions to particular interest groups within society and to society at large. As such it involves extending the accountability of organisations (particularly companies) beyond the traditional role of providing a financial account to the owners of capital, in particular shareholders. Such an extension is predicated upon the assumption that companies do have wider responsibilities than simply to make money for their shareholders.[11]

Social accounting, according to Gray, Owen and Adams, is a combination of accounting for different things (i.e., other than accounting strictly for economic events); accounting in different media (i.e., other than accounting in strictly financial terms); accounting to different individuals or groups (i.e., not necessarily only accounting to the providers of finance); and accounting for different purposes (i.e., not necessarily accounting only to enable the making of decisions whose success would be judged in financial or even only cash flow terms).[12] Gray, Owen and Adams elaborate on this definition by explaining the main features of social reports. Thus they tend to be informal rather than formal accounts, prepared by organisations either for themselves or which are (less commonly) disclosed to others. Social reports are generally prepared about certain areas of activity, typically those which affect the natural environment; employees; and wider 'ethical' issues which typically concentrate upon: consumers and products; local and international communities.[13]

As the activity of narrative reporting in these areas develops, definitions of social and environmental reporting may also change. In particular it is

---

[10] Accounting Standards Steering Committee, *The Corporate Report* (ICAEW,1975), para. 6.46 at pp. 57–8.

[11] R. H. Gray, D. L. Owen and K. T. Maunders, *Corporate Social Reporting: Accounting and Accountability* (Prentice Hall, London, 1987), p. ix.

[12] Rob Gray, Dave Owen and Carol Adams, *Accounting and Accountability: Changes and Challenges in Corporate Social and Environmental Reporting* (Prentice Hall, London, 1996), pp. 3–11.

[13] Gray, Owen and Adams acknowledge that this is a narrow range of concerns and the ethical consumer may be interested in animal testing; armaments; environment; irresponsible marketing; land rights; nuclear power; oppressive regimes; South Africa; trade union relations; wages and conditions: at pp. 11–12.

possible to witness a progression from separate environmental reports, to social reports and then sustainability reporting. Sustainability reports are more rounded reports and can be defined essentially as environmental accounts that include social and economic aspects. The two main features of sustainability reporting are that, first, they attempt to deal with the three strands of social, environmental and economic dimensions in one report and, secondly, they express a commitment to involving stakeholders directly in the reporting process. Another term used to define this kind of reporting is triple bottom line reporting, again signifying reporting of economic, social and environmental indicators.

More broadly and more conceptually, Gray, Owen and Adams explain that all accounting and, as a result, all of corporate social reporting, 'implicitly begs a whole range of fundamental questions about the structure of and power in society, the role of economic as opposed to social and political considerations, the proper ethical response to issues and so on'.[14]

In essence, corporate social and environmental reporting involves disclosure of the effects of a company's activities on all stakeholders and such information being presented to all stakeholders. Corporate social and environmental reporting goes beyond financial reporting and addresses not only shareholders but stakeholders too.

What are the objectives of social and environmental reporting and accounting?

Clear objectives are necessary if social and environmental disclosure is to have any true significance. Social and environmental reporting arguably have two similar overall objectives of improving the behaviour of companies and making them accountable generally for their actions. According to Brophy the goals of environmental reporting were initially to demonstrate a company's commitment to the environment. The basic goal is to communicate environmental performance. A company may produce an environmental report with the aim of differentiating itself from its competitors but it may also, through its environmental report, signal acknowledgement of a shared responsibility for the state of the environment. A company might also seek to obtain social approval for its operating practices and through its report the company may be aiming to demonstrate regulatory compliance.[15] Similarly, a social report might be used to demonstrate a company's commitment to its relationships with

---

[14] *Ibid.*, at p. 12.
[15] M. Brophy, 'A Stakeholder's View of Environmental Reporting' at www.environmental-expert.com/articles/article20/article20.htm.

its workers and with the community. It might, for example, highlight its role in maintaining the local economy and in providing public services. Charitable donations might be highlighted as a demonstration of the company's commitment to helping others and thereby enhance the company's image.

In the area of environmental responsibility a company could be exposed to financial penalties if it fails to meet environmental performance targets or if its operations cause damage, such as pollution, to the environment. From this perspective, the process of reporting and disclosure arguably increases awareness both by the company and by the public recipients of the information. In this way, the more corporate actions are subject to public scrutiny, the more likely businesses will avoid borderline or questionable environmental practices.[16] Thus disclosure potentially has the effect of encouraging companies to avoid misdemeanours where they are required to expose their conduct. Disclosure requirements might then help to eliminate malpractice. According to Ferman, as corrective costs and penalties under environmental laws 'skyrocket', the regulatory authorities may find themselves in the position of being able to eliminate, rather than expose and punish, environmental non-compliance. Ferman suggests that many companies liquidate themselves when the costs of environmental clean-up are assessed. Disclosure thereby operates in such a way as to avoid permitting companies to engage in misconduct to a point where they cannot afford either the penalties or remedial costs, and allows the regulatory authorities to intervene at an earlier stage. By requiring the disclosure, the regulatory authority can prevent further escalation of environmental non-compliance.[17]

This potential role of environmental reporting demonstrates that disclosure could play a role in improving corporate behaviour and improving performance. This 'house cleaning' role[18] means that the knowledge that certain activities will be disclosed might also influence corporate managers to use their power prudently and properly and encourage them to review their policies in order to make them more acceptable to the public. In turn this can have beneficial effects on the company's achievements of its objectives.

According to Ferman, businesses recognise the inherent advantages of self-regulation. Such benefits range from saving money by assessing risks

---

[16] See Risa Vetri Ferman, 'Environmental Disclosures and SEC Reporting Requirements' (1992) 17 *Delaware Journal of Corporate Law* 483, p. 508

[17] Ferman, at p. 509, note 154.

[18] Mark A. Sargent, 'State Disclosure Regulation and the Allocation of Regulatory Responsibilities' (1987) 46 *Maryland LR* 1027, at p. 1045.

before acting, to improving a firm's relationship with government regulatory agencies and the investing public. The hallmark of a responsible corporation is that it polices its own environmental practices, whatever its ultimate motivation may be.[19] Internal cost savings might also be made from environmental reporting. For example, DuPont found that once it started measuring and reporting on the environmental impact of its activities its annual environmental costs dropped from US$1 billion in 1993 to $560 million in 1999.[20]

In Gray's view the objectives of social and environmental reporting could include discharging accountability to stakeholders, controlling stakeholders and moving towards sustainable reporting or acting as an exercise in self-justification.[21] If accountability is the real goal of such reporting this has important consequences for company law because, as Gray argues, accountability places society at the heart of the analysis and questions the legitimacy of an organisation's actions, or perhaps even its right to exist.[22]

Regulatory approaches to social and environmental reporting

The UK

In the UK there are very few regulations that demand environmental or social disclosures. The Companies Act 1985 covers principally financial information requirements but, as has been discussed in the previous chapter, the directors' report must contain a fair review of the development of the business of the company during the financial year and of the company's position at the end of that year. Schedule 7 sets out certain specific information to be contained in the directors' report. This includes particulars of any important events affecting the company or any of its subsidiaries which have occurred since the end of the financial year; an indication of likely future developments in the business of the company and of its subsidiaries; and an indication of the activities of the company and its subsidiaries in the field of research and

---

[19] Ferman, p. 506, at footnote 146. On the other hand some corporate entities neither disclose nor monitor their environmental practices for fear that such activity will alert government agencies to their misconduct. Still others do not disclose because they do not plan to take any corrective action and do not want to notify the public of 'the havoc they wreak in the environment': see Ferman, p. 507, at footnote 147.

[20] *Ibid.*

[21] Gray, 'Thirty years', at p. 11.

[22] *Ibid.*

development.[23] In addition, details about charitable and political donations should be included in the report.[24] Companies employing more than 250 employees should also include details relevant to information and consultation of employees and special provisions for appointing, training, career development and promotion of disabled employees.[25] The Government, however, plans to remove the requirements for disclosures in respect of the employment of disabled persons and employee involvement, because these are covered by substantive requirements in other legislation such as the Disability Discrimination Act.[26]

The (now repealed) OFR Regulations would have required quoted companies to provide details of social and environmental matters in their operating and financial review if they were necessary for giving a balanced and comprehensive analysis and assisting members to assess the company's strategies.[27] The Accounting Standards Board's Reporting Standard made clear that a balanced and comprehensive analysis would be required of the development and performance of the company's business during the financial year; the position of the company at the end of the year; and the main trends and factors underlying and likely to affect in future the development performance and position of the business. Such information should assist members to assess the strategies adopted by the entity and the potential for those strategies to succeed.[28] The Reporting Standard listed information that was to be reported to the extent necessary for members to assess the strategies relating to the nature, objectives of the business, the development and performance of the business, its resources, risks and uncertainties and relationships that may affect the entity's long-term value; and the position of the business. The information listed included employees, environmental matters and social and community issues. The Standard suggested therefore that these matters should be included if they are necessary for the members to be able to assess the company's strategies. However, if the directors did not consider such items necessary they would not be obliged to include them in the review. It is also important to note that the Directors' Report is intended (as would have been the OFR) to be general

---

[23] Schedule 7, para. 6.

[24] Schedule 7, paras. 3–5.

[25] Schedule 7, paras. 9–11.

[26] See White Paper, *Company Law Reform* (DTI, March 2005) para. 4.10.

[27] Companies Act 1985 (Operating and Financial Review and Directors' Report) Regulations 2005, SI 2005/1011, reg. 9, inserting Sch. 7ZA into the Companies Act 1985.

[28] Accounting Standards Board, *Reporting Standard 1: Operating and Financial Review* (May 2005) paras. 28–76.

reports and so is unlikely to provide the level of detail that a single full and independent environmental report or social report would contain.

The recently introduced Environmental Information Regulations 2004 and the Environmental Information (Scotland) Regulations 2004[29] implement the EC Directive on Public Access to Information[30] and these require certain companies, as well as public authorities, to provide the public with access to environmental information when a request is made. Public utilities companies, public private partnerships and private companies with environmental functions such as those in the energy, water and waste sectors are covered by the Regulations which form part of a legislative triumvirate on freedom of information.[31] The Pensions Act 1995 also contains provisions requiring pension fund trustees to state their policy in their statement of investment principles, including details on the extent to which social, environmental or ethical consider-ations are taken into account in the selection, retention and realisation of investments disclosures.[32]

In addition to the legislative provisions a number of financial reporting standards issued by the Accounting Standards Board contain require-ments for environmental information. For example, FRS12 obliges companies to disclose the amount of their environmental provisions and contingent liabilities and the circumstances surrounding them. FRS 10 and FRS 11 also require companies to account for changes to asset values that result from environmental factors if such factors are financially material.

These minimal and discrete legislative and regulatory requirements for information on social and environmental matters are supplemented by various voluntary schemes and award programmes such as the ACCA UK Environmental Reporting Awards in 2001 which has since been named the ACCA Awards for Sustainability Reporting. This scheme has three categories – social reporting, environmental reporting and sustainability reporting. Similarly, the Association of British Insurers published *Disclosure Guidelines on Social Responsibility*[33] which aim for companies to report on social, ethical and environmental considerations and thereby facilitate 'constructive . . . engagement between companies

---

[29] SI 2004/3391.
[30] [2003] OJ L 41.
[31] The Data Protection Act 1998, the Freedom of Information Act 2000 and the Environ-mental Information Regulations 2004.
[32] Section 35, Pensions Act 1995, as amended by reg. 2(4), the Occupation Pension Schemes (Investment, and Assignment, Forfeiture, Bankruptcy etc.) Amendment Regulations 1999, SI 1999/1849.
[33] See ABI, *Investing in Social Responsibility: Risks and Opportunities*, App. 1.

and their shareholders.'[34] The position in the UK is similar to that at the general European level where there is a minimal amount of legislation supplemented by recommendations and support for voluntary disclosure schemes as part of corporate social responsibility and corporate environmental management strategies.

EC law

The Regulations for the OFR and Directors' Report were intended to implement, in part, the European Accounts Modernisation Directive[35] which requires an enhanced review of a company's business in the directors' report. Thus large and medium-sized companies would be required, since January 2005, to provide 'a fair review of the development and performance of the company's business and its position'.[36] The review 'shall be a balanced and comprehensive analysis of the development and performance of the company's business'.[37] The Directive adds that to 'the extent necessary for an understanding of the company's development, performance and position, the analysis shall include both financial and, where appropriate, non-financial key performance indicators . . . including information relating to environmental and employee matters'.[38]

The European provisions consist of Regulations and Recommendations that lend support to and encourage the development of voluntary schemes. For example, in 1993 a Council Regulation allowing voluntary participation by companies in the industrial sector in a Community eco-management and audit scheme[39] was introduced. This Regulation encourages industry to adopt a proactive approach to managing the environmental impact of its activities. The Regulation calls on companies to establish and implement environmental policies, objectives and programmes and effective environmental management systems and not only to comply with regulatory requirements but also to promote the reasonable continuous improvement of environmental

---

[34] *Ibid.*, see further John Parkinson, 'Disclosure and Corporate Social and Environmental Performance: Competitiveness and Enterprise in a Broader Social Framework' (2003) 3 *JCLS* 3, at p. 6.

[35] Directive 2003/51/EC of the European Parliament and of the Council of 18 June 2003 amending Directives 78/660/EEC, 83/635/EEC and 91/674/EEC on the annual and consolidated accounts of certain types of companies, banks and other financial institutions and insurance undertakings (2003, OJ L 178/6, 17.7.2003).

[36] Article 1, para. 14, amends Art. 46 of the Fourth Directive with new para. 1(a).

[37] Article 1, para. 14, amends Art. 46 of the Fourth Directive with new para. 1(a).

[38] Article 1, para. 14, amends Art. 46 of the Fourth Directive with new para. 1(b).

[39] No. 1863 of 29 June 1993, OJ L168, 10.7.1993.

performance. The Regulation gives guidance on the character of such programmes. For example, it suggests that companies should seek to ensure employee awareness and that an environmental management system should include environmental auditing procedures.

The provision of information to the public is considered an essential element of good environmental management and a response to the growing interest of the public in such information. The 1993 Regulation suggests that companies should be encouraged to produce and disseminate periodic environmental statements containing information for the public on the factual environmental situation in their industrial sites and on their environmental policies, programmes, objectives and management systems. Credibility is increased if the information receives assessment by accredited environmental verifiers. Companies involved are required to undertake an initial environmental review and to establish an environmental programme and an environmental management system. The scheme requires a three-yearly environmental audit. A company that participates in the scheme is required to provide an environmental statement containing the following elements: a description of the organisation and its activities, products and services; the organisation's environmental policy and a brief description of its environmental management system. This requires a description of all the significant direct and indirect environmental aspects of the organisation and an explanation of the nature of the impacts as related to these aspects; a description of its environmental objectives and targets in relation to the significant environmental aspects and impacts; a summary of the organisation's year-by-year environmental performance data which may include pollution emissions, waste generation, consumption of raw materials, energy, water and noise; other factors regarding environmental performance including performance against legal provisions; and the name and accreditation number of the environmental verifier, the date of validation and deadline for submission of the next statement.

In May 2001 the European Commission issued a recommendation on the recognition, measurement and disclosure of environmental issues in the annual accounts and annual reports of companies.[40] The Commission recognised two problems: that any or all of the different stakeholder groups could feel that the disclosures were insufficient or unreliable and that there was a low level of voluntary disclosure, even in sectors which have a significant impact on the environment. The lack of harmonised guidelines also has the consequence that investors and others are unable

---

[40] OJ L 156, 13.6.2001, p. 33.

to compare companies or adequately assess environmental risks affecting the financial position of the company.

The Recommendation highlights the need to avoid burdensome reporting obligations and also to ensure that any such rules should be compatible with the Fourth and Seventh Directives. In this light the Commission recommends disclosure if the issues are material to the organisation's financial performance or financial position. Organisations should then disclose in their annual and consolidated reports the policies that have been adopted and reference to any certification such as EMAS; improvements made in key areas with physical data if possible, for example on emissions; progress on implementing environmental protection measures; information on the enterprise's environmental performance such as energy use, materials use, water use, emissions and waste disposals; and reference to any separate environmental report produced. Balance sheets should contain details of provisions and environmental liabilities and the notes to the annual accounts and consolidated accounts should contain details of valuation methods applied on environmental issues, extraordinary environmental expenditures, details relating to provisions in the balance sheet as well as details about contingent environmental liabilities and costs incurred as a result of fines and penalties for non-compliance with environmental regulations and compensations paid to third parties.

It is notable that the European legislative provisions, like those in the UK, do not lay down requirements for separate full reports on environmental or social impacts. Rather, these aspects are to be included in the general annual reports and accounts. In part this reflects an intention to avoid costly reporting burdens and it arguably also highlights the relevance of social and environmental aspects to the financial performance of the company. Indeed, the European Commission's Recommendation aims to make separate environmental reports and the annual accounts and annual reports more consistent, cohesive and closely associated. The Recommendation seeks to ensure that the environmental disclosures are incorporated in the annual reports and annual accounts in a way that complements the more detailed and wide-ranging separate environmental reports. The Recommendation also aims for appropriate disclosure that is relevant to users' understanding of the financial statements, and to identify relevant disclosures to allow for comparability and consistency.

In addition, the European Environmental Reporting Awards were established in 1997.[41] Such schemes give to environmental reporting a

---

[41] In 2000 the overall winner was Shell International (UK)!

higher profile and contribute to increased quality of such reports. These schemes also have persuasive influence and companies refer to them in their reports.

Other European jurisdictions have adopted a stronger stance than the European Union or the UK towards environmental reporting. In Denmark the Environmental Protection Act 1996 requires relevant companies to produce 'green' accounts disclosing consumption of energy, water, raw materials and the type and quantity of pollutants to the air, land and water. In the Netherlands the Environmental Management Act 1999 requires high impact companies to produce reports on environmental impact to the government and to the public. In Norway the Law of Accounts of 1999 requires companies to give an account in their Directors' Report of their impact on the environment and on planned measures to reduce this impact. In Sweden companies are required by the Law of Accounts to provide information on their impact on the environment and their level of compliance with environmental codes. France recently introduced a new company law code in 2003 requiring listed companies to report on their impact on the environment, any environmental expenditure and any management controls in place.[42]

With regard more specifically to social reporting and accounting, again most aspects tend to be left to voluntary initiatives. Increasingly, public initiatives support the development of social and environmental reporting. For example, the Danish Social Index is a self-assessment tool for measuring the degree to which a company lives up to its social responsibilities. Similarly, in 1998 the High Level Group on Economic and Social Implications of Industrial Change invited companies of more than 1,000 employees to publish voluntarily a Management Change Report – an annual report on employment and working conditions.

A variety of organisations have developed standards for social accounting, reporting and auditing. They have varied approaches – from process to performance standards, from voluntary to mandatory standards and from single issue to multi-issue standards. International initiatives focus on the globalisation of social standards, public disclosure of information and the development of social reports such as Social Accountability 8000 and the Global Reporting Initiative.

At the European level support has been given for triple bottom line reporting. For example, the European Commission Communication concerning Corporate Social Responsibility noted that 'triple bottom

---

[42] This information has been taken from Table 2 Accounting and reporting standards, in Environment Agency, *Environmental Disclosures* (July 2004), available at www.environment-agency.gov.uk, at p. 14.

line reporting' of economic, social and environmental indicators is emerging as good practice and made reference to the Global Reporting Initiative that sets down guidelines for this type of reporting activity.[43] The EU Multi-stakeholder Forum on Corporate Social Responsibility aims to promote transparency and convergence of corporate social responsibility practices and instruments and to create guiding principles on development of commonly agreed guidelines and criteria for corporate social responsibility measurement, reporting and assurance. Reporting is regarded as part of an overall strategy for better environmental impact by corporate actions.

A recent European Commission proposal to amend the accounting directives, published in October 2004,[44] includes a proposed mandatory corporate governance statement on the basis of a 'comply or explain' approach – including a statement about risk management processes. The Commission proposes a corporate governance statement for listed EU companies along the lines set out in its Action Plan thereby limiting information requirements to what is strictly necessary, i.e., reference to the corporate governance code to which the company submits, the extent to which that code is complied with, information about shareholders' meetings, and the composition and operation of the board and its committees.

International standards and programmes

As was noted above, the legislative efforts of individual states and of the European Union with regard to environmental and social reporting are relatively undeveloped. However, at the international level a number of influential programmes have been created to provide benchmarks and guidelines for environmental and social reporting. For example, the United Nations Environmental Programme resulted in the Montreal Protocol 1987 on Substances that Deplete the Ozone Layer, whereby in 1996 industrialised countries ceased production and consumption of a significant proportion of all ozone-depleting substances. The United Nations Environmental Programme has also initiated the development of environmental guidelines for sports federations and countries bidding

---

[43] European Commission Communication concerning, 'Corporate Social Responsibility: A business contribution to sustainable development', para. 5.3, p. 14.

[44] Proposal for a Directive of the European Parliament and of the Council amending Council Directives 78/660/EEC and 83/349/EEC concerning the annual accounts of certain types of companies and consolidated accounts COM/2004/0725 final – COD 2004/0250, Brussels 27.10.2004, not yet published in Official Journal but available at http://europa.eu.int/scadplus/leg/en/lvb/l26009.htm.

for the Olympic Games. Similarly, the International Organization for Standardization (ISO), a non-governmental organisation established in 1947, comprises a worldwide federation of national standards with the aim of establishing international standards to reduce barriers to international trade. ISO 14001, for example, sets out requirements for establishing an environmental management system. Companies must satisfy the requirements of ISO 14001 in order to qualify for ISO certification. The benefits of the system are that it ensures involvement of top-level management, it promotes environmental management, and it provides a framework for continual improvements.

The OECD Principles of Corporate Governance[45] provide basic principles of disclosure and transparency, including the principle that disclosure for the purpose of corporate governance should include material information on employees and other stakeholders. The notes to the Principles advise that issues material to employees and other stakeholders include those issues that may materially affect the performance of the company. Therefore, disclosure may include management/employee relations, and relations with other stakeholders such as creditors, suppliers and local communities. The Principles annotations also state that human resource policies, such as programmes for human resource development or employee share ownership plans, can communicate important information on the competitive strengths of companies to market participants. The OECD has supplemented these Principles with *Guidelines for Multinational Enterprises*[46] and these also contain principles relating to disclosure. These expressly encourage enterprises 'to apply high quality standards for non-financial information including environmental and social reporting where they exist.'[47] The Guidelines state that enterprises should disclose material information on financial and operating results of the company, its objectives, major share ownership and voting rights and other matters. The Guidelines also state that enterprises are *encouraged*

to communicate additional information that could include value statements or statements of business conduct intended for public disclosure including information on the social, ethical and environmental policies of the enterprise and other codes of conduct to which the company subscribes. In addition, the date of adoption, the countries and entities to which such statements apply and its performance in relation to these statements may be communicated; information on systems for managing risks and complying with laws, and on statements or

---

[45] Draft Revised Text (January 2004).
[46] OECD, *The OECD Guidelines for Multinational Enterprises* (revised 2000).
[47] III, Disclosure, para. 2, at p. 20.

codes of business conduct; and information on relationships with employees and other stakeholders.[48]

It is interesting to note however, that in its Guidelines, the OECD makes the point that: 'Disclosure requirements are not expected to place unreasonable administrative or cost burdens on enterprises. Nor are enterprises expected to disclose information that may endanger their competitive position unless disclosure is necessary to fully inform the investment decision and to avoid misleading the investor.'[49]

Although there are no mandatory standards at international level there are more focused international initiatives towards bottom line reporting, such as the Sustainability Reporting Guidelines issued in 2000 by the Global Reporting Initiative Steering Committee. The Committee membership comprises representatives from bodies such as ACCA, the Institute of Social and Ethical Accountability, the New Economics Foundation and Sustainability Ltd from the UK. These voluntary sustainability reporting guidelines make links between the three dimensions – economic, environmental and social – and the aim is to assist organisations to report information that complements existing reporting standards. This information should be consistent, comparable and easy to understand, so that parties contemplating a relationship have a clear picture of the human and ecological impact of the business in order to be able to make an informed decision. Such information should also enable management to have the means to develop information systems to provide the basis for monitoring performance, facilitating inter-company comparisons and reporting to stakeholders. According to the GRI, a sustainability report has six parts: a statement from the Chief Executive Officer describing key elements of the report; a profile providing an overview of the organisation and the scope of the report which sets the context for the next four parts; an executive summary and key indicators to assist stakeholders to assess trends and make inter-company comparisons; a statement of the vision for the future and how that integrates economic, environmental and social performance – policies, organisations and systems; an overview of the governance and management systems to implement this vision with a discussion of how stakeholders have been engaged; and a performance review.[50]

---

[48] III, Disclosure, para. 5, at p. 20.
[49] Commentary on Disclosure, para. 18, at p. 45.
[50] See Global Reporting Initiative, *Sustainability Reporting Guidelines* (2002), especially Part Four.

Features of environmental and social reporting

The voluntary nature of most social and environmental reporting means that such reports are difficult to compare and that their contents will vary. Without clear requirements, companies have discretion about what to put into their report and with different corporate objectives this will inevitably create variations. However, it is possible to identify a basic set of common elements in environmental reports, social reports and sustainability reports.

Features of environmental reports

Brophy observes that environmental reports range from a simple public relations statement to a detailed and in-depth examination of the company's environmental performance, policies, practices and future direction.[51] Within this range there are, according to Brophy, five stages of environmental reporting: (i) green 'glossies' or newsletters or short statements in the annual report; (ii) one-off environmental reports, often linked to first policy statements; (iii) annual reporting linked to an environmental management system; (iv) provision of full TRI-style performance data on an annual basis; (v) sustainable development reporting, linking environmental, economic and social aspects of corporate performance.

Whilst Brophy does not identify specific elements common to environmental reports it is possible to identify common elements in statements produced under the Voluntary European Eco-Management and Audit Scheme. These include: an introduction from the Chief Executive; background information about the organisation; a description of the organisation's environmental policy; a statement about the organisation's overall position regarding the environment; an assessment of progress made towards specific targets established in previous reports; and a description of new targets or actions to improve the organisation's environmental performance in the future.

Features of social reports

The main social indicators seem to depend on which code or guidelines are followed. Business in the Community's *Winning with Integrity* takes

---

[51] See Brophy, 'A Stakeholder's View of Environmental Reporting' at www.environmental-expert.com/articles/article20/article20.htm.

the business case for social and sustainability issues and identifies seven areas which can impact on the success of most companies: purpose and values, workforce, marketplace, environment, community, human rights, guiding principles.[52] The Better Business Bureau in Maniland, BC, identifies nine areas covered by a corporate social report: community, diversity, employee relations, environment, international operations, product and business practices, military weapons, nuclear power and 'other'.[53] One problem is that social accounting often appears as a series of 'add-ons'– a little on charity donations, a little on disabled recruitment policy – so that it is not always possible to identify features in common between different social reports. Consequently, social performance indicators have not been clearly established. For example, Ella Joseph observes that only a few companies report on the ethnic diversity of their companies, and she finds no company providing information on child labour in their supply chains.[54] Joseph also observes that some sectors report less than others. Thus in insurance, communications, retail and banking environmental issues are seen to be less relevant.[55] Smaller companies are also less likely to report.[56] These observations reveal considerable variation among social reports, possibly arising from the different guidelines adopted by companies and the individual priorities and objectives of companies.

Features of sustainability reports

Values-based organisations, such as Body Shop and Co-op Bank, pioneer more socially-rounded reports through social and ethical accounting, auditing and reporting. The main feature of a sustainability report is that it includes social, environmental and economic dimensions in one report. The report puts forward a 'triple bottom line', and will normally contain an expressed commitment to involve stakeholders directly in the reporting process.

Poor quality of reporting

Not only has the broad voluntary framework resulted in varied reports from companies, but also most reports contain insufficient details on

---

[52] Business in the Community, *Winning with Integrity*, Summary (2000) at p. 4.

[53] See Better Business Bureau, Maniland, BC at www.bbbmbc.com/csreport.htm.

[54] Ella Joseph, 'Promoting corporate social responsibility: is market-based regulation sufficient?' (Institute for Public Policy Research, 2002) *New Economy* 96–101, available at www.ippr.org/research at p. 98.

[55] Joseph, *ibid.*

[56] Ella Joseph, *ibid.*

specific issues. For example, the European Commission, in its Green Paper *Promoting a European Framework for Corporate Social Responsibility* in 2001, expressed the view that 'companies' approaches to social reporting are as varied as their approaches to corporate social responsibility. In order for these reports to be useful, a global consensus needs to evolve on the type of information to be disclosed, the reporting format to be used, and the reliability of the evaluation and audit procedure.'[57] The Green Paper continued, 'few of them provide much detail on their policies and performance on human resource management and on employment issues such as bargaining and recognition, staff consultation and training and board accountability'. Similarly, the European Commission[58] recognises that the level of diversity on corporate social responsibility and the fact that companies operating in different countries have to adapt to the specific situations in such countries has helped to create an 'impressive richness of voluntary enterprise initiatives, which often include innovative elements, but also implies challenges, namely the lack of transparency and comparability'.[59] The Communication adds that:

The interest in benchmarks has resulted in an increase of guidelines, principles and codes during the last decade. Not all of these tools are comparable in scope, intent, implementation or applicability to particular businesses, sectors or industries. They do not answer to the need for effective transparency about business social and environmental performance.[60]

Other factors in combination with the variation of social and environmental reports also reduce their quality. For example, such reports are seldom verified by third parties. Further, companies rarely use quantitative performance data to support the policy assertions made in the social or environmental reports.[61] Ella Joseph observes that although seventy-nine of the top 100 FTSE produce social reports, much of it is corporate gloss and only sixteen such companies used quantitative data to back up their performance claims.[62]

---

[57] *Promoting a European Framework for Corporate Social Responsibility*, Brussels, 1.7.2001, COM (2001) 366 final, at p. 16 heading 3.2.
[58] European Commission, 'Communication concerning Corporate Social Responsibility: A business contribution to sustainable development' (COM 2002) 347 final, Brussels, 2.7.2002.
[59] *Ibid.*, at p. 12.
[60] At p. 12–13, para. 5.
[61] Deborah Doane, 'Market Failure: the case for mandatory social and environmental reporting', *New Economics Foundation*, March 2002.
[62] Joseph, at p. 97.

Often such reports amount to saying no more than that 'the company values its employees and is concerned to look after their well-being' or that 'the company is committed to its customers'.[63] Stittle provides a survey of the social reporting of ten leading FTSE 100 companies and notes that their approach to ethical reporting is largely subjective and often unstructured. He also observes that many of the companies make claims that are not supported with evidence or examples. For example, AstraZeneca plc, in its 2001 report, states that the company 'aims to promote a culture of integrity and high ethical standards', but does not show supporting evidence or explanation for this claim.[64] Similarly, British Telecommunications plc claims to have assessed its policies under the criteria established by the UN Declaration of Human Rights and its environmental management system under ISO 14001 but does not provide the result of this assessment.[65]

The reports are not all bad and it is fair to say that they have improved over time. Owen, for example, has observed improvement in structure and content, and 'fewer blatant public relations exercises, a willingness to convey bad news, quantified targets, more verification statements and steady development of industry-wide performance indicators enabling intra-sectoral comparisons'. He adds, however, that the better quality reports are produced by the best companies but that the 'vast majority of companies supply brief rudimentary information at best and second tier companies and SMEs tend not to have such reports'.[66]

The voluntary framework

The variations and variable quality of corporate social and environmental reports are a result of the predominantly voluntary focus of regulation in this area. This leads to the question: why is the emphasis on voluntary practice rather than on mandatory regulatory requirements? There are several possible explanations and justifications for this voluntary approach and reliance on best practice. One is that it avoids the problems

---

[63] David Owen and Tracey Swift, 'Introduction, Social accounting, reporting and auditing: Beyond the rhetoric?', *Business Ethics: A European Review* (2001), Vol. 10, Issue 1, pp. 4–8. Owen and Swift refer to John Pilger who calls such activity 'specious gloss, the work of fixers, known as spin doctors and assorted marketing and public relations experts. . .' See John Pilger, *Hidden Agendas* (Vintage, London, 1998), at p. 5.

[64] John Stittle, at p. 359.

[65] John Stittle, at p. 361.

[66] David L. Owen, 'Recent developments in European social and environmental reporting and auditing practices – A critical evaluation and tentative prognosis' Research paper series, international centre for corporate social responsibility, No. 3 2003, (www.nottingham.ac.uk/business/ICCSR).

of boiler plating that frequently arises in a compliance culture. Voluntary reporting could give rise to better reports because they are created willingly. Indeed, a particular problem with compliance approaches is that they can allow companies to set low objectives for improvement and report these achievements with little confidence that there has been significant environmental benefit.[67] Of course that is true if the compliance approaches themselves set low standards and this might well be the case where they attempt to cover a diverse range of companies and activities and focus on the lowest requirements that all companies may achieve. It could be argued in response that the market will provide sufficient incentive for companies to be transparent about their social and environmental impacts since the market will ensure that companies will be rewarded for managing risk by better financial performance.[68]

However, the evidence would suggest otherwise. Deborah Doane for example notes that market mechanisms rely on informed consumers even though the perfectly informed ethical consumer is non-existent. Doane suggests that fewer than 5 per cent of consumers make an active and informed choice in the majority of their purchasing decisions. Furthermore, the incentives for business are insufficient since, in reality, even businesses that do not report on their social and environmental impacts are still rewarded by their customers. Often such companies still enjoy access to capital and have a broad customer base to enable them to profit. Moreover, companies may resist social reporting because they fear that it leads to resentment and suspicion of their motives.[69] Indeed there are real disincentives for companies to produce social or environmental reports as is noted by Tixier. For example, such reports can actually lead to discontent among the public and in the marketplace, such as where a company refuses to be held responsible or where the company produces an incomplete or inaccurate piece of information. These dangers lead companies generally to be discreet about their patronage for fear of being accused of commercial manipulation. Furthermore, publicised responsible behaviour induces public anger if problems then occur, making the company vulnerable and subject to boomerang effects.[70]

---

[67] Barry Elliott and Jamie Elliott, *Financial Accounting and Reporting* (8th edn, FT, Prentice Hall, London, 2004) at p. 841.
[68] Deborah Doane, above.
[69] Maud Tixier, 'Note: Soft vs Hard Approach in Communicating on Corporate Social Responsibility' *Thunderbird International Business Review* (2003) Vol. 45, 71–91.
[70] Maud Tixier, *ibid.*, pp. 71–91.

Connected problems are that the short-term demands of the capital market stand in the way of long-term incentives for social and environmental reporting by companies, such as developing long-term markets, protecting natural assets, and ensuring an educated and diverse source of labour.[71] In addition, the voluntary system is open to capture and management control. Owen and Swift describe this as managerial and professional interests capturing the business case so that 'true accountability slips off the agenda'.[72] They cite Elkington's view of the triple bottom line thesis, which is that social responsibility provides a major means of achieving long-term economic success, with the effect that socially-responsible companies will prosper. However, as Owen and Swift suggest, this is 'consultant speak' the use of which is likely to 'displace necessary in-depth analysis of the tensions and problems encountered in holding powerful economic organisations to account'.[73] The result is, as Owen highlights, problems of over-aggregation of data and poor links to financial reporting that are often unclear; and that explanations of performance variations are often lacking; report verification is very poor tending to focus exclusively on systems compliance issues; such verification mechanisms through which managers appoint auditors lack independence in contrast with the financial reporting process where auditors are appointed by shareholders.[74] This managerial capture of the process means also that stakeholder views and concerns do not get included in corporate decision-making. Rather, stakeholders are told that their interests coincide with those of the corporate management and the capital providers. The effect is that the institutional framework does not allow stakeholders to hold management accountable for their decisions.[75]

The voluntary framework results in a lack of enforcement mechanisms and stakeholders are forced to rely on business to uphold the codes.[76] This inevitably leads to a negative assessment of the ability of social and

---

[71] Deborah Doane, 'Market Failure: the case for mandatory social and environmental reporting' Paper presented to ippr seminar, The Transparent Company (20 March 2002), available at www.ippr.org/research.

[72] David Owen and Tracey Swift, 'Introduction, Social accounting, reporting and auditing: Beyond the rhetoric?' *Business Ethics: A European Review* (2001), Vol. 10, Issue 1, pp. 4–8.

[73] *Ibid.*

[74] David L. Owen, 'Recent developments in European social and environmental reporting and auditing practices – A critical evaluation and tentative prognosis', Research paper series, international centre for corporate social responsibility, No. 3 2003, (www.not tingham.ac.uk/business/ICCSR).

[75] Owen and Swift, at p. 7.

[76] Doane.

environmental reporting to make management and companies accountable for their environmental and social impacts, arguably one of the
primary theoretical objectives of this type of reporting. As Owen observes:

> corporate governance mechanisms have not evolved so that stakeholders can
> effectively use information provided, or highlight information not provided, with
> a view to influencing corporate decision-making. In essence stakeholders within
> the environmental reporting process, unlike shareholders within the financial
> reporting process, appear largely disenfranchised and therefore unable to hold
> corporate management accountable in any meaningful sense.

If stakeholders do not get an opportunity to respond to social and
environmental reports then the democratic aspect of this activity is also
lost. As is stated by Owen, 'the whole raison d'etre for social and
environmental accounting lies in its potential to make certain aspects
of corporate activity more transparent to external stakeholders who may
then be empowered to hold corporate management accountable for their
actions insofar as they are affected by them'.[77] Owen continues:

> accounting's preoccupation with financial performance as the sole yardstick of
> organisational success leads inevitably to its implication in the environmental
> destruction, social dislocation and exploitation of the weakest members of soci-
> ety consequent upon such a narrow interpretation of 'success'. Current corpor-
> ate social and environmental reporting initiatives are therefore to be judged
> on the basis of whether they offer more emancipatory alternatives that may
> improve the situation in terms of delivering greater levels of organisational
> accountability.[78]

From this point of view a system for comparing reports produced by
companies might assist in encouraging companies to provide useful
information, if only to avoid a negative comparison with other companies who produce such reports more willingly. A number of schemes
have been established to assist in this way. For example, the London
Benchmarking Group, which was established in 1994, and the Impact
on Society website created in 2001, are designed to assist companies in
assessing and targeting their community programmes and also to provide users with access to comparative data about companies using a
common set of indicators against which those companies may be measured. The information on the Impact on Society website contains company profiles which can be measured against specific indicators that

---

[77] David L. Owen, 'Recent developments in European social and environmental reporting
and auditing practices – A critical evaluation and tentative prognosis', Research paper
series, international centre for corporate social responsibility, No. 3 2003, (www.not
tingham.ac.uk/business/ICCSR), at p. 2.
[78] Owen, *ibid.*, at p. 2.

enable the companies to be compared and contrasted.[79] The point remains, however, that though these are helpful measures their voluntary nature means that companies are not bound to comply with them. Similar measures would be made much stronger if there were a compulsory registration system for social and environmental impact reports that would be accessible to all interested users, as is the case with the annual accounts.

Should social and environmental reporting be linked to financial measures?

As has been noted above, shareholders may have an interest in social and environmental reports, particularly if they demonstrate a link with the company's profit levels. Additionally there is a growing body of ethical investors who demand the companies in which they invest to have a socially responsible approach to their activities and such investors refuse to make investments in companies that cause harm or are indifferent to the environment.[80] Not only so-called ethical investors show a concern with social and environmental reports. Indeed, traditional economic investors will also become increasingly concerned with this kind of information if it has a material impact upon the company's financial condition and prospects; so they too would require full disclosure of environmental and other liabilities and obligations. Indeed, they could claim to have been financially damaged by companies that have failed to disclose any such social or environmental problems.[81] However, to encourage shareholders to become active requires a demonstration of the link between environmentally friendly practices and economic growth – sustainable development. Elliott and Elliott anticipate that the more transparency achieved the less volatile the share prices will be.[82]

---

[79] See Ella Joseph, 'Promoting corporate social responsibility – Is market-based regulation sufficient?' (IPPR, New Economy, 2002) and for more details see LB Group: www.lbg-online.net, and Impact on Society website 2001 www.iosreporting.org.

[80] Ferman at p. 512. For details of the increasing numbers of socially responsible investors in the UK see CSR Campaign, 'A question of business fundamentals: Socially responsible investment goes mainstream in the United Kingdom almost' available at www.csrcampaign.org/publications/excellencereport2002/uk2/printpage/content.aspx. See also Michele Sutton, 'Between a rock and a judicial hard place: corporate social responsibility reporting and potential legal liability under *Kasky* v. *Nike*' (2004) 72 *UMKC L Rev* 1159, at p. 1163.

[81] See, e.g., Perry E. Wallace, 'Disclosure of Environmental Liabilities Under the Securities Laws: The Potential of Securities-Market-Based Incentives for Pollution Control' (1993) 50 *Washington and Lee Law Review* 1093, at 1101, note 29 and accompanying text.

[82] Barry Elliot and Jamie Elliott, *Financial Accounting and Reporting* (8th edn, FT, Prentice Hall, London, 2004), at p. 842.

The extent to which shareholders are interested in social and environmental disclosure is open to question. Of course, as was discussed in chapter 4, shareholders are not a homogenous group necessarily. The interests of institutional investors may differ from the interests of individual investors and short-term and long-term investors will also have different priorities. Furthermore, there may be specific aspects of social and environmental information that may be of interest whilst other aspects may be considered less significant. Indeed, empirical evidence does suggest that shareholders do take an interest in certain aspects of social and environmental information. First, there is evidence that the market reacts to social disclosures[83] thereby indicating that they do have significance for shareholders, and it appears that individual investors do display an interest in social disclosures. Individual investors, according to Epstein and Freedman, are interested in having their companies report on certain aspects of social activities.[84] They particularly demand information on product safety and quality and about the company's environmental activities, and they show an interest in ethics, employee relations and community involvement.[85] As has already been observed above, there is also evidence to suggest that increasingly more investors are adopting the Socially Responsible Investing principles, with ethical investment funds being valued at over US\$ 2,000 billion in 1999.[86] This might lead to shareholders being prepared to challenge misleading reports by management. Such a challenge took place in the US, where shareholders challenged Nike inc for statements relating to treatment of workers in developing countries. *Kasky* v. *Nike* showed the dangers involved in making erroneous statements.[87] As Tixier suggests, companies are reluctant to report for fear of negative comments and suspicion that their reports are simply public relations measures.[88] Yet worse is to be caught concealing information or telling lies which may cast a long-lasting stain on the company's image.

The subject matter of social and environmental reporting shows inherently that shareholders are not the only or even the primary relevant

---

[83] See, e.g., A. Belkaoui, 'The Impact of the Disclosure of the Environment Effects of Organizational Behavior on the Market' (1976) *Financial Management* Winter, 26–31; J. C. Anderson and A. W. Fraankle, 'Voluntary Social Reporting: An Iso-beta Portfolio Analysis' (1980) *The Accounting Review*, July, Vol. 55, No. 3, 467–479.

[84] Marc J. Epstein and Martin Freedman, 'Social Disclosure and the Individual Investor' (1994) 7 *Accounting, Auditing and Accountability Journal* 94–109.

[85] *Ibid.*, at p. 107.

[86] Joseph, above.

[87] See Sutton, above, for an account of the proceedings.

[88] Maud Tixier, 'Note: Soft vs Hard Approach in Communicating on Corporate Social Responsibility', *Thunderbird International Business Review* (2003) Vol. 45, 71, at p. 76.

user group. As David Owen suggests, 'a wider audience is envisaged'.[89] Owen notes that recognition of other interest groups tends to be limited to reports on the physical environment 'to the almost complete exclusion of the social'.[90] Yet, as Owen argues, 'there are links between poverty, inequality and environmental degradation, so to exclude consideration of the social dimension results in attention being focused merely on the symptoms and not the causes of environmental problems. Stakeholders other than shareholders are likely to be concerned with social as well as purely environmental concerns.'[91]

The steps towards addressing the interests and needs of stakeholders other than shareholders raise new challenges for those involved in the social accounting and reporting process, not least the accountants and auditors. They need to consider, according to Elliott and Elliott, whether their primary concern will be to serve the interests of the shareholders or the interests of management, or to focus on equity issues and social welfare.[92]

Role of auditors in social and environmental reporting

Accountants and auditors have traditionally been the friend of the collective body of shareholders and their practice has been to deal with and verify the financial accounts. Thus the notion of involving them in social and environmental reporting presents a sea change in their role for the company. However, O'Dwyer offers at least four positive reasons for accountants to have a role in social and ethical reporting.[93] First, accountants can offer significant technical expertise in the process of reporting, whether it be financial reporting or social and environmental reporting. The production of accounts relies on collection and dissemination of information and in large organisations these will involve complex information systems. Frequently, such systems are developed and maintained by accountants. The same technique is relevant for social accounting and clearly accountants have the skills to help develop the information systems necessary for social accounting. Secondly, the quantitative aspects of social and environmental reports, such as employee turnover, financial donations, number of clients served, are

---

[89] Owen (2003).
[90] Owen (2003).
[91] Owen (2003).
[92] Elliott and Elliott, at p. 833.
[93] Brendan O'Dwyer, 'The legitimacy of accountants' participation in social and ethical accounting, auditing and reporting' (2001) 10 *Business Ethics: A European Review* 27, at pp. 29–31.

within the skills of accountants. Thirdly, the large accounting firms that have a global reach are equipped to cope with the complex information systems across multinational companies. Fourthly, financial auditors possess the skills to assess the truth of some of the information provided in social, ethical and environmental reports, such as numerical accounts, and the integrity of the internal management systems. O'Dwyer makes clear that these positive contributions are dependent on a stakeholder/risk management conception of social and ethical accounting, auditing and reporting. This approach regards such reporting activity as complementary and instrumental to the company's financial performance.

However, the role of accountants in social, ethical and environmental reporting is more questionable if the concern is accountability to stakeholders. O'Dwyer observes the inevitability of trade-offs between economic and social objectives. In this context, the ability of accountants to pursue accountability to stakeholders is limited by their own self-interest as profit-based businesses concerned to perform a service for their customer rather than seeking to assist in accountability processes to protect the public interest.[94] Mathews refers to this problem as a narrow view of ethics in the professionalism of accountants.[95] Their codes of professional ethics, for example, are designed for the purpose of regulating the conduct of professional and professional, and professional and client, and no other relationship. 'Professional codes are not designed or intended to relate to the wider world', claims Mathews.[96] In addition, much of social reporting contains non-financial and qualitative aspects 'on which accountants may find it difficult to make a judgement given the absence of "hard" numbers'.[97] The consequence of their lack of expertise and experience on these qualitative matters is not only to raise suspicion regarding their competence but also 'raises the risk of the auditor increasingly relying on client management in terms of asking questions and assessing responses and poses an initial threat to the independence of the financial auditor in an area where he/ she may feel less competent'.[98] Their independence may also be undermined by the fact that they may well be providing other, more lucrative, services for the social audit client, such as financial audit, and this in turn will

---

[94] *Ibid.*
[95] M. R. Mathews, 'Social and Environmental Accounting: A Practical Demonstration of Ethical Concern?' (1995) 14 *Journal of Business Ethics* 663–71, at p. 663.
[96] *Ibid.*
[97] O'Dwyer, at p. 32.
[98] O'Dwyer, *ibid.*, at p. 32. See also T. Lee, 'A stakeholder approach to auditing' (1998) 9 *Critical Perspectives on Accounting*, 217–26.

discourage them from engaging in the conflict which could be regarded as an inevitable part of external social auditing.

The stakeholder-wide potential of social and environmental reports and the subject matter which may be sociological or scientific will also present challenges which accountants and auditors are arguably not qualified to resolve. Indeed, both Doane and Joseph observe that accountant verification is very poor and frequently ignores matters that have not been included in the report.[99] Often, verification procedures consist only of a fact-checking exercise and frequently they are linked to the consultancy role of auditors regarding the direction of overall strategy thereby reducing their level of independence. Yet, at the same time, verification by independent third parties of the information published in social responsibility reports is needed in order for the reports to avoid criticism that they are public relations schemes without substance.

Stittle goes further in his attack on accountants, accusing them of hindering the development of social reporting, arguing that the lack of real concern by the accountants has been a major factor allowing companies to develop their own restricted interpretation of ethical reporting. He cites Cowe who claims that 'most individual accountants and all accountancy bodies seem to have perceived the ethical and social issues as political rather than professional concerns so that they are not issues with which the profession should concern itself'.[100]

Any verification process requires clarification of the measures against which a company's performance and the statements in its report will be assessed. The Global Responsibility Initiative on sustainability reports suggests a number of specific indicators for such reviews. Economic indicators include profits, intangible assets, investments, wages and benefits, labour productivity, community development and suppliers. Environmental indicators include products and services, disposal of waste, suppliers, travel objectives and targets such as product distribution, fleet operation, miles travelled. Social indicators include quality of management, health and safety, wages and benefits, training and education, and freedom of association.[101]

Effectively, as Owen and Swift suggest, the role of verification depends on what is wanted from social and environmental reporting: if it is a

---

[99] Deborah Doane above and Ella Joseph above.

[100] Stittle, 'UK Corporate Ethical Reporting', at pp. 354–5, referring also to R. Cowe, 'Green Issues and the Investor: Inadequacies of Current Reporting Practice and Some Suggestions for Change' in D. Owen (ed.), *Accountancy and the Challenge of the Nineties* (Chapman and Hall, London, 1992) 125–36, at p. 126.

[101] Global Reporting Initiative, *Sustainability Reporting Guidelines* (2002), esp. at pp. 45–51.

stakeholder management or strategic risk exercise then the accountants may offer expertise and technical skills; but if social and environmental reporting is to be concerned with accountability then the relevance of accountants is open to question. In this case, it might be better to have a civil society organisation such as an NGO to do the audit in order to give legitimacy to the process.[102] Perhaps if stakeholders cannot be involved in the production of such reports an alternative would be to involve them in the verification process. Another possibility is for external bodies to conduct a social or environmental audit of the company. Such a move is regarded by the general public as desirable, according to a MORI poll conducted for *The Guardian* in 2004.[103] This might involve audits like those carried out in the European Providing Assurance on Environmental Reports programme assisted by the European Federation of Accountants Sustainability Working Party since 1999. These audits generally involve assessments of physical systems and staff appraisal – with site inspections, scientific testing of air samples, off-site testing and inspections, systems inspections to review the state of management and control systems, operational reviews to review actual practices in comparison with the stated systems, compliance audits for certification schemes, and awareness tests for staff about their knowledge of the systems and practices used in the organisation. Such audits might also include an assessment of the company's future – such as planning and design processes and preparedness for emergencies: the process would include the review of planning procedures, design reviews, review of emergency procedures and crisis plans. An Environmental Audit Report will contain a comprehensive review and comment on current operational practices, a list of action required turning on areas of immediate concern as well as areas for improvement over a set period of time, a qualitative assessment setting out the overall environmental risk being faced by the organisation and an action plan with a schedule of improvement and encouragement of good practice.

These issues of report contents and audit are covered in detail by the sustainability reporting guidelines provided by the Global Reporting Initiative and the Accountability AA 1000 standard. Whilst these have not been universally adopted by companies, and their voluntary nature allows companies to select aspects that suit them for their reporting process, they do at least provide a detailed indication of what would amount to good practice by companies if they were followed.

---

[102] Owen and Swift, at p. 7.
[103] Murray Armstrong, 'We're all off message' *The Guardian, The Giving List*, 8 November 2004, 11.

Sustainability reporting

A move to sustainability reporting rather than single areas such as environmental or social reporting separately has the potential to address the problems of information deficiency, such as lack of social information, and stakeholder exclusion.[104]

The most developed sustainability reporting initiatives are produced by the Global Reporting Initiative and the Institute of Social and Ethical Accountability Standard AA1000. The ISEA Foundation Standard AA1000, launched in 1999, is not directly concerned with prescribing reporting formats but aims to improve stakeholder engagement by specifying the appropriate internal processes necessary for reporting quality and for ensuring an inclusive approach. Together with guidelines and a professional qualification the standard makes up an AA 1000 Framework. The Framework is 'designed to improve accountability and performance by learning through stakeholder engagement'. The framework was 'developed to address the need for organisations to integrate their stakeholder engagement processes into daily activities'. The Framework does not prescribe what should be reported on but *how*. In this way it is designed to complement the GRI Reporting Guidelines. Notably, the AA 1000 standard highlights the connection between accountability to stakeholders and corporate financial performance. This has been interpreted as demonstrating its focus on a strategic stakeholder management approach, supporting in effect an 'instrumental stakeholder theory'.[105]

The Global Reporting Initiative Sustainability Reporting Guidelines 2002 are voluntary requirements that recognise that governance systems are increasingly expected to extend beyond their traditional focus on investors to address diverse stakeholders.[106] They act as a framework for reporting on an organisation's economic, environmental and social performance. The Guidelines present reporting principles and specific content to guide the preparation of organisation-level sustainability reports. The Guidelines assist organisations in presenting a balanced and reasonable picture of their economic, environmental and social performance and they aim to promote comparability of sustainability reports, while taking into account the practical considerations related to disclosing information across a diverse range of organisations, many with

---

[104] Owen (2003).
[105] See Brendan O'Dwyer, 'The legitimacy of accountants' participation in social and ethical accounting, auditing and reporting' (2001) 10 *Business Ethics: A European Review* 27, at p. 28.
[106] GRI, Sustainability Reporting Guidelines, at p. 2.

extensive and geographically dispersed operations. They also support benchmarking and assessment of sustainability performance with respect to codes, performance standards, and voluntary initiatives, and they serve as an instrument to facilitate stakeholder engagement.

As has been noted in other aspects of social and environmental reporting, the GRI Guidelines encourage the coordination of the processes of financial reporting and sustainability reporting, anticipating that over time financial performance measurement increasingly will benefit from the measurement of economic, environmental and social performance.

Various aspects contribute to the credibility of reports produced by organisations. Thus a report will gain credibility through the use of stakeholder consultation panels, strengthened internal data collection and information systems, issue-specific audits by appropriate experts, internal audits of data collection and reporting systems, use of the GRI Guidelines as the basis for report preparation (and indicating so), reviews and commentaries by independent external experts and use of independent assurance processes.[107]

The Guidelines adopt specific reporting principles. The principles of transparency, inclusiveness, and auditability form the framework for the report. Completeness, relevance and sustainability context inform decisions about what to report. Accuracy, neutrality and comparability are concerned with ensuring quality and reliability. Clarity and timeliness inform decisions about access to the report. Supporting these principles the Guidelines indicate what should comprise the content of the report. Thus the report should contain a statement of the company's vision and strategy, describing the reporting organisation's strategy with regard to sustainability, including a statement from the CEO. The report should include a profile which provides an overview of the reporting organisation's structure and operations and of the scope of the report. The governance structure and management systems should be described with reference also to stakeholder engagement efforts. To make the report more accessible it should contain a GRI content index – a table supplied by the reporting organisation identifying where the information is located within the organisation's report. The report should set out the performance indicators used to measure the impact or effect of the reporting organisation divided into integrated, environmental, and social performance indicators.

[107] GRI, Sustainability Reporting Guidelines, p. 18.

The Guidelines emphasise particular indicators. For example economic indicators cover direct economic impacts and so include customers, suppliers, employees, providers of capital, and the public sector. Environmental indicators include materials, energy, water, biodiversity, emissions, effluents, waste, suppliers, products and services, compliance, transport and the company's overall impact. Social indicators include labour practices and decent work: employment, labour/ management relations, health and safety, training and education, diversity and opportunity. The human rights social indicators include strategy and management, non-discrimination, freedom of association and collective bargaining, child labour, forced and compulsory labour, disciplinary practices, security practices and indigenous rights. Society-based social indicators include community, bribery and corruption, political contributions, competition and pricing. Product responsibility indicators include customer health and safety, products and services, advertising, respect for privacy.

The Guidelines refer to international conventions such as the ILO Tripartite Agreement, and the OECD *Guidelines for Multinationals*, in order to give measurement yardsticks and presumably allow for comparability. Whilst the GRI Guidelines remain voluntary they have gathered an increasing level of authority and this has encouraged the GRI to seek formal endorsement of the guidelines at national and European levels. They are also referred to in the US by shareholders seeking to persuade companies to provide corporate social responsibility reports. Thus in 2003 shareholders filed resolutions against fifteen companies seeking to obtain social reports based on the GRI Guidelines.[108]

It is clear from these Guidelines that they aim to improve the quality and usefulness of sustainability reports. They focus on stakeholder dialogue as a key stage in the reporting process, with reporting meant to facilitate stakeholder dialogue. As the GRI Guidelines state: 'reports alone provide little value if they fail to inform stakeholders or support a dialogue that influences the decisions and behaviour of both the reporting organisation and its stakeholders.'[109] It is clear that stakeholder dialogue involving ideas running both ways is a primary function of sustainability reporting.[110] This is emphasised by the main bodies and institutions concerned with such reporting. However, it is also important

---

[108] Anthony Harrington, 'Global Reporting Initiative picks up momentum', *Scotland on Sunday*, 18 April 2004.

[109] GRI Guidelines, 2002, at p. 2.

[110] See also Business in the Community, *Winning with Integrity, Summary* (November 2000), at p. 14.

to ensure that the stakeholder dialogue is not controlled in such a way as to prevent the achievement of accountability. Otherwise the ultimate objective of such reports – to achieve social change and better corporate behaviour – is unlikely to be fulfilled.

Conclusion

A Mori poll for *The Guardian* newspaper suggests that more than half of the population do not trust the motives of big business, and 82 per cent think that most companies try to get away with as much as they can. At the same time more than a third say that corporate responsibility is important to their purchasing decisions and evidence suggests that sales of ethical products such as fair trade goods and recycled items are rising.[111]

A broad range of voluntary sources have shaped the process of social and environmental reporting resulting in a confused 'pick and mix' arrangement for companies intending to engage in such practice. As is described by Clarke, the development of social reporting has been *ad hoc*, incomplete and produced in a hotchpotch fashion.[112] Some confusion remains about the stakeholder groups the company is communicating with and how those groups are to use the reports to hold the companies to account. Whilst this amounts to a soft form of accountability what remains is a distrust of corporate management by stakeholder groups seeking a positive duty to account upon the organisation in order to get true accountability. Such distrust is increased by the fact that companies may target issues that they perceive to be the major concerns affecting their activities. Moreover, they are able to dominate the process 'with a managerial turn'. This amounts to stakeholder management displacing any meaningful moves to corporate accountability towards stakeholders. In response to this problem Owen argues that what is required is not more focus groups or a place where people can express themselves but some countervailing power, some force that resists the imperatives of profit in the name of economic democracy.[113]

---

[111] Murray Armstrong, 'We're all off message', *The Guardian, The Giving List*, 8 November 2004, 11.

[112] J. Clarke, 'Corporate Social Reporting: An Ethical Approach' in C. Gowthorpe and J. Blake (eds.), *Ethical Issues in Accounting* (Routledge, London, 1998), 185, quoted by John Stittle, 'UK Corporate Ethical Reporting – A Failure to Inform: Some Evidence from Company Annual Reports' (2002) 107:3 *Business and Society Review* 349–70, at p. 351.

[113] Owen (2003).

A clear rationale for mandatory social and environmental reporting is required. As is argued by Joseph, a critical question for policy-makers is how far disclosure of social and environmental impacts can be an effective means to improve corporate behaviour. To make it effective a number of other criteria for reporting must be met: the issues that can be reported on must match the interests of stakeholders; there must be a measure or a metric that accurately captures performance and can be applied across organisations; that measure or metric should be audited; that measure or metric should be communicated to the appropriate stakeholders; and the relevant stakeholders should respond.[114] These points indicate that more than just transparency is required. Public response to corporate activity is also necessary, entailing a two-way discussion that leads to influence on the decision-making process and activities of the company. Indeed, as Monaghan states,

reporting is not an end goal in itself. It should instead be considered as one of many tools that can potentially enhance corporate accountability. The intended benefits of reporting are, or should be, to better allow a company to: coherently communicate its position as a good corporate citizen on material issues; influence stakeholder decision-making; and inform organisational learning. Yet . . . little evidence exists of social and sustainability reporting providing an effective tool in making a real difference to corporate decisions, practices and outcomes.[115]

---

[114] Joseph (2002).
[115] Philip Monaghan, 'Does Reporting Work? The Effect of Regulation' (2003) *Accountability Quarterly* (September 2003) (AQ21), at pp. 4–5.

11   Corporate reporting and employees

Introduction

'Economic entities are concerned with the use of monetary, material and human resources. As employers they are accorded a position of trust by their employees who look to the entity for employment security and prospects. In our view this relationship carries with it a responsibility to report to and about employees.'[1] When the Accounting Standards Steering Committee made this statement in *The Corporate Report* in 1975 the Committee acknowledged that employees were almost totally ignored in the Companies Acts and in corporate reports. Today, however, there is increasing recognition of the fact that companies' asset structures are in a state of change as the Western economy moves its focus from manufacturing towards service-based industries. This has brought about a change of emphasis from tangible assets, such as buildings, plant and machines, towards intangible assets, not least intellectual capital. This change raises challenges for corporate reporting practice because traditional accounting methods no longer give a full picture of a company's worth since they do not deal adequately with intangible assets. When employee issues are reported they tend to be treated as a cost rather than as an investment. Yet, despite this economic change, little has altered in the way companies report on employee issues since *The Corporate Report* was published. Indeed, one commentator observed recently that conventional reporting structures have failed to evolve to capture the extent and value of human capital, that the accounting profession has displayed a negative attitude and lack of commitment and that other regulators and legislators have also 'largely ignored the reporting of human capital'.[2]

---

[1] Accounting Standards Steering Committee, *The Corporate Report* (London, 1975), at p. 51, para. 6.13.
[2] John Stittle, 'UK Corporate Reporting of Human Capital: A Regulatory Failure to Evolve' (2004) 109 *Business and Society Review* 311, at pp. 311–2.

There are two dimensions in which employees are relevant to the debate on corporate disclosure. First, how does a company value its employees and report on its relationship with them? Secondly, how does a company relate to its employees? The first of these aspects of the company's relationship with its employees is largely unregulated. Indeed, there are very few formal requirements for a company to report *about* its employment relations. However, how a company relates *to* its employees has recently been the subject of legislative reform; new rules having been introduced in the UK in order to implement a European Directive on employee involvement.[3]

With regard to reporting about the company's employees and their contribution to the company's financial performance, there has been recent discussion about the benefits of human capital reporting, in particular its value in predicting a company's prospects of future success, since it is now recognised that human capital is an important asset relevant to a company's productivity and profitability. Thus, how employees are managed is part of a company's strategy and will influence that company's performance. One of the major challenges in this area is how to measure the value of human capital and how to relate it to the investors' interests in the company. A different perspective is that of employee relations in which employees' interests are to be considered in order to improve a company's ability to adapt to market and technological changes. By involving employees in company decision-making, they are more likely to remain motivated and adaptable in order for a company to develop and continue to profit.[4] Although discussion centres on the contribution that both employee reporting and employee involvement may provide towards the company's prospects, the two activities have

---

[3] See below.
[4] See for example, Directive 2002/14/EC of the European Parliament and of the Council of 11 March 2002 establishing a general framework for informing and consulting employees in the European Community OJ L 80/29, 23.3.2002, recital 7, preamble: 'There is a need to strengthen dialogue and promote mutual trust within undertakings in order to improve risk anticipation, make work organisation more flexible and facilitate employee access to training within the undertaking while maintaining security, make employees aware of adaptation needs, increase employees' availability to undertake measures and activities to increase their employability, promote employee involvement in the operation and future of the undertaking and increase its competitiveness.' According to the DTI in the UK also: 'A wide body of evidence has demonstrated that good practice in human resources, work organisation and employee relations can help raise employee commitment and engagement, helps reduce absenteeism and staff turnover, and leads to higher levels of productivity, performance and customer satisfaction.': DTI Guidance on the Information and Consultation of Employees Regulations 2004, para. 2, p. 3, available at www.dti.gov.uk/er/consultation/proposal. htm.

different emphases. One focuses on how a company will be perceived in the marketplace by the way in which it demonstrates its employment relations to the outside world, and the other focuses on how a company can maintain a committed workforce by ensuring that its employees are given an opportunity to participate in decisions by which they will be affected. Ultimately, it is possible to see in both areas that the traditional legal model of the company, which aims primarily to achieve shareholder value, has shaped the development of these aspects of company disclosure.

Human capital reporting

Human capital reporting has been largely a matter of voluntary initiative. It has been a 'cyclical and fashion driven issue'[5] with very little required by the companies legislation to be reported in the company's annual report. Indeed, in its discussion paper in 1975, the Accounting Standards Steering Committee stated that '[N]othing illustrates more vividly the nineteenth century origin of British company law than the way in which employees are almost totally ignored in the present Companies Acts and in corporate reports.'[6] Even the provisions for the operating and financial review did not guarantee that information about employee relations would feature in a company's narrative qualitative report. Indeed this fact has been the subject of negative criticism by a number of commentators who argue that employee matters could not be considered as immaterial to an understanding of the company's position and future prospects.[7]

What is human capital?

One of the first issues of controversy in human capital reporting is the definition of human capital. The lack of a settled definition perhaps contributes to the failure to develop this aspect of corporate disclosure. Westphalen adopts and refines an OECD definition and provides the following definition of human capital: 'the knowledge,

---

[5] John Stittle, 'UK Corporate Reporting of Human Capital', at p. 315.

[6] Accounting Standards Steering Committee, *The Corporate Report* (London, 1975), at p. 51, para. 6.12.

[7] See, for example, Select Committee on Trade and Industry Sixth Report on the Operating and Financial Review, Appendix 2, Memorandum by Tomorrow's Company, Written Evidence available at www.publications.parliament.uk/pa/cm200203/cmselect/cmtrdind/439/439ap13.htm.

skills, competencies and other attributes embodied in individuals or groups of individuals acquired during their life and used to produce goods, services or ideas in market circumstances.'[8] In the 2003 *Accounting for People* Consultation Paper human capital was defined as 'the relevant knowledge, skills, experience and learning capacity of the people available to the organisation'.[9] Stiles and Kulvisaechana argue that human capital is broader than human resources. Human capital emphasises collective knowledge but also the individuals must commit or engage with the organisation if effective utilisation of human capital is to happen. Thus, from their perspective, a company requires social capital and organisational (structural) capital as well as human capital. These three forms contribute to intellectual capital.[10] Guimón also focuses on intellectual capital and in doing so adopts the definition provided by Edvinsson and Malone as 'the sum of a company's intangible resources (including knowledge, technology, brand reputation, competencies etc)'.[11] From this range of definitions human capital is arguably at the narrower end with intellectual capital at the wider end, taking in not just knowledge, skills and experience of individuals, but also the collective results of employing such skills, knowledge and experience.

For human capital to be of practical value it requires a commitment to use it in such a way that enhances the company's reputation and ultimately that benefits the company in the long term. A company also needs to have a clear human capital management policy in operation in order to benefit from that human capital. Reporting on human capital is a necessary aspect of human capital management since the process of collecting and presenting information enables managers to assess the contribution of their employees and others to the company's success. In addition reporting is an important part of the process of dialogue in

[8] Sven-Åge Westphalen, *Reporting on Human Capital; Objectives and Trends*, paper presented to Technical Meeting 'Measuring and Reporting Intellectual Capital: Experience, Issues and Prospects', 9–10 June 1999, at p. 10. See also Organisation for Economic Cooperation and Development (OECD), *Measuring what people know* (Paris, 1996) and OECD, *Human Capital Investment* (Paris, 1998).

[9] Task Force on Human Capital Management, *Accounting for People: Consultation Paper* (May 2003), p.1 para. 2.

[10] Philip Stiles and Somboon Kulvisaechana, *Human Capital and Performance: A literature review* (University of Cambridge, Business School, 2003).

[11] José Guimón, 'Recent European models for intellectual capital management and reporting: A comparative study of the MERITUM and the Danish Guidelines'. See also L. Edvinsson and M. Malone, *Realizing your company's true value by finding its hidden brain power* (Harper Collins Publishers, New York, 1997).

which human capital contributions to the company's productivity and success are considered.

It is clear that human capital now represents a major part of a company's financial value. Whilst the key resources of enterprises since the industrial revolution have been perceived to be tangible assets such as plant and machinery, the last twenty years in the UK, and the Western economy generally, has shifted from a manufacturing base to a service base. This has created an 'organisational and operational emphasis on intellectual capital and other intangible assets'.[12] As O'Connor states: 'the distinctive feature of the emerging economy is an increasing emphasis on human capital – the knowledge of employees – rather than physical capital.'[13] This growing importance of intangible assets[14] requires new accounting methods for companies to be able to present their true value in their reports. Assessing a company's financial position and status also demands reference to the employee input. Bearing in mind the importance of human capital to a company's performance, why has a human capital reporting practice not been widely established?

Why has human capital reporting not developed in the same way as financial reporting?

Financial reporting rules and practice are a fundamental institution within the field of corporate activity. The financial markets operate largely by reference to financial information disclosed by companies. As has been shown in the previous chapters this has led to a sophisticated financial reporting system with complex rules and professional input. The same observations cannot be made for human capital reporting. Despite growing recognition of the importance of human capital to a company's value and position human capital reporting remains a sketchy and under-developed practice. There are a number of reasons for this poor development.

As has already been discussed in this book, the shareholder focus that has predominated in corporate law and theory has meant that corporate reporting requirements have tended to be designed to accommodate the

---

[12] Stittle, at p. 312. *Accounting for People*, Taskforce Report (DTI, London, October 2003), at p. 11.

[13] Marleen A. O'Connor, 'Rethinking Corporate Financial Disclosure of Human Resource Values for the Knowledge-Based Economy' (1998) 1 *University of Pennsylvania Journal of Labor and Employment Law* 527, at p. 528.

[14] European Commission, Enterprise Directorate General, *Study on the Measurement of Intangible Assets and Associated Reporting Practices* (EC, Brussels, 2003).

interests of shareholders. This approach has resulted in very little emphasis on human capital because in practice shareholders have shown a lack of interest in human resources matters.[15] The CIPD reports on a study carried out on behalf of Central London Focus which found that human resources indicators currently play little part in investors' decisions. According to the study, investors see no proven causal link between corporate performance and strategies directed at employee and human resources development and investment such as the Investors in People standard. The study suggested that investors are not very interested in human capital issues apart from senior management. In addition the study found that senior managers were cautious about the value of human capital reporting because it gives only 'snapshot views' when in reality human capital is a part of a dynamic picture of development in which people management is embedded in the business.[16]

Not only do shareholders demonstrate little interest in human capital reporting but also, according to Westphalen, a number of other stakeholders do not show sufficient interest in developing strategies for human capital reporting. Whilst they express an interest, many stakeholder groups have not really been active in creating frameworks or providing support structures for a system of reporting. For example, international state organisations such as the OECD and the European Commission have promoted investments in and reporting on human capital but they have not made clear recommendations or sought to influence the development of human capital reporting directly by creating support frameworks. Similarly, governments and trade unions, except in Scandinavia, have expressed an interest in human capital reporting but they have not taken specific steps to guide enterprises or organisations on how to report on human capital. Enterprises tend to have specific reasons for human capital reports, such as their contribution to improving the performance of the enterprise. Employees do not initiate or express an interest in human capital reports until after the enterprise introduces them. Westphalen concludes from his observations of the stakeholder groups that support is still at the level of testing and theorising rather than decision-making on or active promotion of reporting frameworks.[17] What appears to be the case is that even though

---

[15] Westphalen, at p. 19; O'Connor, at p. 548.

[16] CIPD, *The Change Agenda*, (2003), at pp. 3–4, describing the Central London Focus Report: PIRC, *Assessing the value of human capital: the experience of investors and companies* (Focus, London, 2001).

[17] See Westphalen, *Reporting on Human Capital: trends and objectives* (1999), pp. 18–20. See also Jens V. Frederiksen and Sven-Age Westphalen, *Human resource accounting: Interests and conflicts* (CEDEFOP, Thassaloniki, 1998).

academic research and management intuition suggests a clear link between human capital management reporting and measuring and profitability and competitiveness, very few companies are actively measuring and reporting. Other more administrative tasks take priority and accounting departments are not trained and lack the requisite experience to measure and report on human capital.[18] Human capital indicators tend to be used internally rather than reported externally and where they are reported they are generally aimed at external consultants, employees and prospective applicants.[19]

Another potential reason for the failure to establish itself as a key aspect of reporting is that human capital developments tend to be compliance driven with the result that the reporting side is merely instrumental to a different objective separate from the reporting activity itself. In its discussion on the OFR as a potential mechanism for human capital reporting the ICAEW notes, for example, that the Accounting for People Taskforce was set up to address the problem of the continuing gender pay gap. The Taskforce suggested that statutory reporting requirements on gender equality in pay within human capital reporting might reduce the gap.[20] The emphasis on the reporting is thus lost in a broader agenda or other motive.

Other reasons for the lack of an established practice of human capital reporting include a reluctance to reveal this type of information to competitors, the absence of legal requirements to do so and the inadequacy of accounting methodology for appropriate measurement of human capital.[21] Stittle blames the accounting profession and other regulators and legislators, since the accountants and their professional accountancy bodies, as the key drivers of implementing changes in UK reporting practice, have failed to show any meaningful or sustained initiatives in human capital reporting, and the regulators have largely ignored the reporting of human capital.[22] Consequently, the lack of clear guidance or any established standards to help 'kick-off' human capital reporting give no incentive for companies to start up the practice.[23]

---

[18] Ken Foong and Richard Yorston, *Human Capital Measurement and Reporting: A British Perspective* (London Business School, 2003), at p. 38.

[19] Foong and Yorston, *Human Capital Measurement and Reporting* (2003), at p. 38.

[20] ICAEW, *The Operating and Financial Review and Human Capital Reporting: Is the OFR the Place for Human Capital Reporting?* (London, 2003) p. 3, available at www.icaew.co. uk/policy.

[21] O'Connor, at p. 528.

[22] Stittle, at pp. 311–2, and 319–22. See also L. Parker, K. Ferris and D. Otley, *Accounting for the Human Factor* (Prentice Hall, New York, 1989), at p. 3.

[23] Foong and Yorston, at p. 32.

From the above account it appears that despite recognition of the potential value of human capital reporting, it has not become an established practice and remains a voluntary exercise by companies seemingly at the forefront of best practice. The Accounting for People Taskforce was set up with the aim of producing practical guidance for companies in order to encourage them to engage in human capital reporting. Such guidance would entail a survey of the features of human capital reporting and its benefits and potential disadvantages.

What are the features of human capital reporting?

Human capital, according to the Chartered Institute of Personnel and Development, represents the fit between the demand for and supply of human capabilities – the contribution of human capital is 'contingent upon the supply and relevance of employee competences to the business needs of the organisation as determined by its strategy'.[24] This context-dependent quality of human capital makes standardised measures problematic. This fact might explain why human capital reporting has developed through a number of stages since it was first introduced during the 1960s. In the first stage, human capital reporting was pre-dominantly based on accounting principles. Then, during the 1970s, a second stage was initiated from a management perspective, focusing on the optimised use of human capital 'as a means to gain the competitive edge'.[25] From the 1990s the third stage involved a 'balanced scorecard' operating within a global perspective. In other words the enterprise and its human capital interacts with the surrounding world and treats human capital as a dominant element upon which strategies are formulated and implemented and form a major input to the assessment of the enter-prises' total value.[26] The fourth stage was also developed during the 1990s and combines basic information on investments in human capital with human capital strategies and evaluation of returns. This represents a less ambitious approach than the balance scorecard but is more prag-matic and can therefore be a useful mechanism internally. The report

---

[24] Chartered Institute of Personnel and Development, *The Change Agenda* (2003), at p. 2.

[25] Westphalen, *Measuring and Reporting Intellectual Capital: Experiences, Issues and Prospects* (1999), at p. 14.

[26] See Robert S. Kaplan and David P. Norton, 'The Balanced Scorecard – Measures that Drive Performance' (1992) 70 *Harvard Business Review*, No. 1, January–February 71–9; Robert S. Kaplan and David P. Norton, *The Balanced Scorecard – Translating Strategy Into Action* (Harvard Business School Press, Boston, 1996); Robert S. Kaplan and David P. Norton, *The Strategy-focused Organization: How Balanced Scorecard Companies thrive in the New Business Environment* (Harvard Business School Press, Boston, 2001).

could in this way also be used to benchmark enterprises within and across sectors as well as countries but it is incomplete because it does not provide all the relevant information needed relating to the growing dominance of intangible inputs to production.[27]

Another model of human capital is the 'investment in people' model. This model is a standard on training investments and has been in operation since 1991. It has four principles – commitment, planning, action and evaluation – and these are pursued through an 'action line' of review, action, assessment, achievement and continuous improvement.[28] Since these are relatively broad principles each 'investment in people' plan is highly individualised.[29] Such an approach is problematic if standardisation is sought, but it allows investment in people to be a usable model. Companies pursue this award scheme because it improves their image, encourages better management of training and improved training processes and it improves employee morale and motivation.[30] These are all factors that indirectly impact on the company's overall performance. However, the restriction of the award to training aspects makes it too narrow for use as a general human capital management and reporting process. Such a process requires management and measurement and reporting of a potentially broad range of factors.

The contextual nature of human capital measurement could lead to a problem of meaningful reporting and comparable reporting. However, there are certain items that are generally recognised as relevant for a human capital report. These items include the size and composition of the workforce; retention and motivation of employees; the skills and competences necessary for business success and training to achieve these; remuneration and fair employment practices; leadership and succession planning.[31] In the UK the areas commonly reported on include staff turnover and retention, absenteeism, employee satisfaction, training, workforce demographics and diversity.[32]

The *Accounting for People Report* suggests that good human capital management reporting combines narrative and hard data about areas such as recruitment, skill, development and training, remuneration, job design, and organisational culture. This requires an evolutionary

---

[27] Westphalen, *Measuring and Reporting Intellectual Capital*, at p. 14.

[28] Westphalen, at p. 23.

[29] Westphalen, at p. 23.

[30] J. Hillage and J. Moralee, *The Return on Investors*, ies report 314 (Brighton, 1996).

[31] Taskforce on Human Capital Management, *Accounting for People*, Report (October 2003), p. 17, para. 22.

[32] Foong and Yorston, *Human Capital Measurement and Reporting: A British Perspective* (June 2003), at p. 24.

approach combining a strategic focus with safeguards to ensure balance, objectivity and progressive improvements in comparability to reconcile conflict between recognising individual company context and gaining common standards to allow comparability and reliability. On this basis the Taskforce recommends that human capital management reports should have a strategic focus communicating clearly, fairly and un- ambiguously the Board's current understanding of the links between the human capital management policies and practices, its business strat- egy and its performance; and including information on the size and composition of the workforce, retention and motivation of employees, the skills and competences necessary for success and training to achieve these, remuneration and fair employment practices, leadership and suc- cession planning. In addition, reports should be balanced and objective, following a process that is susceptible to review by auditors, and should provide information in a form that enables comparisons over time and uses commonly-accepted definitions where available and appropriate.

There is no single set of human capital management practice that can be described as best practice applicable to all organisations, nor agree- ment on a set of universal indicators. However, any report would need to combine qualitative and quantitative information on measures that shape the quality and sustainability of human capital within an organisation and their 'fit' with its business. The report should at least include an account of the firm's people strategy and the relation of this to its business strategy, evidence of how the organisation recruits, develops, manages and retains human capital, and an assessment of the effectiveness and performance of its human capital policies and practices.

What are the potential benefits of human capital reporting?

Several studies show a positive link between human capital, competitive- ness and performance and shareholder value. For example, the Char- tered Institute of Personnel Development research suggests that the quality of people management is a better predictor of performance than business strategy, research and development or quality management.[33] Successful firms are more likely to focus on employee measurement recognising that workers' feelings about their jobs and companies impact on their performance and the companies' performance.[34] According to a

---

[33] CIPD, *The Change Agenda*, at p. 1.

[34] See e.g., J. H. Lingle and W. M. Schiemann, 'From Balanced Scorecard to Strategic Gauges: Is Measurement Worth It?', *Management Review* (March 1996), pp. 58–60.

study published by an international consulting firm, Watson Wyatt LLP, key HC practice dimensions associated with increase in shareholder value include clear rewards and accountability, excellence in recruitment and retention, a collegial, flexible workplace, communications integrity and prudent use of resources. The study revealed that organisations with the best human capital management practices have a higher performance reflected in market value and shareholder returns.[35] Stiles and Kulvisaechana also observe a shift away from external positioning in the industry, and the relative balance of competitive forces, towards an acknowledgment that internal resources be viewed as crucial to sustained effectiveness.[36] Indeed, human capital may gain competitive advantage because it is difficult to imitate.

A number of benefits have been demonstrated by organisations that have adopted the Investment in People approach. Such a strategy presents a positive image of the organisation, it offers better management of training and improved training processes. The model has been shown to improve employee morale, motivation, commitment etc., and there are business benefits and other miscellaneous reasons for adopting a human capital management policy such as improved workplace relationships, improved skills and quality of workforce, increased quality of goods and services, improved customer satisfaction, improved financial performance.[37]

As there is a significant amount of evidence to suggest a link between human capital and a company's financial performance this gives rise to an argument for reporting on human capital management practices. For example, according to the *Accounting for People Report*:

> for most organisations the link between HCM policies and practices and performance is sufficiently central to be a material factor whose disclosure might reasonably be expected to influence assessments of their value and effective stewardship by management. In such cases disclosure increases the value of financial reports and will be important for the effective operation of capital markets . . . More generally, people are looking for reports that demonstrate to other stakeholders (such as customers, suppliers, employees and regulators) that the organisation is focusing on all the drivers of value.[38]

---

[35] Watson Wyatt, *The HC Index: Linking HC and Shareholder Value*, Survey Reports (1999, 2000, 2002). Discussed by Foong and Yorston in *Human Capital Measurement and Reporting: A British Perspective* at pp. 16–7.

[36] Philip Stiles and Somboon Kulvisaechana, *Human Capital and Performance: A literature review* (University of Cambridge, Business School, 2003), at p. 3. See also P. M. Wright, B. B. Dunford and S. A. Snell, 'Human resources and the resource-based view of the firm' (2001) 27 *Journal of Management* 701–21.

[37] J. Hillage and J. Moralee, *The Return on Investors*, ies report 314 (Brighton, 1996).

[38] Taskforce on Human Capital Management, *Accounting for People Report* (October 2003), p. 8, para. 5.

The report of the Taskforce suggests that there are a number of benefits in reporting on human capital. Reporting on human capital management helps employees and prospective employees to understand their contribution to overall performance and how they are valued.[39] This improves the organisations' ability to attract, motivate and retain the people they need.[40] Reporting increases organisations' ability to evaluate the contribution of workforce policies and practices to performance and make more informed and effective decisions on investment in workforce development.[41] Information assists in matching skills and organisational needs. Shareholders also benefit from the demonstration of sound management and a greater understanding of the factors that influence future performance. High quality reporting on human capital management will, according to the Taskforce, assist investors seeking long-term performance.[42] By causing organisations to focus on their key drivers of value in people management, through strategic analysis and measurement, reporting increases organisations' ability to evaluate the contribution of workforce policies and practices to performance and to make more informed and effective decisions on investment in workforce development. Workers benefit more generally, as a result of their improved ability to manage their own future employability and prospects. Their ability to keep up with necessary skills and requirements depends upon availability of information on the skills most valued by different employers and identification of the opportunities that different organisations offer to acquire and develop those skills. Shareholders benefit from the demonstration of sound management and a greater understanding of the factors that influence future performance.

Other benefits considered to result from external reporting on human capital management include demonstration of commitment to diversity and inclusiveness, health and safety and respect for employees, achievement of buy-in and support from senior level; improvement of stakeholder confidence; provision of internal benchmarks on which to improve year to year; facilitation of prioritising of resources and efforts to improve performance.[43]

Human capital reporting can also improve communications for a company, especially in situations in which there is uncertainty about

---

[39] Taskforce, *Accounting for People Report* (October 2003), p. 9, para. 6.
[40] *Ibid.*
[41] *Ibid.*
[42] *Ibid.*
[43] Foong and Yorston, *Human Capital Measurement and Reporting: A British Perspective* (2003), at p. 34.

a company's performance or about its future performance. The company's expressed attitude towards its employee contribution and how it values its employees may provide others with a deeper insight into the character of the company. Human capital and intellectual capital reports may complement and reinforce claims made in the financial statements, since only a small proportion of a firm's intangibles are reflected in financial statements.[44] Indeed, external reporting of human capital may improve accounting standards and company valuation and thereby make possible better decision-making by senior managers, investors, analysts and other organisational stakeholders.

This highlights the relevance of human capital reporting to investors. It is increasingly recognised that this is no longer a 'stakeholder' issue or soft reporting issue but, in fact, has real impact on the financial performance of the company. The investors are showing an increased interest in the subject. That may be a result of education or it may be a result of economic trends. Thus, as Murray observes, in a low inflation environment investors are more interested in how the company will be performing in the medium to long term. Traditional accounts are less helpful in this respect. Consequently investment analysts rely on sources other than published accounts, such as their own and others' research, industry surveys and meetings with boards of directors and management, in order to assess the future prospects of a company.[45] It becomes necessary in such a context to give investors more detail about management's future strategy for the company, market position, brands, investment, research and development.[46] Furthermore, as Murray observes, if a company or its board is accused of some unethical practice it can have an immediate and devastating impact on the company's share price. Thus by having its policies already laid out, explained and understood, then even if the company is operating in potentially sensitive areas, investors will be able to assess the impact on the company's reputation.[47]

If human capital is a constraining factor there is an increasing need for companies to explain to investors what kind of people the organisation employs, the skills they have, the way they are trained, the amount of money invested in their training and the strategies to ensure that the best possible candidates are recruited. The fact that there are more

---

[44] Guimón, at p. 4.
[45] Peter Murray, 'Reporting on Intangibles and Future Prospects: Meeting Market Needs' in ICAEW, *Human Capital and Corporate Reputation: Setting the Boardroom Agenda* (ICAEW, London, 2000) at p. 4.
[46] *Ibid.*, at p. 4.   [47] *Ibid.*, at p. 5.

knowledge-based organisations in the economy makes it increasingly important for investors to have an idea of the quality of people employed. Arguably this approach then becomes important across the economy as a whole because investors make comparisons. If some companies supply this type of information investors might inquire why others are not providing it. Such an approach requires companies to provide detailed reports to help investors understand how human capital builds long-term corporate value. In short, the main reasons for companies introducing human capital reports are to attract investors; to establish an internal information system on human resource issues; to pursue a cost-benefit analysis of investments in human resources; and to improve human resource management. They also seek to build the company's image and indicate their social responsibility and ethical values to the outside world in order to attract and retain customers and qualified employees.[48]

What are the potential limits of human capital reporting?

Despite the potential benefits of human capital reporting it is easy to idealise and overstate them. Currently, the return side of human capital is not easily measured and so companies are left with benchmarking which is not an exact science and tends to concentrate on the investments and processes and indirect measures rather than on the direct gains arising from human capital.[49]

A number of obstacles stand in the way of effective human capital reporting. First, the information may be commercially sensitive because it could reveal a competitive advantage.[50] Other sensitivities include the potential reaction of employees and trade unions to information disseminated in the reports.[51] Secondly, the costs involved in human capital reporting may outweigh the benefits[52] and thereby reduce the incentive to engage in this reporting process. Thirdly, lack of guidance,[53] for example with regard to measures and comparators make the task of human capital reporting more difficult, in particular in transnational or group companies where there may be different human resources demands and priorities. Fourthly, human capital reports rarely provide a full picture of the human capital dimensions in the company. This lack of completeness makes

---

[48] Westphalen, at p. 20.
[49] Westphalen, at pp. 7–8.
[50] Foong and Yorston, at p. 31.
[51] Stiles and Kulvisaechana, at p. 20.
[52] Foong and Yorston, at pp. 31–32 and O'Connor, at p. 538.
[53] O'Connor, at p. 538; Foong and Yorston, at p. 32.

human capital reports difficult to use in terms of evaluating the company's performance. Fifthly, human capital reporting tends to have a low status with little support from senior management.[54]

Foong and Yorston suggest that external reporting on human capital currently does not mean reporting in annual reports but rather that such information is shared with 'FTSE for Good' or third party consultants with an interest in human capital management.[55] In reality external stakeholders do not see the reports and, where they are reported, they tend to be incomplete, only covering matters such as diversity statistics, health and safety statistics, aggregate employee survey results, recourse to fair treatment systems, quality of leadership, employee headcount, work overtime, training spend.[56] Stiles and Kulvisaechana observe that many firms lack databases and audited information that can give strong and relevant information to investors.[57] Ultimately their failure to show how they affect profitability and competitiveness and how the issues impact on shareholder value causes such reports to be of limited value to investors.

Indeed, the type of measurement presented in human capital reports tends to be limited to compliance with legal requirements or sometimes other incentives such as government procurement policies.[58] Companies also tailor their human capital reports to respond to local conditions and their own particular circumstances and needs.[59] This reduces their comparability for investors and stakeholders. The strategic value of human reporting, such as attempts to recruit or retain, tend to govern the frequency and method and style of human capital reporting. Thus internal reporting is more widespread than external reporting in the UK.[60] Generally, the information does not appear in the company's annual report and accounts but on the company's website or corporate social responsibility report; or the data is passed to other actors, assessors, and consultants.[61]

It might be argued that measuring human capital is playing to the accountants' rules and requires adoption of their methodologies, such as cost-based approaches, market-based approaches and income-based approaches. Such methodologies might be inappropriate for human capital

---

[54] Foong and Yorston, at p. 32.
[55] Foong and Yorston, at p. 33.
[56] Foong and Yorston, at p. 34.
[57] Stiles and Kulvisaechana, at p. 20.
[58] *Accounting for People Report*, para. 52, at p. 32.
[59] *Ibid.*
[60] *Accounting for People Report*, para. 59, at p. 33.
[61] *Ibid.*, para. 59, at p. 34.

reporting. For example, financial valuations highlight market prices rather than value; and financial information on revenue and payroll costs is retrospective rather than prospective, so indicating the historical strength of the company's market position rather than the potential created by the skills of its employees.[62]

Companies using the Danish guidelines have been shown not to be providing consistent reports and nor do they provide sufficient information for analysis.[63] In addition comparability is not achieved because over time there are frequent changes in form and structure of such reports and they also mix historical developments with planned future actions. Nor is understandability achieved because companies do not explain what is meant by intellectual capital reporting and there is a lack of pedagogically formed statements.[64] On the other hand, as Rimmel *et al* observe, since intellectual capital statements are not governed by the boundaries of traditional corporate annual reports they can go further and may provide much more useful information.[65] However, analysis of such statements is often also of poor quality because there is no traditional way to read and interpret them as there is for analysing numbers in a traditional financial statement analysis.[66]

The lack of meaningful measures to communicate the value of a company's human capital in the marketplace is clearly an obstacle to effective reporting. Even though the Centre for Excellence in Management and Leadership Report offered some possible measures that may be helpful, including morale, motivation, investment, long-term development, external perception, it recognised that the problem with this menu approach is that it does not allow for comparability either at a sector or economy level.[67] In addition it is necessary to find a causal link between the human resources policies and practices and the company's performance and to be able to demonstrate that in the report. This may be difficult to achieve although some studies suggest that such a link exists. For example, it might be possible to see a connected chain from

---

[62] Stittle, at pp. 317–8.

[63] Rimmel, Blom, Lindstrii, and Persson, *The Danish Guidelines on Intellectual Capital Reporting: Towards a European Perspective on Human Resource Disclosures?* (paper presented at the 6th SNEE Conference on Economic Integration in Europe, Molle, Sweden, May 2004).

[64] Rimmel, Blom, Lindstrii, and Persson, *The Danish Guidelines on Intellectual Capital Reporting*, at p. 17.

[65] *Ibid.*

[66] *Ibid.*, at p. 4.

[67] Centre for Business Performance, *The case for corporate reporting: overwhelming or over-hyped?* (CBR, Report to the Centre for Excellence in Management and Leadership, Cranfield, 2002), discussed in CIPD, *The Change Agenda*, at pp. 4–6.

effective HR practices to aspects of employee attitudes and behaviour, and from this to organisational outcomes, such as higher comparative productivity, and in turn higher financial performance.[68]

These obstacles might create the impression that a meaningful practice of human capital reporting cannot be achieved. However, examples from other jurisdictions might also provide direction at least for getting the practice started.

Other jurisdictions

The Scandinavian countries appear to have the most advanced human capital and intellectual capital reporting systems, although these remain at an experimental stage and are not yet firmly established in the regulatory framework. The Danish 'Guideline for Intellectual Capital Statements – A Key to Knowledge Management', developed by a taskforce coordinated by the Danish Agency for Trade and Industry, provides an Intellectual Capital Statement Model that identifies four interrelated elements relevant to a description of a corporation's resources: employees, customers, processes and technologies.[69] Within the model each element comes with a knowledge narrative, a set of management challenges, a set of initiatives, and a set of indicators. The Danish Ministry of Science Technology and Innovation also published a report, *Analysing Intellectual Capital Statements*,[70] offering analysts a systematic method for reading and interpreting the information contained in the Intellectual Capital statements. Three criteria are suggested for evaluating the company's treatment of its customers, employees, processes and technologies: effects, activities and resources. A systematic analysis enables users to make comparative analyses rather than being directed by each individual company in their evaluations. The accounts of Rimmel *et al* and Guimón of this Guideline suggest that it is not perfect and is largely user driven.[71] Rimmel *et al*, for example, found in their study that companies applied it in different ways and its flexible approach made comparability difficult to achieve.[72]

An alternative model has been developed in Spain by researchers in Madrid: the 'Guidelines for the Management and Disclosure of Information on Intangibles' otherwise known as the MERITUM

---

[68] Guest, *Effective People Management* (2000), p. 35.
[69] See Danish Ministry of Science, Technology and Innovation, *Intellectual Capital Statements – The New Guideline* (Copenhagen, Denmark, 2003).
[70] Danish Ministry of Science, Technology and Innovation, *Analysing Intellectual Capital Statements* (Copenhagen, Denmark, 2003).
[71] Rimmel et al, and Guimón.   [72] Rimmel et al, at pp. 15–8.

Guidelines.[73] The MERITUM model advises companies on how to utilise their intangible resources effectively and how to report on them. Effective use of intangible resources is a process involving three phases. In the first phase, the intangibles required to attain the firm's strategic objectives are identified. In the second phase, the company's activities and the role of the intangible resources in those activities are measured with reference to specific indicators. The third phase involves consolidation of the intangibles management system and its integration within the firm's management routines. This three-stage model comprises a learning process of monitoring and evaluating how different activities affect the firm's intangible resources, critical intangibles and strategic objectives. With specific reference to the intellectual capital report the MERITUM Guidelines suggest that this should consist of three parts: the vision of the firm; a summary of the firm's intangible resources and activities; and a system of indicators which allow the reader to assess how well the company is managing to attain its objectives. The Guidelines advise on how to collect information; who should prepare it for the report; and how frequently the company should report. Both the Danish and the Spanish models support the use of a common intellectual capital account that is likely to make measurement easier for the company and evaluation easier for the report users.

Finland has also generated a project on human resource accounting. Indicators identified as relevant to such reporting include knowledge about development of personnel in numbers and in structure, usage of working hours, personnel-related costs, personnel resources and their development, state of personnel, both physical and mental well-being, reward systems, efficiency and service ability, value. In addition, information on how cost-effectively human resources are managed, how the organisation has taken care of its personnel so that they have quantitatively and qualitatively adequate human resources, how the quality of work and working conditions, personnel resources, efficiency and personnel well-being have been taken care of.[74] Currently in Finland human capital accounts are only required to be published internally as an extra to company reports.

A well-publicised company project on human capital reporting is that provided by Skandia Navigator, a financial services group, which publishes an intellectual capital report as a supplement to its annual

---

[73] MERITUM Project, Guidelines for Managing and Reporting on Intangibles (Intellectual Capital Report) (Airtel-Vodafone Foundation, Madrid, 2002) available at www.eu-know.net. See Guimón for an analysis.
[74] Westphalen, at p. 24.

report and seeks to integrate its traditional and intellectual capital reports.[75] The report incorporates about 30 indicators, grouped into five interactive categories: financial focus, customer focus, process focus, renewal focus, human focus. Parker explains each focus. The financial focus requires a change in role of the financials from a direct indicator of a company's worth to a means by which the overall value of the company can be judged. The customer focus seeks to understand the position of the company in the marketplace in connection with its intellectual capital position. The process focus relates to the firm's infrastructure; what it does and how. This covers technology and how it is applied; metrics include the number of contracts concluded without error, the time required for particular operations, the number of accounts and transactions per employee etc. The renewal focus is concerned with the capacity of the company to respond to future trends and events such as changes in customer base, changes in consumer demands, expenditure on research and development etc. This focus also considers the readiness of the company to respond; for example, the age profile of the workforce, or training provided. The human focus concentrates on diversity, number of employees with degrees etc., number and reasons for opting for part-time work, languages spoken by employees and cultures within the organisation.[76]

In the USA the Stakeholder Alliance published a set of 'sunshine standards' that aim to provide direction for corporate reporting to stakeholders and are intended to complement and extend generally accepted accounting principles issued by the FASB. Whilst these are not compulsory they do provide guidance on the type and level of detail for a human capital report. The fundamental principle of these standards is that:

Corporations must provide information that stakeholders need in order to make rational, informed decisions in a free market system, and to protect themselves from negative consequences of corporate actions. Disclosure must be complete, accurate, timely, objective, understandable, and public. Stakeholder 'right to know' takes precedence over cost, inconvenience, or risk to the corporation.

With regard to employees, the sunshine standards require information to be provided that will enable

(a) present and potential employees to make fully informed employment decisions, and to protect themselves in the workplace and in other relations with the corporation; and (b) consumers, government agencies, and other stakeholders to

---

[75] Derek Parker, *Towards IC Reporting – Developing New Measures*, (Australian CPA, 1998), available at www.cpaustralia.com.au/Archive/9806/pg_aa9806_towardsicr.html.
[76] *Ibid.*

fairly assess the company's workplace conditions on issues such as fair pay, child labor, sweatshop conditions, and the right to organize.[77]

It is clear from these sunshine standards that a worthwhile human capital report would require details on a broad range of employee relations issues in order to provide the reader with an opportunity to evaluate the company's treatment and use of its human capital. It needs to see employees not only as part of its strategic financial assets, but also to consider its employees from the point of view of their safety and security, and to what extent they are treated fairly. These elements are arguably independent of the company's financial performance.

What is the appropriate way forward?

Enthusiasm for human capital or intellectual capital reporting is un-doubtedly growing and this has been supported by publication of the *Accounting for People Report*. Other influential and authoritative organisations have also expressed support for the development of human capital reporting. However, the form that such reporting should take and to whom it should be addressed have not been settled. Current practice is *ad hoc* and appears still to be left to companies that are either 'progressive' or that are really only seeking a positive image with shareholders and stakeholders. There are no detailed legal or regulatory requirements to report on human capital except to the very limited extent laid down in Schedule 7 of the Companies Act 1985, covering details about disabled employees and employee involvement.[78] The requirement to provide information about the company's employees in the operating and financial review Regulations was limited to the need to disclose that information 'to the extent necessary to comply with the general requirements' of the review[79] which were essentially to 'be a balanced and comprehensive analysis' of the company business's development and performance during the financial year, the company's position, the main trends and factors underlying its development and performance and position and likely to affect its future development and performance and position.[80]

---

[77] The Stakeholder Alliance – Sunshine Standards, available at www.stakeholderalliance. org/sustds.html.

[78] The Government is proposing removing these requirements; see White Paper, *Company Law Reform* (March 2005), para 4.10.

[79] Schedule 7ZA, Companies Act 1985, paras. 3–4, inserted by the Companies Act 1985 (Operating and Financial Review and Directors' Report etc.) Regulations 2005, SI 2005/1011, reg. 9.

[80] Schedule 7ZA, Companies Act 1985, para. 1, inserted by the Companies Act 1985 (Operating and Financial Review and Directors' Report etc.) Regulations 2005, SI 2005/1011, reg. 9.

The review was to be prepared so as to assist the members of the company to assess the strategies adopted by the company and the potential for those strategies to succeed.[81] Thus, any information about the company's employees that assists the members in this way would be necessary. However, that would have been a matter for individual company boards of directors to decide.

The main problems to date causing a failure to establish a comprehensive and universal human capital reporting practice have included use of simplistic valuation methods that are inappropriate for measuring human capital. Measurement and valuation techniques must be identified if human capital reporting is to get genuinely established. An established standard would provide common metrics worth comparing. Compulsory measures would avoid a whole variety of incomparable indicators. Of course, companies differ in type of business, size and organisation. Such differences will be reflected also in their employment relationships. In this respect, it might be appropriate for any regulations to lay down a primary set of compulsory details to be supplemented by different types of information depending on the type of sector or organisation concerned. These steps are necessary because, as Blair *et al* state, such information 'is just a fog if it is not reported regularly and collected in a consistent and sensible way'.[82] Such steps also require more enthusiasm and practical support from the accounting professions as well as from the legislators and regulators.

Currently there are no real measures available for human capital reporting and it might be the case that such reporting cannot be subject to a numerical formula. Instead it is likely to remain a descriptive and judgmental narrative for which the operating and financial review could be regarded as the appropriate place. This proposal has the merit of reducing the costs of providing a separate report and might encourage it to be read more carefully because it appears with other explanations of the company's financial position and future prospects. The Operating and Financial Review was also intended to be a forward-looking document, and this would certainly be relevant in the human capital area. Relating the human capital resources and their use to the financial performance of the company may draw the interest of the shareholders more easily, since the human capital report would then demonstrate that there is a link between the ways in which people are managed and how

---

[81] Schedule 7ZA, Companies Act 1985, para. 1, inserted by the Companies Act 1985 (Operating and Financial Review and Directors' Report etc.) Regulations 2005, SI 2005/1011, reg. 9.

[82] Blair, at pp. 59–60.

the business performs. This might be achieved by linking human capital information to other measures such as customer satisfaction, product quality, supplier relations and innovativeness.[83] In this respect the OFR might have been regarded, according to the ICAEW, 'as a bridge between "hard" numbers and "soft" people issues'.[84] The Accounting for People Task Force recommends the OFR as the natural place for the human capital management report since human capital management is in most cases a material factor in organisational performance. The Task Force also recommends that the report be balanced and objective by covering the whole workforce, with due emphasis given to the various factors in play and by covering both historic and prospective trends as well as being accurate and verifiable.[85] In addition, the Task Force recommends that the report is created by a process that is susceptible to review by auditors.[86]

A number of counter arguments might be made to dissuade companies from inserting this report into the Operating and Financial Review and tying it to the financial performance and prospects of the company. First, as is noted above, the OFR Regulations did not make such reporting compulsory. Employee-related information need only be included to the extent necessary for an understanding of the company's performance and position and future prospects. The *Financial Times* recently reported that 'more than 40 of senior managers have no plans to include reports on employee developments in operating and financial reviews'. In a survey *Water for Fish*, noted by the *Financial Times*, the consultants stated: 'Many organisations appear to be putting this new Department of Trade and Industry requirement on the back burner, either because their year-end is some way off; or, simply they see other information as more critical to their business.'[87] Secondly, the human capital report might have been overshadowed by the Operating and Financial Review. Thirdly, information overload may be a problem if the Operating and Financial Review were to become too long. Fourthly, tying the human capital dimension to the company's financial prospects may lead to considering the employees as instrumental to the company's

[83] O'Connor, 'Rethinking Corporate Financial Disclosure. . .' above, at p. 530.

[84] ICAEW, *The Operating and Financial Review and Human Capital Reporting: Is the OFR the Place for Human Capital Reporting?* (London, 2003) available at www.icaew.co.uk/policy.

[85] Taskforce on Human Capital Management, *Accounting for People* (October 2003), p. 21, para. 30.

[86] Taskforce on Human Capital Management, *Accounting for People* (October 2003), p. 22, recommendation 1.

[87] 'Only half will keep new reporting rules', *Financial Times*, 30 May 2005.

objectives without recognising their own needs and seeing the relationship as two sided. Financial performance is also problematic because of different accounting practices across countries so that the human capital report could be interpreted in different ways through its connection to the financials. By contrast, a 'balanced scorecard' approach would support the stakeholder perspective as it is intended to weigh the interests of various stakeholders.

Ultimately, by connecting the human capital report to financial performance could be viewed as more pragmatic or realistic since the evidence currently shows that the investors are only interested if they see this connection. Thus from this point of view Marleen O'Connor suggests that firms should include human resources disclosure in the notes to the financial statements. First, this location would not sharply disrupt established convention by affecting the financial statements. Secondly, placement in the notes emphasises that this information directly impacts the financial statements. Thirdly, auditors review the notes to financial statements more thoroughly, thereby providing a higher degree of reliability than assertions made in managements' reports to shareholders.[88] Lack of investor interest also needs to be tackled if human capital reporting is to be taken up by companies. This might require investors to be re-educated by showing them how human capital creates new valuation and reporting issues. One reason for their lack of interest is the fact that this type of reporting has tended to be of uncertain reliability and comparability. They also need guidance on how to analyse and compare reports.

The contents of a human capital report must be tailored to the needs of a particular business but at the same time it should include discussion of certain specific aspects of human capital management whatever the type of company. The basic elements of any human capital report, in order to be of value, would include them looking forward as well as back and they should also set out the organisation's human capital management strategy and show how it is aligned with the business strategy. The report should outline the human capital management practices relating to the strategy; set out the performance indicators in use; report progress; and outline intended remedies for problems revealed. An assessment would consider not only what workforce skills are relevant to the business but also how such skills are to be matched with business needs. Aspects of human capital management to be included in the report that are likely to be relevant in all companies include: employee engagement

---

[88] O'Connor, 'Rethinking Corporate Financial Disclosure . . .', above, at p. 551.

and satisfaction; recruitment and retention; employee turnover; absenteeism; training and development; talent management and succession planning; workforce profile; remuneration and pensions; fair employment policies; profit or revenue per employee; human capital return on investment; organisational culture, ethics and codes of conduct. According to the CIPD, in each category there should also be a distinct section on management and leadership.

What is not discussed in the literature is what might happen as a result of publishing the human capital report. Attention is focused on the contents and reasons for such reporting, but how the report is to be used is not addressed. Clearly, if it were to form part of the OFR the report would have been presented to the members in the first instance. The argument of O'Connor suggests that the members are the primary recipients also. However, what is the next stage following the publication of the report likely to be? As an indicator of the company's profit-making potential, the report would appear to act as a source of information relevant to the investment decisions of the company's existing and potential members.

To what extent does human capital reporting demonstrate regard for the interests of the employees? The Company Law Review, when debating directors' duties and the OFR, suggested that the new statutory duty would signify the disappearance of section 309 of the Companies Act 1985. Section 309 requires directors to take into account the interests of the employees when carrying out their functions for the company. Whilst section 309 has long been criticised as window dressing because it does not give to employees standing to challenge the actions of directors,[89] its disappearance from the Companies Act might worsen the employees' position further.[90] Even when accounts are strongly regulated it is not impossible to create false impressions. The proposal to include the human capital report within the OFR, which would be a document primarily for the use and benefit of a company's members, would not necessarily guarantee any high regard for the employees' interests. Indeed, the intention was that shareholders may challenge boards of directors for inaccuracies in the OFR, but other stakeholders would not be able to do so. Thus, even though the human capital report might show a commitment to the employment relationships, the company

---

[89] See Charlotte Villiers, 'Section 309 of the Companies Act 1985: Is it Time for a Reappraisal?' in Hugh Collins, Paul Davies, and Roger Rideout, *Legal Regulation of the Employment Relation* (Kluwer, 2000) 593.

[90] See Lord Wedderburn of Charlton, 'Employees, Partnership and Company Law' (2002) 31 *ILJ* 99.

need not fear employee reactions to statements made about their development and contribution to the company's performance.

If publication of a human capital report is meant to demonstrate the company's appreciation of the contribution of its employees to its profit-making abilities one might argue that the employees should be the prime recipients with an opportunity to engage in dialogue with the company about employment arrangements. However, this aspect of the company's relationship is dealt with independently of the company reporting regime.

Employee involvement in corporate decision-making

Arguably, a more appropriate way of utilising employees and demonstrating respect for their contribution to the company's performance is to ensure that they are involved in decision-making activities in the company. At the very least employees require information and consultation rights. In the UK such rights have been shaped by European initiatives. Until recently there were very limited information and consultation rights concerned with specific issues.[91] More recently, following a European Directive, Regulations were introduced for the provision of general information and consultation arrangements. In particular, the Information and Consultation of Employees Regulations 2004 were introduced to implement the Directive on employee involvement.[92] Space limits the discussion of this aspect to a brief overview and comment on the Regulations in the context of human capital management and company law.

The Regulations give to employees in larger undertakings rights to be informed and consulted about the business they work for. They are presented on the basis that the principle of informing and consulting employees 'is good for the employees themselves and good for the organisations they work for'.[93] The Regulations apply to undertakings[94] with fifty or more employees. Their application has been phased so that since 6 April 2005 they have become applicable to undertakings with

---

[91] These covered collective redundancies, health and safety and transfers of undertakings.

[92] Directive 2002/14/EC of the European Parliament and of the Council of 11 March 2002 establishing a general framework for informing and consulting employees in the European Community OJ L 80/29, 23.3.2002. See the implementation by the Information and Consultation of Employees Regulations 2004, SI 2004/3426.

[93] See DTI Guidance on the Information and Consultation of Employees Regulations 2004, para. 2, p. 3, available at www.dti.gov.uk/er/consultation/proposal.htm.

[94] The registered office, head office or principal place of business is situated in Great Britain (reg. 3(1)(b)).

150 or more employees, then from 6 April 2007 they will apply to undertakings with 100 or more employees and from 6 April 2008 they will apply to undertakings with fifty or more employees.[95] The Regulations do not automatically require the establishment of an information and consultation arrangement but can be triggered either by the employer voluntarily commencing negotiation of an agreement or by a request from the employees.

If there is a pre-existing information and consultation agreement the employer may then hold a ballot of the workforce to determine whether the employees endorse the employee request.[96] Such a request is endorsed by at least half of those voting, and at least 40 per cent of the undertaking's employees must vote to validate the endorsement.[97] In that case the employer will then be required to enter into negotiations for a new information and consultation agreement. However, if fewer than 40 per cent of the workforce vote or less than a majority of those voting support the request, the employer will not be obliged to negotiate a new agreement and the existing arrangements for information and consultation may continue to operate, with a moratorium of three years on any further employee request.[98] Where there is a pre-existing agreement and an employee request is made, if the employer does not hold a ballot he will then be obliged to enter into negotiations for a new agreement.[99] Similarly, if there is no pre-existing agreement and at least 10 per cent of the employees make a valid request, the employer will be obliged to enter into negotiations for an information and consultation agreement.[100]

If, following a valid employee request or a valid employer notification to initiate negotiations, such negotiations are not carried out or an agreement is not reached within the time limit, the statutory default procedure will be triggered in which standard information and consultation provisions will become applicable.[101] The standard information and consultation provisions will require the employer to inform and consult the representatives with information on the recent and probable development of the undertaking's activities and economic situation; the situation, structure and probable development of employment within the undertaking, including anticipatory measures envisaged and threats to employment; and decisions likely to lead to substantial changes in the work organisation or contractual relations, including redundancies or transfer situations.[102] The Regulations also require that the information

[95] See reg. 3 and Sch. 1.   [96] See regs. 8 and 9.
[97] Regulation 8(6).   [98] Regulation 12(1).
[99] See regs. 7(1), 10(3) and 11.   [100] Regulation 7(1).
[101] Regulation 18.   [102] Regulation 20(1).

must be given 'at such time, in such fashion and with such content as are appropriate' to enable the representatives 'to conduct an adequate study and, where necessary, to prepare for consultation'.[103] Under the Regulations the employer is required to ensure that consultation is conducted

> in such a way as to ensure that the timing, method and content of the consultation are appropriate; on the basis of the information supplied to the representatives and of any opinion which those representatives express to the employer; in such a way as to enable the information and consultation representatives to meet the employer at the relevant level of management depending on the subject under discussion and to obtain a reasoned response from the employer to any such opinion; and in relation to certain matters regarding work organisation or contractual relations with a view to reaching agreement on decisions within the scope of the employer's powers.[104]

A number of points emerge from these Regulations. First, their complexity is likely to result in disputes. This complexity arises partly because the Regulations take advantage of the flexibility opportunities offered in the Directive. Thus the Regulations seek to accommodate the individual needs and interests of different undertakings rather than impose a uniform information and consultation structure. The attempt to accommodate different undertakings with different needs and priorities and also with different levels of development of information and consultation structures has resulted in numerous possible arrangements for informing and consulting employees. One might argue that the Regulations and the Directive deepen the two-tier employment and workplace protections available in organisations, giving greater protection to those granted the status of employee compared to those treated as workers. Such a reference to employees also potentially limits the number of workplaces and organisations to which the Regulations will apply. Already the DTI's explanatory memorandum indicates that the Regulations will apply to only 3 per cent of organisations, although they will cover three-quarters of UK employees.[105]

The use of the pre-existing agreement is potentially a way of avoiding the standard requirements because it need not contain information or consultation requirements on the areas specifically identified in the standard provisions of the Regulations. A pre-existing agreement gives freedom to the parties on the issues for which information will be relevant and therefore a pre-existing agreement could provide for a limited range of information to be provided to the employees or their

---

[103] Regulation 20(2).   [104] Regulation 20(4).
[105] DTI, Explanatory Memorandum to the Information and Consultation of Employees Regulations 2004, para. 7.2.

representatives so long as the employees approve it. This will generate differential treatment of employees throughout the UK in an area in which they might expect a degree of uniformity and consistency. Moreover, a pre-existing agreement does not have to provide for consultation. A further point one might make against this light touch response towards pre-existing agreements is that it does not sit comfortably with the research findings that underline the Regulations. Such findings emphasise the importance of consultation and two-way dialogue. Indeed, the responses to the DTI's consultations reported in the 2003 Consultation Paper included those who 'stressed the importance of two-way communication – that there was more to it than simply keeping staff informed of what was going on; the decision-making itself could be improved through a process of genuine dialogue where minds could be changed.'[106]

Despite the apparent neutrality and balance in the Regulations, a closer inspection of the language may lead to an alternative interpretation of the Regulations. The Regulations specify that 'the parties are under a duty, when negotiating or implementing a negotiated agreement or when implementing the standard information and consultation provisions, to work in a spirit of co-operation and with due regard for their reciprocal rights and obligations, taking into account the interests of both the undertaking and the employees'.[107] These provisions would suggest that the interests of employers and employees are given equal regard in the Regulations. The DTI's Explanatory Memorandum gives a positive impression when it says that the Government 'believes that genuine on-going consultation can help to develop a climate of trust and co-operation that can make implementing business decisions easier, as well as ensuring that employees are treated fairly and informed about decisions affecting their future'.[108] Yet 'trust' carries with it some potentially negative implications for employees. As I have argued elsewhere the notion of trust implies vulnerability on the part of the worker who is economically dependent on the employer. This fact may encourage a more passive stance on the part of the employee rather than invite the employee to get involved and self-protect by seeking directly to influence the decisions of the manager.[109] Indeed, the Government's consultation

---

[106] DTI, *High Performance Workplaces – Informing and Consulting Employees*, Consultation Document (July 2003) para. 2.6.
[107] Regulation 21.
[108] DTI Guidance, para. 7.
[109] See Charlotte Villiers, 'Workers and Transnational Corporate Structures: Some Lessons from the BMW-Rover Case' (2001) 3 *International and Comparative Corporate Law Journal* 271, at p. 291.

paper makes clear that such trust should mean that employees better understand the challenges and the changing needs of the organisation and respond more effectively:

> Effective employee dialogue can help staff feel more involved and valued by their employer, *make them better aware of the business climate in which the organisation is operating and help them be more responsive to and better prepared for change. This in turn can benefit the business through better staff retention and lower absenteeism, increased innovation and adaptability to change. This should allow a greater ability to react rapidly to opportunities and threats, thereby ultimately enhancing a company's productivity.*[110]

Conclusion

Employee relations are not a well-recognised aspect of the legal model of the company. However, the increasing importance of intangible assets and the contribution of employees to the profit-making abilities of the company are pushing this subject into the reporting and accounting debate. Unfortunately, in the human capital reporting developments as well as in the legislation recently introduced at European level and in the UK with regard to employee information and consultation rights, an instrumental role is attributed to the employee. Reporting on human capital, according to the Accounting for People Task Force, should show a link between high performance human capital management practices and the financial performance of the organisation.[111] This might itself be a problem of interpreting narrowly the concept of human capital. Indeed, one could go so far as to argue that a concept of human capital that uses and evaluates labour from the standpoint of its efficiency in the productive sphere dehumanises and depersonalises the labour process.[112] The metrics of the cost-benefit calculus leads to valuation in pecuniary terms, reducing investments in human capital such as education and training to be judged by their monetary output.[113] Such an approach focuses on maximising productivity or economic growth for a whole society rather than on the rights and interests of each individual severally. This incurs the danger of viewing employees and human capital only in terms of the company's needs and subject only to an efficiency calculus.[114] Certainly this is the risk when the evidence

---

[110] DTI, *High Performance Workplaces*, para. 1.1. Emphasis added.
[111] See *Accounting for People: Consultation Paper* (DTI, London, May 2003).
[112] Alan Gewirth, *The Community of Rights* (University of Chicago Press, Chicago, 1996), at p. 138.
[113] *Ibid.*, at p. 139.   [114] *Ibid.*, at p. 139.

suggests that investors, and governments, are only really interested in the efficiency sense of human capital.[115] One might be forgiven for accusing the whole debate about human capital reporting as missing the point! Demonstrating recognition of the contribution of employees and maintaining their loyalty and motivation clearly requires more than a good human capital management report!

A more positive viewpoint would be to look at human capital in terms of individual rights where the employee has control of his or her own capital. As is suggested by Gewirth, 'because human capital is oriented toward increasing one's levels of purpose-fulfillment and one's economic capabilities, it is a dynamic notion as part of a person's economic biography. It involves the idea of the agent's self-improvement, his development of certain personal virtues and sense of personal responsibility with a view to being able to participate more effectively in the productive process.'[116] This approach would enable the individual employee, and employees collectively, to control their use of human capital, and it stops him from being subject to 'an efficiency calculus' whereby investment in his education or wealth, for example, is determined by comparing its rate of return with alternative uses of available funds. Under this version of human capital, 'even if the entrepreneur views his workers' human capital only in terms of maximising his profits, and even if, in the macro-economic sphere, human capital is viewed only as a means of fostering economic growth, it does not follow that the individual worker must also view his human capital in the same way. Instead, he may view it as a means to, or as a component of, his overall freedom and well-being.'[117] Thus while economic growth and corporate success are relevant, they should not be regarded as the only role of human capital. Governments and organisations are required to assist employees to participate in the productive process in a way that develops their own sense of personal responsibility.[118] Within the context of human capital reporting this requires at the very least participation by employees in the reporting process rather than it being controlled by management. The fact that this area was intended to be left as a matter of discretion for directors in the production of the OFR indicates the limited viewpoint from which human capital is regarded in the

---

[115] Westphalen, at p. 19; O'Connor, at p. 548.
[116] Gewirth, *The Community of Rights*, at p. 137.
[117] Gewirth, *ibid.*, at pp. 140–1.
[118] Gewirth, *ibid.*, at p. 141.

UK. Moreover, a genuine recognition of the contribution of human capital arguably requires the participation of employees in decision-making. Even the Government has acknowledged this as a possible key to success. At the very least, providing employees and their re-presentatives with information and consulting them or making decisions jointly with them is likely to advance the company further than another annual report.

Part IV

A way forward

12 Conclusions – rethinking the disclosure agenda

Introduction

The overview of disclosure presented in this book exhibits a complex system comprising a variety of regulatory mechanisms. Disclosure is an essential company law device that is increasingly relied upon as a method of control of corporate activity. The disclosure regime has evolved with changing business priorities and behaviours, but the essential shareholder-centred profit-maximisation objective that underpins company law generally has also shaped the character of that regime. Consequently, the disclosure system emphasises the need for information on the company's financial position with a view to assisting shareholders in making economic decisions.

There are many levels upon which the disclosure system operates, with an extensive body of statutory and professional requirements as well as voluntary schemes to encourage best or good practice. Companies provide information centrally and publicly on the Companies Register as well as on the internet and they present more specific information to different groups relevant to their needs and discussions. Information is presented internally within the company and externally to the public, and is generated both by the company itself and externally by organisations such as the media or financial analysts. Indeed, a broad range of participants are involved in the disclosure process. Those responsible for providing information may include the company secretary, the board of directors, accountants, lawyers, employees and others. Recipients range from internal managers, shareholders and employees, to the wider public such as consumers and campaign organisations.

Disclosure has numerous objectives. It is intended to protect the integrity of the capital markets by preventing fraud and by enabling investors to make informed decisions. Accountability of managers to the shareholders and others gives to disclosure a house-cleaning function as well as a role in assisting managers to answer the questions of others. However, the extent to which the disclosure regime achieves these objectives is debateable. Whilst there has been an increase in transparency as the disclosure system has developed many problems have been identified with company reports, including their complexity, their failure to meet the information needs of the recipients, their emphasis on the past and on the short term. The narrow focus and lack of adequate comparability of corporate reports reduce their value. At the same time an increasing emphasis on companies' intangible assets is altering the information demands of recipients and regulators. In this way, the attempt at introducing a mandatory operating and financial review for quoted companies reflected a recognition of the need for broader and more qualitative and forward-looking information.

What has been revealed in this study of corporate reporting is a system that struggles to keep up with business trends and developments. This struggle arises because the disclosure regime rests on a legal model which places the relationship between directors and shareholders at the centre of the company. The regime has evolved into an arrangement that is predominantly focused on regulating the presentation of financial claims so as to protect investors and potential investors, and the integrity of the markets. A complex and sophisticated structure has been created for financial reporting with input from professional organisations. However, the methods used for financial reporting have tended to be historically based and therefore limited in their ability to assist shareholders in making economic decisions. Recognition of this limitation, coupled with the increasing importance of intangible assets, has, as already noted, resulted in the introduction of a formal requirement for forward-looking narrative information.

The stakeholder movement sought to use the operating and financial review requirements as the basis of a new mandatory social and environmental reporting regime. The problem is that the financial interest bias necessitated that the OFR would address the shareholders primarily, thereby maintaining the company law status quo. The remainder of the social and environmental reporting agenda currently continues to depend predominantly upon voluntary codes and schemes with the result that reports are of variable quality and are difficult to compare.

An alteration of the emphasis away from financial information and profits would require a rebalancing of the regulatory structure so that social and environmental and human capital reporting would be given the same or equally strong regulatory support mechanisms as the financial reporting aspects. The role of those responsible for providing information would also have to be redirected. Whilst the operating and financial review was intended to reflect an 'enlightened shareholder view' requiring directors to take a long-term view of the company's interests, arguably this would not have been sufficient to change the emphasis away from the shareholders' profit-maximisation objective. A more radical directors' duty would be necessary. Similarly, the role of the gatekeepers, including non-executive directors and auditors, would also need to change. Their current focus on protecting shareholders and ensuring that the company's accounts provide a true and fair view of the company's financial position is both narrow and vague at the same time. Arguably, there could also be a role for non-financial auditors from among the stakeholder groups themselves.

One cannot deny the relevance of stakeholder interests, especially when intangible assets have gained recognition as an important contribution to a company's success. However, the usual problem for stakeholder advocates is that such a perspective presents the directors with 'too many masters' so that effectively they become accountable to nobody. In addition, within the disclosure context the stakeholder position is challenged by the potential cost implications of reporting to all stakeholder interests. The ASSC's proposal for separate reports was met with little enthusiasm. Such a step would be too expensive, especially when the company faces other challenges such as globalisation. Yet not to recognise such interests misses the point that intangible assets are increasingly important to a company, as is its reputation value among stakeholders.

Three possible responses may alleviate, if not resolve, these problems. These responses include recognition and use of communication processes as essential to effective decision-making, of which the reporting element forms only a part; an arrangement of stakeholders into organised networks with whom effective communication may become possible; and wider take up of electronic facilities such as eXtensible Business Reporting Language.

A communicative approach

The delivery of information is not an isolated activity, nor does it occur without a purpose. Rather, information is normally part of a communication process whether or not that information is received passively or actively. As Arthur Levitt, previous Chairman of the SEC, has stated, 'Disclosure is not disclosure if it does not communicate'.[1] David Tweedie,

---

[1] Arthur Levitt, 'Plain English in Prospectuses' (1997) 69 *New York State Bar Journal*, November 36, at p. 36 (hereinafter 'Levitt'). See also, Isaac C. Hunt, Jr, 'Plain English – Changing the Corporate Culture' (1997) 51 *University of Miami Law Review* 713, at p. 714.

then Chairperson of the Accounting Standards Board, has stated, 'Financial Reporting is useless if it fails to communicate'.[2]

A number of key documents published by the accountancy professions over the years have expressed concern with communication. Thus, for example, the ASSC's document, *The Corporate Report*, stated expressly that 'the fundamental objective of corporate reports is to communicate economic measurements of and information about the resources and performance of the reporting entity useful to those having reasonable rights to such information'.[3] Similarly, some of the major financial accounting and reporting texts emphasise communication as the primary objective. The opening paragraph in *Elliott and Elliott* for example states: 'Accountants are communicators. Accountancy is the art of communicating financial information about a business entity to users such as shareholders and managers. The communication is generally in the form of financial statements that show in money terms the economic resources under the control of the management. The art lies in selecting the information that is relevant to the user and is reliable'.[4] Alexander, Britton and Jorissen also state in their book: 'The accountant has to provide figures to the user. But "provide" does not just mean "send". It is not enough to send, to deliver, sheets of paper with words and figures on it. There has to be communication, there has to be understanding by the user. The point about communication, the point about information, is that the receiver is genuinely informed'.[5]

These statements make the point that disclosure has more than one dimension. First, information is made available to investors, and secondly it requires information that actually gets across to investors.[6] Thirdly, it is part of an overall process of communication involving dialogue. The AA 1000 Framework, for example, emphasises the point that engagement needs to: allow stakeholders to assist in the identification of other stakeholders; ensure that stakeholders trust the social and ethical accountant; be a dialogue, not a one-way information feed; be between parties with sufficient preparation and briefing to make well-informed decisions; involve stakeholders in defining the terms of the engagement; allow stakeholders to voice their views without restriction

---

[2] See ASB Press Notice 157, relating to discussion paper, *Year-End Financial Reports: Improving Communication*, 17 February 2000.

[3] ASSC, at p. 28.

[4] Barry Elliott and Jamie Elliott, *Financial Accounting and Reporting* (FT, Prentice Hall, London, 2004), at p. 3.

[5] David Alexander, Anne Britton and Ann Jorissen, *International Financial Reporting and Analysis* (Thomson, London, 2003), at p. 9.

[6] Arthur Levitt, at p. 37.

and without fear of penalty or discipline – stakeholders must know that if their opinions are taken seriously and acted upon this will have consequences for them and other stakeholder groups; include a public disclosure and feedback process that offers other stakeholders information that is valuable in assessing the engagement and allows them to comment upon it. Similarly, the GRI Guidelines state that a 'primary goal of reporting is to contribute to an ongoing stakeholder dialogue. Reports alone provide little value if they fail to inform stakeholders or support a dialogue that influences the decisions and behaviour of both the reporting organisation and its stakeholders. However, GRI clearly recognises that the engagement process neither begins nor ends with the publication of a sustainability report.'[7] In short, according to the GRI: 'Effective reporting is part of a broader dialogue between the reporting organisation and its stakeholders that should result in new actions by both parties.'[8]

It is also possible to underpin this communicative approach with a more theoretical justification. Here, we might turn to Jürgen Habermas who, concerned with the legitimacy of actions, has constructed a deliberative or communicative course of action.[9] Essentially, Habermas is concerned with an 'ideal speech situation' in which the parties seek a mutual understanding which serves to bring reason and will together and leads to convincing positions to which all individuals can agree without coercion. This discursive process is a legitimating force in which all parties affected would agree to a course of action on the basis of good reasons.

Habermas has developed his discourse theory over a period of more than thirty years. The theory is an idealised construct which consists of a procedure by which the participants reach a mutual understanding and consensus to a law or policy. This procedure consists of a free and open discussion in which all the participants are given an equal opportunity to present their views and for them together to reach an agreement based upon full knowledge of the issues and choices before them. Habermas offers an inclusive model in which all the participants have the same

---

[7] GRI, *Sustainability Reporting Guidelines*, at p. 9.

[8] *Ibid.*, at p. 17.

[9] See Jürgen Habermas, *The Theory of Communicative Action* vol. 1 *Reason and the Rationalization of Society*, vol. 2 *Lifeworld and System: A Critique of Functionalist Reason* (translated by T. McCarthy, 1984 and 1987); *Communication and the Evolution of Society* (translated by T. McCarthy, Boston 1979); *Justification and Application: Remarks on Discourse Ethics* (translated by C. P. Cronin, Cambridge, Mass, 1993); *Moral Consciousness and Communicative Action* (translated by C. Lenhardt and S. W. Nicholsen, Cambridge, Mass., 1990); *Between Facts and Norms: Contributions to a Discourse Theory of Law and Democracy* (translated by William Rehg, Cambridge, Polity Press, 1996).

opportunities to initiate debate and both to question and provide reasons for and against the claims made. The beliefs and norms held must not be based upon power or be imposed by domination but instead should be founded upon generalisable interests and exist in a context in which the parties are given equal and mutual respect.[10] The participants in this context are persuaded by the force of the better argument in a rational discussion. The legitimating force of the discursive process of opinion and will-formation is that 'illocutionary binding forces of a use of language oriented to mutual understanding serve to bring reason and will together – and lead to convincing positions to which all individuals can agree without coercion'.[11]

Habermas' theory is a counterfactual construction that requires a move from contract to consensus and in this sense moves from strategic action to a deliberative or communicative process.[12] The contractual or strategic approach involves participants regarding others as instrumentalities in the pursuit of their own objectives. Yet the existence of inequalities in bargaining power, information, and rhetorical skills means that this strategic approach is unlikely to be in the equal interests of all contractors or even of the group as a whole.[13] By contrast, the communicative or deliberative course aims at reaching a common understanding concerning the rightness of the norms under consideration.[14] The result is that the participants would only accept as legitimate those norms upon which all those possibly affected would agree upon together on the basis of good reasons.[15]

Habermas' theory rests on a number of assumptions and preconditions. One of the ground rules for the effectiveness of the discourse procedure is that assertions made in the discussions are true or that the facts alluded to are correct. Without truth there cannot be a rational discourse. Additionally there can exist no coercion or economic or political domination in reaching the decision. There must be total freedom of choice which depends upon all relevant information being made equally accessible to all participants. The construct also contains an assumption of accountability so that all beliefs and actions can be justified through the giving of reasons. The result would be that action norms would be accepted as legitimate by all those possibly affected

---

[10] Tony Prosser, 'Towards a Critical Public Law' (1982) 9 *Journal of Law and Society* 1, at pp. 9–12.

[11] Habermas, *Between Facts and Norms*, at p. 103.

[12] Michel Rosenfeld, 'Law as Discourse: Bridging the Gap Between Democracy and Rights' (1995) 108 *Harvard LR* 1163, at p. 1168.

[13] Rosenfeld, at p. 1168.

[14] Rosenfeld, at p. 1169.   [15] Rosenfeld, at p. 1169.

through their agreement to assent on the basis of good reasons. The only thing that counts 'is the compelling force of the better argument based on the relevant information'.[16] The notion is that reason and will come together and steer the participants towards convincing positions to which all individuals can agree without being coerced into such agreement. In this process, the goal of each participant is to reach a common understanding rather than personal success. In short, according to Habermas,

Rational discourse is supposed to be public and inclusive, to grant equal communicative rights for participants, to require sincerity and to diffuse any kind of force other than the forceless force of the better argument. This communicative structure is expected to create a deliberative space for the mobilization of the best available contributions for the most relevant topics.[17]

Habermas suggests that communication is aimed at achieving an objectively rational result. It is not an instrumental device nor does it seek to persuade, or worse, manipulate, those involved in the process. Habermas' theory is grounded upon a scientific process of communication. It therefore seems appropriate at this point to provide a general description of communication and its key elements and how these might appear in a corporate context. This might provide some clues as to identifying the relevant parties and how lawyers and corporate actors might successfully establish when and how such communication processes should be operated.

The process of communication

Communication theory has developed within a broad range of contexts – from mathematics and engineering to advertising and management systems. However, from these different contexts it is possible to identify a general set of characteristics of communication that could be used to inform rule-makers and those concerned with corporate disclosures.

The key aspects of communication include the existence of a relationship between sender and receiver which enables messages passed between the participants to be understood and appropriate or meaningful responses to be made. The use of language and knowledge of culture and background experiences of the participants will influence the form of presentation of information for purposes of communication as will the

---

[16] Habermas, *Between Facts and Norms*, at p. 103.

[17] Jürgen Habermas, 'Introduction' in a Special Issue of *Ratio Juris*: 'A Discursive Foundation for Law and Legal Practice – A Seminar on Jurgen Habermas' Philosophy of Law' (1999) 12 *Ratio Juris* 329, at p. 332.

structure of an organisation. It is to these aspects that I will now turn, and I will consider how they might occur in the company law context.

Communication is a form of social behaviour and involves sharing and common understanding between the participants. As Cherry remarks, 'communication is essentially a social affair'.[18] The behaviour of the participants becomes 'concerted, co-operative, and directed toward some goal'.[19] The sender and receiver of information are involved in a relationship in which they hold in common a language or a mutual co-orientation and a measure of understanding. They may also share time and experience.[20] Communication means generally that the passing and receipt of the information will itself increase the shared experience or knowledge between the senders and recipients and will involve a degree of interaction between them generally by way of a response to the message or information conveyed. The interaction between the participants signifies that communication is a dynamic and circular process so that the participants exchange roles as sender and receiver as the original receiver provides feedback to the sender.

The diverse range of relevant interest groups and individuals could pose problems for the company in its disclosure activities since the variety of recognised interests calls for a potentially broad range of information to be supplied in different ways. One potential control on the diversity of such information might be achieved by taking account of the background knowledge and experiences of the identified and recognised participants. This might curtail dissemination of at least some irrelevant information. Background knowledge and experience of the participants may be shaped by their own cultures or contextual situations. The works of Peirce and of Ogden and Richards have demonstrated that the meaning of signs will be connected to an individual's background and environment and to their past experiences.[21] Perception has a dynamic element so that new information becomes related to old information in a structured way that makes us ready to handle further information.[22] Additionally, it is the user's needs or circumstances and his or her experiences that will determine how useful or

[18] Colin Cherry, *On Human Communication* (2nd edn, MIT, Cambridge, Mass., 1966) at p. 3.
[19] Cherry, at p. 17.
[20] Denis McQuail, *Communication* (2nd edn, Longman, London, 1984) at p. 3.
[21] C. Hartshorne and P. Weiss (eds.), *Collected Papers of Charles Sanders Peirce* (Harvard University Press, Cambridge, Mass., 1931–35); C. K. Ogden and I. A. Richards, *The Meaning of Meaning* (Routledge and Kegan Paul, London, 1949) discussed in Cherry, pp. 266–7.
[22] K. Lovell, 'The Philosophy of Jean Piaget' (1966) *New Statesman*, 11 August, discussed in Parry, at pp. 96–104.

even how reliable information may be.[23] These background experiences might also raise barriers to effective communication if the sender should fail to take them into account when delivering the message. If the sender or receiver are unaware of the other's background knowledge or experiences this is likely to create 'cross-purpose talking'.[24]

In the company context, where information is published or presented the directors should take into account what the recipients of that information already know when seeking to convey new information to them. For example, when communicating with shareholders it might be necessary to provide new investors with more background information about a proposal than is necessary for long-established members, in order for those new members to participate more fully in the decision-making process. In publishing a prospectus the issuer should consider who is most likely to read it and make use of it. The limited experience of other stakeholders in reading and using financial information might require for those recipients the provision of narrative explanations rather than accounts figures and tables.

One requirement is that the signs used to convey the information or the message are known and understood in the same way by the participants.[25] The participants must each know the code used and it must have a common meaning for them. In communication theory, the smaller the differences between the message sender and the recipient the more successful will be the communication. Conversely, the greater the differences in mind set between the sender and receiver the higher the probability of misunderstandings and cross-purpose talking between the parties or even of a breakdown in communication.[26]

The use of language rests on a foundation of information that is shared by the participants.[27] Language use engages the participants in a collective, cooperative and collaborative process in that the speaker makes 'utterances' that have meaning and the listener coordinates with the speaker in trying to understand what the speaker means. The speaker also designs his or her utterances for their particular audience.[28] This collaborative process is essential to the achievement of successful

---

[23] Cherry, at pp. 228–9.

[24] John Parry, *The Psychology of Human Communication* (University of London Press, London, 1967), at p. 91.

[25] A. Schutz, *Phenomenology of the Social World* (Heinemann, London, 1972) cited by McQuail, at p. 56.

[26] Parry, at p. 17.

[27] For analysis of language use see Herbert H. Clark, *Arenas of Language Use* (University of Chicago Press, Chicago, 1992) and *Using Language* (Cambridge University Press, Cambridge, 1996).

[28] *Ibid.*

communication. Thus in the same way that communication is a social activity, so too is language use (itself an element of the communication process) a species of joint action. Ambiguities can occur as a result of different connotations of general terms or shifting meanings.[29] For example, in the corporate context the profit and loss account and the balance sheet tend to be produced without a consistent conceptual basis.[30] Such ambiguities will limit the effectiveness of the communication. Shifts of meanings may arise because of the different contexts in which language may be used.

If the target recipients of company information are not familiar with the technical language or terminology being used then that information should either be presented differently or the terminology should be explained. The role of informational intermediaries is clearly of relevance since, for example, accountants agree on a common language and standardise disclosure.[31] The simplification of language project in the European harmonisation programme might go some way towards alleviating language barriers to communication in the company law context.

The sender of information should avoid ambiguities and may have to tailor the information for the different groups involved. Thus, as suggested above, different formats might need to be used for delivering the same information to different participants. For example, a lay customer might respond better to visual images as a way of informing him or her about what they are considering for purchase, whereas an analyst might prefer to see graphs or figures about sales turnover comparing the company to others in the same sector.[32] Charkham and Simpson suggest that words and narrative are very important as these give a clearer, more complete picture.[33] Within each interest group there could also be sub-categories. For example, institutional investors have different information needs from private investors. However, the key is not necessarily to offer less information to one group than is given to the other but to present it in ways appropriate to the needs and understandings of the different constitutents.

Another example might be the need for familiarity with the accounting methods and the manner of presentation of the accounts in order for the reader of the accounts to be given a meaningful indication of the

---

[29] Parry, at pp. 91–2.   [30] ICAS, at p. 21.

[31] F. H. Easterbrook and D. R. Fischel, *The Economic Structure of Corporate Law* (Harvard University Press, 1991) at p. 293.

[32] Richard Pildes and Cass R. Sunstein, 'Reinventing the Regulatory State' (1995) 62 *University of Chicago Law Review* 1, who draw a distinction between experts and lay people who will require different information. They also note that different types of risk will also generate different styles of disclosure: at pp. 108–11.

[33] Jonathan Charkham and Anne Simpson, *Fair Shares: The Future of Shareholder Power and Responsibility* (Oxford University Press, 1999) at pp. 198–200.

company's financial situation. If, for example, in the company the sender and recipient are using different methods of valuation and the sender does not take account of that fact in the delivery of the accounts, the recipient will perhaps be given a different impression of the company's financial situation than the sender has conveyed or has sought to convey. Thus the accounts need to be accompanied by an explanation of the accounting methods used. Additionally, Turner suggests replacing terms such as 'debtors' and 'creditors' with 'accounts receivable' and 'accounts payable' since these are in his view clearer.[34] Redundancy can dispel doubt. Thus the aim should not necessarily be to pare down the information to the bare minimum but, on the contrary, to build redundancy deliberately into accounting and other management information systems.[35] Use of graphs and other visual images might also assist provided these are used as redundancy techniques to enhance rather than to obscure understanding. One danger is that information can be presented in a style that is instrumental since it may influence the reaction of the recipients.[36] It is important to recognise this danger in company law where the potential for abuse of power by the directors is already recognised, thus giving rise to the existence of fiduciary duties as well as stringent disclosure obligations where there are potential conflicts of interest between the directors and the company.

Related to these codes and cultures that shape the information are the media used to transmit the information. These may have an impact upon degrees of understanding and how much can be assimilated by the recipient. One problem in assessing the capacity of a recipient to receive information is that there is no single way of measuring information[37] and individuals vary in their capacity to handle information.[38] However, psychological research has identified some ways in which information processing capacity and understanding might be maximised, while 'noise' might be reduced. It is clear that memory span and absolute judgement span limit the amount of information that individuals are able to receive, process and remember.[39] Some of these problems can be reduced by

[34] Turner, at p. 156.

[35] Anthony G. Puxty, *Organisation and Management: An Accountant's Perspective* (Pitman, London, 1986), at p. 217 (hereinafter 'Puxty').

[36] Ota Weinberger, 'Information and Human Liberty' (1996) 9 *Ratio Juris* 248, at p. 255. See also for an overview of the issues and the literature, Sonja Gallhofer, Jim Haslam, Stephen Morrow and Robin Sydserff, 'Accounting, Transparency and the Culture of Spin: Re-Orientating Accounting Communication in the New Millenium' (December 1999/January 2000) 11 *Pacific Accounting Review* 97.

[37] Parry, at p. 79.

[38] Parry, at p. 54.

[39] George Miller, *The Psychology of Communication: Seven Essays* (Allen Lane, Penguin, London, 1968), at pp. 41–2.

breaking information down into smaller chunks. Increasing the number of alternative stimuli may also improve the communication, although there appears to be a ceiling upon the appropriate number of stimuli above which the communication benefits are reduced.[40] Thus, data could be presented in visual as well as written form. For example, the accounts, in which numbers are used, could be explained in word narrative as well as in graphs or diagrams. By repeating the information in different ways – redundancy – the recipient has a greater chance of noticing the information and of understanding it and retaining it in his or her memory. Avoidance of competing pieces of information will also minimise the risk of noise or distraction.[41] Simplicity of design and absence of cluttering of diagrammatic presentation is also more likely to be successful.[42] The form of information provided may also be influenced by the character of the organisation.

Organisational structure

According to Puxty, 'information is the life-blood of an organisation. The only way a manager can know what to do is on the basis of the information he or she gets. The only way the manager can act is to impart information. Managers are from one point of view just aspects of a communication and control system'.[43] For Cherry communication *means* organisation.[44] He states that 'when members or elements are in communication with one another, they are associating, co-operating, forming an organization, or sometimes an organism. The organization possesses a structure and the possession of this structure allows the whole organization to be better adapted or better fitted for some goal-seeking activity.'[45]

In this way communication works to provide members with shared knowledge about an organisation's goals and can mediate the inputs and outputs of an organisation.[46]

The structure of an organisation both enables and constrains communication. By constraining activities within a structured environment more information can actually be conveyed less chaotically and more predictably, thereby preventing 'overload' and missed information.

---

[40] *Ibid.*, p. 18.   [41] Parry, at p. 88.   [42] Parry, at p. 114.

[43] Puxty, at p. 213.

[44] Cherry, at p. 5.

[45] Cherry, at p. 6.

[46] Everett M. Rogers and Rekha Agarwala-Rogers, 'Organizational Communication' in Gerhard J. Hanneman and William J. McEwen (eds.), *Communication and Behaviour* (Addison-Wesley, Reading, Mass., 1975), 218, at p. 219.

Structure allows information to be processed more efficiently by means of delegated responsibility.[47] In a small organisation, the group may more easily develop its own private language and rules for communication. In a larger organisation groups may be formalised and communication may occur both horizontally and vertically.[48] Horizontal information tends to be less formal and more fluid, whereas vertically transmitted information is usually more formal and more slowly transmitted.[49] Horizontal information in large organisations tends to be related to task coordination whereas top-down vertical information tends to consist of authoritative orders.[50] There is a complementarity between horizontal and vertical information channels in a successfully communicating organisation.[51] Etzioni, noting the possibility of information flowing vertically and horizontally in the rank structure and that vertical information may flow upwards or downwards, suggests that the amount of information carried by the various networks and the direction of the flow are central determinants of organisational effectiveness and level of participation in the organisation.[52]

Organisation also has connection with the exercise of power and can have some negative aspects since those with power may control the flow of information and who has access to it. This allows control of the premises of discussion and the outcomes.[53] Thus organisation can enable those in power to manipulate the communication process. This manipulation or influence can be achieved by use of 'gatekeepers' who, whilst having a positive role of preventing overload, might filter information through the communication channels in hierarchical organisations. This filtering process could be used to distort or omit essential information.[54] Power can also be exercised in the manner in which information is transmitted. Thus words can be used to mislead the recipient or to persuade him or her to the speaker's purpose or point of view.[55] From this perspective the role of non-executive directors and auditors cannot be underestimated. They are in a position to be able to direct the process of communication, by the way in which they influence the flow of information to and from those reliant on corporate reports.

---

[47] J. David Johnson, *Organizational Communication Structure* (Ablex, Norwood, New Jersey, 1993) at pp. 3–5.

[48] McQuail, at pp. 105–15.

[49] Rogers and Agarwala-Rogers, at p. 228.

[50] *Ibid.*, at p. 228.

[51] *Ibid.*, at p. 228.

[52] Amitai Etzioni, *A Comparative Analysis of Complex Organizations: On Power, Involvement and their Correlates* (Free Press, New York, 1961), at p. 138.

[53] Johnson, at pp. 3–5.

[54] Rogers and Agarwala-Rogers, at p. 223.   [55] Parry, at pp. 18–19.

Organising the stakeholders

As has already been stated, company law's traditional model of the company which focuses on the relationship between the directors and shareholders, is becoming increasingly outdated whilst the moral and commercial relevance of stakeholders are gathering momentum. Recognition of this fact is extremely significant for the debate on corporate reporting and disclosure. The increasing importance of intangible assets and value of reputation to companies means that they cannot ignore their stakeholders. Corporate reports can no longer be tailored to the needs only of shareholders and potential investors. The Government's own admission of this fact lies behind its endorsement of the 'enlightened shareholder value' rhetoric.

If the stakeholder claim to recognition is accepted this raises a practical challenge for the disclosure regime: how are all the interests to be satisfied? There are a number of possible alternative responses to this question. One is to consider the claims of stakeholders as competing claims which would require a process by which their claims can be arranged in an order of priority. Another response is to view them as equally worthy of recognition in which case a method is required for engaging with them all without the prohibitive cost implications this might create for companies. This is a matter which I hope to explore in future research in greater depth but a starting point might be provided by the suggestions of theorists such as Scholes and Clutterbuck[56] and Clarke.[57] Their recognition of the importance of intangible assets and the contribution of constituents other than shareholders persuades them to consider placing another body at the centre of the company for the purposes of effective communication. All these theorists suggest that employees should be placed at the centre of the communication circle. Clarke argues this point from a moral perspective, based on the value of the employees' contribution to the company's success, whilst Scholes and Clutterbuck rest their argument on the reputational relevance of employees – their level of contentment is the strongest form of advertisement for a company. Part of this placing of employees (or any other constituents) at the centre of the communication circle is an

---

[56] Eileen Scholes and David Clutterbuck, 'Communicating with Stakeholders: An Integrated Approach' (1998) 31 *Long Range Planning* 227.

[57] Thomas Clarke, 'The Stakeholder Corporation: A Business Philosophy for the Information Age' (1998) 31 *Long Range Planning* 182. See also Margaret Blair, *Ownership and Control* (Brookings Institute, Mass., 1998).

attempt to organise stakeholders into communication networks[58] that enables all stakeholders to be provided with information and to be given opportunities for dialogue with the company's management through forums in which stakeholders share expectations, values and understanding and that involves them in the creation of values and in auditing how the company adheres to its policies and values.[59] This approach could decentralise the annual general meeting as the key forum in which the management board is held to account by shareholders and where discussion of the company's reports and accounts take place. Instead, an integrated approach is required which builds communication into corporate strategy and aims to align the needs of rather than satisfy or pacify individual groups. This should not become stakeholder management but should be management with stakeholder involvement.

Electronic communication

Part of the solution for the problems involved in communicating with large and multiple groups with different needs and interests rests in the use of electronic communication through facilities such as the internet and email. The Department of Trade and Industry has consistently supported modernisation of communications via electronic mechanisms. The Company Law Reform Bill, for example, pursues measures to allow companies to default to electronic communications with shareholders. This can improve the immediacy and quality of communications between companies and their shareholders; enhance the exercise of shareholder rights; and facilitate cost-savings by eliminating the unnecessary use of paper. As the DTI has observed: 'It is now feasible for companies to supplement the shareholder communications required by statute by placing on such websites much of the information now available only to institutions and analysts, thus reducing the present disparity of information, at least for those individual shareholders able to receive electronic communications.'[60]

Of course there are problems that could arise through electronic deliberations. For example, some constituents remain without computer access with the result that concentration on electronic resources could disenfranchise them. Additionally, electronic communications

---

[58] See Timothy J. Rowley, 'Moving Beyond Dyadic Ties: A Network Theory of Stakeholder Influences' (1997) 22 *Academy of Management Review* 887.

[59] Scholes and Clutterbuck, at p. 237.

[60] Department of Trade and Industry, *Company General Meetings and Shareholder Communication*, Consultation Paper (1999) para. 63, at p. 28.

could encourage prolonged discussion and many more questions than would an annual general meeting, leading to different inefficiencies.[61] However, the potential for electronic communications to reach a large number of participants in a cost-effective manner cannot be underestimated. One of the problems that was highlighted by the Enron demise was the lack of timely information. However, new facilities are being developed to overcome these problems as well as to provide consistent and standardised information more easily. The growing popularity of the eXtensible Business Reporting Language, a standard based on eXtensible Markup Language, is a major step forward in the activity of information provision and corporate reporting. XBRL is an electronic format for simplifying the flow of financial statements, performance reports, accounting records, and other financial information between software programs. The XBRL standard provides a consistent format for business reporting and streamlines how companies prepare and disseminate financial data, and how that data is to be reviewed and analysed.[62] The Securities and Exchange Commission has recently adopted a voluntary program for reporting financial information using the XBRL system. The system allows for presentation of information in various languages and the tagging facility enables users to search, retrieve and analyse information automatically.[63]

The developing electronic communications systems have transformed the disclosure process considerably already, notably in the way in which the Companies Registrar holds and makes information available. Clearly the potential opportunities may alleviate some of the pressures created by the growing information demands of larger numbers of interested participants and globalisation.

Ultimately, the disclosure process is of enormous significance to company law. This book has sought to provide an overview and to present its basic features. As an evolving regulatory process it will continue to change and new demands will be made of it. No longer can it afford to rest on the traditional company law philosophy of shareholder primacy and profit maximisation. Companies are more complex than that philosophy would suggest, and corporate reporting must recognise that fact. The alternative is the introduction of more intrusive regulatory techniques.

---

[61] Elizabeth Boros, 'Corporate Governance in Cyberspace: Who Stands to Gain What from the Virtual Meeting?' (2003) 3 *Journal of Corporate Law Studies* 149.

[62] See Editorial, 'PricewaterhouseCoopers: Keep your eye on XBLR' *Silicon Valley Business Journal*, 6 May 2003.

[63] For information on XBRL see Michael Ohata, 'XBRL', available at www.realcorporatelawyer.com/faqs/xblr.html.

Bibliography

Accounting Standards Board, *Foreword to Accounting Standards*, available at www.frc.org.uk/asb

Reporting Standard 1: Operating and Financial Review (May 2005)

Statement of Principles for Financial Reporting (London, December 1999) circulated in *Accountancy* (March 2000) 109

Year-End Financial Reports: Improving Communication (ASB, Milton Keynes, 2000)

Accounting Standards Steering Committee, *The Corporate Report*, (ASSC, London, 1975)

AICPA, Special Committee on Financial Reporting, *Improving Business Reporting – A Customer Focus: Meeting the Information Needs of Investors and Creditors* (1994)

Akerlof, G., 'The Market for "Lemons": Quality, Uncertainty and the Market Mechanism' (1970) 90 *Quarterly Journal of Economics* 629

Alchian A. A., and Demzetz, H., 'Production, Information Costs, and Economic Organization' (1972) 62 *American Economic Review* 777

Alexander, Kern, 'The Need for International Regulation of Auditors and Public Companies', (2002) 23 *Company Lawyer* 341

Amnesty International UK Response to the Operating and Financial Review Working Group on Materiality (DTI, September 2003)

Anderson, J. C., and Fraankle, A. W., 'Voluntary Social Reporting: An Iso-beta Portfolio Analysis' (1980) *The Accounting Review*, July, Vol. 55, No. 3, 467

APB Ethical Standard 1, *Integrity, Objectivity and Independence*, (October 2004)

Armstrong, Murray, 'We're all off message' *The Guardian, The Giving List*, 8 November 2004, 11

Arnold, John, 'The Information Requirements of Shareholders' in Carsberg, Bryan, and Hope, Tony (eds.), *Current Issues in Accounting* (Phillip Allan, Oxford, 1977) 107

Association of British Insurers, *Investing in Social Responsibility: Risks and Opportunities*

Azzi, John, 'Disclosure in Prospectuses' (1992) 9 *Company and Securities Law Journal* 205

Bartlett, Susan A., and Chandler, Roy A., 'The Corporate Report and the Private Shareholder: Lee and Tweedie Twenty Years On' (1997) 29 *British Accounting Review* 245

Barton, A. D., *Objectives and Basic Concepts of Accounting*, (Australian Accounting Research Foundation, Melbourne, 1982)

Beattie, Vivien (ed.), *Business Reporting: The Inevitable Change?* (Institute of Chartered Accountants in Scotland, Edinburgh, 1999)

Beaver, William H., *Financial Reporting: An Accounting Revolution* (Prentice Hall, 3rd edn, New Jersey, 1998)

Belkaoui, A., 'The Impact of the Disclosure of the Environment Effects of Organizational Behavior on the Market' (1976) *Financial Management* Winter, 26

Benjamin, James J., and Stanga, Keith G., 'Differences in Disclosure Needs of Major Users of Financial Statements' (1977) *Accounting and Business Research* 187, at p. 191

Benston, G., 'Required Disclosure and The Stock Market: An Evaluation of the Securities Exchange Act of 1934' (1973) 63 *American Economic Review* 132

Berle, Adolf A., and Means, Gardiner C., *The Modern Corporation and Private Property* (1991) (originally published in 1932 by Harcourt, Brace and World Inc.)

Bird, Peter, 'Group Accounts and the True and Fair View' (1982) *JBL* 364, at p. 365

'What is a "True and Fair View"?' (1984) *JBL* 480

Birds, John (et al), *Boyle and Birds' Company Law* (5th edn, Jordans, Bristol, 2004)

Birkinshaw, Patrick, *Freedom of Information: The Law, the Practice and the Ideal* (2nd edn, Butterworths, London, 1996)

Blair, Margaret M., 'For Whom Should Corporations Be Run?: An Economic Rationale for Stakeholder Management' (1998) 31 *Long Range Planning* 195
Ownership and Control: Rethinking Corporate Governance for the Twenty-First Century (Brookings Institution, Washington DC, 1995)

Blair, Mark, and Ramsay, Ian M., 'Mandatory Corporate Disclosure Rules and Securities Regulation' in Walker, G., and Fisse, B. (eds.), *Securities Regulation in Australia and New Zealand* (Oxford University Press, Melbourne, 1994) ch. 12, 264

Blanchard, Julian, 'Corporate Accountability and Information – Lessons from Democracy' (1997) 7 *Australian Journal of Corporate Law* 326

Boros, Elizabeth, 'Corporate Governance in Cyberspace: Who stands to Gain What from the Virtual Meeting?' (2003) 3 *Journal of Corporate Law Studies* 149

Bowers, Simon, 'Rover questions must be answered' *The Guardian* 1 June 2005, 18

Boyle, A. J., 'Economic considerations in Part 3 of the Law Commission's paper on company directors' (1999) 20 *Co Lawyer* 210

Brandeis, L., *Other People's Money* (1933)

Brophy, M., 'A Stakeholder's View of Environmental Reporting' at www.environmental-expert.com/articles/article20/article20.htm

Brown, J. Robert, Jr and De Tore, Stephen M., 'Rationalizing the Disclosure Process: The Summary Annual Report' (1988–89) 39 *Case Western Reserve Law Review* 39

Buck, Tobias, and Jopson, Barney, 'Europe softens line on audit committees', *Financial Times*, 22 June 2005, 1

Business in the Community, *Winning with Integrity*, Summary (2000)

Cadbury Committee, *Report on the Financial Aspects of Corporate Governance* (Gee, London, 1992)

Cary, W., 'The Case for Higher Corporate Standards' (1962) *Harv Bus Rev*, Sept.–Oct. 53

Catanach Anthony H., and Rhoades-Catanach, Shelley, 'Enron: A Financial Reporting Failure?' (2003) 48 *Vill LR* 1057

Central London Focus Report: PIRC, *Assessing the value of human capital: the experience of investors and companies* (Focus Central London, London, 2001)

Centre for Business Performance, *The case for corporate reporting: overwhelming or over-hyped?* (CBR, Report to the Centre for Excellence in Management and Leadership, Cranfield, 2002)

Charkham, Jonathan and Simpson, Anne, *Fair Shares: The Future of Shareholder Power and Responsibility* (Oxford University Press, Oxford, 1999)

Cheffins, Brian R., *Company Law: Theory, Structure and Operation* (Clarendon Press, Oxford, 1997)

Cherry, Colin, *On Human Communication*, (2nd edn, MIT, Cambridge, Mass., 1966)

CIPD, *The Change Agenda* (2003)

Clark, Herbert H., *Arenas of Language Use* (University of Chicago Press, Chicago, 1992)

Using Language (Cambridge University Press, Cambridge, 1996)

Clarke, J., 'Corporate Social Reporting: An Ethical Approach' in Gowthorpe, C., and Blake, J. (eds.), *Ethical Issues in Accounting* (Routledge, London, 1998), 185

Coffee, Joe, and Somnier, Jonathan Overett, 'The Market Abuse Directive – The First Use of the Lamfalussy Process' (2003) 18 *Journal of International Banking Law and Regulation* 370

Coffee, John C., 'Market Failure and the Economic Case for a Mandatory Disclosure System' (1984) 70 *Va L Rev* 717

Coffee, John C., Jr, 'Gatekeeper Failure and Reform: The Challenge of fashioning Relevant Reforms' in Guido Ferrarini et al (eds.), *Reforming Company and Takeover Law in Europe* (Oxford University Press, Oxford, 2004) 455

Commission of the European Union, *Reinforcing the statutory audit in the EU* Communication of the Commission (2003/C 236/02)

The Statutory Audit in the European Union, the way forward (OJ C 143, 8.5.1998, p. 12)

Commission of the European Union, *Financial Services: Implementing the Framework for Financial Markets: Action Plan*, Communication of the Commission COM (1999) 232

Committee of European Securities Regulators, *Proposed Statement of Principles of Enforcement of Accounting Standards in Europe*, Consultation Paper (October 2002), CESR/02 – 188b, available at www.europefesco.org

Committee of Wise Men, *Final Report of the Committee of Wise Men on the Regulation of European Capital Markets* (Lamfalussy Report, Brussels, 2001) available at http://europa.eu.int/comm/internal-market

Committee on Corporate Laws, 'Changes in the Model Business Corporation Act – Amendments to Financial Provisions' (1979) 34 *Business Law* 1867

Companies House, *Annual Report 2003–2004*
  Development Plan 2001–2004
  Strategic Direction 2003–2006 – *The Future of Companies House*
Company Law Review Steering Committee, *Modern Company Law for a Competitive Economy: Final Report* (July 2001)
CORE, *Coalition Response to the UK Government's Draft Regulations on the Operating and Financial Review and Directors' Report Consultation Document* (6 August 2004), available at www.corporate-responsibility.org
  'What's wrong with the OFR?' (November 2004), available at www.corporate-responsibility.org
Cornelius, I., and Davies, M., *Shareholder Value* (FT Financial Publishing, London, 1997)
Cottrell, *Industrial Finance: 1830–1914* (Methuen, 1979)
Cowe, R., 'Green Issues and the Investor: Inadequacies of Current Reporting Practice and Some Suggestions for Change' in Owen, D. (ed.), *Accountancy and the Challenge of the Nineties* (Chapman and Hall, London, 1992), 125
Cox, Charles C., 'Accounting Standards from and Economist's Perspective' (1985) 7 *Journal of Comparative Business and Capital Market Law* 349
Cross, Simon, 'Companies House' *International Accountant* (October 2002)
CSR Campaign, 'A question of business fundamentals: Socially responsible investment goes mainstream in the United Kingdom almost' available at www.csrcampaign.org/publications/excellencereport2002/uk2/printpage/content.aspx
Danish Ministry of Science, Technology and Innovation, *Analysing Intellectual Capital Statements* (Copenhagen, Denmark, 2003)
  Technology and Innovation, *Intellectual Capital Statements – The New Guideline* (Copenhagen, Denmark, 2003)
Davies, Paul, 'Post-Enron Developments in the United Kingdom' in Guido Ferrarini et al (eds.), *Reforming Company and Takeover Law in Europe* (Oxford University Press, Oxford, 2004) 185
Davies, Paul L. (ed.), *Gower's Principles of Modern Company Law* (6th edn, Sweet & Maxwell, London, 1997)
  (ed.), *Gower's Principles of Modern Company Law* (7th edn, Sweet & Maxwell, London, 2003)
de Búrca, Gráinne, 'The Institutional Development of the EU: A Constitutional Analysis' in Craig, Paul, and de Búrca, Gráinne (eds.), *The Evolution of EU Law* (Oxford University Press, Oxford, 1999)
Dearing Committee, *The Making of Accounting Standards* (ICAEW, London, 1988)
Department of Trade and Industry, *Accounting Simplifications: A Consultative Document* (DTI, London, May 1995)
  Accounting Simplifications: Re-arrangements to Companies Act Schedule on Small Company Accounts: A Consultative Document (DTI, London, July 1996)
  Audit and Accounting Requirements for Very Small Companies: A Consultative Document (DTI, London, April 1993)
  Director and Auditor Liability, Summary of responses to the Government's consultation (2004) available at www.Department of Trade and Industry.gov.uk

Director and Auditor Liability: A Consultative Document (DTI, London, December 2003)

Draft Regulations on the Operating and Financial Review and Directors' Report, Consultation Document (DTI, London, May 2004), available at www.dti. gov.uk/

Final Report of the Review of Companies House (July 2000) Companies House, Guidance Booklet, *Annual Return*, available at www.companieshouse.gov.uk/

High Performance Workplaces – Informing and Consulting Employees, Consultation Document (July 2003)

International Accounting Standards: A Consultation Document on the Possible Extension of the European Regulation on International Accounting Standards (30 August 2003) URN 02/1158

Modern Company Law for a Competitive Economy: Company General Meetings and Shareholder Communication (DTI, London, October 1999)

Modern Company Law for a Competitive Economy: Completing the Structure (November 2000)

Modern Company Law for a Competitive Economy: Final Report (DTI, June 2001)

Review of the Regulatory Regime of the Accountancy Profession (October 2002), URN 02/1340

Review of the Regulatory Regime of the Accountancy Profession: Report to the Secretary of State for Trade and Industry (January 2003), URN 03/589

Small Companies Audit Exemption: Consultation on Proposed Amendments: A Consultative Document (DTI, London, January 1997)

Small Company Accounts: A Possible Standard Format: A Consultative Document (DTI, London, September 1996)

Dezalay, Yves, 'Territorial Battles and Tribal Disputes' (1991) 54 MLR 792

Dickerson, Claire Moore, 'Ozymandias as Community Project: Managerial/ Corporate Social Responsibility and the Failure of Transparency' (2003) 35 *Connecticut Law Review* 1035

Doane, Deborah, 'Market Failure: the case for mandatory social and environmental reporting', *New Economics Foundation* (March 2002)

Dowling, J., and Pfeffer, J., 'Organizational Legitimacy: Social Values and Organizational Behavior' (1975) *Pacific Sociological Review* 122

Doyle, Louis, 'Change in the wind on common law defective-prospectus liability?' (1996) 17 *Co Law* 279

Easterbrook, F. H., and Fischel, D. R., *The Economic Structure of Corporate Law* (Harvard University Press, 1991)

Eccles, Robert G. and Mavrinac, Sarah C., 'Improving the Corporate Disclosure Process' (1995) *Sloan Management Review*, Summer Issue, 11

Edvinsson, L., and Malone, M., *Realizing your company's true value by finding its hidden brain power* (HarperCollins Publishers, New York, 1997)

Elliott, Barry and Elliott, Jamie, *Financial Accounting and Reporting* (8th edn, Financial Times, Prentice Hall, London, 2004)

Environment Agency, *Environmental Disclosures* (July 2004), available at www. environment-agency.gov.uk

Epstein, Marc J., and Freedman, Martin, 'Social Disclosure and the Individual Investor' (1994) 7 *Accounting, Auditing and Accountability Journal* 94

Ernst & Young, *Corporate Governance: Greenbury Implementation* (Ernst & Young, London, 1996)

Etzioni, Amitai, *A Comparative Analysis of Complex Organizations: On Power, Involvement and their Correlates* (Free Press, New York, 1961)

European Commission, *Communication concerning Corporate Social Responsibility: A business contribution to sustainable development*

Communication: *EU Financial Reporting Strategy: the way forward*, COM (2000) 359 final, Brussels 13.6.2000

Enterprise Directorate General, *Study on the Measurement of Intangible Assets and Associated Reporting Practices* (EC, Brussels, 2003)

Green Paper on *The Role, Position and Liability of the Statutory Auditor in the EU* (OJ C 321, 28.10.1996, p. 1)

Mapping Instruments for Corporate Social Responsibility (European Commission, Directorate-General for Employment and Social Affairs, 2003)

Promoting a European Framework for Corporate Social Responsibility, Brussels, 1.7.2001, COM (2001) 366 final

Fama, Eugene, 'Efficient Capital Markets: A Review of Theory and Empirical Work' (1970) 25 *J Fin* 383

Fama, E. F., and Jensen, M. C, 'Separation of Ownership and Control' (1983) 26 *Journal of Law and Economics* 301

Ferman, Risa Vetri, 'Environmental Disclosures and SEC Reporting Requirements' (1992) 17 *Delaware Journal of Corporate Law* 483

Ferran, Eilis, *Company Law and Corporate Finance* (OUP, Oxford, 1999)

Financial Reporting Council, *Regulatory Strategy* (December 2004) (available at www.frc.org.uk)

Audit Committees – Combined Code Guidance (January 2003)

The State of Financial Reporting (FRC, London, 1991)

Financial Services Authority, *Review of the Listing Regime*, Consultation Paper CP203 (2004)

The Listing Review and Implementation of the Prospectus Directive, Consultation Paper, CP04/16 (2004)

Foong, Ken and Yorston, Richard, *Human Capital Measurement and Reporting: A British Perspective* (London Business School, 2003)

Frederiksen, Jens V., and Westphalen, Sven-Age, *Human resource accounting: Interests and conflicts* (CEDEFOP, Thassaloniki, 1998)

Freedman, Judith and Power, Michael, 'Law and Accounting: Transition and Transformation' (1991) 54 *MLR* 769

Fuller, Jane, 'Setting the standard: does Europe's accounts overhaul add up for business?' *Financial Times*, 23 November 2004, 17

Garcia, Rafael Arenas, 'Registry Disclosure in Europe. Towards a European Registry Space' available at www.ecrforum.org/sevilla last accessed 25.8.04

Gewirth, Alan, *The Community of Rights* (University of Chicago Press, Chicago, 1996)

Gilson, Ronald J., and Kraakman, Reinier H., 'The Mechanisms of Market Efficiency' (1984) 70 *Va LR* 549

Global Reporting Initiative, *Sustainability Reporting Guidelines* (2002)

Gower, L.C.B., *Principles of Modern Company Law* (4th edn., Sweet & Maxwell, London, 1979)

Review of Investor Protection (1984) Cmnd. 9125

Gray, R. H., Owen, D. L., and Maunders, K. T., *Corporate Social Reporting: Accounting and Accountability* (Prentice Hall, London, 1987)

Gray, Rob, 'Thirty years of social accounting, reporting and auditing: what (if anything) have we learnt?' (2001) 10 *Business Ethics: A European Review* 9

Gray, Rob, Owen, Dave, and Adams, Carol, *Accounting and Accountability: Changes and Challenges in Corporate Social and Environmental Reporting* (Prentice Hall, London, 1996)

Greenbury Committee, *Report on Directors' Remuneration* (Gee, London, 1995)

Grienberger, Warren F., and Lee, Michael C., 'Should the Board of Directors Have a Disclosure Committee?' available at www.lawhost.com/lawjournal/98spring/committee.html

Grier, Nicholas, 'Watch out for share-pushers' (1998) 19 *Co Law* 311

Griffiths, Ian, 'Breaking Down the mechanics of the money', *The Guardian*, 15 April 2005

'Rover's £400m accounting puzzle', *The Guardian*, 15 April 2005

Groves, R., 'Financial Disclosure: When More is Not Better' (May–June 1994) *Financial Executive* 11–14

Guardian, Notebook, 27 August 2004, 'Curbs have done little to shrink bosses' pay', p. 27

Guest, *Effective People Management* (2000), p. 35

Guimón, José, 'Recent European models for intellectual capital management and reporting: A comparative study of the MERITUM and the Danish Guidelines' available at www.idde.org/files/mcmaster2.doc, last visited 1 July 2005

Habermas, Jürgen, 'Introduction' in a Special Issue of *Ratio Juris*, 'A Discursive Foundation for Law and Legal Practice – A Seminar on Jurgen Habermas' Philosophy of Law' (1999) 12 *Ratio Juris* 329

Communication and the Evolution of Society (translated by T. McCarthy, Boston 1979)

The Theory of Communicative Action Vol. 1; *Reason and the Rationalization of Society* Vol. 2; *Lifeworld and System: A Critique of Functionalist Reason* (translated by T. McCarthy, 1984 and 1987)

Between Facts and Norms: Contributions to a Discourse Theory of Law and Democracy (translated by William Rehg, Polity Press, Cambridge, 1996)

Justification and Application: Remarks on Discourse Ethics (translated by C. P. Cronin, Cambridge, Mass., 1993)

Moral Consciousness and Communicative Action (translated by C. Lenhardt and S. W. Nicholsen, Cambridge, Mass., 1990)

Hampel Committee, *Final Report on Corporate Governance* (London, Gee, 1998)

Hannigan, Brenda in *Company Law* (Lexis Nexis, London, 2003)

Hargreaves, Deborah, and Tricks, Henry, 'New accounting rules raise questions of accountability', *Financial Times*, 9 December 2004, 20

Harrington, Anthony, 'Global Reporting Initiative picks up momentum', *Scotland on Sunday*, 18 April 2004

Hertig, Gérard and Lee, Ruben, 'Four Predictions About the Future of EU Securities Regulation' (2003) 3 JCLS 359

Higgs, Derek, *Guidance on the Role of the Non-Executive Director*, published with the Combined Code on Corporate Governance, July 2003, available at www.frc.org

Review of the role and effectiveness of non-executive directors (DTI, London, January 2003)

High Level Group of Company Law Experts, *Report on a Modern Regulatory Framework for Company Law in Europe* (Brussels, 4 November 2002)

Hillage, J., and Moralee, J., *The Return on Investors*, ies report 314 (Brighton, 1996)

Hilton, Steve, 'Identikit bureaucrats or romantic crusaders?', *The Guardian, The Giving List*, 8 November 2004, 12

Hines, R. D., 'The Usefulness of Annual Reports: the Anomaly between the Efficient Markets Hypothesis and Shareholder Surveys' (1982) *Accounting and Business Research* 296

Hirschman, Albert O., *Exit Voice and Loyalty: Responses to Decline in firms, Organizations and States* (Harvard University Press, Cambridge, Mass., 1970)

HM Treasury, Financial Services Authority and Bank of England, *After the EU Financial Services Action Plan: A new strategic approach* (HMSO, London, May 2004)

The EU Financial Services Action Plan: Delivering the FSAP in the UK (HMSO, London, May 2004)

Hoffman, Leonard, QC and Arden, Mary H., 'The Accounting Standards Committee Joint Opinion', *Accountancy*, November 1983, 154

Hopt, Klaus J., 'Modern Company and Capital Market Problems: Improving European Corporate Governance after Enron' (2003) 3 *JCLS* 221

Hutton, Will, *The State We're In* (Vintage, London, 1996, first published by Jonathan Cape, 1995) Royal Society of Arts, *Tomorrow's Company* (1995)

Inel, Burcak, 'Assessing the First Two Years of the New Regulatory Framework for Financial Markets in Europe' (2003) 18 *Journal of International Banking Law and Regulation* 363

ICAEW, *Additional Guidance on Independence for Auditors* (2004)

Reviewing Auditor Independence: Guidance for Audit Committees (ICAEW, London, 2003)

The Operating and Financial Review and Human Capital Reporting: Is the OFR the Place for Human Capital Reporting? (London, 2003) available at www.icaew.co.uk/policy

Institute of Chartered Accountants in England and Wales, *Guidance for audit committees: Monitoring the integrity of financial statements* (March 2004), available at www.icaew.co.uk

Inside Out: Reporting on Shareholder Value (ICAEW, 1999)

Preparing an Operating and Financial Review: interim process guidance for UK directors (January 2003)

The 21st Century Annual Report (ICAEW, London, 1999)

Institute of Chartered Secretaries and Administrators, *Role of the Company Secretary*, Guidance Document (1998) available at www.icsa.org.uk

International Accounting Standards Committee, *Foundation Constitution*, last revised on 8 July 2002, available at www.iasc.org.uk

Investment Management Association, Letter to David Loweth, Accounting Standards Board, 28 February 2005, available at www.iasc.org.uk

Jensen and Meckling, 'Theory of the Firm: Managerial Behavior, Agency Costs and Ownership Structure' (1976) 3 *Journal of Financial Economics* 305

Johansson, Sven-Erik, and Östman, Lars, *Accounting Theory: Integrating Behaviour and Measurement* (Pitman, London, 1995)

Jopson, Barney, 'Accountants put champagne on ice as party loses its fizz', *Financial Times*, 21 June 2005, 3

'Mid-cap groups at risk from IFRS', *Financial Times*, 9/10 July 2005, M3

'Stringent rules now squeeze shareholders', *Financial Times* 9/10 July 2005, M3

'Warning on threat to quality of auditing', *Financial Times*, 21 June 2005, 1

Joseph, Ella, 'Promoting corporate social responsibility: is market-based regulation sufficient?' (Institute for Public Policy Research, 2002) *New Economy* 96–101, available at www.ippr.org/research

Kant, Robert S., 'The New Annual Report to Shareholders' (1974–75) 20 *Villanova Law Review* 273

Kaplan, Robert S., and Norton, David P., 'The Balanced Scorecard – Measures that Drive Performance' (1992) 70 *Harvard Business Review*, No. 1, January–February 71

The Balanced Scorecard – Translating Strategy Into Action (Harvard Business School Press, Boston, 1996)

The Strategy-focused Organization: How Balanced Scorecard Companies thrive in the New Business Environment (Harvard Business School Press, Boston, 2001)

Kay, J., and Silberstone, A., 'Corporate Governance' (1995, August) *NIESR* 84

Kerr, Janet E., 'A walk through the circuits: the duty to disclose soft information' (1987) 46 *Maryland LR* 1071

Knauss, Robert L., 'A Reappraisal of the Role of Disclosure' (1964) 62 *Michigan Law Review* 607

KPMG, *The Combined Code: A Practical Guide* (Gee, London, 1999)

Kraakman, Reinier, 'Disclosure and Corporate Governance: An Overview Essay' in Ferrarini, Guido, et al (eds.), *Reforming Company and Takeover Law in Europe* (OUP, Oxford, 2004) 95

'The Emerging Framework for Disclosure in the EU' (2003) 3 *JCLS* 329

Kripke, Homer, 'The Myth of the Informed Layman' (1973) 28 *Business Lawyer* 631

Lannoo, Karel, 'The Emerging Framework for Disclosure in the EU' (2003) 3 JCLS 329

Lasok, K. P. E. and Grace, Edmond, 'Fair Accounting' (1988) *JBL* 235

Lee, T. A., and Tweedie, D. P., 'The Private Shareholder: his Sources of Financial Information and his Understanding of Reporting Practices' (1976) *Accounting and Business Research* 304

'Accounting Information: An Investigation of Private Shareholder Understanding' (1975) *Accounting and Business Research* 3

'Accounting Information: An Investigation of Private Shareholder Usage' (1975) *Accounting and Business Research* 280

Lee, T., 'A stakeholder approach to auditing' (1998) 9 *Critical Perspectives on Accounting* 217–226

Levitt, Arthur 'Plain English in Prospectuses' (1997) 69 *New York State Bar Journal*, November, 36

Lewis, Norman D., *Choice and the Legal Order: Rising Above Politics* (Butterworths, London, 1996)

Lingle, J. H., and Schiemann, W. M., 'From Balanced Scorecard to Strategic Gauges: Is Measurement Worth It?', *Management Review*, March 1996 58

Litan, Robert E., et al, 'The Enron Failure and the State of Corporate Disclosure' (The Brookings Institute, Washington DC, 2002) extract from book, available at www.brookings.edu

Litan, Robert, and others, *Following the Money: The Enron Failure and the State of Corporate Disclosure* (Brookings, US, Mass., 2002)

London Stock Exchange et al, *News Dissemination and the EU Transparency Directive* (October 2003), available at www.londonstockexchange.com

Loss, Louis, 'Disclosure as Preventive Enforcement' in Hopt, K., and Teubner, G., *Corporate Governance and Directors' Liabilities* (deGruyter, New York, Berlin, 1985) 327

Lowenstein, Louis, 'Financial Transparency and Corporate Governance: The United States as a Model?' in Grantham, Ross, and Rickett, Charles, *Corporate Personality in the 20th Century* (Hart, Oxford, 1998) 279

Mahoney, Paul G., 'Mandatory Disclosure as a Solution to Agency Problems' (1995) 62 *University of Chicago Law Review* 1047

Manning, Bayless, 'Thinking Straight About Corporate Law Reform' (1977) 41 *Law and Contemporary Problems* 3

Martorell, Rafael Guasch, 'La Armonización en el Marco del Derecho Europeo de Sociedades: La Obligación de Resultado Exigida por las Directivas Societarias a los Estados Miembros' (1994) 596 *Revista General De Derecho* 5651

Mathews, M. R., 'Social and Environmental Accounting: A Practical Demonstration of Ethical Concern?' (1995) 14 *Journal of Business Ethics* 663

McBarnet, Doreen and Whelan, Christopher, *Creative Accounting and the Cross-Eyed Javelin Thrower* (Wiley, Chichester, 1999)

'The Elusive Spirit of the Law: Formalism and the Struggle for Legal Control' (1991) 54 *MLR* 848

McGee, Andrew, 'The True and Fair View Debate: A Study in the Legal Regulation of Accounting' (1991) 54 *MLR* 874

McKee, Michael, 'The Unpredictable Future of European Securities Regulation: A Response to Four Predictions About the Future of EU Securities Regulation by Gerard Hertig and Ruben Lee' (2003) 18 *Journal of International Banking Law and Regulation* 277

McQuail, Denis, *Communication* (2nd edn, Longman, London, 1984)

Meier-Schatz, Christian J., 'Objectives of Financial Disclosure Regulation' (1986) 8 *Journal of Comparative Business and Capital Market Law* 219

MERITUM Project, 'Guidelines for Managing and Reporting on Intangibles' (Intellectual Capital report) (Madrid, Airtel-Vodafone Foundation, 2002) available at www.eu-know.net

Merkt, Hanno, 'Disclosing Disclosure: Europe's Winding Road to Competitive Standards of Publication of Company-Related Information' in Ferrarini, Guido, et al (eds.), *Reforming Company and Takeover Law in Europe* (OUP, Oxford, 2004) 115

Millon, David, 'Theories of the Corporation' (1990) 193 *Duke Law Journal* 201

Mims, Robert, 'The SEC and Corporate Financial Disclosure: A View from the Press' (1985) 7 *Journal of Comparative Business and Capital Markets Law* 387

Mogg, John F., 'Regulating Financial Services in Europe: A New Approach' (2002) 26 *Fordham International Law Journal* 58

Moloney, Niamh, 'Time to take stock on the markets: the financial services action plan concludes as the company law action plan rolls out' (2004) 53 *ICLQ*, 999

Monagan, Philip, 'Does Reporting Work? The Effect of Regulation' (2003) *Accountability Quarterly*, September 2003 (AQ21)

Murray, Peter, 'Reporting on Intangibles and Future Prospects: Meeting Market Needs' in ICAEW, *Human Capital and Corporate Reputation: Setting the Boardroom Agenda* (ICAEW, London, 2000) 4

O'Connor, Marleen A., 'Rethinking Corporate Financial Disclosure of Human Resource Values for the Knowledge-Based Economy' (1998) 1 *University of Pennsylvania Journal of Labor and Employment Law* 527

O'Dwyer, Brendan, 'The legitimacy of accountants' participation in social and ethical accounting, auditing and reporting' (2001) 10 *Business Ethics: A European Review* 27

Organisation for Economic Cooperation and Development, *Human Capital Investment* (Paris, 1998)
  Measuring what people know (Paris, 1996)
  The OECD Guidelines for Multinational Enterprises (revised 2000)

Ormrod, P., and Cleaver, K. C., 'Financial Reporting and Corporate Accountability' (1993) 23 *Accounting and Business Research* 431

Owen, David L., 'Recent developments in European social and environmental reporting and auditing practices – A critical evaluation and tentative prognosis' Research paper series, international centre for corporate social responsibility, No. 3, 2003 (www.nottingham.ac.uk/business/ICCSR)

Owen, David, and Swift, Tracey, 'Introduction, Social accounting, reporting and auditing: Beyond the rhetoric?' *Business Ethics: A European Review* (2001), Vol. 10, Issue 1, 4

Parker, Derek, *Towards IC Reporting – Developing New Measures* (Australian CPA, 1998), available at www.cpaustralia.com.au/Archive/9806/pg_aa9806_towardsicr.html

Parker, L. , Ferris, K., and Otley, D., *Accounting for the Human Factor* (Prentice Hall, New York, 1989)

Parkinson, J. E., *Corporate Power and Responsibility: Issues in the Theory of Company Law* (OUP, Oxford, 1993)

Parkinson, John, 'Disclosure and Corporate Social and Environmental Performance: Competitiveness and Enterprise in a Broader Social Framework' (2003) 3 *JCLS* 3

Parry, John, *The Psychology of Human Communication* (University of London Press, London, 1967)

Patfield, Fiona Macmillan, 'Challenges for Company Law' in Patfield, Fiona Macmillan (ed.), *Perspectives on Company Law: 1* (Kluwer, London, 1995) 1

Peirce, C. S., *Collected Papers of Charles Sanders Peirce*, 6 volumes, C. Hartshorne and P. Weiss (eds.) (Harvard University Press, Cambridge, Mass., 1931–35)

Pettet, Ben, *Company Law* (2nd edn, Longman, London, 2005)

Pijper, T., *Creative Accounting: The Effectiveness of Financial Reporting in the UK* (MacMillan, London, 1993)

Pildes, Richard and Sunstein, Cass R., 'Reinventing the Regulatory State' (1995) 62 *University of Chicago Law Review* 1

Pilger, John, *Hidden Agendas* (Vintage, London, 1998)

Pratley, Nils, 'Fears over new "fair value" accounts', *The Guardian*, 3 January 2005, 18

Prentice, D. D., 'A Director's Right of Access to Corporate Books of Account' (1978) 94 LQR 184

Prosser, Tony, 'Towards a Critical Public Law' (1982) 9 *Journal of Law and Society* 1

Puxty, Anthony G., *Organisation and Management: An Accountant's Perspective* (Pitman, London, 1986)

Report of an Investigation under section 165(6) of the Companies Act 1948 (HM Stationery Office, 1954)

Research Committee of the Institute of Chartered Accountants of Scotland, *Making Corporate Reports Valuable* (ICAS, Kogan Page, London, 1988)

Review Group – *Review of the Regulatory Regime of the Accountancy Profession: A Consultative Document* (October 2002), URN 02/1340

Rimmel, Blom, Lindstrii, and Persson, *The Danish Guidelines on Intellectual Capital Reporting: Towards a European Perspective on Human Resource Disclosures?* Paper presented at the 6th SNEE Conference on Economic Integration in Europe, Molle, Sweden (May 2004)

Rogers, Everett M., and Agarwala-Rogers, Rekha, 'Organizational Communication' in Gerhard J. Hanneman and William J. McEwen (eds.), *Communication and Behaviour* (Addison-Wesley, Reading, Mass., 1975)

Rosenfeld, Michel, 'Law as Discourse: Bridging the Gap Between Democracy and Rights' (1995) 108 *Harvard LR* 1163

Ruder, David S., 'Disclosure of Financial Projections – Developments, Problems and Techniques' (1974) *Fifth Annual Institute on Securities Regulation*, Vol. 5, 5

Sage, William, 'Regulating Through Information: Disclosure Law and American Health Care' (1999) 99 *Columbia Law Review* 1701

Sargent, Mark A., 'State Disclosure Regulation and the Allocation of Regulatory Responsibilities' (1987) 46 *Maryland LR* 1027

Schiffren, Deborah, *Approaches to Discourse* (Blackwell, Cambridge, Mass. and Oxford, 1994)

Schneider, Carl W., 'Financial Projections – Practical Problems of Disclosure' (1974) *Fifth Annual Institute on Securities Regulation*, Vol. 5, 47

Schneider, Carl W., Manko, Joseph M., and Kant, Robert S., 'Going Public: Practice, Procedure and Consequences' (1981) 27 *Villanova Law Review* 1

Scholte, J. A., 'Civil Socity and Democracy in Global Goverance', CSGR Working Paper, No 65/01 available at www.warwick.ac.uk/fac/soc/csgr/wpapers/wp6501.pdf

Schutz, A., *Phenomenology of the Social World* (Heinemann, London, 1972)

Sealy, Leonard, 'The "Disclosure Philosophy" and Company Law Reform' (1981) 2 *Company Lawyer* 51

Seligman, Joel, 'The Historical Need for a Mandatory Corporate Disclosure System' (1983) 9 *Journal of Corporation Law* 1

'The SEC and Accounting: A Historical Perspective' (1985) 7 *Journal of Comparative Business and Capital Market Law* 241

Sharpe, Note (170) 25 *J Fin* 418

Shocker, A. D., and Sethi, S. P., 'An Approach to Incorporating Social Preferences in Developing Corporate Action Strategies', in Sethi, S. P. (ed.), *The Unstable Ground Corporate Social Policy in a Dynamic Society* (Melville, California, 1974)

Siegel, Stanley, 'A Critical Examination of State Regulation of Accounting Principles' (1985) 7 *Journal of Comparative Business and Capital Market Law* 317

Sommer, A. A., Jr, 'The Annual Report: A Prime Disclosure Document' (1972) *Duke LJ* 1093

Stamp, Edward, 'First steps towards a British conceptual framework' (1982) *Accountancy* (March 1982) 123

Stevenson, Russell B., 'The Corporation as a Political Institution' [1979] 8 *Hofstra LR* 39

Stigler, J., 'Public Regulation of the Securities Markets' (164) 37 *J Bus* 117

Stiles, Philip and Kulvisaechana, Somboon, *Human Capital and Performance: A literature review* (University of Cambridge, Business School, 2003)

Stittle, John, 'UK Corporate Reporting of Human Capital: A Regulatory Failure to Evolve' (2004) 109 *Business and Society Review* 311

Stokes, Mary, 'Company Law and Legal Theory' in W. Twining (ed.), *Legal Theory and Common Law* (Blackwell, Oxford, 1986) 155

Sutton, Michele, 'Between a rock and a judicial hard place: corporate social responsibility reporting and potential legal liability under *Kasky v Nike*' (2004) 72 *UKMC L Rev* 1159

Task Force on Human Capital Management, *Accounting for People: Consultation Paper* (May 2003)

Taylor, Andrew, 'Kingsmill denies review diluted' *Financial Times*, 11 April 2005, 4

Teather, David, 'Andersen cleared by Supreme Court over Enron', *The Guardian*, 1 June 2005, 18

The Stakeholder Alliance – Sunshine Standards available at www.stakeholderalliance.org/sustds.html

Tixier, Maud, 'Note: Soft vs Hard Approach in Communicating on Corporate Social Responsibility', *Thunderbird International Business Review* (2003) Vol. 45, 71

Trade and Industry Select Committee, Sixth Report of Session 2002–03, HC 439

Tricks, Henry, and Hargreaves, Deborah, 'Accounting watchdog sees trouble', *Financial Times*, 10 November 2004

Turner, R., 'Clear and Simple', *Accountancy*, October 2000, vol. 126, No. 1286, 156

Villiers, Charlotte, 'Workers and Transnational Corporate Structures: Some Lessons from the BMW-Rover Case' (2001) 3 *International and Comparative Corporate Law Journal* 271, at p. 291

　European Company Law – Towards Democracy? (Ashgate, Aldershot, 1998)

Wallace, Perry E., 'Disclosure of Environmental Liabilities Under the Securities Laws: The Potential of Securities-Market-Based Incentives for Pollution Control' (1993) 50 *Washington and Lee Law Review* 1093

Watson Wyatt, *The HC Index: Linking HC and Shareholder Value*, Survey Reports, 1999, 2000, 2002

Wedderburn of Charlton, Lord, 'Employees, Partnership and Company Law' (2002) 31 *ILJ* 99

Weetman, Pauline and Collins, Bill, *Operating and Financial Review: Experiences and Exploration* (Institute of Chartered Accountants of Scotland, Edinburgh, 1996)

Weiss, Elliot, 'Disclosure and Corporate Accountability' (1979) 34 *The Business Lawyer* 575

Weiss, Elliott J., and Schwartz, Donald E., 'Using Disclosure to Activate the Board of Directors' 63

Westphalen, Sven-Åge, *Reporting on Human Capital; Objectives and Trends*, paper presented to Technical Meeting 'Measuring and Reporting Intellectual Capital: Experience, Issues and Prospects', 9–10 June 1999

Wheeler, David and Sillanpää, Maria, 'Including the Stakeholders: the Business Case' (1998) 31 *Long Range Planning* 201 at p. 205

White Paper, *Modernising Company Law* (July 2002), Cm. 5553-I

White, James Boyd, 'How Should We Talk About Corporations? The Languages of Economics and of Citizenship' (1985) 94 *Yale LJ* 1416

Whitney, Jack M., II, 'Disclosure in the Annual Report to Shareholders' (1974) *Fifth Annual Institute on Securities Regulation*, Vol. 5, 103

Woods, Lorna, and Villiers, Charlotte, 'The Legislative Process and the Institutions of the European Union: A Case Study of the Development of European Company Law' in Craig, Paul and Harlow, Carole (eds.), *Lawmaking in the European Union - Proceedings of W G Hart Legal Workshop 1996* (Sweet & Maxwell, London, 1998)

Working Group on Materiality, *The Operating and Financial Review: Practical Guidance for Directors* (DTI, London, May 2004)

Wright, P. M. , Dunford, B. B., and Snell, S. A., 'Human resources and the resource-based view of the firm' (2001) 27 *Journal of Management* 701

Zeff, Stephen A., '"Political" Lobbying of Proposed Standards: A Challenge to the IASB', *Accounting Horizons*, Vol. 16, March 2002

　'US GAAP confronts the IASB: Roles of the SEC and the European Commission' (2003), 28 *North Carolina Journal of International Law and Commercial Regulation* 879

Index